TROUBLED BY FAITH: INSANITY AND THE SUPERNATURAL IN THE AGE OF THE ASYLUM

TROUBLED
BY FAITH

INSANITY AND THE
SUPERNATURAL IN THE
AGE OF THE ASYLUM

OWEN DAVIES

OXFORD
UNIVERSITY PRESS

OXFORD
UNIVERSITY PRESS

Great Clarendon Street, Oxford, OX2 6DP,
United Kingdom

Oxford University Press is a department of the University of Oxford.
It furthers the University's objective of excellence in research, scholarship,
and education by publishing worldwide. Oxford is a registered trade mark of
Oxford University Press in the UK and in certain other countries

Published in the United States of America by Oxford University Press
198 Madison Avenue, New York, NY 10016, United States of America

British Library Cataloguing in Publication Data
Data available

Library of Congress Control Number: 2023932990

ISBN 978–0–19–887300–6

DOI: 10.1093/oso/9780198873006.001.0001

Printed and bound in the UK by
Clays Ltd, Elcograf S.p.A.

Acknowledgements

Some of the research for this book was kindly funded by the Leverhulme Trust as part of the project, 'Inner Lives: Emotions, Identity, and the Supernatural, 1300–1900' (RPG-2015-180). I would like to thank the project team of Malcolm Gaskill (PI), Sophie Page, Ceri Houlbrook, James Brown, and Kathleen Walker-Meikle for their collegiality, knowledge, and sense of fun. It was one of those rare collaborative projects that was far more than the sum of its parts. I would like to thank especially Ceri Houlbrook for enthusiastically immersing herself in the oft-curious world of asylum archives, and for searching through and transcribing casebook entries as part of the project. The publisher's anonymous peer reviewers, and the commissioning editor Luciana O'Flaherty, provided thoughtful and helpful suggestions that informed the final manuscript.

Preface

It is a common refrain that 'we live in a mad world'. People wonder with frustrated bemusement at the ideas, actions, and decisions of swathes of the population that seem incomprehensible to their own logic and understanding. They do not necessarily mean these 'others' are literally clinically insane, but 'madness' sums up their frustrations, puzzlement, and anger with those who do not think as they do, who hold what are deemed irrational political, religious, or cultural notions that are impervious to argument or evidence. Perhaps, you the reader, have experienced this frustration, convinced of the rationality of your convictions and conceptions just as the objects of your criticisms are of theirs. This book is the story of this debate, those feelings, at a time when old beliefs about the supernatural were tied to new medical beliefs regarding insanity.

What did it mean to be insane in the nineteenth century? What was an irrational religious or supernatural notion? Who decided? And what were the consequences for patients and practitioners at any point in time? I approached researching and writing this book as a work of mental archaeology, a forensic excavation through layers of thought about the supernatural in an age when magic was considered by the nascent psychiatric profession to be a diseased survival of a benighted medieval past. And just like soil strata in an archaeological excavation, we will see how layers of belief became disturbed and confused as opinions changed, beliefs were redefined, and new expressions of the supernatural intruded into the bedrock of established faith.

I have written many books and articles on the history of witchcraft, magic, ghosts, and popular religion across centuries and different countries and cultures. In researching and writing this book, more than any other, I have been confronted with existential thoughts about the relationship between what *I* think is rational or irrational, and conceptions of what beliefs are *normal* from a societal and medical perspective in both the past and the present. Indeed, is any *belief* really a mark of insanity or just on a spectrum of aberrant thinking as defined at any given time? I hope that this book will also provoke readers to question their own preconceptions about the mental worlds of the past in relation to the 'mad world' we live in today.

Contents

PART II. INNER LIVES

.

List of figures

PART I

A world of insanity

Introduction

Persons whose eccentricities of conduct would scarcely have interfered with public order or private comfort, as they were understood in the time of Queen Anne, would be felt to be intolerable in the present state of society under Queen Victoria.[1]

(John Sibbald, Deputy Commissioner in Lunacy for Scotland, 1877)

The early nineteenth century witnessed the birth of a new medical science that fundamentally changed how insanity was labelled and understood. Psychiatrists not only thought they could cure the ills of the present but also explain the great human mysteries of the past. They bristled with confidence that in an era of massive population growth, industrialization, and urbanization, unlocking the secrets of the mind was essential to an ordered and progressive society. As a result, the influence of religion and the supernatural became a significant measure of insanity in any given population at any moment in time, and thereby a means of assessing collective and individual mental states. Beliefs and behaviour were divided up into the pathological and the healthy. While insanity could not be eradicated as an aspect of the human condition, the further societies distanced themselves from the mindsets of such 'dark times' as the era of the witch trials and the Inquisitions, the healthier they would become. But the swelling number of asylum patients through the nineteenth century, and the beliefs, fears, and emotions many expressed about the supernatural, confronted the psychiatrists, and society at large, with the possibility that what were now deemed irrational beliefs were not irreconcilable with modernity after all. As the century went on, simplistic assumptions about Enlightenment progress began to look decidedly rickety. The rise of spiritualism, evangelical revivals, the strength of popular tradition, and juridical resistance to expert medical witnesses in court, all tested to the limits what psychiatrists judged to be rational in the modern world. This entangled, contradictory, baffling, and at times admirable attempt to make sense of the human experience is the focus of the first half of this book.

Foundations

Psychiatric medicine did not appear out of nowhere. For centuries physicians and philosophers had pondered over the nature and origin of the signs of mental distress and disorder. Both Protestant and Catholic churches also recognized spiritual and emotional sickness and provided services to aid sufferers.[2] Indeed, the broad understanding of insanity, and the terms used to describe its various manifestations, did not change fundamentally from antiquity to the twentieth century, though there were advances in knowledge and definitions shifted over the centuries. Take 'hysteria', for instance, which the reader will hear more about. Ancient Greek and Roman physicians considered it as a loose set of symptoms arising from the condition of the womb (the ancient Greek '*hysterikos*' meant 'from the womb'). During the seventeenth century, new medical insights resulting from autopsy and dissection led to doubts about such classical diagnoses. Women who suffered from hysterical manifestations were found to have perfectly healthy wombs, and so hysteria was recategorized as a 'nervous distemper', to use a phrase from the time, and not as a uterine disorder. Then, during the second half of the nineteenth century, psychiatrists reconfigured the definition of hysteria once again with profound consequences for how supposed manifestations of witchcraft and possession were interpreted.[3]

'Mania' was another term and concept with origins in the ancient world. It had long been used to describe an uncontrollable delirious or frenzied state that seized mind and body. It was a 'raging madness' accompanied by delusions. The image of the maniac chained to the wall came to define public perception of the eighteenth-century madhouse. Mania's twin was 'melancholia', a subdued state of anguish, low spirits, silence, sullen resentment, and fixed obsessions that sometimes led to suicidal tendencies or morphed into mania. While in the twentieth century melancholy would often come to be equated with what we call 'depression' today, it should be used and understood only in its historic context rather than seeking equivalence with contemporary categories of mental illness. Dementia was also a venerable broad category of insanity, though, again, in the past it was not understood in the same way as it is today. Well into the age of the asylum it was defined as a chronic, often irreversible failure of mental function that could strike both young and old. The demented suffered from hallucinations and delusions and were unable to hold prolonged rational conversation.[4]

While for the sake of simplicity I use 'psychiatrist' and 'psychiatry' throughout this book, these terms only came into widespread usage in Europe and America during the twentieth century. For most of the period covered here the terms 'psychological medicine', 'mental medicine', and 'asylum physician' were used in the English-speaking world, although the French title of 'alienist' was also widely adopted. It derived from Phillipe Pinel's pioneering conception of '*l'aliénation mentale*' or 'mental alienation' to describe mental disorders or the estrangement from reason. Pinel (1745–1826) became a god-like figure in the early history of psychiatry.[5] As a physician at the venerable Bicêtre Hospital, Paris, which housed criminals as well as mental patients, and then, in 1795, during the turbulent years following the French Revolution, as chief physician of the huge Salpêtrière hospice, Pinel instituted radical improvements in the care of the insane. His 'moral treatment' of the alienated led to the unchaining of those considered maniacs and the application of simple therapeutic methods, such as encouraging recreational activities, exercise, fresh air, and other means of providing relief from intense mental preoccupations. Orthodox medicines such as purges and vomits were still given to patients following personal consultation rather than indiscriminate application, but the secret to curing the insane now lay in the mind. Moral treatment required time, patience, and space. Pinel recounted one of his successes, a maid who had come to believe she was persecuted by the Devil. She was ever seeing him in the corner of her room and under the bed blanket: she was overcome with fright and from time to time cried out terribly as she succumbed to the illusions of her 'wild imagination'. She was taken to another lodging to break the physical reminders that inspired her fears, and her attendants made her examine every part of the new room to show that there were no demons. Regular baths and tonics gradually helped calm her melancholic delirium until she made a full recovery.[6] But Pinel readily admitted such careful and sensitive treatment was not always possible.

Pinel's mythic status was not assiduously constructed by the man himself, though, but by a new profession seeking to create a clear, triumphant narrative of Enlightenment progress. He became a milestone in a carefully constructed

history of medicine.[7] While he was not without his critics in France and
abroad, in both his psychiatric practice, and his conceptual understanding of
insanity, he inspired a new generation of asylum doctors in Europe and
overseas. In April 1846, for instance, the New York State Lunatic Asylum
celebrated 101 years since Pinel's birth, with odes, hymns, recitations, and an
exhibition. When Joseph Workman (1805–1894), a Unitarian lay preacher and
one of the founders of Canadian psychiatry, gave a paper on the psychiatry
of the witch trials to an annual meeting of asylum superintendents in
Toronto, he honoured Pinel in God-like terms: '*He* drove out Satan, by
unchaining him. The brute could not look Pinel in the face, for heavenly
charity beamed from *his* bewitching eyes.'[8] The story of Pinel's moderniza-
tion of the treatment of the insane was more complex than such paeans
suggest. Psychiatry was a global endeavour that began in Europe and
America and then spread across the colonial world; meanwhile moral treatment had parallels in the work of other eminent physicians at the time,
some of whom we shall encounter later. Asylum doctors toured the institutions of other countries on fact-finding missions. Dozens of psychiatric
journals sprung up filled with new theories, experimental treatments, international asylum reports, and patient case studies. To understand how psychiatrists made sense of supernatural beliefs, therefore, requires an awareness of
the international debates at the time, and the different types of belief
expressed by patients from different countries and cultures.

Despite the impressive international collaborative effort, however, deep
veins of national, religious, political, and racial bias revealed themselves.
When the pioneering French psychiatrist and pupil of Pinel, Jean-Étienne
Dominique Esquirol (1772-1840), surveyed the current mental state of
nations in his much-read book *Des maladies mentales* (1838), translated into
English a few years later under the title *Mental Maladies: A Treatise on Insanity*,
he was not sparing in his sweeping criticisms of the psychological make-up
of other countries. He considered that the English were more prone to
insanity than any other nation due to their possessing 'all the caprices, as
well as the excesses of civilization'. They also had a hereditary predisposition
to the illness, while the indolence of the rich, the abuse of wine and brandy,
and the activities of Methodist preachers furthered the problem.[9] The
Italians were more prone, though, to erotomania, while in France there was
less insanity in the countryside but the cities had a problem due to the
influence of radicalism, intellectual quandary, and thwarted ambitions in
the urban milieu.[10] All this was contested with patriotic vigour. In their

influential and long-running *Manual of Psychological Medicine* (1858), the British psychiatrists Daniel Hack Tuke (1827–1895) and John Charles Bucknill (1817–1897) countered the charge of widespread English madness, explaining proudly that the supposed epidemic was due to the country's advances in the statistical assessment of insanity, and also because there was a greater knowledge and awareness of mental illness amongst the English than elsewhere.[11] Religion became a significant aspect of this international psychiatric politics: Catholics and Protestants fought over which faith generated the most insanity; mainstream Protestants pathologized evangelical and prophetic movements; in Catholic countries psychiatry developed an anticlerical wing; and 'strange' popular religious beliefs, such as possession, were considered indicative of insanity by both Catholic and Protestant psychiatrists.

The rise of the asylum

A massive public asylum-building programme took place across Europe and North America from the 1830s onward. There was also a growth in private asylums catering for wealthy clients. By 1870, there were fifty county and borough asylums in England and Wales and another 126 institutions dealing with the insane. In Scotland there were thirty-one asylums in total and fifteen lunatic wards in poor houses, while in Ireland there were twenty-three district asylums and twenty private asylums. Elsewhere in the world, around the same time, there were sixty-six public and private asylums in the United States, ninety-nine asylums in France, and, on the eve of German unification, there were fifty-nine private and public asylums in Prussia alone, and around seventy-five in other German states.[12] From the 1870s the proliferation of new institutions slowed, though many well-established asylums were enlarged to meet the increasing demand. By 1900 there were more than 100,000 certified insane patients in Britain alone. That means that over the century hundreds of thousands of people spent weeks, months, or years in an asylum.[13]

The reasons for this supposed massive increase in insanity are multifarious and were as much debated at the time as they are today by historians.[14] There was the simple fact of exploding population growth so one would expect exponential increase in insanity diagnoses. The expansion of public asylums for the poor enabled many more people to take the opportunity to have their friends and family cared for at the expense of the state. Whether they were all insane or not is another matter. One of the big discussion points at the time was whether the increase was a consequence of the recent advance of civilisation since the so-called Enlightenment. The more educated, complex, and intense the society, such as in modern urban environments, the more chance there was that more minds would become frazzled by sensory overload and constant decision-making. This plainly contradicted the other psychiatric dictum that ignorance and superstition were the founts of much insanity.

The theories and explanations put forward by historians during the midtwentieth century focussed strongly on the political and class aspects of the rise of the asylum. Various claims were made that the asylum movement was less about societal wellbeing and more about the intrusive extension of the state and the political economy of dealing with 'undesirables' in a changing social landscape. The French philosopher and historian of ideas Michel Foucault argued, for instance, that the asylum was a tool of social control, an expression of 'disciplinary power' to enforce conformity. Suffice it to say, the reasons for the development of psychiatry and the rise of asylums are far more complex than any overarching political theory can encompass. The vast body of historical research that has been conducted on asylums over the last few decades shows a move away from broad political theorizing to much more forensic explorations of the administration of asylums and a focus on patients and their families. Recent historians have used a far greater array of archival sources as well, which show that rather than being some conspiratorial, sinister imposition, asylums, for all their faults, became an accepted part of the medical strategies of the poor even if they were not necessarily well-regarded.

In the second half of this book we turn to a history of insanity from below, an exploration of the inner lives of hundreds of patients from all walks of life.[15] The huge increase in asylums, and the governmental requirements to create official records of their 'business', generated millions of pages of archival records that are also of great value for the understanding of popular mentalities in the nineteenth century. With the extension of insanity diagnoses to ways of *believing* as well as to ways of *behaving*, many thousands were taken to the asylum for beliefs that would have been thought normal in the past but were now considered estranged from rational thought. So, the focus shifts to the lives of those who found themselves in asylums in part because of their belief in witches, fairies, and ghosts; their conviction that they were prophets, the Virgin Mary, or the Messiah; that they communicated with angels or were tormented by devils; or because they believed new technologies operated in supernatural ways. The asylums became mental clearing houses where such people were given space to reflect on their pre-occupations and encouraged to divest themselves of what were considered their irrational or outmoded ways of thinking. I should note that the term 'supernatural', used here to describe phenomena or a state of existence seemingly inexplicable in relation to the verifiable material world, or laws of science at any given period, comes with its own historical baggage. The main point to make, though, is that the asylum casebooks show that the holding of supernatural and scientific beliefs were not mutually exclusive at all. In a transformative technological age, most patients did not need to reject one of way thinking to subscribe to the other in their explanations for what was influencing them.

I have limited the focus to the archival case notes of patients in several asylums in England and Scotland, but also use some examples from Ireland that help contextualize the experiences of the many recent Irish immigrants in Britain at the time. But the range of beliefs and concerns they all expressed, what they believed in, what they feared, and what comforted them with regard to supernatural relations, represented the ideas of many more who were never certified as insane. In this sense the asylum patients' thoughts were not just an expression of individual mental health, but also provide a unique reflection of society at the time.[16]

★　★　★

Troubled by Faith is not intended as another critique of psychiatry. I highlight the contradictions and twists and turns in the psychiatric interpretation of the belief in the supernatural, and also the naivety, condescension, and over-confidence of many in the profession in this respect. Along the way I also show how some psychiatrists were motivated by a sense of public good, a thirst to understand humanity, and a desire to better the lives of the individuals under their care. But this book is primarily a social history of ideas about the supernatural across society through the prism of medical history and its archives. It is a story of how people continued to make sense of the world and rationalize their experiences in supernatural terms, and how belief came to be pathologized and categorized through the invention of medical theories and suppositions that sometimes look deluded from a contemporary perspective.

The book ends in the early twentieth century for two main reasons. One is practical in that public access to patient records is closed to the general public for a century after their creation for obvious reasons of sensitivity regarding living relatives. The other is conceptual. It was 100 years ago that the name 'asylum' was widely abandoned after accruing the same public opprobrium as 'madhouse' a century before. Care for the certified insane now became the remit of 'mental hospitals'.[17] Behind the decision to abandon the language of the 'asylum' lay fundamental shifts in medical theory, practice, and cure regarding mental illness. By 1920, the psychiatric profession, its diagnostic tools, terminology, and ideas, were very different to those of a century before. And, as we shall see, the rise of psychology and psychoanalysis in the late nineteenth century also altered how supernatural beliefs were understood outside of a pathological framework. Yet, the roots of early psychiatric thinking continue to reach into our contemporary world and influence perceptions of the supernatural. To understand fully how this came to be we must begin by exploring the early psychiatric obsession with the age of the witch trials, for the mental world of the distant past determined how psychiatrists interpreted their present and informed the early classification of psychiatric illness.

I

Explaining away the witch trials

The annals of demonology can no longer be separated today from the field of mental medicine, as the analogies that exist between these two orders of knowledge are numerous and so great they are increasing every day, thanks to the progress made in recent years in this last branch of pathology.[1]

(French psychiatrist Claude-François Michéa, 1862)

Early psychiatrists were attracted by the horror stories of the witch trials like moths to a flame. They sought a concrete foundation of historic material on which to establish their ideas of mental pathology as a fundamental aspect of the human condition, and in the trial records, confessions, and lurid demonologies of the sixteenth and seventeenth centuries they found an extraordinary wealth of delusions, hallucinations, anxieties, and fears. The mental health of whole societies could be uncovered from the archives, their new theories of insanity acting as a stethoscope tapping into the impulses of the collective mind of the past. And all this was conducted with the great comfort of being far divorced from the generations of those 'benighted' times and a smug sense of Enlightenment progress since.

Using the medical advances of the present to explain the medical 'dark ages' was seen as a public good to show how society had evolved. But psychiatrists were not the only new profession looking at the witch trials. The emerging academic disciplines of history and anthropology were also seeking to understand the beliefs of past societies and place them on the timeline of human progress. Historians eagerly adopted the early pioneers of psychiatry to their cause. The eminent Irish historian William Lecky (1838–1903), author of the influential *History of the Rise and Influence of the*

Spirit of Rationalism in Europe (1865), drew upon the work of Pinel, Esquirol, and others in his depiction of the witch trials as inspired by a mix of ignorance, religious bigotry, and insanity. 'The theological notions about witchcraft either produced madness or determined its form', he explained.[2] But the historians made few attempts to engage properly with the swiftly developing medical literature. Meanwhile the psychiatrists tended to rely on each other's historical musings and ignore the increasingly rigorous approaches of the historians to the interpretation of the archives. The result was a deeply problematic pathologizing of the past that had profound ramifications that continue to the present in both disciplines. This was the moment in the mid nineteenth century which gave birth to the language of 'witch mania', 'witch craze', and 'witchcraft hysteria'.

The term 'witch mania' first seems to have appeared in print in the 1820s, used by an American local antiquarian in relation to the Salem witch trials of 1692.[3] But its widespread adoption was largely due to the popularity of Charles Mackay's *Memoirs of Extraordinary Popular Delusions* (1841), which included a chapter entitled 'Witch Mania'. Mackay was a journalist, newspaper editor, and ballad writer. He was experienced at writing for a general audience and he was not bound by scholarly or professional conventions. For Mackay, the witch trials were just another entertaining example of the 'madness' of fads and crowd behaviour along with financial bubbles, tulipomania, alchemists, prophets, and mesmerists. He told his readers about 'popular madness with regard to witchcraft' and the 'cruel and absurd delusions' of those who accused and tried suspected witches.[4] In using the term 'mania' Mackay was instrumental in spreading the notion amongst the educated public that the witch trials could only be understood as an insane delusion rather than as a clear intellectual response to theological and political challenges in the world at the time.

The German term '*Hexenwahn*', which is usually taken to mean 'witch craze' but is more accurately translated as 'witch delusion', was used a couple of times in the late 1700s but proliferated in the following century after the German historian Wilhelm Soldan (1803–1869) adopted it in his influential academic study of the witch trials published in 1843. The term 'witch craze' then spread in Britain and America from the 1880s onward. It was often used to explain Salem, but it was also employed by the eminent American medieval scholar Henry Charles Lea (1825–1909) to refer to the rise of the European trials. Hugh Trevor Roper's widely read but now very dated book *The European Witch-Craze of the 16th and 17th Centuries* (1969) further boosted its widespread usage. Both 'witch craze' and '*Hexenwahn*' are still used in history books today in problematic ways (it is embedded in the current A Level syllabus in Britain), leading the eminent scholar of German witchcraft, H.C. Erik Midelfort, to make a plea in 2011 that they be retired as condescending to the past.[5] Finally, the term 'witch hysteria' was popularized in the twentieth century thanks to the cultural influence of Freudian psychoanalysis, though its origins lie at the very heart of the development of the psychiatric profession during the nineteenth century.

The redesignation of the witch trials as the consequence of mass mental pathology, replacing the older Enlightenment interpretation in terms of popular ignorance, was made even more problematic by the common conviction at the time that the trials took place in the Middle Ages. There had been heresy trials in Europe in the fourteenth and early fifteenth centuries that involved lurid accounts of Satanic worshippers, but secular laws against witchcraft and witches only spread from the early sixteenth century onward, at the same time as the rise of Protestantism and the print revolution. The notion of *medieval* witch hunts was partly born of rudimentary historical periodization. The term 'early modern' which historians today use to describe the period broadly between 1450 and 1750 only really started to appear in history books from the 1880s onward. But there was also a pernicious willingness by historians, early novelists, and psychiatrists to portray the Middle Ages as a period of benighted Catholic superstition and persecution across Christendom, and thus the fitting location in which to situate the witch trials.[6] This suited both Protestant propagandists and anti-clerical psychiatrists in nineteenth-century Catholic France and elsewhere.

Invisible fluids and brain organs

Pinel's work appeared at a moment in the history of medicine when phrenology and mesmerism were offering competing and complementary ideas about insanity. We may describe them as pseudo-sciences today but at the time they were as much in the swirl of medical science as psychiatry, and while they all attracted controversy and criticism, they also led to cross-fertilization of ideas about the past and present, for good and bad.

Mesmerism or animal magnetism was based on the ideas of the German physician Franz Anton Mesmer (1734–1815), whose university medical thesis concerned the influence of the moon and planets on the human body.

He also experimented with magnets. His research on patients led him to believe that he had discovered an invisible fluidic force inside the body that could be influenced and channelled by external forces such as magnets and electric currents, but also by certain people, including himself. Through will power or touch the flows in other humans could be altered and unblocked, thereby restoring a balanced healthy mind and body. The theory was hugely controversial but also highly attractive, and generated a new medical vocabulary of occult or hidden forces and their influence.[7] The mesmerized state was sometimes referred to as 'artificial somnambulism', for instance, a trance-like level of consciousness, while the term 'hypnotism' similarly had its origins in the same notion that people in a sleep-like mesmeric state were neurologically very active and so were highly sensitive to suggestion from the mesmerist.

Phrenology held out the profound promise that character and mental capacity could be identified from the physical shape of the head. One did not need to understand the workings of the mind to determine mental health because the skull provided a historic physical diagnosis. The idea originated with the Viennese physician Franz Joseph Gall (1758–1828) who developed upon earlier medical notions regarding physiognomy—the science of judging character from facial characteristics. Gall suggested that the size of different 'organs' of the brain, each of which related to specific aspects of intellect and moral character, shaped the contours of the skull as the bones ossified during infancy. Deficiency or excess in the size of some brain organs indicated a natural propensity to certain types of mental illness. Gall's ideas were further developed and popularized by one of his former pupils, Johann Gaspar Spurzheim (1776–1832). From cranial studies and surgical dissections the two of them identified twenty-seven organs of the brain.

Pinel certainly took an interest in these two medical theories. When he took over editorship of the *Gazette de Santé* in 1784, he wrote a series of articles assessing animal magnetism and concluded that if there was a therapeutic effect then it was likely caused by the positive power of the imagination rather than by any magnetic vital fluid. Years later, in 1812, Pinel apparently invited the leading French mesmerist, the Marquis de Puységur (1751–1825), to the Salpêtrière where they talked about magnetism and the Marquis demonstrated his magnetic treatment on a young patient that he had brought with him. There is no evidence Pinel changed his mind on the subject, but he remained inquisitive as ever concerning the revolutionary medical claims of others.[8]

When, in 1810, one of Pinel's former students, Jean-Étienne Dominique Esquirol (1772–1840), published his description of a new category of insanity called 'monomania', new vistas opened up for the advocates of phrenology as well as psychiatry. For Esquirol and his early followers, a 'monomaniac' was someone who held a pathologically fixed idea or single obsession but who was otherwise a perfectly sane and socially-functioning individual. Conceptually this was a replacement for some symptoms encompassed by the old term melancholia. The Scottish physician William Cullen (1710–1790), who Pinel much admired, had already proposed the idea of 'partial mania' to define the melancholia that exhibited itself in terms of a monothematic delusion. Gall had also referenced the idea of partial insanity as a self-evident corollary of the phrenological theory of multiple brain organs, where one organ may have been pathological but all the others remained normal. As Spurzheim explained, 'how is it possible to combine partial insanities with the unity of the brain?'[9] The brain had to be made up of separate organs with different functions. While redefining Pinel's classification of melancholia, Esquirol also came up with the category of 'lypemania' as a form of depressive monomania, mostly hereditary, that mapped directly onto venerable conceptions of depressive melancholia. While monomaniacs were excited and expansive in their delusions and fears, lypemaniacs were, by contrast, sober and morose. Lypemania never really caught on as a term, but monomania became widely adopted—raising profound new issues for jurisprudence which we will explore later. For the moment, suffice it to say that through the early nineteenth century the concept of monomania helped support the practice of phrenology amongst receptive asylum specialists and it has been argued, in turn, that the enthusiasm for phrenology in Britain brought the term monomania into fashionable usage beyond France.[10]

Both mesmerists and phrenologists had their own ideas about the mental and physical state of those who expressed supernatural beliefs in the past. The German physician Joseph Ennemoser (1787–1854), one-time Professor of Medicine at Bonn University, was a rather late proponent of mesmerism, taking up the cause around 1819 and writing numerous works on the subject as well as applying it in his own medical practice. What interests us here, though, is his book *Geschichte der Magie* (1844) or the *History of Magic*, which was translated into English in 1854. He was also one of those responsible for perpetuating the mistaken idea that the witch trials were a matter of the Middle Ages. Ennemoser's purpose in delving into history was to show how, across time and space, in essence and in practice, magic was revealed to be an expression of mesmeric or somnambulistic influence. By the end of his *History*, Ennemoser hoped the reader would be apprised of how 'many wonderful stories can be explained and connected most naturally with well-known facts', and that having 'compared together historical facts, it is possible that he may have discovered traces of a more extended universe than that of the senses or of worldly experience'.[11]

Between the publication of the German and English editions of Ennemoser's *History*, animal magnetism advocate and lawyer John Campbell Colquhoun (1785–1854), who had spent some time in Germany and drew upon the same German intellectual traditions as Ennemoser, wrote his own two-volume *History of Magic, Witchcraft, and Animal Magnetism* (1851), that explored in great depth his conviction that mesmerism 'lay at the foundation of all fables of magic and sorcery' from across the 'barbarous ages'.[12] Colquhoun had been working away at this idea for some fifteen years. In 1836 he had expressed the hope that if mesmerism could be demonstrated as a fact, then 'it might serve, perhaps, to explain some of the extraordinary powers attributed to witches, such as flying in the air, &c'.[13] By way of possible proof of such historic powers of levitation he referred to the recent case of Sophie Laroche, a sixteen-year-old labourer's daughter from Virieu, France, who had caused quite a sensation for her prophetic revelations, her ability to detect lost property, and the miraculous ability to speak Latin and Greek while in a somnambulistic, mesmeric state. While in this condition she also acquired a peculiar bodily lightness so that she could be lifted as though she only weighed a few ounces. Colquhoun also cited a patient of the chief Scottish surgeon John Abercrombie (1780–1844). She was a 24-year-old woman who had uncontrollable twitches and paroxysms, and whose body manifested a 'convulsive spring' so great that she catapulted herself onto a cupboard five feet high. She apparently recovered once a full and healthy menstruation occurred after an absence of several years.[14]

Both books were deeply problematic as works of history. One English reviewer of Ennemoser's tomes was brutal. 'Such a subject, adequately handled by a competent and scientific thinker might furnish a fertile theme for comment', said the reviewer, 'but it can only be a matter of regret that Dr. Ennemoser's innocent, but very moon-struck speculations have not been allowed to rest in the obscurity of their primitive tongue'.[15] Yet Ennemoser's *History* continued to be cited periodically in psychiatric literature as a source for historic examples of hysteria well into the twentieth century, long after animal magnetism had been consigned to the history of medicine. It was also a significant influence on the occult revival of the late nineteenth century, including the Theosophy movement.[16]

The medical doctor, Thomas Stone, a Fellow of the London Medico-Chirurgical Society, was also struck by the similarity of the behaviour of people under mesmeric influence and those who claimed to be possessed by witches and devils in the era of the witch trials. But, unlike Ennemoser and Colquhoun, he was not searching for universal truths about magic as mesmerism, but patterns of behavioural diagnostics. Stone was, for a time, Medical Superintendent at Wyke-house Asylum, Brentford, and Haydock Lodge Asylum, Manchester, and had attracted some controversy in 1828 by conducting a cranial study of twenty-two hardened criminals, including the infamous Burke and Hare, which forensically undermined phrenological claims about criminal head shapes.[17] Stone was more open to the reality of mesmerism, however, and he pored over various sixteenth- and seventeenth-century French and English tracts concerning witchcraft and possession in search of evidence. He read about the case of the Frenchwoman Martha Brossier, who, around 1600, claimed she was possessed by demons and would display all sorts of extreme contortions, and he also perused the Elizabethan sceptical text *Discoverie of Witchcraft* (1584) by Reginal Scot—more on which later. These confirmed to him that there was historic evidence that mesmerism had long been an unidentified natural force: 'It would appear that many who professed these Satanic arts discovered in the exercise of their skill the development of a power within themselves to affect others, of which they were originally unconscious, and which confirmed them in the idea of their being really supernaturally possessed.'[18] Stone urged caution in making retrospective diagnoses, however, advising that each case of reputed mesmerism in the annals had to be investigated on its own merits. He noted, for instance, that 'hysterical affections' such as convulsions, incoherent talking, and the like could assume a mesmeric character.

The phrenologists could also see patterns in the past. Spurzheim proposed that the development of the Organ of Marvellousness, which was located under what was described as the frontal bone of the skull, had, from the dawn of humankind, shaped people's fascination with tales of wonder and miracles. It was more or less morbidly active, not only from individual to individual but also between entire nations. An enlarged organ made people all the more preoccupied with sorcery, amulets, magic, and astrology, and influenced their actions. It also predisposed people to radical religion. It was no surprise, noted Spurzheim, that the founder of Methodism, John Wesley (1703–1791), had a remarkably prominent 'Organ of Marvellousness'. Spurzheim had originally described the fascination with the miraculous engendered by this organ as 'supernaturality' but later plumped for 'marvellousness' to better describe the 'kinds of astonishment caused by natural and supernatural circumstances'.[19] The dogged phrenologist George Combe (1788–1858) preferred the term 'Organ of Wonder' as he was of the opinion that philosophy did not allow for the existence of the supernatural. He observed that, 'some individuals, so endowed, have informed me, that when any marvellous circumstance is communicated to them, the tendency of their minds is to believe it *without examination*'.[20] In 1815 the astronomer and phrenologist Thomas Forster (1789–1860) had also proffered that there was an 'Organ of Mysterizingness', which when fully developed, 'persons are much disposed to be superstitious, to have visions, to believe in ghosts, astrology, &c'.[21]

The disciples of phrenology and animal magnetism propounded *physical* explanations for past and present belief in the supernatural. So, while they interacted with the early psychiatrists, and the likes of Spurzheim drew upon the work of Pinel and Esquirol, their medical systems were ultimately incompatible with the ideas developing around moral insanity during the first half of the nineteenth century. Psychiatry would slowly but surely undermine both phrenology and animal magnetism from one side, while the doctors of physiology would squeeze them to extinction from the other side through accumulated scientific evidence about the brain. Psychiatry found a way through and, ironically, would break new ground with the redefinition of a spectral term that had its origins in the era of the witch trials.

Demonomania and the new demonologists

The term 'demonomania' was coined in 1580 with the publication of one of the most influential demonological texts of the witch trial era, *De la démonomanie des sorciers*. The book went through twenty-three editions and it was published in several languages. Its author, Jean Bodin (1530–1596), was a well-established French political philosopher with a number of significant books on political theory and history to his name by the time he wrote *De la démonomanie*. Bodin considered witches as the Devil's agents and so a fundamental threat to the Christian state. 'I decided to write this treatise which I have entitled The Demonomania of Witches', he explained in the preface, 'on account of the madness [*rage*] which makes them run after devils: to serve as a warning to all those who read it, in order to make it clearly known that there are no crimes which are nearly so vile as this one, or which merits more grievous penalties.'[22] Bodin became a *bête noire* amongst the early historicizing psychiatrists, held up as a classic example of the bigotry and zealotry of the time.

The second publication to use the term, a treatise entitled *La démonomanie de Lodun, qui montre la véritable possession des religieuses urselines* (1634), had, perhaps, even more of an influence on nineteenth-century psychiatrists. It concerned the notorious case of the supposed possession of nuns at a convent in Loudun in the west of France in 1634. At the ensuing trial, a troublesome local priest, Urbain Grandier, was accused of having made a pact with the Devil and of having cast a spell over the nuns. He was executed. The behaviour of the nuns, which included the uttering of blasphemies, barking like dogs, convulsions, and talking and shouting in strange voices, was much discussed in later psychiatric literature and became the archetypal example of temporary insanity and mass hysteria. Then 'demonomania' largely fell into disuse for the rest of the seventeenth century, cited mostly in reference to Bodin and the Loudun tract, until it was resurrected in the mid eighteenth century and redefined in new medical rather than supernatural terms.

As the ancient systems of medicine were slowly abandoned along with the supernatural origin of illness during the late seventeenth and eighteenth centuries, those in the vanguard of the new medical orthodoxy set about re-classifying medical conditions of the past and present. With regard to mental illnesses, over thirty different types were now classified depending on the nosologies of various authors.[23] One of the most influential of the classifiers was the French physician and botanist François Boissier de Sauvages (1706–1767), professor at Montpellier University, who followed a botanical model of classification for human diseases inspired, in part, by his Swedish contemporary Carl Linnaeus (1707–1778) who founded the modern classification of the plant world. Sauvages gave over some seven pages in his *Nosologie méthodique* (1763) to the subject of *démonomanie*, which he described as 'a delirium true or deceitful, by which sorcerers, the wicked and imposters are seen to be obsessed, or possessed by a demon'. By 'true' he did not mean real diabolic influence on the human body, but true delirium involving the *belief* in such diabolic influence.[24] Sauvages expressed brief but trenchant criticism of the witch trial demonologists. We could laugh, he said, at the credulity of Bodin, and express anger and sadness for the hundreds condemned to death by the French witch-hunting judge Nicholas Rémy (1530–1616). He argued that those that had been sent to the pyres should have instead been cared for compassionately in the *petites Maisons*—a reference to the sixteenth-century Parisian hospice for beggars and the insane.[25]

Sauvages identified an impressive nine different species of the disease supported by historic sources. There was *dæmonomania sagarum* or the demonomania of the witches, which Sauvages defined as 'the delirium of those who, by a diabolic art, and an agreement with the demon, make manifest surprising things, and gain credit amongst fools'. According to Sauvages, it explained those 'old women' who imagined they had the power to hurt children and livestock, to render men impotent, and all the other things blamed on witches. He referenced examples from the six-volume *Magical Investigations* of the Jesuit demonologist Martin Delrio (1551–1608).[26] He also cited the French philosopher Pierre Gassendi (1592–1655) who had apparently experimented on a poor man who believed himself a witch, by giving him a pessary containing psychoactive stramonium seeds. This sent him into a profound sleep and on awakening he reported he had been to a witches' sabbat, whereas Gassendi observed that he had never left his bed. Sauvages' description of *Dæmonomania vampirismus* was based on an account written by the French botanist Joseph Pitton de Tournefort (1656–1708). He was on a royal expedition to Greece when he found himself on the island of Mykonos around 1701 where he witnessed an apparent vampire epidemic. He wrote about it in his *Relation d'un voyage du Levant* published in 1717. According to Sauvages, vampires were either active or passive. The active were straightforward imposters while the passive concerned the living or the dead on whom people inflicted cruelty for supposedly being vampires. The Romanian physician, Martinus Martini (1750–1800), expanded considerably on Sauvages' category of *vampirismus* in his published Latin medical thesis on 'Demonomania and its various subclasses' presented to the University of Vienna in 1782. Martini provided further historical evidence and accepted that true demonomania and true vampirism had probably occurred in the past but that there was no evidence for it still occurring in his lifetime, when only simulated and falsely ascribed forms of demonomania existed, in some cases resulting from hysteria.[27]

The category of *dæmonomania coribantisme* or *simulata* concerned the supposed demonic possession of a person by a demon to fool the credulous and attract attention, which Sauvages also categorized as simulated epilepsy. He drew upon the nuns of Loudun as an example. *Coribantisme* referred to the ancient Greek mythology about the Korybantes, who were male ecstatic dancers that worshipped the goddess Cybele. He went on to describe some of the methods that had been used to unmask such impostors, and also noted a recent report in a French medical journal of a woman ventriloquist who could imitate the sound of a drum with her farts.[28] Various symptoms caused by intestinal worms, such as convulsions, contortions and delirium, but interpreted by the ignorant as signs of possession, made up the species *dæmonomania à vernubes* or *vermibus*. This curious category was justified by a terse reference to 'Cardan'. We know from other sources that it was based on a story concerning the Dutch priest and humanist Erasmus (1466–1536) recounted by the Italian mathematician and physician Gerolamo Cardano (1501–1576). Erasmus apparently once came across an Italian suffering from worms who could speak fluent Dutch even though he had never learned it. The man was thought to be possessed by a devil as a consequence. But when he voided all his intestinal worms and recovered his health, he had no knowledge that he had ever spoken Dutch.[29] A good dose of emetics and purgatives soon cured this demonomania, Sauvages suggested. *Dæmonomania fanatica* was dealt with briefly as describing those possessed with extreme zealotry or fanaticism, particularly of a religious nature, which had led to wars and all sorts of crimes up to the present day.

Sauvages then moved on to a species that would resonate across the next century of psychiatry—*dæmonomania hysterica*. This account was based on contemporary observation, particularly a case communicated by Jean-Baptiste Auclerc-Descottes of Argenton, a recently graduated medical student from Montpellier University. It concerned two housemaids aged twenty. They were good friends, and both were diagnosed as hysterics, though locals considered they were the victims of 'obsession' (when a devil had external control over its victim). They would go into terrible convulsions and then fall into profound sleep during which they were completely insensible to burning and pinching. They experienced *lipothymia* (fainting fits) and suppression of their menstruation. Sauvages was consulted. He concluded that the young women suffered nothing more than a melancholic hysterical condition, and said that people had been gullible to attribute this 'sort of comedy' to anything else. After his recommended treatment of taking baths, drinking whey, and dosing with opium syrup (*syrop de karabé*) during their fits, the two women eventually recovered and were married—the ultimate eighteenth-century proof of sound female mental health. In 1772, the Scottish physician, James Makittrick Adair (1728–1802), also highlighted the relevance of *demonomania hysterica* in contemporary medical practice, referring to it in lay terms as 'a species of nervous disease from which the ignorant suspect the person to be bewitched'.[30]

Opium was the cause rather than the cure of Sauvages' seventh species, *dæmonomania Indica* or *Indienne*. It was based on an account by the German naturalist and explorer Engelbert Kämpfer (1651–1716) who travelled around Asia on behalf of the Dutch East India Company. Kämpfer described in 1712 how opium was consumed in the East Indies and that it sometimes provoked a state of insensible fury that led to homicidal knife-wielding attacks in the streets. Yet, once the effects had worn off, they were unable to remember anything of their violent madness. Sauvages referred to it as the '*rage de l'hamuck*' or what we know in English as 'running amok'.[31] *Dæmonomania Polonica* was another of Sauvages' region-specific species. Since the sixteenth century there had been reports of a mysterious disease plaguing the lands of Poland and Lithuania. It was called *plica Polonica* and supposedly caused extraordinarily matted hair growth. Cutting the hair could cause death. Other symptoms included convulsions, seizures, and headaches. In popular culture the affliction was attributed to witches, possession, and punishment from God. By the end of the nineteenth century *plica Polonica* was dismissed as a medical misunderstanding born of 'prejudice and lack of hygiene'.[32] Sauvages' final species was *dæmonomania à cardiogmo*. As the name suggest this was concerned with the heart, more specifically those suffering aortic aneurysm, noting that some attributed the condition to hysteria and others to poison. He referenced the pioneering work on the circulation of blood by the English physician William Harvey (1578–1657).

The Scottish physician and intellectual William Cullen (1710–1790), while remaining respectful, clearly had little time for Sauvages' eclectic ethnographic and historical classifications of demonomania. He rejected outright there was any true demonomania as argued by the early demonologists, and in his own influential nosology, demonomania was merely considered as a sub-category of melancholia. All the species recorded by Sauvages could be subsumed into four classes of physical and mental disorder. First, *dæmonomania Indica* and *fanatica* were either expressions of melancholia or mania. The second category concerned those cases where spectators to the illness, rather than those afflicted, diagnosed the demonic influence, such as *vermibus*, *plica Polonica*, and *cardiogmo*. Then, as a third category, there were the feigned diseases, namely *sagarum*, *vampirismus*, and *simulata*. Finally, there were the diseases that were partly real and partly feigned, principally *demonomania hysterica* but also aspects of the other categories on an individual basis.[33]

The redefinition of demonomania at this time was not just some abstruse, academic matter. The classifications developed by the likes of Cullen and Sauvages formed the basis of later encyclopaedia entries on the topic, which disseminated beyond the universities and bookshelves of the medical professionals. While cutting-edge medical treatises and theses were still being published in Latin during the eighteenth century, from the mid century onward there was a boom in vernacular medical literature.[34] Increasing literacy, the growth of the middle-classes, the advent of public libraries, and the popularity of literary genres such as newspapers, dictionaries, and encyclopaedias, meant there was a growing market for learned but accessible scientific medical knowledge. As a review of George Motherby's *A New Medical Dictionary* (1775) explained, 'the chief use of a dictionary is, to explain, in a familiar manner, the terms of the art, and to assist the practitioner, who wants immediate assistance, and cannot turn to the more elaborate systems, or is unable from his situation to procure them'.[35]

During the early nineteenth century these dictionaries and encyclopaedias were also important vehicles for the dissemination of cutting-edge medical thinking to the wider public and from one country to another.[36] They soon began to reflect the recent work on moral insanity as well as long-held notions about physical ailments borrowed from early modern works. In Britain, for instance, Abraham Rees's *The Cyclopædia; Or, Universal Dictionary* (1819) included a lengthy entry on 'dæmonomania' that provided a synopsis of Sauvages' classification as well as reference to Cullen's opinion. The volume containing the entry was first written in 1808, and it began with the observation that, 'it is unnecessary, at the present day, to enter into arguments, with a view to confute the opinions that prevailed, in the ages of ignorance and superstition'. The whole matter of possession and demonomania could be 'accounted for by a consideration of physical and moral causes'.[37]

The new medical classifications of insanity also had 'real world' application in terms of the religious debate over the continued manifestation of diabolic possession. This was ignited at a local level in England during the early 1820s, for example, when two cases of possession excited the people of Plymouth Dock, south Devon.[38] The first Plymouth Dock case concerned the four daughters of a grocer and lay preacher named John Kennard. The girls, aged between seven and sixteen, exhibited such characteristic symptoms as fits, running up walls, and vomiting pins. Then the contagion spread to a boy named John Evens who said he had been bewitched. He went into convulsions, barked like a dog, and swore profusely. He also had 'a furious antipathy to anything sacred'. Local Wesleyan Methodist preacher, John Heaton, involved himself deeply with the affair and wrote an account of the events along with his Bible-evidenced conviction that these were true cases of diabolic possession.[39] According to Heaton there were no better collective proofs than the word of God, one's own eyes, and the 'faithful testimony of men of sound judgement and unimpeachable veracity'.[40] His own views ran contrary to those of the eminent Dr Cullen whose sceptical classification of demonomania Heaton had read about in the entry for 'Melancholy' in the *Encyclopaedia Perthensis; Or Universal Dictionary*. It shows how this new educational literary tradition was cascading more recent scientific and medical knowledge beyond the medical profession.[41] Heaton's second-hand understanding of demonomania nosology led him to state incorrectly that the 'eminent' Sauvages had allowed that demons could cause madness. He then contrasted this with Cullen's dismissal of the possibility. Heaton complained that Cullen's nosology made 'a laborious effort to vindicate the "*wicked one*" from the accusation of doing injury to the bodies and minds of men'. He even accused Cullen of hiding evident cases of the *true* form among his 'unaccountables (mania obscura)', and concluded: 'wherever even a learned man opposes what is *truth*, he must involve himself in absurdity'.[42]

During the publishing lifespan of Pinel's *Nosographie philosophique*, which first appeared in 1798 and went through six editions over twenty years, he gently pulled away from the methodologies of the eighteenth-century classifiers. Although initially inspired by the nosologies of Cullen, Sauvages, and others, Pinel simplified the criteria. Whereas Sauvages had detailed some 2400 diseases, Pinel reduced the number to under 200.[43] Demonomania was not given any particular attention and was seen simply as an expression of melancholia, as 'the idea of being possessed by a demon'.[44] But Esquirol would soon turn the whole concept on its head.

Esquirol first set out his radical redefinition of *démonomanie* as a category of mental illness in an article published in the huge, multi-volume *Dictionnaire des Sciences Médicales* in 1814.[45] The study of history was at the heart of it, for Esquirol wanted to understand the manifestation and frequency of mental illness over time and in response to major crises and upheavals. With regard to the French Republic, he tried to determine whether there was more insanity before or after the Revolution.[46] He was interested more generally to see if moral insanity could unlock the medical experiences of the past, and what that, in turn, said about the progress of medical science. Esquirol wanted to learn from the evidence provided by the demonologists rather than spend much time lambasting them for their ignorance and bigotry, as others had already done. The demonological texts were a source of psychiatric case histories, and he set about comparing early modern accounts of the possessed with those he had observed first-hand in the asylum. Esquirol was at pains to point out that his definition of demonomania did not refer to demons as solely evil spirits in an early modern Christian sense. He began his 1814 article by explaining that in the ancient world the world 'demon' signified a 'spirit, genius, intelligence' rather than solely a devil or evil entity. Demonomania encompassed all spirits, good and bad, that the insane claimed to be influenced by or in communication with.

He set out a sweeping historical narrative with a broad societal take on the experience of insanity, beginning with a delve into antiquity to explore the relationship between religion and insanity in the mental world of the ancients who claimed divine inspiration or who practised or believed in astrology, magic, and sorcery. Moving on to the early centuries of Christianity, Esquirol concluded that the belief in the powers of the spirit world over body and mind were further exaggerated, with the fear of yielding to the machinations of the Christian Devil inspiring new worries. And so, the demonomaniacs multiplied and the early church offered up its exorcisms in response, while solemn ceremonies were established in several cities for the healing of the possessed.[47] The advent of Protestantism, Calvinism in particular, made things worse, he said. Fanaticism and religious melancholy now triggered an epidemic of insanity. The demonomaniacs were forced to confess to diabolic pacts and were burned at the stake as witches rather than healed through the old rites and rituals. The more they were hunted, the more ways were found to torture them, the more the number of these patients increased by 'exalting the imagination, by dealing with chimerical fears'. Not only were these poor melancholics and maniacs the victims of the church and state, but they were also prey to charlatans and cunning-folk who trafficked 'in the ignorance and superstition of their fellow men'. A few beacons of light shone out of the darkness, physicians and philosophers who fought against the bigotry and ignorance of the Bodins of the time. He referred to the doctors who were commissioned by the bishop of Paris to examine the supposed possession of Marthe Brossier. One of them, Michel Marescot (1539–1606), published an account of their findings, namely that Brossier was not possessed: there was 'nothing of the Devil, much fakery, a bit of illness'.[48] The report, said Esquirol, was a model of reason and knowledge that undermined the machinations of the Catholic clergy who had organized her exorcism.

For Esquirol, the annals of history showed that demonomania was most frequent at times when religious issues were uppermost in people's minds, collectively and individually, and when it was the constant preoccupation of public and published discussion. During the Enlightenment, better science, popular education, and the development of a more rational, sober Christianity meant the popular imagination was calmed and no longer gave birth to mass fears and delusions of witches and magicians. The trials came to an end. In his own time, he suggested, religious institutions had lost their influence and governments had found other ways to ensure the docility of the people and control their behaviour.

Esquirol's search through the old demonologies and treatise also led him to make a set of diagnoses and clinical observations about those who suffered from demonomania in the past. He noted that pre-pubescent children rarely succumbed to demonomania, and that the most favourable age to get the illness was between forty and fifty. The stereotype of the old witch was based on the dry, thin, wrinkled, decrepit exterior of demonomaniacs, he observed, 'who, by the pains they experience, and the aches and privations they suffer, age outwardly long before age'. The hereditary principle in insanity was proven by the accounts of the power of supposed witchcraft being passed from one generation to the next. The glaring data from the witch trials that most of the accused and the supposedly possessed were women merely confirmed that women were more prone to nervous disease, and more exposed to all kinds of 'alienation', such as melancholy, hysteria, and monomania. The epidemic nature of historic demonomania really intrigued him. 'Like all nervous maladies', he said, 'it propagates itself by a kind of moral contagion, and by the power of imitation.'[49] He found examples drawn from demonological texts to illustrate the point. He referred obviously to Loudun, but also to an episode in Rome in 1554 where eighty-two women, mostly recently baptized Jews, claimed to be possessed, and also to the possession of some nuns at a German convent at Kentorp around the same time. The latter account derived from Bodin's *Démononmanie*, and Bodin had, in turn, lifted the story unacknowledged from an early sceptical work, *De præstigiis dæmonum*, by the Dutch physician Johann Weyer—more on whom later.[50]

These cases clearly demonstrated to Esquirol 'the power of imagination over our organization'. He made four concluding clinical observations that defined the condition of demonomania: it was a species of religious melancholy; its originating cause was the ignorance, prejudices, feebleness, and pusillanimity of the human mind; it was provoked by fear and dread; and that the delusions and actions of demoniacs depended upon false notions of religion, and a frightful depravation of morals.[51]

Pinel and his contemporaries had talked of 'religious mania' and 'religious melancholy' as two sides of the coin of mental illness caused by excessive religious preoccupations. Then, Esquirol went on to create the category of 'religious monomania' as the twin of demonomania, each defined by the nature of the delusions and fears expressed by the insane. Esquirol also proposed 'theomania' as a subcategory of religious monomania which described 'those alienated souls who believe themselves to be God, who imagine that they hold intercourse and intimate communication with the Holy Spirit, with the angels and with the saints; who pretend to be inspired and to have received a mission from Heaven for the purpose of converting man'. Alexander Morison, President of the Royal College of Physicians, put it more succinctly; theomania occurred when 'pride and vanity are united to religious hallucinations'.[52] Joan of Arc was considered the classic, historic archetype of the theomaniac. So, prophets who preached they were the new messiah were diagnosed as suffering from theomania, while their followers were prone to more general religious monomania manifest by their preoccupation with prophecies and their fulfilment.

By the 1830s, Esquirol's demonomania had been included in several French medical and scientific dictionaries and encyclopaedias. In 1823 a new journal of the sciences and the arts, *Le Musée d'Aquitaine*, dedicated an article to demonomania, reprinting illustrative case studies from Pinel and Esquirol.[53] The author of the article, Jean-Baptiste Saincric, stated that such important medical developments were of great interest to humanity but were usually contained in books that were rarely read by the general public. The journal was doing a public service in printing the essence of Esquirol's account of demonomania as mental alienation rather than 'superstition'. Its circulation from medical discourse to the wider educated public is evident from a letter written by the Romantic poet Gérard de Nerval (1808–1855) to his friend Ida Ferrier, wife of the famed novelist Alexandre Dumas, in 1841. Nerval suffered from what would be termed today as nervous breakdowns.

> I had formally admitted that I had been sick which costs a lot to my self-esteem and my honesty. Confess! Confess! They shrieked at me, as they used to do to sorcerers and heretics, and to settle the matter, I allowed myself to be classified as afflicted with a malady defined by doctors and variously labelled Theomania or Demonomania in the medical dictionaries.[54]

The Italian medical profession was quick to adopt Esquirol's term, with the phrenologist and forensic doctor Antonio Fossati, who spent much of his time in Paris, referring to demonomania as an expression of 'superstitious monomania' in an Italian study of suicide in 1831.[55] It was also well received across the channel. In 1828, Alexander Morison rejected Gall's phreno-logical nosology, and considered Esquirol's new classifications as more 'suited to the present state of our knowledge'. In his casebook on mental disease for medical students, published in 1828, Morison included a case of demonomania from his own professional observations of the mentally ill. It was a fifty-year-old woman who amongst other delusions believed she had sold herself, her husband, and her son to the Devil. Morison noted that this 'deplorable' type of insanity was fortunately uncommon, though he had recently heard of 'a miserable instance of it in one of the country asylums'. He also knew of a clergyman who suffered periodic attacks of demonoma-nia during which he believed the Devil entered his brain and he tried to dislodge the Devil by beating his head severely, causing nasty injuries. In 1835, the early American psychiatrist and founding member of the Association of Medical Superintendents of American Institutions for the Insane, Amariah Brigham (1798–1849), wrote glowingly of Esquirol's 1814 essay on demonomania and included extensive approving quotes from it in his *Observations on the Influence of Religion upon the Health and Physical Welfare of Mankind*. He agreed that from his own medical experience it was a deplorable disease that was also apt to lead to suicide.[56]

The psychiatrist as historian

The publication of Esquirol's hugely influential tome, *Des maladies mentales* in 1838, which included a slightly revised and updated version of his 1814 dictionary entry, further boosted interest in demonomania as well as the value of historical comparisons. From the 1840s to the 1860s it seems as though French psychiatrists spent as much time rootling through old religious and demonological books as they did with their own patients. The age of retrospective diagnoses had begun.

In 1836 medical doctor Louis-Francisque Lélut published a study of the mental state of the Greek philosopher Socrates based on the 'application of psychological science to history' and concluded that Socrates suffered from insanity.[57] Over in Germany, physician Justus Friedrich Karl Hecker (1795–1850) gave lectures at the University of Berlin on the history of medicine and 'historical pathology' during the 1830s. He published several influential books on medieval epidemics and infant mortality, as well as medical encyclopaedia entries on the same subject. The year 1845 was a major moment in the study of witch trial pathology with the publication of *Des Hallucinations, ou Histoire raisonnée des apparitions, des visions, des songes, de l'extase* by the French psychiatrist Alexandre Brière de Boismont (1797–1881). It was soon translated into English with the preface stating, 'in giving a less scholastic turn to his treatise, and introducing questions of historic psychology, [he] has succeeded in electrifying both the press and the public'. The same year, Louis-Florentin Calmeil published his monster two-volume work *De la folie* (*On Insanity*), which he described as a philosophical, historical, and judicial study stretching from the 'revival of the sciences in Europe to the nineteenth century'. The French psychiatrist and historian of medicine Claude-François Michéa (1815–1882) once stated that Lélut 'served as a torch for Mr. Calmeil to dissipate the darkness spread over the history of witchcraft and demonic possession during the last three centuries'.[58]

The long-lived Calmeil (1798–1895) had been an assistant to Esquirol at the Charenton asylum, and he later became its director. Over 1000 pages in length, *On Insanity* was the first systematic attempt to apply cutting-edge psychiatry to the witch trials. Calmeil borrowed heavily from notorious printed demonological texts by the likes of Bodin, the zealous witch-hunting judge Pierre de Lancre (1553–1631), fellow French judge Henri Boguet (1550–1619), Nicholas Rémy who boasted of executing over 800 witches, and the *Magical Investigations* by Martin Delrio. Calmeil made sense of all this material by medicalizing it. The description of Rémy's work in the contents pages, for instance, states simply that the magistrate 'interrogates the sick and exposes the symptoms of their delirium'.[59] He used Esquirol's categories of monomania, theomania, and demonomania, but also carved out his own sub-categories, namely 'prophetic monomania', 'demonolatry', 'demonopathy', and 'hystero-demonopathy'. One English reviewer heaped great praise on the book, stating that 'no one was better fitted to be an historian' than Calmeil, and that he had performed the Herculean task 'with an energy and skill, which must add greatly to his reputation'. The reviewer went on to conclude that Calmeil had convincingly 'shown that persons who were burnt, or otherwise executed for magic and other offences, ought instead, if psychological science had been sufficiently advanced, to have been sent to lunatic asylums'.[60]

By the 1860s, three main classes of demonomania had become more or less established, identified primarily from historical analysis rather than contemporary clinical study. There was Calmeil's 'demonolatry', a term he no doubt borrowed from Rémy's book *Daemonolatreiae libri tres* (1595). The sufferers of demonolatry were those who, for one reason or another, believed they were members of a diabolic witch cult who worshipped the Devil at sabbats and committed horrible crimes in his name. Michéa described it as the rarest form. 'You could even say that the latter variety no longer exists', he reflected. 'It ended with the superstition of evil pacts, that it has disappeared since we no longer believed in sorcerers, and especially since the courts no longer deliver them to the flames'.[61] The study of demonolatry was, agreed fellow French alienist Antoine Ritti, only of historical interest to the psychiatrist and mainly because of the way it had nearly always expressed itself as an epidemic illness.[62] The second category, 'demonopathy', or epidemic 'hystero-demonopathy' in women, concerned those who considered themselves bodily possessed and who had the conviction that an evil spirit or devil was inside them controlling what they did. Calmeil gave the case of the nuns of Cambrai as an example. For several years in the 1490s it was reported that some nuns of the Augustinian convent at Quesnoy le Conte, near Cambrai, were possessed by devils that made them climb trees, run wild like dogs, and fly in the air like birds. One demon appeared repeatedly in the guise of the nuns' recently deceased father confessor. Exorcism largely failed and Pope Alexander VI even gave a special mass to try and end the crisis.[63] The third main class of demonomania, 'damnomania', was quite widely, albeit briefly, adopted as a term in Italian and French psychiatry, but less so in anglophone literature. Sufferers were convinced their souls were lost and believed that the Devil taunted them with damnation and visions of the flames of Hell and tempted them to commit suicide.

The term had originally been coined back in 1817 by François-Emmanuel Fodéré (1764–1835), one-time director of the Marseille asylum, to distinguish between demonomania as supposed diabolic possession and those whose insanity expressed itself in terms of a melancholic fear of personal divine damnation or demonic threat. It was given new currency mid century due to the influential work of Maurice Macario—who we shall hear more of in the next chapter. Belgian psychiatrist Joseph Guislain (1797–1860) also proposed an alternative term—'demonophobia'—for the same set of fears and persecutions that were considered, at base, symptoms of a form of melancholic terror.[64]

What about witches?

Claude-François Michéa was the author of one of the more original exercises in retrospective diagnoses at this time. While his fellow psychiatrists were preoccupied with a relatively small number of notorious possession cases, he turned his gaze to the thousands of people accused, tortured, and executed for witchcraft and their supposed victims.[65] In 1862 he surveyed the historic material in light of the latest research in physiology as well as psychiatry, and even referred to some of the retrospective diagnostic work by the mesmerists. Michéa's key aim was to overturn, once and for all, the 'insulting hypothesis of simulation' that had long been promoted as an explanation for those who claimed they were bewitched and possessed in the past. One way or another, all the aspects of witchcraft could be accounted for medically; sometimes by psychiatry, sometimes by physiology. To begin with, he drew upon the metaphysics of the early modern experimental scientist and philosopher Francis Bacon (1561–1626), who wrote of the power of envy in witchcraft accusations. Vehement wishes, Bacon observed, 'frame themselves readily into imaginations and suggestions'.[66] Michéa suggested that witchcraft had been real in some senses rather than a foolish belief. To what extent, he wondered, could the mind act on the body or on the mind of another person by the sole force of his or her imagination? When projected through look or voice, fear, envy, hatred, and revenge might work on the imagination and affect mental and physical states in people and so cause the symptoms that were attributed to the supernatural. There was no fakery and there was no magic, just the influence of the mind on the body and vice versa.

Michéa found various references to suicide amongst those who were accused of and tried for witchcraft, mostly in the work of Nicolas Rémy. He rather overstated the frequency of suicide amongst accused witches from what we now know, but he saw suicide as a convincing link with contemporary psychiatric research, explaining that 'melancholic lunatics' or demonopaths, were particularly prone to end their anxieties of damnation by killing themselves.[67] He applied a similar diagnostic process to a passage in Henri Boguet's *Discours exécrable des sorciers* (1602) that concerned how witches blasphemed and mumbled, noting that they were 'phenomena that mental medicine has long since converted into symptoms of religious melancholy'.[68] The issue of witches flying and their victims levitating remained a perennial puzzle ripe for new explanation. Michéa referenced a case reported by Bodin of a young girl who was suspended in the air and also the accusations the nuns at Louvier, Normandy, made against the young priest Thomas Boullé in 1647.[69] Amongst them was the claim that he forced some nuns to fly with him to a sabbat. Michéa recognized the long-held view that hallucinogenic drugs may have led to such accusations but also noted how in some nervous diseases the insane lost consciousness of the weight of their own bodies. So, it was understandable that they might earnestly report the sensation of flying.

Michéa seemed particularly pleased with his extensive detective work on the issue of the insensitive Devil's marks that accused witches across Europe supposedly bore on their bodies as a proof of their satanic pact. Thomas Boullé was searched, for example, and found to bear such a stain. Michéa noted the 'bites, the scratches and the abrasions which are made daily in the insane asylums by patients in the grip of melancholy' by way of explaining the origin of these marks. As to their insensitivity, there was by way of analogy the asylum patient observed by Bénédict Morel (1809–1873) who plunged his arm into boiling water to show that he could handle the flames of Hell.[70] He ended his survey triumphantly: 'The very recent conquests of pathology of the nervous system therefore remove the last traces of the shadows spread over the history of demonology.' And he had harsh words for the authorities of the fifteenth and sixteenth centuries. 'By establishing confusion between real crimes and chimerical facts imagined in good faith by sick minds', he said, the law against witchcraft was 'perhaps a greater evil than the one it sought to destroy'.[71]

But were the witch hunters Michéa denounced just as insane as the witches who confessed? This was an issue that never really got reconciled in

the psychiatric literature. It was easy enough to explain away blithely the
delusions and stories of the poor and uneducated as aspects of insanity, but
what of the learned judges, philosophers, and theologians who believed
exactly the same thing? The question was clearly an uncomfortable one. The
British psychiatrist Forbes Benignus Winslow (1810–1874), founder and editor of the *Journal of Psychological Medicine*, observed in 1860 that 'the practice
of judging the so-called witches and sorcerers seems, indeed, to have developed an insanity all its own'.[72] He did not pursue this thought any further,
though. One of the few others to comment on the matter was William
Tennant Gairdner (1824–1907), Professor of Medicine at Glasgow University
and Royal Physician. He had researched the Scottish witch trials, read the
work of Calmeil, and confidently stated by way of conclusion that it was
'now universally conceded' that those accused of witchcraft were in many
cases insane. As to the men who operated the laws against witchcraft, well
their beliefs 'may well be called, in a very real though not technical sense of
the word, an insane opinion; but the men who held it in those days were by
no means individually insane'.[73] He seemed to suggest in a mealy-mouthed
way, in other words, that if you were learned then you could be an ardent
witch hunter and be sane while those poor people tortured were insane by
way of holding the same beliefs.

Too many manias

By the 1870s there was some concern that categories of insanity were spreading like a disease. Joseph Guislain was grumbling about it already in the 1850s,
noting twenty-three forms of mania at that point—and that was only his short
list. He commented wryly that this terminological baggage was proving rather
heavy on the memory. An English medical reviewer was blunter in 1866,
complaining of 'the useless verbiage of name inventors in classification'.[74]
From the days when Pinel radically reduced the number of diseases in his
nosology, including the eradication of Sauvages' nine demonomanias, the
growing number of psychiatrists and asylum superintendents had generated an
international proliferation of new terms and categories of mental illness, as well
as the resurrection of old ones. There seemed a mania or insania for everything
based on symptoms alone. It was becoming a joke. One British journalist
joshed that all the people who continued to buy the 'worthless' astrological
Moore's Almanack must be sufferers of 'almanack monomania'.[75]

The growth of categories and symptoms was driven, in part, by the preoccupation with explaining all the curious beliefs and symptoms found in the demonologies and witch trial records of the past. A case in point was the werewolf prosecutions in France and Germany. In 1855 the Assistant Physician at the London Hospital, Nicholas Parker, wrote an article for the *Asylum Journal* on this variety of 'Insania Zoanthropica', a term that had been recently made current by the German psychiatrist Johann Baptist Friedreich (1796–1862). Parker observed that 'some delusions, indeed, being founded upon passions which always exist in the human breast, are common to every people in every age. But it is only during the middle ages that we observe numerous instances of the rapid spread of such epidemics.'[76] Choreomania, an obscure term coined in the late eighteenth century (orchestromania also floated briefly in the literature), was reinvigorated in the mid nineteenth century as psychiatrists delved deeper into the history archives.[77] It derived from the ancient Greek word 'choreia' meaning 'to dance'. From the fifteenth century, reports emerged across Europe of outbreaks of compulsive collective dancing with people collapsing from exhaustion or breaking bones. During one such outbreak in Strasbourg in 1518, the legendary exorcist Saint Vitus was called upon by the Church to intercede and cure the disease.[78] From here on the condition became widely known as Saint Vitus' Dance. Influential sixteenth-century physician Paracelsus gave it a place in medical nosology and termed it *Chorea Sancti Viti*. In fact, Paracelsus identified three main types of chorea: *chorea imaginativa*, which arose from the imagination, *chorea lasciva*, arising from sexual arousal and desire, and *chorea naturalis*, which had nothing to do with holy intervention and arose from troubled mental states. The following century Thomas Sydenham identified 'chorea minor', or what is still known today in neurological medicine as Sydenham's chorea, to define not a dancing disease but the rapid, spasmodic convulsions he had seen in pre-pubescent children. The whole topic was given a renewed high profile in the psychiatric world with the publication of Justus Hecker's essay *Die Tanzwuth, eine Volkskrankheit im Mittelalter* (1832), which was a history of 'Dancing Mania'. Hecker was fascinated by the diseases of the medieval period and had just published a well-received book on the Black Death. He juxtaposed the 'mental plague' of dancing mania with the physiological bubonic plague. An English translation was published in 1844 by the Sydenham Society, which had been set up the previous year to support the diffusion of medical literature.[79]

The growing influence of medical jurisprudence on psychiatry as well as clinical asylum research would begin to whittle away at the necessity for so many categories, particularly the ones with such historical baggage. During the late 1870s and the 1880s various International Committees for the classification of mental diseases were also held to arrive at a consensual, streamlined list of insanities. But around this time the profusion of manias and insanias was swept away by the psychiatric profession's brief but powerful embrace of hysteria as an all-encompassing explanation for the mental 'aberrations' of the past.

Writing hystory

The famed French psychiatrist Jean-Martin Charcot (1825–1893), professor of anatomical pathology at the Salpêtrière, and tutor to Sigmund Freud, is sometimes credited with creating the field of retrospective diagnosis.[80] Yet, as we have seen, historical psychiatry was well-established by the time Charcot rose to prominence in the 1870s, and it had already profoundly shaped psychiatric classifications. What Charcot and his fellow hystorians did, then, was to use their new definition of hysteria to promote such retrospective medicine as never before, and also to make the early modern witch trials a vibrant contemporary religious and political talking point.[81]

In essence, Charcot and his followers used the evidence of history to argue that rather than being an unstable and erratic condition, 'hysteria' was governed by immutable medical 'laws' that were evident across time and cultures and had clearly defined physical manifestations.[82] By establishing such an overarching explanation, Charcot rendered redundant the endless attempts at precise symptomatic diagnoses and chased the references to demons from medical classification. This new hysteria was not considered a category of insanity, but, rather like epilepsy, it was defined as a related condition that could lead to insanity. Charcot and his disciple Paul Richer (1849–1933) admitted, for instance, that not all cases of demonic possession in the past could be classified as hysteria, since epilepsy, hypochondria and insanity could all produce similar symptoms. Hysteria, although still mostly associated with women, was freed of its lingering gynaecological associations and so men and boys were also 'discovered' to suffer from the same set of symptoms.

According to Charcot, major hysterical attacks consisted of four phases, each identifiable by performative physical signs. The first began with spasmodic or convulsive fits rather like chorea or epilepsy. Then came extraordinary, gymnastic contortions and arching of the back. The third phase consisted of passionate emotions and gestures, and then the patient entered a final phase of melancholic delirium with crying and laughter subsiding into dazed confusion. Each phase could also manifest itself alone and Charcot identified the second phase of violent distorted movements with the behaviour of those thought possessed in the past, while the third phase explained the ecstatic experience of religious mystics recorded in history.[83] Charcot also invented the category of hystero–epilepsy to describe patients with nervous conditions who acquired or imitated the symptoms of epileptics. Unlike the suddenness of epileptic seizures, hystero–epileptics exhibited premonitory hysterical symptoms. This term generated confusion as to its relation with hysteria, with some suggesting they were synonymous.[84]

Charcot not only turned to the old familiar demonologists for evidence but also explored the world of early modern art. He became an avid collector of prints of historic paintings and engravings of the possessed which he displayed in his reception room. One visitor described the scene: 'on the walls of this room we seem to be intentionally brought face to face with the whole past history of nervous diseases in some of the strangest and most unique aspects'.[85] Charcot and his disciples compared these depictions with the many photographs and artistic representations of the female hysterics in the Salpêtrière, which were published in *La revue photographique des hôpitaux de Paris* and a dedicated journal, *Iconographie de la Salpêtrière*. The most striking product of Charcot's retrospective diagnoses was the book he wrote with Paul Richer, *Les démoniaques dans l'art* or *The Possessed in Art* (1887). As well as being an anatomist and psychiatrist Richer was also an artist, sculptor, and later a professor of artistic anatomy, though he had no formal training.[86] Their book included numerous sketches of the four hysteric forms copied from paintings and engravings of demoniacs from the fifth to the eighteenth century, and its aim was 'to deliver these sick people from the ill-founded reputation that was imposed on them so long ago'.[87]

The book was received well in the psychiatric world where Charcot now had international star quality. The *Journal of Mental Science* praised it fulsomely for its artistic and medical qualities.

> No one, at any rate, could leave the wards of the Salpêtrière and proceed to visit the picture galleries of the old masters, of the churches where Art has been employed to represent the miraculous scenes of ecclesiastical history,

without being struck with the accuracy with which the painters have delineated
those convulsions and nervous distortions which may be seen in so concentrated
a form in the great Paris Hospitals.[88]

But there was an inevitable adverse reaction in Catholic circles. Joseph de
Bonniot, science editor for the Jesuit periodical *Études religieuses, historiques
et littéraires*, led the charge. He was not fundamentally antagonistic to psychiatry, and he would later endorse work at the Salpêtrière on hypnotism,
suggesting that possession and hypnotic influence were close neighbours.
But he fundamentally disagreed with what was proposed in *Les démoniaques
dans l'art*. He both critiqued Charcot's conception of hysteria in scientific
terms and he upheld the miraculous and divine as depicted in works such
as Rubens' *Miracles of St Ignatius of Loyola*, painted for the high altar of the
Jesuit Church in Antwerp in 1617–1618, which shows the co-founded of the
Jesuits exorcizing a woman whose face is contorted and body convulsed.[89]
The Catholic periodical the *Dublin Review*, which was actually published in
London, endorsed Bonniot's criticism, observing that 'Charcot has probably
got hysteria on the brain'. If his views remained unchecked, it warned,
works such as *Les démoniaques dans l'art* could cause harm, undermining
the venerable evidence for demoniacs in history and the divine power of
exorcism.[90]

    Charcot's ideas about hysteria in the past and present were hugely influ-
ential far beyond the borders of France and the closed world of medical
journals and doctoral theses. He was a showman and courted publicity. He
gave public lectures and demonstrations where he hypnotized his female
hysterical patients. Through the 1880s and 1890s English-language medical
journals reported admiringly on his activities and ideas, which were popularized in newspapers and periodicals around the world. In 1880, for instance,
the American *Popular Science Monthly* printed an article on 'Hysteria and
Demonism' by one of Charcot's interns at the time, Charles Richet, which
was translated from the literary and cultural magazine, *Revue des Deux
Mondes*. The cultural reach of the new hysteria was also manifest in art
and literature.[91]

    Charcot's experiments with hypnosis on hysterical patients also triggered
a related wave of retrospective diagnoses. His use of hypnosis validated, to a
degree, some of the old claims for mesmerism in this respect. There was no
fluidic force involved now, but the new hypnosis nevertheless reinvigorated
the notion that there could exist an invisible bond between individuals and

that people were prone to involuntary suggestive influences.[92] Charcot believed hypnosis only worked on hysterical patients, but up in the north-eastern city of Nancy physician Ambroise-Auguste Liébeault (1823–1904), who had long researched induced sleep states, and his student Hippolyte Bernheim (1840–1919), vociferously rejected this and promoted the view, which would become pervasive, that the hypnotic state was not patho-logical in nature and could be induced in everyone. This had implications for interpreting the supposed role of hypnosis in the past. Stimulated by the experiments of Charcot and Bernheim, in 1887 Swedish Professor of Psychiatry Fredrik Björnström wrote a history of hypnotism in which he confidently stated that all those persecuted as witches were 'nothing but somnambules who easily entered into the hypnotic state'. A few years later, the French physician and medical author Louis Raoul Regnier also wrote a book entitled *Hypnotism and Ancient Beliefs* which contained a section on the witch trials presenting evidence culled from all the usual demonologies and cases. In the early 1890s the Harvard Professor of English Barrett Wendell (1855–1921) was newly convinced that the Salem witchcraft accusations could now be explained away as an epidemic of hypnotism. The bewitched girls were 'victims of hypnotic excess', he claimed. 'In all probability they had learned, willingly or unwillingly, to hypnotise themselves.'[93]

What Charcot attempted through art history his fellow French psych-iatrist Désiré Magloire Bourneville (1840–1909) attempted through litera-ture. He was a disciple of and collaborator with Charcot, first as an assistant at the Salpêtrière and then as the head of the children's section at the Bicêtre. Unlike Charcot, Bourneville's political and medical agendas became deeply entwined. As an ardent secularist and anticlerical politician he was involved in successful campaigns to remove nuns from acting as nurses in public hos-pitals and to end compulsory church attendance for patients. He was also a leading campaigner for cremation.[94] For Bourneville the days of the witch trials were a period that demonstrated the very worst influence religious institutions had on society, general intellect, and mental health. In the face of the power of the Church the development of psychiatry represented the great flourishing of secularism and scientific endeavour under the French Republic. But the war was not yet won. The category of hysteria, and the application of psychiatry to the past were tools for undermining the remain-ing influence of the Church.

Between 1882 and 1902 Bourneville published nine edited volumes on diabolic possession, religious ecstasy, and corporeal miracles, including some key demonological texts from the sixteenth and seventeenth centuries. The series has been neatly described as representing 'the crossroads of science, history and politics'.[95] Bourneville called it the *Bibliothèque diabolique* or Diabolic Library, partly to describe its contents and partly, with amusement, to reflect how his religious opponents would certainly denounce such an enterprise. The first volume, *Le sabbat des sorciers*, published in 1882 with the assistance of his friend Edouard Teinturier, was hardly explosive. It consisted mostly of extracts from Bodin and the *Compendium maleficarum* (1608) by the Italian priest and exorcist Francesco Maria Guazzo. Guazzo's book, which borrowed heavily from Nicholas Rémy and Martin Delrio, considered at length the witch's pact with the Devil, and also the use of drugs and poisons by witches. It was evocatively illustrated with numerous woodcuts of witches and devils that have been widely used since. Somewhat surprisingly, considering the rich material, Bourneville only made one innocuous professional observation on the text, a brief note concerning the strong breath and odour of hystero-epileptics.[96]

There was talk of producing editions of the notorious texts by Bodin and Boguet that had long been cited by psychiatrists, but they never appeared.[97] Instead the next in the series was a manuscript in the French National Library, edited by the archivist Armand Bénet, that recounted the exorcisms of a young chambermaid named Françoise Fontaine at Louvier, Normandy, in 1591. She claimed she was possessed by an evil spirit and exhibited all the usual symptoms, but she was arrested as a suspected witch. She was pricked for the Devil's mark and confessed to making a pact with him. At her trial she also said she had been raped by soldiers.[98] Bourneville's edition was prefaced by a lengthy essay on the historical, literary, and psychiatric aspects of the case, and included some of his case notes to give comparative examples of women suffering the same hysterical symptoms in the present day. It was concluded that Françoise Fontaine was a clear hystero-epileptic. Other historic texts in the series likewise concerned 'hysterical' young women, including the personal account of the Dominican nun Jeanne Féry who was possessed and exorcized in 1584–1585 and wrote about her experience. The most heavily annotated with retrospective diagnostic observations was the volume on *Soeur Jeanne des Anges* (1886), which reprinted the autobiography of the Ursuline nun Jeanne de Belcier who was at the centre of the Loudun possession sensation of 1632.[99] It was the only volume in the series with a preface by Charcot, while doctor Gabriel Legué (1847–1913) and Charcot's former intern George Gilles de la Tourette (1857–1904), who was brought up near Loudun and who gave his name to Tourette's Syndrome, provided the annotated notes. But the most influential of all the historic texts published under the series was a reprint of the 1579 French edition of Johann Weyer's *De praestigiis daemonum* or *On the Tricks of Demons* (1563).[100] When the Viennese bookseller Hugo Heller asked Sigmund Freud in 1907 to name ten good books, he wrote back that amongst the most 'significant' books to his mind were 'those of Copernicus, of the old physician Johann Weier on the belief in witches, Darwin's *Descent of Man*'.[101]

Johann Weyer (1515–1588) is certainly an intriguing figure. He was a Dutch physician who had been a student of the great German physician and occult philosopher Heinrich Cornelius Agrippa (1486–1535), who posthumously attracted a Faustian reputation for satanic relations. Weyer was, then, a link between the intellectual world view of the Renaissance 'magicians', before the witch trials escalated, and the witch-hunting demonological authors of the second half of the sixteenth century.[102] In various respects, *On the Tricks of Demons* was similar to other demonological texts of the period. Weyer did not deny the existence of devils or that they held influence over some of those accused of witchcraft or who claimed to be possessed. The Devil was a powerful force in the world within God's boundaries. What marked Weyer out as a maverick was his denial of physical diabolic pacts between witches and devils, and his view that women accused of witchcraft were, by and large, not guilty of their supposed crimes. Women were much more prone to melancholy, he considered, and therefore easy prey for the Devil and his illusions, seductions, and deceptions, which fed their foolish imaginings about their magical powers. Their persecution and execution served no purpose, said Weyer. Such deluded women required the help of physicians and priests. Wicked male magicians who deliberately sought out evil spirits through adjuration and conjuration, or who employed poisons, were, on the other hand, complicit and guilty in the eyes of God and the law. This distinction incensed the ardent witch-persecutors such as Bodin, who refuted Weyer in an appendix to *De la démonomanie*. Female witches were as guilty as the learned conjurors, said Bodin, and it was an outrage to suggest that they were innocent because they were sick and weak. It was an attack on the godly state and its authority.

A last Latin re-edition of *De praestigiis daemonum* was produced in Amsterdam in 1660 and then Weyer's medical reputation rather fell into obscurity until resurrected by the psychiatrists.[103] In the 1780s, the English physician and early psychiatrist Thomas Arnold (1742–1816) referenced *De praestigiis daemonum* along with Sauvages' *Nosologie*, as sources for understanding the 'absurdity' that was the epidemic insanity of the belief in possession and witchcraft.[104] Pinel was also well aware of Weyer's work and recognized that he was a rather lone voice in a world governed by what he saw as prejudice, ignorance, and intolerance. But Weyer was sadly tainted with the 'common errors' of the time, said Pinel, and so a 'blind belief in demonomania or the tricks of the devil should not be surprising in the writings of Wierus'.[105] In the early 1830s, Joseph Guislain was much more generous and was the first to promote Weyer to the pantheon of early psychiatry. Guislain commended Weyer as starting a new enlightened era in the understanding of mental illnesses after the darkness of the fifteenth century, and he later recommended Weyer's book along with the works of Esquirol, Macario, and Calmeil with regard to the study of demonomania.[106] Several decades later, in 1865, the Parisian Professor of General Pathology Alexandre Axenfeld (1825–1876) gave a widely reported and well-received lecture on 'Jean Wier and the witches' to the Paris Medical Faculty. Delivered with great verve in front of a packed house, it was not an exercise in retrospective diagnosis or a swingeing polemic, though he did take a swipe at religion when he stated that 'witches were the crime of the church'. The main thrust was to establish Weyer as a founding father of rational medicine. A newspaper report on the lecture agreed that Weyer should now 'be considered as the true precursor of Pinel, of Esquirol'.[107]

In 1893 William Tennant Gairdner wrote to his friend the physician Professor Clifford Allbutt (1836–1925), who had recently been commissioner in lunacy in London, to correct him about a claim Allbutt had made that Weyer was an Englishman. Gairdner described Weyer's work as 'a wonderful book for its day', but told Allbutt that it was 'not so wonderful (I think), or at least so thorough-going as the nearly contemporary one of Reginald Scot'. Axenfeld had also given an approving mention to Scot in his lecture.[108] Yet Scot (c.1538–1599) was no doctor but a modest landed gentleman and surveyor. The reason for his name appearing briefly in the annals of psychiatry was due to a remarkable book he wrote in 1584 called *The Discoverie of Witchcraft*.[109] Scot roundly critiqued and condemned the arguments for the persecution of suspected witches and the Catholic church's role in fostering magical beliefs. He relied heavily on Weyer for his medical evidence for the mental health of supposed witches and their melancholic tendancies. The main thrust of his argument was that post-menopausal women were particularly prone to the condition. But Scot went further than Weyer in arguing the medical case over the supernatural. While Weyer suggested that women's delusions of being witches were because their gender and mental state made them vulnerable to the Devil's machinations, Scot thought that melancholic women simply *imagined* their diabolic relations. This advancement of the medical arguments was presumably one of the reasons why the *Discoverie* was translated into Dutch by members of Leiden University's medical faculty in the early seventeenth century.[110]

Gairdner was adamant that Scot was far in advance of the Dutchman 'in the clearness of his views and the unwavering steadiness of his leanings to the side of humanity and justice'.[111] It is no surprise, then, that Gairdner had a hand in ensuring that the first new edition of Scot's *Discoverie* since the seventeenth century appeared a year after Bourneville's edition of Weyer. He encouraged his old friend from student days, Richard Brinsley Nicholson (1824–1892), a distinguished military surgeon, to produce a new edition. Nicholson was already an active editor of early modern folios for the New Shakspere Society and in 1883 sent round a circular proposing the first edition and asking for subscribers. The editors of the *Journal of Mental Science* printed the circular and heartily wished for its success. Only 250 copies were printed and among the subscribers were numerous medical men, including the likes of the British psychiatrist Daniel Hack Tuke (1827–1895). A review in the *Journal of Mental Science* expressed 'feelings of admiration and gratitude' towards Scot, 'who was in advance both in knowledge and boldness of even the physicians of his day'.[112] But despite such advocacy, Nicholson's edition of Scot did not get widely reviewed in the medical press at home or abroad, and Scot never got the attention and praise that Gairdner hoped. The fact that he was not a physician and so did not fit into the narrative of the profession explains part of it. Scot's *Discoverie* was also never published in French like Weyer's book. We can also detect some signs of nationalism at play, perhaps, at a time in the late nineteenth century when cultural, military, and political rivalry with Bismarckian Germany was really ramping up. In 1894 an article in the *Journal of Mental Science* stated that German psychiatrists were promoting Weyer as the first to attack demonology and witchcraft, before offering a questioning footnote that referred to Gairdner's admiration for Scot as the true pioneer.[113]

The new witch prickers

In his 1859 study of hysteria, Paul Briquet (1796–1881), who had a great influence on Charcot's ideas of the condition, particularly the view that men could also be hysterics, devoted considerable thought to various forms of anaesthetic hysteria, including those which affected patches of skin. Briquet based much of his study on clinical observation and testing of his own patients, as well as on some earlier studies of insensibility. But he also drew on the evidence of the early modern demonologists, including the usual suspects, Bodin, Rémy, and Boguet. He was interested too in the witch-pricking activities of the notorious Witchfinder General, Matthew Hopkins, regarding whom he had read about in Sir Walter Scott's *Letters on Demonology and Witchcraft* (1830), which had been translated into French in 1832.[114] In the years 1645–1647, during the British Civil Wars, Hopkins, who was the son of a Puritan clergyman, and his sidekick John Stearne, travelled through the counties of eastern England gathering evidence against suspected witches which lead to the execution of well over 100 people, mostly women. Hopkins died in 1647 but Stearne wrote about the witch's mark in his 1648 guide to witch hunting, and explained, 'I confess that it is very difficult to be known, and very few ever attained to the discovery thereof: but it is to be known by the insensiblenesse thereof.'[115] Briquet wondered how many sufferers of lypemania, hypochondria, and hysteria had perished because of insensitive skin patches.

Michéa added recent research on pain theory to his explanation of these witch marks, and in particular the pioneering work of the neuroscientist Charles Bell (1774–1842) on muscle nerves, phantom limbs, and analgesia. This, he thought, explained the analgesia experienced by hysterics and maniacs under torture, while the slowing down of capillary circulation in the organs affected by analgesia explained the lack of blood reported when suspected witches were pricked for Devil's marks. In 1871, William Alexander Hammond (1828–1900), Professor of Diseases of the Mind at New York University, and the first professional neurologist in America, also observed the frequency of skin anaesthesia experienced by hysterics in his charge. 'In the days of witchcraft', he noted, 'many a hysterical woman with anaesthetic spots on her skin, went to the gallows or the stake'.[116] Unperturbed by the problematic historical associations, Hammond had even applied the wire brush of a powerful induction coil to the insensitive spot of one patient, but she felt no irritation.

A couple of decades later, John Michell Clarke, then assistant physician and neurologist at Bristol General Hospital, England, explored Charcot's conception of hysteria in the journal *Brain*. He noted Briquet's pioneering work on the matter before observing that 'hysterical anaesthesia was not generally recognized until the popularization of the subject by M. Charcot'. For Clarke, the only way to get a thorough understanding of hysteria was by the experimental method. So out came the needles again. He cited the opinion of the seventeenth-century French physician Jacques Fontaine, professor of medicine at the University of Aix, who wrote a book on witches' marks and gave evidence at the infamous trial of Father Louis Gaufridy, who was executed for making a pact with the Devil and causing the possession of Ursuline nuns at Aix-en-Provence in 1611.[117] Fontaine had concluded that the Devil applied hot iron to the body of his converts without producing a scar. Clarke mused that, 'today the physician proceeds in the same way as the judges of the middle ages; when he suspects a person of hysteria he begins by trying to obtain moral proof of the existence of the neurosis in the morbid tendencies—hereditary and personal—of the patient'.[118] Now re-defined as 'hysterical stigmata' or 'marks of hysterical possession', the experiment was described by Clarke as follows, 'a fine sharp point is used; it is necessary to make the pricks sufficiently profound, and to go over an extensive surface of skin, or at any rate to prick the skin in several places widely separated from each other. The results may be then, for convenience, marked out on a chart.'[119]

It was, of course, women on whom this was practised, partly because of the link between anaesthesia and hysteria, but it was also due to the preoccupation with analogous evidence from the witch trials. The fact that some psychiatrists freely equated their experiments on hysterics with early modern torturers and prickers has rightly invited criticism from more recent scholars about the explicit and implicit misogyny inherent in the writings and actions of the psychiatrists of hysteria.[120] This is most evident, and unsettlingly so, from a case study published by William Tennant Gairdner, which he called 'A Modern Witch, medically investigated'. Asylum patient Mrs X.Y. had not been accused of witchcraft and neither had she expressed any thoughts about witchcraft, it was Gairdner who called her a 'Modern Witch' from his clinical observation of her appearance, mental state, and physical condition. From reading the old witch trial cases he found in her a modern archetype of the women who were tried and executed in the early modern period. She could not remember her age but she was several years

past child bearing and had experienced a 'deal of trouble' in her marriage.
She lived on the verge of poverty and was tired of life. When brought to the
asylum in 1879 she was examined for ovarian hyper-aesthesia (hyper physical sensitivity), which was considered a classic symptom of hystero-epilepsy.
No symptoms were found, and, indeed, no other obvious signs of hysteria.
Yet Gairdner noticed 'a kind of tremor or "shudder"', which combined
with Mrs X.Y. also having a wry neck (slightly twisted or tilted), and unsociable ways, 'gave her at times a rather "weird" appearance'. In other words,
she looked like an old-time witch to Gairdner. Furthermore, he never personally saw her shed any tears in his presence over the years, which he
described as 'an indubitable sign of a witch, according to ancient opinions'.
The next proof required the pricking test. Mrs X.Y. spent much of her time
knitting, so she had no fear or concern with jabbing herself with a sharp
point. When medical attendants tried her with pins they found that all over
the surface of the body the sense of pain was extremely deficient. This varied from the usual hysterical surface anaesthesia that manifested in terms of
patches of skin. As Gairdner reported, 'a pin can be stuck into any part of
her surface so far as hitherto tried, or even passed through a fold of integu-
ment again and again without her wincing in the slightest degree, or giving
even the least evidence of pain'. This was, he concluded, the ' "raw material"
of a witch'.[121]

Gazing into the subconscious

Charcot's hysteria went out of fashion by the end of the 1890s. Hystory was
history, psychiatrists began to close their books of demonology, and the
pricking needles were put back in their cases. The new star of psychiatry, the
German Emil Kraepelin (1856–1926), was on the rise, and he proposed a
transformative new nosology based solely on clinical observation. He made
a determined break with the long-held notion that certain symptoms were
characteristic of specific illnesses. Symptoms of insanity were shared with
too many other conditions for them to be the basis of psychiatric classification. Hence there was no need to search across the centuries for precedents.
Others had made a similar point before, but Kraepelin successfully reconfigured psychiatric classification in response, based on studying the occurrence,
evolution, and outcome of mental diseases free of the old associations.[122]
The most lasting consequences of his approach were the establishment of

two major categories, namely 'manic depressive insanity' and '*dementia praecox*' (early-onset dementia), which would later be redefined as schizophrenia. But the impulse to search for historical truths in the mental worlds of the distant past were inherited by the emerging sciences of psychoanalysis and psychology.

The modern discipline of psychology was forged in universities rather than hospitals and asylums and had its origins in mid nineteenth-century Germany, where the likes of Wilhelm Wundt (1832–1920) repositioned psychology away from its old philosophical concerns with the Christian soul and towards experimental work on human mental behaviour. The philosopher and psychologist George Trumbull Ladd (1842–1921), who introduced German experimental and statistical psychology to the United States, defined the new discipline simply as 'the description and explanation of the states of human consciousness'.[123] It was a behavioural rather than a medical science. There was considerable overlap between the interests and ideas of psychology and psychiatry, of course, with the field of 'abnormal psychology' concerned with the reasons for the onset of mental illness. Broadly speaking, though, the psychologists were interested in the totality of the human consciousness rather than just its pathological aspects. Wundt's laboratory, for instance, pioneered work on word association, space perception, and mental reaction times. But psychology also had its unorthodox histories and pathways that entangled with the older pseudo-sciences, and with issues of the supernatural already explored in this chapter. And, today, the investigation of the paranormal and magical thinking is still within the remit of academic psychology.[124]

In the early 1880s the American neurologist George Miller Beard (1839–1883) was walking the streets of Salem with a friend one day and began to muse on the origin of the notorious trials:

> I formed a resolution to search out and solve, if might be, the psychological problems that were the basis of that delusion; and to present the solution in such a way that it should be at once an original contribution to science and a practical guide for the present and the future.

The result was a book entitled *The Psychology of the Salem Witchcraft Excitement of 1692*. He claimed grandly but incorrectly that it was 'the first systematic attempt that has ever been made to lift the general subject of witchcraft—or this special manifestation of it—out of narrative and tradition into the science of psychology'.[125] There was a reason why he chose the term 'excitement' rather than 'craze' or 'mania', for he believed that Salem was all about the nervous system. The neurological causes for the behaviour of those who said they were bewitched, and those accused of witchcraft, were 'more complex phenomena than those of insanity alone'.[126] Beard was a leading promoter of the condition termed neurasthenia, which was adopted widely in American medicine into the twentieth century. It was a nervous, depressive disorder manifest in terms of headaches, fatigue, mental exhaustion, moodiness, dyspepsia, and high blood pressure. Beard and others considered it a disease born of the stresses of modern life, as he outlined in a book called *American Nervousness* (1879). Beard obviously did not, then, retrospectively diagnose the presence of neurasthenia in the witch trials. He concluded, instead, that the basis of the Salem 'excitement' was a mix of hypnotic trance, insanity, and hysteria, and it was the ignorance of such conditions, and of the nervous system more generally, that made the trials possible. Beard was not a trained psychologist and his approach to witchcraft and Salem was not particularly 'psychological' with respect to the burgeoning academic discipline. Indeed, the *Detroit Lancet* thought it the very worst of Beard's publications, 'words, words, but no ideas'.[127]

For insight into the new 'psychological turn' we go, instead, to one of the founding fathers of American psychology, William James (1842–1910), who taught the first university class in psychology at Harvard in the 1870s and wrote the monumental founding text, *The Principles of Psychology* (1890). James had met with Beard, his library contained a copy of *Psychology of the Salem Witchcraft Excitement*, and we can detect some trace of his views in James's teaching. James referred only very briefly to the witch trials in *The Principles*, though, merely observing: 'the whole history of witchcraft and early medicine is a commentary on the facility with which anything which chances to be conceived is believed the moment the belief chimes in with an emotional mood'. His views were more fully expressed in his 1896 public lecture series on abnormal psychology, which explored how morbid ideas were part of the healthy as well as the diseased mind. One of the lectures was on historic demoniacal possession and another on witchcraft.[128] His manuscript lecture notes referenced Boguet, Calmeil, and Weyer, and he also cited the notorious *Malleus Maleficarum* or *Hammer of Witches*, a deeply misogynistic, demonological text written by Heinrich Kramer, a Dominican inquisitor, which was published in 1487. The work was well-known to early historians of the witch trials, such as Lecky, Charles Lea, and Johann Gieseler, but it was largely ignored by the early psychiatrists, with the exception of

Jean Baptiste Parchappe (1800–1866), who wrote a long commentary on it in 1843. Reading through the various demonological accounts gave James 'the most curious gruesome rathole feeling'.[129]

One comment stands out in the lecture notes: 'History shows that mediumship is identical with demon-possession. No one regards it as insanity.'[130] James was a co-founder of the American Society for Psychical Research, attended seances, and believed in psychic phenomena such as telepathy, though he never fully came down on the side of there being a spirit world; but it was a possibility. He once said of his favourite trance medium Leonora Piper that she 'has supernormal knowledge in her trances; but whether it comes from "tapping the minds" of living people, or from some common cosmic reservoir of memories, or from surviving "spirits" of the departed, is a question impossible for *me* to answer'.[131] Note the use of 'supernormal'. If communications with the spirit world were real, then this was not a matter of the 'supernatural'. That was why scientists were interested because it would prove a new dimension in the workings of the natural world. James's working knowledge of modern trance mediums convinced him that if they were not hysterical or insane then those sup-posedly possessed in the era of the witch trials need not be understood in such terms either. Perhaps some of *them* also possessed supernormal knowledge and even channelled spirits. 'If there are devils—if there are supernormal powers', he reflected, then 'it is through the cracked Self that they enter!'[132]

With spiritualist mediums at their disposal, psychologists no longer needed to search through old demonologies looking for analogous examples of abnormal mental states exhibited through supernatural beliefs. In Switzerland, James's good friend Théodore Flournoy (1854–1920), Professor of Psychology at the University of Geneva, and a student of Wundt, worked with a medium for five years but reached different conclusions to his American counterpart. It took him a while to get the confidence of a medium willing to be studied but he eventually struck gold with a woman in her thirties he called 'Hélène Smith', but whose real name was Catherine-Elise Müller (1861–1929). She had 'discovered' her mediumistic powers in 1892, and Flournoy described her as 'a remarkably intelligent and gifted person'. In another letter he described to James, 'this woman is a veritable museum of all possible phenomena and has a repertoire of illimitable variety: she makes the table talk,—she hears voices,—she has visions, hallucinations, tactile and olfactory,—automatic writing—sometimes complete somnambulism, catalepsy, trances, etc'.[133] She believed she had been reincarnated several times, once as the wife of a Hindu princess, at another time Marie-Antoinette. She also described how she had visited the inhabitants of Mars, depicting the planet's vegetation, and showing Flournoy examples of the Martian language. As a psychologist why bother looking at accounts of sixteenth-century possessed people when such rich material poured forth from mediums? Unlike psychical researchers, Flournoy was not looking for evidence of proof but for inner-life histories, evidence for the mental past of Smith's multiple reincarnation fantasies, looking for clues to unconsciously remembered experiences in her real life. His conclusions were written up in the sensational *Des Indes à la planète Mars* (*From the Indies to the Planet Mars*) published in 1899.[134]

With *Des Indes à la planète Mars* selling well in English and French, James wrote to Flournoy, 'Upon my word, dear Flournoy, you have done a bigger thing here than you know, and I think that your volume has probably made the decisive step in converting psychical research into a respectable science.'[135] In Britain, Italy, and France the boundaries between psychology and psychical research, indeed, remained entangled for a while.[136] But in America, all this dabbling with psychical research was too much for James's fellow psychologists. Wundt had rejected psychical research as unscientific back in 1879, and some of his American students, such as Granville Stanley Hall (1846–1924), first president of the American Psychological Association, vigorously ensured that the new discipline in North America was not tainted by association with mediumship research. Joseph Jastrow (1863–1944), well known for his work on the psychology of optical illusions, was quite clear that engagement with spiritualism was 'dangerous to mental sanity'.[137] The new adherents of experimental and social psychology also focused determinedly on the present rather than seeking to pathologize or explain the past. Their interest in history was more deep-time, concerned with the development of human cognition and the personal, experiential histories embedded in the individual subconscious. In the 1890s, for instance, Stanley Hall conducted a mass survey of contemporary popular fears, including those regarding the supernatural.[138] During the early twentieth century the psychology of contemporary 'superstition' would become well established in America and Europe, and the First World War provided an ideal laboratory for exploring the psychology of such belief in relation to stress and physical hardship.[139] Belief in witchcraft, magic, and the occult may have been considered symptomatic of abnormal psychology, but psychologists were also showing it was not just a mental throwback to the past but a fundamental part of the human condition.

We need not delve into the bitter factional disputes about who founded psychoanalysis as an enduring therapeutic treatment for mental disorders. Suffice it to say that both contenders, Sigmund Freud and Pierre Janet, were one-time students of Charcot and shared his interest in the witch trials as a means of exploring the unconscious. Their aim was to find the subconscious 'pathogenic secrets' of their patients, unlock them, and thereby enable a restorative cure.[140] This could only be achieved by exploring the emotional history of the individual.

Frenchman Pierre Janet (1859–1947) was a pivotal figure in the cross-fertilization between psychiatry, psychology, and psychoanalysis at the turn of the twentieth century. He became highly critical of Charcot's conception of hysteria as a universal condition—it became just a 'mere formula', he complained. Like William James, he was deeply interested in hypnosis and somnambulism, and he coined the term 'subconscious' and 'psychological analysis' before they became associated with Freud. In 1894 he gave a paper at Lyon University, subsequently published, in which he discussed the case of one of his patients at the Salpêtrière who believed himself possessed.[141] 'Achille' was a modest businessman brought up in a rural part of France. He was educated, did not share the 'superstitions' of his fellow villagers, and was lukewarm in religion. He married young, had children, and then in his thirties he experienced a series of medical problems including angina. He had also apparently been unfaithful to his wife on his business trips. His mood changed. He lay down in bed motionless for two days saying nothing and then suddenly burst into convulsive laughter. He had been possessed by the Devil.

Janet introduced his study of Achille by referencing the early modern Kentorp and Loudun nunnery possession cases, and he also recommended a recent article by Henry Meige (1866–1940) on the iconography of possession in the art of antiquity. Meige was one of Charcot's last interns and had worked with Richer and Charcot on their 'great art as psychiatric evidence' project.[142] Janet also quoted from the Diabolic Library's *Mémoires de sœur Jeanne des Anges*. Esquirol had explained 'this singular delirium as much as one could do in his time', Janet concluded, but 'all enlightened minds are now fully convinced that these possessions were mere mental illnesses, and that exorcisms, when they have had any effect, have played a role analogous to that of suggestions in hypnosis research'. As to Achille, Janet found him very resistant to hypnosis but eventually gained the revelation of his pathogenic secret—his adultery. But therapeutic cure proved elusive until Janet decided to act as exorcist and address the supposed Devil possessing Achille. Inspired by the automatic writing used by spiritualist mediums he began a dialogue with Achille/the Devil that eventually led to his cure.

It was Sigmund Freud, more than any other, perhaps, who ensured that retrospective diagnoses became deeply engrained in the twentieth-century public consciousness regarding the witch trials. As early as 1888 he wrote an encyclopaedia entry on hysteria in which he stated, 'In the Middle Ages neuroses played a significant part in the history of civilization, they appeared in epidemics as a result of psychical contagion, and were at the root of what was factual in the history of possession and witchcraft.'[143] In January 1897 he wrote a letter about it to his friend Wilhelm Fliess (1858–1928), a German crank surgeon who believed there was a direct neurological link between the nose, the genitals, and menstruation, and also conducted operations to sever the link. Freud told Fliess that the old possession cases were 'identical with our theory of a foreign body and the splitting of consciousness'— which obviously echoed Janet's recent work on Achille.[144] Thirty-five years later, he was still pursuing retrospective diagnoses in his paper, 'A Seventeenth Century Demonological Neurosis' (1923). It concerned a sick Bavarian painter named Christoph Haitzman who claimed he had made a pact with the Devil to keep him alive for another nine years. When time was nearly up he began to have convulsions, underwent exorcism, and wrote down an account of his life and his visions. When Freud was made aware of the manuscript in the Austrian National Library he read what he wanted to see and concluded Haitzman's state was the result of his libido and that he was suffering from a sexually neurotic condition. The case has attracted numerous psychoanalytical studies since.[145]

Back to January 1897 and Freud's mind was whirring on early modern possession cases as proof of the theory of split consciousness. He ordered a copy of the *Malleus Maleficarum* seeking historic evidence. 'I shall study it diligently', he told Fleiss.[146] There were no translations of this notorious book at the time. The first German edition appeared only in 1906, and no Latin reproductions had been printed for many years, so Freud presumably picked up an old early modern edition. Its contents seeped into his own subconscious as he wrote that he was beginning to dream 'of an extremely primitive devil religion'. Freud's interest in the *Malleus* made it the 'go to' demonological text amongst his disciples, and with the publication of a new

German edition in 1922–1923 it also became one of the most internationally accessible works of all the old demonologists. One of those disciples who worked through its lurid content was the Welsh psychiatrist, Ernest Jones (1879–1958), Freud's friend and official biographer, who gave a rousing defence of the Freudian interpretation of the witch trials in his book *On the Nightmare* (1931), which was based on research he had published twenty years earlier.[147] Jones began to engage with Freud's work around 1905, and he was particularly interested in repressed sexual memories, masturbation, and symbolism in mythology and folklore. This led him to explore old demonological texts for details of werewolves, nightmares, vampires, incubi, succubae, and witches. He used the recent 1906 German translation of the *Malleus*, as well as the already familiar works of Bodin, de Lancre, and Reginald Scot. He also drew upon the recent contextual work of historians, anthropologists, psychologists, as well as early psychiatrists.

Jones noted that the histories written by Ennemoser, Soldan, and others of their generation, had now been superseded by the more refined studies of Charles Lea and a handful of new German histories of the trials by the likes of the archivist Joseph Hansen (1863–1943). Jones consequently accepted the historical complexities of the early modern witch trials, but he was convinced, nevertheless, that the fundamental psychoanalytic explanation for the *belief* in witches and possession was quite simple. It was not a matter of insanity after all. It was, instead, 'in the main an exteriorization of the repressed sexual conflicts of women, especially those relating to the feminine counterpart of the infantile Oedipus situation'. This exteriorization of unconscious thoughts about themselves and their mothers explained 'why Witches were for the most part either very old and ugly or very young and beautiful'. Any historian of the trials today would tell you this gross generalization is arrant nonsense. But on we go. The symptoms of hysteria were also present, thought Jones, which, according to Freudian thinking by this point, were mostly convulsive hysterical attacks that symbolized coitus.[148] The reason why the trials happened when they did was due to social conditions at the time and the Church's misogyny and attitude towards sexual matters. It was an extreme form of repression that brought about widespread jealousy and dissatisfaction among women, which was then internalized and suppressed.

We end our journey into the world of retrospective diagnoses with an influential history of medicine written by the psychoanalyst Gregory Zilboorg (1890–1959), who emigrated from Ukraine to America in 1919 and set up his practice in NewYork. In *A History of Medical Psychology* (1941) he gave a substantive account of the 'burning horror' of the *Malleus* by way of contrast with his promotion of Johann Weyer's enlightened *De praestigiis daemonum*.[149] This built on his earlier study, *The Medical Man and the Witch During the Renaissance* (1935). The whole premise of Zilboorg's books was built on the century or so of psychiatric re-writing of history charted in this chapter. The familiar narrative was that during the benighted Middle Ages demonology replaced early psychiatric knowledge with disastrous consequences, and that those who confessed to being witches and demoniacs were psychotic and insane. 'For many years the world looked like a veritable insane asylum without a proper mental hospital', he wrote. Johann Weyer was the great beacon of light that shone out in this world of psychiatric darkness. Zilboorg further sealed the reputation of the *Malleus* as the key text in explaining the role of early modern demonology, and by this time the1928 English edition of the *Malleus* edited by Montague Summers had whipped up a lot of interest. Summers (1880–1948) became well-known for his popular histories of witchcraft and his sensational stance that people at the time had truly been possessed by the Devil.[150] So anglophone readers of Zilboorg's books could now easily follow up the references to the *Malleus* and have all their preconceived ideas confirmed.

Come the 1960s and such flawed histories came under sustained attack by the so-called 'anti-psychiatric movement' whose advocates argued that psychiatry was a tool of state oppression and even questioned whether established medical categories of mental illness existed at all. In 1970 the controversial psychiatrist and psychoanalyst Thomas Szasz (1920–2012), who argued that mental illness was more metaphor than actual illness, launched a scathing attack on Zilboorg and the prevalent psychiatric interpretation of the witch trials. It had 'become psychiatric dogma', he complained, 'so that today no "serious" student of psychiatry doubts that witches were insane.'[151] He was right in this sense. Further attacks continued through the 1970s and 1980s. A study of twenty student textbooks on abnormal psychology published between 1978 and 1981 found that they overwhelmingly repeated and endorsed Zilboorg's narrative as fact. These textbooks completely ignored the considerable body of critical work by historians and anthropologists on witchcraft and possession since the 1930s.[152] And, so, this chapter ends where we started really—with bad or outdated history.

★   ★   ★

The enthusiasm of psychiatrists, psychologists, psychoanalysts—and historians—to find an overarching explanation for the witch trials was fuelled by the zeal to prove that the past could be understood scientifically, that there was a key to such strange conundrums and that the lock was embedded in the pathology of the mind or body. In this determination they wilfully conflated, confused, and misunderstood the nature of early modern witchcraft. Little distinction was made between the small number of sensational diabolic possession and sabbath cases and the tens of thousands of more mundane accusations of neighbourly witchcraft, which often involved everyday misfortunes concerning bewitched livestock, dairying, and crops, rather than satanic orgies and extraordinary contortions. The role of torture in generating lurid fantasies of satanic conspiracies and experiences was largely ignored.[153] The likes of Michéa were more interested in understanding how people endured torture rather than reflecting on it being the source of 'insane' beliefs. A rare, perspicacious reviewer of Calmeil's book made just this observation in 1849: 'In some instances, it is probable that weak timid persons, in dread of torture, or overcome by pain, confessed that which they knew to be false. All who were executed as demon-worshippers were not, in all probability, monomaniacs.'[154]

This urge to find a simple, overarching cause has not gone away in the contemporary world. Computational methods have been employed to crack the 'mystery' of the witch trials by crunching data on the climate and crop failure in relation to large-scale hunts. The notion that delusions caused by fungal ergot poisoning were responsible remains widespread in popular culture. Others argue that the trials can be explained solely by the misogyny of emergent capitalism. All this tells us more about the world today, frankly, than that of our early modern ancestors. A huge amount of archival research has been conducted on the witch trials over the last fifty years. Hundreds of scholarly books and articles reveal that the trials were a deeply complex episode involving inter-linked legal, scientific, theological, political, cultural, and social developments at the time. And the most resounding refutation of the early psychiatrists' retrospective diagnoses was the ample evidence everywhere that the belief in witchcraft, magic, possession, and miracles continued to abound across modern Western Europe. As we shall now see, the past was not so easily separated from the present in the age of the asylum.

2

Pathologizing the supernatural present

If a man was to tell me that he believed in the existence of fairies or witches, I should not think this alone sufficient; but, if he told me that he was constantly in the habit of seeing the former dance, and being entertained by their music; or, that the latter were continually doing him mischief; I should have good reasons for supposing him mad.

(Thomas Bakewell, 1805)[1]

Thomas Bakewell (1761–1835) was not a qualified physician. He began his working life as a weaver, progressing to being the manager of a tape mill that made narrow strips of woven fabric. But his uncle and grandfather had run private 'mad houses' and, following in the family tradition, he founded his own institution in 1808, Spring Vale Asylum near Stone in Staffordshire.[2] While a good specimen of the burgeoning middle-class of the early nineteenth century, he was not entirely detached from the world of popular belief. He had no pretensions that his book *The Domestic Guide, in Cases of Insanity* (1805) was of any value to trained medical men. His motive for writing it was to draw upon the practical experience of his family's mad houses for the benefit of the poor—and at a price they could afford. Bakewell observed that, only fifty years before, those who successfully cured the insane were considered 'conjurers' by the common people across the Midland counties, but he hoped that the time was not so distant when insanity would be 'as much under the power of medicine' as any trifling ailment.[3] A man of Bakewell's background and time would, no doubt, have heard many stories of local witches, ghosts, and fairies. He was born a generation on from the days when the Witchcraft and Conjuration Act of

1604 was still on the statute books, and in his own time the likes of John Wesley (1703–1791) openly declared the reality of witchcraft and the eminent lawyer William Blackstone (1723–1780) said he could not deny the existence of witches because it was confirmed by the Bible.[4] The courts of Europe continued to deal with mob attacks on suspected witches, which were widely reported in the increasing number of provincial and national newspapers during the late eighteenth and early nineteenth centuries. So, it was still perfectly reasonable to believe in witches and fairies, but at the same time questions were beginning to be asked at what point that belief became a mental disease.

Bakewell was not the only one at the turn of the nineteenth century pondering where the boundaries lay and what caused people to believe in supernatural beings in the 'enlightened' world. Across the Atlantic, the Delaware physician John Vaughan (1775–1807) mused on the matter in the *Medical Repository* in 1802.[5] His thoughts were triggered by a case of supposed witchcraft and possession that he described as 'family-mania'. He thought it a highly unusual and sensational case. Indeed, he declared: 'I am flattered with the belief that it will be ranked amongst the wonders of the nineteenth century'. The family lived near Wilmington, and on 3 August 1801 the young man concerned went to see his mother, who had apparently been insane for some time. She caught him round the neck and kissed him, saying he would become a preacher of the gospel. He immediately went 'crazy'. On the next day she kissed four other of her children and two daughters-in-law, who all became 'frantic' as a result. The children became convinced that their mother was possessed by Satan and she had bewitched them with her kisses. They dragged her out of bed and beat her near to death, presumably to pummel the Devil out of her. They were about to set fire to the house to cleanse it when neighbours intervened and separated them. Within a few days they all regained their senses except one son, John, who was chained to the floor with his hands tied. He was released and put under Vaughan's care, making a full recovery after several weeks. 'This case affords ample source of speculation to the metaphysical pathologist who wishes to explain the morbid affections of the mind and body', Vaughan remarked. 'For my part, I confess myself much at a loss to attempt any explanation of this extraordinary form of mania, independent of any previous bodily disease.' He wondered whether it was some sort of sympathetic connection between the stomach and the nervous system. Then again, maybe it was an exclusively mental affection?[6] Twelve years later Esquirol would, of course, provide a clear psychiatric solution to Vaughan's conundrum in his essay on demonomania.

At times during the nineteenth century there was dissonance between the psychiatric language regarding supernaturalism in relation to the past and the profession's reluctant acceptance that the same beliefs were widespread in the present. Two psychiatric discourses developed, the retrospective and the contemporary. Sometimes they aligned and yet, at times, they were frustratingly contradictory. Several decades on from the ruminations of Bakewell and Vaughan, the growth of asylums and their trained medical superintendents revealed many first-hand, observable examples of individuals anguished in mind and tortured in body due to their belief in divine communications, devils, witches, and spirits. For some psychiatrists such people demonstrated aberrant, relict mindsets and beliefs, but collectively they also challenged the psychiatric confidence that the enlightened West had progressed far beyond the benighted era of the witch trials.

Demonomania redux

Esquirol stated in 1814 that of the more than 6000 insane patients he had seen, hardly two out of 1000 suffered from demonomania. He then updated this figure in his 1838 book, *Maladies mentales*, to barely one in 1000 out of the 20,000 patients he had observed up to that point.[7] They were mostly from the 'lowest class of society' and usually women, he stated, and so easy prey for the 'miserable crooks' who professed to have magical powers against witches and devils and stirred up phantasms and delusions in already diseased minds. One case he mentioned in 1814 was that of a 49-year-old female wool-spinner brought to the Salpêtrière. She believed she was bewitched and tried prayers, pilgrimages, and was even magnetized three times, but nothing made her better. She was a quiet woman and spoke reasonably on all other topics except witchcraft and the Devil. With regard to the rare cases of demonomania amongst the literate, he singled out the influence of books of mysticism and magic on susceptible minds. One woman in his care, a fairground trader with three young children, began, at the age of thirty-six, to read books on ghosts and witches, and became fascinated with the biblical Apocalypse. Her sleep started to suffer from the fears and excitement raised by her reading.[8] Esquirol did not think, however, that the perceived decline of belief in witches and devils led to less insanity. In post-Revolution France, he argued, the same people who were most prone to insanity due to hereditary conditions, hysteria, or external influences, were now vulnerable to new fears and apprehensions about the French state instead of the supernatural realm. The new bogeys were the police, prisons, and torture. 'It is always the weakness of the human mind, pusillanimity, disquietude and fear, which acts upon these unfortunate people, just as they were the cause of the maladies of the possessed', he asserted. 'Those who now fear the police, would formerly have been burned because they feared the devil'.[9]

Some of Esquirol's initial admirers were not convinced of his airy dismissal of the belief in witchcraft and possession and its inconsequential role in contemporary mental illness. Alexandre Brière de Boismont, who was the director of a private nursing home at the time, noted in his study of a case of demonomania published in 1843 that, yes, the idea of possession was very common in the Middle Ages, but that the belief in sorcerers was still 'widespread in the countryside and not a year passes without imbeciles or fools coming to testify in court to the truth of this fact'.[10] Over in America in 1835, psychiatrist Amariah Brigham noted that demonomania was not infrequent in his country and he had seen several cases within the previous year alone. The problem was also well observed at the Eberbach asylum in Germany, where at least ninety-three patients, one fourth of the surviving case files from the first half of the nineteenth century, expressed religious or supernatural concerns, delusions, and preoccupations.[11]

In one of his first publications, the young French psychiatrist Maurice Macario (1811–1898), who would later write influential works on the psychiatry of dreams and hallucinations, gave an unusually stinging rebuke to Esquirol's assertion. Esquirol and others were categorically wrong, he said. They were over-confident about the spread of enlightenment rationality among the populace and they had come to conclusions based only on their experience of urban asylum patients: 'If Esquirol had had the leisure to examine asylums in the provinces, he would not have argued that barely one demonomaniac is found in 1,000 insane people.'[12] Macario was the first to conduct a systematic, clinical study of demonomania in the present. His observations were based on his work at the provincial asylum at Maréville in northeastern France, where he had the opportunity to closely observe thirty-three people who claimed to be either suffering from possession, demonic assault, or the conviction of imminent damnation. Among them there were even a few cases of claimed incubi attacks, in other words demonic sexual assaults on women, which as Macario observed, was a condition thought to be obsolete by his peers. One such patient was Charlotte, forty-three years old, gentle, and shy. She believed Satan visited her at night in the form of a pretty boy surrounded by myriad different animals. He caressed her softly and gave her burning kisses on the mouth while making cabalistic signs with his right hand. Then he forced her to have sex. Sometimes he put her to sleep and transported her to Hell, where, one time, she was metamorphosed into a rat and endured the sufferings of the damned for half an hour. Marianne, aged fifty-six, a pious and devoted Catholic who suffered from chronic chest and abdominal pain, said that she lost her virginity to a demon. He came to her at night, smelling like a goat. Once he had copulated with her the demon opened his chest, pierced his heart, and took out a flower—presumably representing her virginity. The poor woman died of consumption after a few weeks in the asylum.

Unlike Esquirol, Macario did not equate demonomania with poverty and lack of education. He suggested, instead, that those involved in sedentary professions, such as tailors, shoemakers, and dressmakers were more prone to demonomaniacal delirium, along with certain types of agricultural workers, such as ploughmen. Macario had known only four completely illiterate demoniacs and he suggested that education as well as adherence to 'superstitious' beliefs, including imbibing tales of ghosts and reading books of magic and witchcraft, were common traits. The youngest demoniac in Maréville was twenty and the oldest seventy-five. The most prone to demonomania were those between forty and fifty years old, and eighteen of the thirty-three patients were women. The occupational categories of patient he identified led more solitary working lives than most and so he believed they were more likely to be preoccupied in reverie and lost in their own thoughts. Then there were the emotional triggers that brought on demonomania, 'sorrows, misery, jealousy, thwarted love, vanity and ambition, a strong moral commotion, a fright, worry, fear, dread, the lively and dark description of the torments of hell'. He also observed a number of physical ailments shared by the demonomaniacs in his care. Haemorrhoids, menstrual difficulties, and drunkenness were thought to provoke demonic delirium. Macario took some satisfaction in further contradicting Esquirol regarding the cure of demoniacs. Esquirol and others had considered the successful treatment of theomania and demonomania very difficult and doubtful. Yet, Macario boasted, 'we have cured almost all the possessed who had not yet fallen into dementia, that is to say seven'.[13] But Macario was not the only one claiming such success.

At a time when the state and the medical profession were increasing their control over the management of the mentally ill, Catholic institutions for the insane were being reinvigorated in France, with several new asylums founded during the 1820s and 1830s by the newly restored lay religious orders *Les Frères de Saint-Jean de Dieu* and the *Frères de Saint Augustin*. The latter also created a regional promotional journal called the *Éclaireur du Midi*, which was described by one reviewer at the time as 'less of a journal and more of a mystical almanac', comparing it to the cheap, popular grimoires that circulated at the time. It was full of miracles, magic, accounts of possession and the supernatural, and critiques of modern medicine. The reviewer concluded by asking his readers not to be too harsh on it, as it was 'more ridiculous than wicked'.[14] A key figure behind this resurgence was the charismatic figure of Joseph-Xavier Tissot (1780–1864), also known as *frère* Hilarion, who was sometimes portrayed as the anti-Esquirol of the age. Tissot had personal experience of mental illness, for in his thirties he had spent four years as a patient at the Charenton diagnosed with mania and melancholy. He later promoted the use of exorcism in therapeutics or what he termed 'religious-moral treatment'. For Tissot, cataleptics, epileptics, convulsives, the delirious insane, and '*les idiots pro-fondes*' were all potentially possessed, the latter from birth, and although he did not completely dismiss physical medical treatment, there was only one infallible cure for possession.[15]

Conflict inevitably resumed when French clergymen attempted to apply spiritual cures to those diagnosed as insane or hysterical. The medical superintendent at the Nantes asylum put out a statement expressing deep concern about the fact that the recently founded Catholic asylums were not only *caring* for the insane but were also *treating* them. Worse, they were engaged in exorcizing patients: 'There is certainly a big difference to be made between the *Frères de Saint Augustin* and *Frères de Saint-Jean de Dieu*, living with the insane, dressing their wounds, going day and night to their bedsides, and considering victims to be snatched from demons.'[16] The ecclesiastical authorities were cautious in sanctioning such exorcisms, though. Around 1840, for instance, Father Chiron, founder of a Catholic asylum for the insane, was refused permission by the archbishop of Lyon to conduct an exorcism on one of his patients who believed he was possessed.[17] But Tissot was a maverick who had no official role as an exorcist, and he did not seem

Figure 1 Joseph Xavier Tissot, in religion Father Hilarion. Lithograph by A. Lalauze.
Credit: Wellcome Collection

to follow the elaborate, sanctioned church ritual of exorcism either. Through his own publications, and the likes of the *Éclaireur du Midi*, he tapped into popular religious sentiment while sowing mistrust of the medical profession.

Exorcizing the demons from medical discourse

In 1857 strange things were afoot in the Alpine village of Morzine.[18] It was a remote mountain commune of some 2000 people in the Duchy of Savoy, which was part of the Kingdom of Sardinia until the French annexed the duchy by treaty in 1860. The nearest town, Thonon, was only twenty miles away but took nine hours on foot or by mule. Several girls at a school run by the Sisters of Saint Vincent in Morzine began to suffer from a strange malady. They blasphemed, cursed the priests, talked in strange tongues, suffered from violent convulsions, and exhibited extraordinary agility in climbing trees. The local doctor, François Buet, notified the authorities. In August Dr François-Joseph Tavernier, who was originally from Morzine but then practising in Thonon, was sent to investigate. Tavernier concluded it was a clear case of contagious *demonomanie*, as defined by Esquirol, which had been triggered by the religious fixation and nervous state of the girls as they experienced their first communion. The first to succumb and infect the others was a 10-year-old named Peronne Tavernier, who claimed to see snakes twisted around her hat. The local priest asserted, however, that the girls were truly possessed by devils, and he took it upon himself to start conducting exorcisms without seeking official sanction from his bishop. Meanwhile, the villagers, while accepting that the devil was at work were fearful that witches were also involved in the affair. The girls claimed they were bewitched by some men in the village, including a defrocked priest. When doctor César Chiara, who practised near Lyon, visited Morzine he interviewed one of the suspected witches, a shoemaker and deputy mayor named Jean Berger, who Chiara described as the Urbain Grandier of the place.[19]

In February 1858, the *mal* or sickness surged with a vengeance and now older women claimed they too were possessed. By June around forty people in the commune had succumbed. There is little evidence, though, that the authorities made any further interventions until after the French authorities took over the region. Then, in 1860, the French Ministry of the Interior sent in the psychiatrist Dr Joseph Arthaud (1813–1883), the director of the l'Antiquaille insane asylum, Lyon. Arthaud was an ardent Catholic and was later appointed the first professor of mental illnesses at Lyon medical school. He found that some 100 people were now affected, nearly all women. He talked to the local doctors, apprised himself of Tavernier's diagnosis, and observed some of the possessed. He said he found only one case of imbecility and one case of epilepsy among them. So something beyond physical 'insanity' was behind it. Citing the work of Calmeil, he concluded it was a case of epidemic hysterical-demonopathy rather than demonomania. The pervasive belief in the supernatural fed the *mal*, and the situation had been exacerbated by the activities of pernicious unbewitchers and charlatans who reinforced the belief in possession in order to exploit people's fears for money and influence. The people had to be instructed that there was no supernatural agency behind their illness. At the same time, Arthaud believed that the Church had a benign role to play in the crisis. It was important to encourage healthy religious devotion, such as prayer and pilgrimage, to calm the spirit and moral state.[20] Following Arthaud's report the local priests were forbidden to continue with exorcisms and there was a subtle threat to transfer forcibly those exhibiting severe signs of possession to hospitals and asylums.

The epidemic continued and the decision was taken to intervene with the full force of the modern state. Augustin Constans (1811–1896), Inspector General of Insane Asylums and President of the *Société médico-psychologique*, was given the task and a substantial budget. He successful argued for a detachment of infantry to be temporarily barracked in the commune, the establishment of a new police office, and the forced removal of some of the possessed to hospitals and asylums in the area. It was a powerful statement of central state intervention. He was respectful but critical of Arthaud's report and considered that the local representatives of the church were part of the problem rather than the solution. The parish priest and several other clergymen were replaced. It was necessary to break the ties in the community that had reinforced the epidemic. But Constans agreed in general with Arthaud's classification of the condition of the Morzine possessed as *hystéro-démonopathie* and the fact that they were insane rather than fakers and fools:

> Esquirol and Calmeil, in their descriptions of epidemics of the same nature, observed in past centuries, did not hesitate to consider the patients of that time as insane. Can the sick of Morzine be classified differently? I do not think so, since among them we find all the principal characteristics of the disease described by the eminent men whom I have just named.[21]

Constans tried to make sense of the small number of males who also claimed to be possessed. They were all adults and none exhibited convulsions like the hysterical women. 'Men, like women, have been influenced by beliefs which depress them all to varying degrees', he opined, 'but in them the effects were less and quite different.'[22] Men were thought to be more prone to digestive tract disturbances than women, and this could have affected their minds. Then the hardship of life along with 'superstitious' fears could have brought out pre-existing conditions that led them to experience the sense of suffocation, strangulation, and the 'hysterical ball'. One of the men was considered an epileptic and a dipsomaniac. Another was described as an 'ordinary drunkard'.

Constans' strategy seemed to work quite well. The soldiers were eventually removed and the situation seemed to be under control for several years. But in 1864 trouble flared again with a new bout of epidemic possession. News from the remote commune spread internationally.[23] The infantry were brought back and some of the possessed, fearing they might be rounded up, locked up and deported, fled across the border to nearby Switzerland. That June, Philippe Kuhn, a doctor at Pau asylum who had also worked as a medical intern at Maréville asylum, was sent to Morzine as Constans' proxy and published his own investigations and analysis of the insanity behind the *mal*. He wrote with the benefit of seven years of psychiatric investigation of the commune's possessed, and he now married this with his own first-hand personal observation. He found there were still 125 possessed women. Thirty-five of them he categorized as simple first-stage hysterics who suffered from abdominal pains and the hysteric ball, but no convulsions. Sixty-three suffered from what he called 'constitutional hystericism', a form of insanity with hallucinations, convulsions, and suicidal tendencies. The rest, some twenty-seven women, suffered from 'imitative hysteria' whereby they could not see the convulsives without temporarily falling into the same state.[24] While 'superstition', credulity, and fanatical faith, were the food that sustained the affair, the medical causes included hereditary insanity, inbreeding, lymphatic nervous temperaments, and chloro-anaemia, which was thought to be caused by poor diet. Any one of these could lead to hysteria, he stated, but they were often to be found collectively in the hysterical Morzine patients. He also considered other types of insanity were involved. With regard to Josephte, aged forty, for instance, he believed she had been hysteric from the age of sixteen, but in her possessed state since 1857 she suffered from dementia passing into lypemania with suicidal tendencies.[25]

The last of the visiting psychiatrists left the village in 1867. Two years later there were only six women still manifesting signs of possession. By 1870 the soldiers and police had packed their bags. The authorities were content they had dealt with a puzzling law and order problem, and the psychiatrists felt vindicated in their diagnoses.

Over the years of the Morzine affair we can detect the medical discourse moving away from Esquirol's notion of demonomania, and facile comparisons with the mass possessions of the witch trials, towards a more complex discourse on mass psychiatry and contemporary health care.[26] While it was still explained, in part, in terms of popular 'superstition', the Morzine outbreak came to be judged by the state as a modern problem requiring novel approaches to mental and physical hygiene. The lessons learned directly informed the psychiatric response to another mass outbreak of possession that occurred a few years later amongst the female population of Verzegnis, a remote mountain village in the Friuli region of northeast Italy. Although now largely forgotten, the case was widely compared to the Morzine affair in the international psychiatric press at the time. It attracted the usual cries of how such things could still happen despite the progress of Western civilization. The *American Journal of Insanity* was typical, stating that the case 'must strike all readers residing in any civilized county, with utter amazement'. It was a throwback to the days of Salem. The origins of the outbreak began in early 1878 when a 26-year-old woman named Margherita Vidusson, who had suffered from convulsions for a number of years, was publicly exorcized.[27] As a consequence, her condition got worse not better. Margherita began to exhibit all the usual signs; she shouted profanities and displayed an angry aversion to the sound of the church bells and the proximity of priests. The contagion began and other women came to exhibit the same symptoms.

In September, a report to the Archbishop's *Curia* described how seven young women were oppressed by 'certain disorders'—'they writhe horribly, scream and shout, lose their senses, and yell'. The Church tried to control the outbreak by authorizing further exorcisms, but as the epidemic spread the civil authorities were finally notified. In December, Fernando Franzolini, a surgeon at Udine District Hospital specializing in ovariectomies, and his colleague Giuseppe Chiap, were instructed to visit Verzegnis to assess the mental state of the now forty women who were thought by villagers to be possessed by the Devil. The two men questioned locals about the diet and sexual lives of the women. As at Morzine, external factors such as a lack of education and isolation from civilization were considered conducive to such outbreaks. Franzolini noted at the end of his 1879 report that, in May that year, villagers, led mostly by men, had formed a public procession demanding that only the expulsion of the devils from their women folk would end the crisis. 'It is certain that if the possessed had requested a human sacrifice', he wrote, 'in that fever of superstition and fanaticism, someone would have been found to execute the demand.'[28]

Franzolini drew upon French psychiatry in determining the women's illness and the best way to treat the epidemic, and his main inspiration was Constans' 1861 report on Morzine. Franzolini was full of admiration for Constans and he set about comparing Verzegnis with Morzine—they were very alike, he said, 'like two drops of water'. They differed only in that the Morzine women exhibited more convulsive symptoms and the Verzegnis women expressed more delusions. They were all suffering from a communicated nervous 'hysterical disorder'. Franzolini had, previously, conducted operations to remove the ovaries of women diagnosed with hysteria but in the Verzegnis women he did not consider the disorder was uterine in origin but instead purely nervous.[29] The demonopathy was merely a secondary condition to hysteria. The cure was to isolate the women from each other and shelter them from religious trigger associations such as the sound of church bells. Seventeen of the women were taken to Udine Hospital for further treatment, and in 1879 Franzolini reported that they had all been cured. By 1883 the epidemic in the village had been completely eradicated. Only a few years after Italian Unification, the Verzegnis affair was seen as a victory of the state and scientific method over Church and popular 'superstition'. The intervention of the *Carabinieri* to enforce high standards of social hygiene in the village was, as at Morzine, also considered key to the success of the containment strategy.

Religion as contemporary disease

Esquirol observed that religious fanaticism had given rise to a lot of insanity in the distant past, but noted in 1814 that 'in modern times, the power of religion has lost its influence on the ideas and conduct of people'.[30] We can take this statement with the same pinch of salt as his confident statement about the decline of demonomania. The notions of possession and exorcism, furthermore, provided early psychiatrists with a convenient distancing measure. Both could be categorized as relic 'superstitions' fostered by ignorance that had no relevance in the present world. But religion per se could not be consigned to the past and dismissed so casually. When contemporary religiosity increasingly became pathologized it also became deeply politicized. Religion continued to shape national identities and generate denominational tensions, propaganda, and prejudice at international, national, and regional levels; and early psychiatrists were no less prone to biases and assumption about the religious beliefs of others than the rest of the population.

Irish psychiatry was deeply entangled with the feverish confessional politics of the nineteenth century.[31] William Saunders Hallaran (1765–1825), physician at the Cork Lunatic Asylum and a former student of William Cullen, claimed in an oft-cited article in 1818 that although there were ten times as many Catholic inmates as Protestants in his asylum the only cases of mental derangement induced by religious excitement or dread were amongst Protestants. The Irish politician and playwright, Richard Lalor Sheil (1791–1851) found this perfect grist to his mill. He was a founding member of the Catholic Association set up in 1823 by the leader of Irish nationalism Daniel O'Connell (1775–1847) to campaign for Catholic emancipation in the United Kingdom. It held impressive mass rallies around Ireland, and at a public meeting in Cork in 1825, where O'Connell and Sheil spoke, the latter turned to a bit of Protestant-bashing by referring to Hallaran's study. Sheil told the audience that the Bible-reading preoccupation of Protestants was a major source of mental turmoil, infecting the country with 'heated imagination' and delirious dreams. 'The lower classes of the Protestant community are driven into a sort of Biblical insanity by this system of excitation', he declared, 'and madness, now-a-day, almost invariably assumes a religious character.' He had visited Cork asylum and talked to its 'benevolent physician' (Hallaran) and found there was not a single Catholic suffering from Bible-induced insanity. There were cries of 'Hear, Hear' from the audience.[32] One anonymous critic published a response to the speech. This author also knew Hallaran and had obtained further information from him. Of 1370 patients at the asylum from 1798 to 1818 only forty were recorded as insane through 'religious zeal', and Halloran apparently confirmed that not one of them had been driven insane by Bible-reading.

The author then moved on to cite Pinel, noting that at the Bicêtre there were numerous priests and Roman Catholics amongst his patients.[33]

Confessional conflict was nothing new in German states either. The most outspoken proponent of the classification of 'religious insanity' or *religiöser Wahnsinn* was Karl Wilhelm Ideler (1795–1860), the son of a pastor who became Professor of Clinical Psychiatry at Berlin University and head physician at the insanity clinic of the Charité Hospital, Berlin. In the late 1840s he wrote a huge two-volume study based on detailed historical examples of religious insanity in the mould of Calmeil's book, but he also observed the 'problem' in his own time and provided further extensive case studies.[34] For Ideler, like many of his fellow psychiatrists, religion was not a concern per se, but religious passions or excitement, and the fostering of popular 'superstition' in the name of religion, could lead to mental imbalances and so insanity. More to the point, fanaticism as a cause of insanity was a threat not only to the individual but to the welfare and functioning of the state. The annals of history proved it, and he could see the same worrying pathological passions in his delusional patients.[35] The early nineteenth century had seen an evangelical Protestant 'awakening' and an upswing in missionary zeal by the old Protestant Moravian Church. At the Eberbach asylum, for instance, we find Margarette K., an innkeeper's wife from Caub diagnosed with 'religious insanity' and 'demonomania' after associating with the Moravian Brethren. The asylum's director Philipp Heinrich Lindpaintner (1794–1848) took vigorous action. He interviewed her husband about where his wife had obtained the Moravian literature and reported the information to the authorities. The husband promised to apprehend the 'theological quack' who peddled the tracts.[36] The mid nineteenth century also saw the growing influence of the Vatican over German Catholicism, which inspired a greater engagement with popular religious sentiment such as the promotion of successful mass pilgrimages, and for some psychiatrists this was a further cause for concern.

Across the Atlantic, the rising number of asylums in early nineteenth-century North America brought with it a distinctive preoccupation with religious insanity. In his book, *Observations on the Influence of Religion upon the Health and Physical Welfare of Mankind*, published in 1835, Amariah Brigham advised American clergymen and preachers to read medical works on insanity and mesmerism so that they would better understand the unhealthy aspects of religious excitement on the populous, and cease their 'gratification of the taste and prejudices of the most ignorant and credulous'. He urged them to tone down the marvellous accounts promoted in the religious newspapers they published, singling out a report concerning a young woman named Narcissa Crippin who was apparently so touched by the Holy Spirit at an evangelical camp meeting that 'her face became too bright and shining for mortal eyes to gaze upon'.[37]

American psychiatrists were concerned that their country was facing a bigger insanity epidemic than Europe. When the young American psychiatrist Pliny Earle (1809–1892) returned from a visit to thirteen European asylums in 1837, including the West Riding Pauper Lunatic Asylum in England, the Salpêtrière, Bicêtre, and Esquirol's Charenton Asylum, he contrasted what he heard and witnessed with the situation in America. He noted, for instance, that of 1375 cases at the Charenton where cause of insanity was given, there was not one case attributed to 'religious doubt, anxiety or perplexity'. By contrast, he knew that nearly 8 per cent or fifty-three out of 678 cases at Massachusetts State Lunatic Hospital were attributed to religion.[38] How to explain this major difference? Earle turned to the views of William Charles Ellis (1780–1839), superintendent at the West Riding Pauper Lunatic Asylum. Ellis had recently written a treatise on the cause and treatment of insanity in which he asserted that at his asylum religion was the largest cause of insanity after distressed circumstances and grief. Ellis, who was a practising Methodist, claimed that there were more 'sectarians' in England than any other part of the world bar America, and so religion was 'more immediately brought home to the poor as a subject of thought and examination. Wherever a variety of opinion exists, and freedom of discussion is allowed, the attention is naturally roused, and the feelings become excited.' In Catholic Europe, by contrast, there was 'ignorance and blind superstitious obedience to the dictum of the priests among the lower classes'. Thus 'the mystery is easily solved', he concluded.[39] But there was no 'mystery' in the first place, as the views of Ellis and others were based on lazy assumptions and old biases rather than rigorous quantitative and qualitative analysis.

James Cowles Prichard (1786–1848), an English physician, psychiatrist, and Commissioner in Lunacy, had thoroughly demolished the basis for such crude comparisons a few years earlier. In his influential book, *A Treatise on Insanity and Other Disorders Affecting the Mind* (1835), which was dedicated to Esquirol, Prichard stated that 'there is no subject connected with the history of insanity on which more crude and ignorant notions are expressed than on what is often termed religious madness'.[40] He believed that far fewer people became insane through religious influence than was generally assumed: 'The circumstance that the mind of a lunatic is occupied during the period of his disease with ideas and feelings connected with an invisible world, is no proof whatever that the derangement of his understanding was produced in the first instance by impressions related to the same subject.'[41] Prichard batted off the claims by the German psychiatrist Johann Michael Leupoldt and Belgian Joseph Guislain, for instance, that insanity was much more prevalent in the Protestant German states of the north than in the Catholic German states in the south. There was little basis for the comparison in terms of comparable asylum statistics, and numerous other factors had to be considered, such as climate, custom, and history. Prichard used the example of trying to compare predominantly Catholic Ireland with predominantly Calvinist Scotland: 'we could not with confidence ascribe any difference that might be found in the proportional numbers of lunatics to the prevalence of the Catholic religion in one and the reformed church in the other, since the habits and characters of these nations are strikingly different in other respects'.[42] The only data comparison Prichard thought of use in the debate concerned a comparison of population size and admission statistics for Catholics, Evangelicals, Mennonites, and Jews in the asylums of five German cities. From this Prichard concluded that Catholic religion was rather more favourable to insanity, thus rather undermining his own arguments against the value of such comparisons. The debate was clearly far from over.

With the huge expansion of asylums from the 1840s onward, a rigorous set of annual asylum statistics became an international benchmark of good psychiatry.[43] Despite Prichard's warnings, with so much new data washing around comparing the statistics on religious insanity proved too tempting for many psychiatrists. But things became even more problematic due to the ever-expanding plurality of opinions, interpretations, and classifications that circulated national and internationally amongst asylum psychiatrists. A person suffering from religious delusions could be recorded and categorized in different ways depending on each institution and the views of its superintendent or director. Terminology varied within institutions as well. The casebooks of Bootham Park Asylum, Yorkshire, between 1817 and 1855 reveal some eighty-seven patients admitted for variously, 'religious ideas', 'ill directed religious feelings', 'religious fears', 'religious excitement', 'religious melancholy', 'religious apprehension', 'religious anxiety', 'religious enthusiasm', and 'mistaken views of religion'. Monomania was mentioned in only a handful of cases dating from 1840 onward.[44]

Nor was the situation as clear cut in France as Earle had made out. Esquirol did not think religion was much of a problem anymore and this evidently showed in how his patients were classified. If we look at other French asylums around the same time the situation appears somewhat different to the Charenton. At the Saint-Yon asylum, Rouen, between 1835 and 1843, religion was recorded as the cause of insanity for 15 out of 433 men (4 per cent) and 31 out of 462 women (7 per cent). Hardly negligible.[45] An 1859 audit in the department of Bas-Rhin, eastern France, also showed that around one in twenty-one asylum patients suffered from what was termed 'religious exaltation', which was essentially another way of saying 'mania' or 'excitement'. Its author, the psychiatrist Henri Dagonet (1823–1902), one-time superintendent at the Stéphansfeld asylum in Alsace, noted that patterns of religious exaltation were sometimes concentrated in certain localities. In Strasbourg, which had a significant minority Protestant population, religion was deemed a particularly dominant cause of moral over-excitement, with it ranking as the eighth highest cause of insanity. For Dagonet, tensions between different faiths living in close proximity, fuelled by popular 'superstition', generated violent passions that could affect reason.[46]

Evangelical super spreaders

The maddening debate over whether Protestants were more prone to religious insanity was shaped considerably by concerns over the evangelical awakenings that periodically broke out across Protestant Europe and North America throughout the nineteenth century, during which followers in their many thousands exhibited uncontrolled emotions and physical paroxysms that suggested they had temporarily lost their senses. While examples of individuals claiming to be possessed by the Devil were not uncommon in Protestant countries, mass *demonic* possession was a Catholic phenomenon and the Catholic Church had its own clear road map for community recovery through exorcism. Protestant countries, by contrast, were prone to mass *divine* possession. Whereas demonic possess was clearly a bad thing for those afflicted, divine possession was welcomed as a gift from God in evangelical communities. There was no need for religious therapy.

Mass divine possession had a long history which was well-known to those psychiatrists interested in retrospective diagnoses. In the second half of the seventeenth century the Religious Society of Friends, also known as the Quakers, had been denounced for frenzied preaching which, it was claimed, drove their followers insane.[47] Their trembling and shaking in the presence of God equated well with the raving symptoms of the mad. This reputation persisted long after the Society had become a sober denomination emphasizing inner divine contemplation rather than physical manifestations of intercession. Writing about his work at the York Retreat, set up in 1796 to care for Quakers with mental health issues, Samuel Tuke noted in 1813 that very few of those brought there were actually suffering from religious concerns.[48] The Retreat soon opened its doors to non-Quakers, and an exchange between Cowles Prichard and Tuke in the 1830s revealed that only eight out of 334 admissions since the beginning of 1812 concerned religious excitement and several of them were not people brought up as Quakers.[49] The Shakers were another group who accrued similar critical condemnation for their ecstatic prayer meetings. They originated from an English splinter group of the Quakers in the mid eighteenth century. Under the leadership of the charismatic Ann Lee (1736–1784), daughter of a Manchester blacksmith, the Shakers became a significant millenarian revival group in America through until the mid nineteenth century.

The Wesleyan Methodists were another magnet for complaints of spreading insanity amongst the poor. The founder, John Wesley, was regularly accused of being mad himself.[50] The biggest English convulsive revival of the early nineteenth century occurred in 1814, on the cusp of the psychiatric revolution, and began at a Wesleyan Methodist chapel in Redruth, Cornwall, before spreading rapidly to other towns in the county. It was estimated at the time that some 4000 people were affected, mostly girls and young women but old men and boys as well, many of them with the usual symptoms of religious excitation, shaking, crying, jumping, and shouting, A local named James Cornish wrote up a first-hand account of the epidemic for the *London Medical and Physical Journal* in which he described it as a convulsive 'disease' that resembled chorea in its incipient stage. 'Some ascribe it to the spirit of God, others to the spirit of the Devil, others to intoxication, others to insanity, and others to the influence of the passions', he observed. But 'those who have considered the subject seriously and without prejudice, think there is no necessity to have recourse either to divine or to diabolical interference to explain it'.[51] As the Wesleyan Methodists, in turn, became a more sober, mainstream, established church during the early nineteenth century so the grass roots Primitive Methodist movement, with its outdoor camp meetings inspired by developments in American evangelical religion, took up the baton of providentialism, supernaturalism, and collective divine inspiration.[52] A study of female insanity and family relationships from the records of the West Riding Pauper Lunatic Asylum shows, for instance, that in the 1840s women were being brought to the asylum by their families on the basis of having apparently become insane through attending Primitive Methodist meetings.[53]

The British and American revivals during the first couple of decades of the nineteenth century were within the memory of many of the first wave of psychiatrists but they obviously only applied their retrospective diagnoses with considerable hindsight. In 1848, for instance, *The New York Journal of Medicine* reprinted an account of a 'singular nervous affection' recorded during the revival in East Tennessee in the early 1800s. It was known in popular idiom as 'the jerks'. The journal's editor likened it to Hecker's accounts of the Dancing Mania. Those revivalists who caught it would exhibit the familiar violent convulsions, their faces became distorted, and 'when the hair was long, it was shaken with such quickness, backward and forward, as to crack and snap like the lash of a whip'. For the editor this was classified as a disease, but for the revivalists at the time, such 'acrobatic Christianity' was the spirit of God at work, and those so struck with the divine hand were not to be restrained.[54] Ann Lee and Joseph Smith (1805–1844), the founder of Mormonism, were also retrospectively diagnosed by critics as theomaniacs or religious monomaniacs and their followers the victims of religious excitement.[55]

By the mid nineteenth century evangelical revivals attracted sympathy from a fairly wide spectrum of Protestants but there were serious concerns about the mental toll of enthusiastic excessiveness. The deleterious influence of 'hellfire and damnation' preaching was particularly worrisome. The London physician Nathaniel Bingham, who ardently espoused the value of religious instruction for the insane but also warned in 1841 of the dangers, collected several examples. There was the genteel young lady who attended the 'vehement harangues of a distinguished preacher' and believed she was in the vicinity of hell and smelt burning sulphur wherever she went. Her parents sent her to stay at the home of a pious clergymen where she fully recovered. A journeyman printer who heard the same preacher got it into his head that he was Saint John the Baptist and stripped naked. He subsequently died of inflammation of the brain.[56] Surprisingly, perhaps, the first major European revival to come under this psychiatric spotlight occurred not in Britain but in Sweden.

Carl Ulrik Sondén (1802–1875), the son of a Lutheran pastor who became one of the first professional Swedish psychiatrists, published a record and analysis of a case of what he considered an epidemic of religious insanity. His account was swiftly translated by Irish and French medical journals, and it was published again in America in 1850 by the American Professor of Theory and Practice of Medicine, Samuel Hanbury Smith.[57] Sondén, who was physician to the Stockholm Lunatic Asylum at the time, was an admirer of Pinel's methods and in 1834 he had, like numerous other budding psychiatrists, toured French asylums and talked to physicians and directors about mental health care and the treatment of the insane.[58] Sweden had only founded its first institution for the treatment of the insane in 1826, and Sondén felt there was much to catch up on and learn from other countries. Then, in the summer of 1841, Swedish psychiatry was given a gift to make its mark on the international psychiatric scene. Liza Andersdotter, a 16-year-old farmer's daughter from Alsarp, began to suffer from a range of disturbing symptoms including persistent hiccups, headaches, cramps, lower abdomen pain, and spasms of the arms and shoulders. She became bed-ridden and occupied herself with reading the Bible, hymn books, and other religious literature. Towards the end of September, she began to sing psalms and seemed to be under some sort of divine influence. She felt the irresistible urge to preach to others about conversion, the sin of pride, and intemperance; after these bouts of intense nervous excitement she would collapse.

On 13 November Lisa prophesied that she would preach just one more time and then she would die. She anointed a 13-year-old girl to continue her preaching mission. Lisa did not meet her maker, though, and a doctor who visited her in April 1842 found that she was still suffering from violent contortions and twitching. In the meantime, other teenage girls, older women, and some men, began to exhibit the same symptoms. One of them, Johanna Persdotter, aged sixteen and described as very pretty and charismatic, became a travelling preacher who enthused crowds with her sermons. They only lasted five to ten minutes and were made up of a mere jumble of common religious phrases, but they had a profound effect on some. As word of mouth and newspapers spread news of this outbreak of religious ecstasy an evangelic movement briefly formed in the region. Hundreds said they experienced the divine spirit as manifested through their paroxysms, rolling around on the floor, leaping in the air, and crying with unbridled emotion. Take Inga Stina, for example, a 27-year-old domestic servant who preached several hours at a time and cursed those who doubted her divine inspiration.

She had been fired up by a 'fanatical' clergyman and this ultimately 'upset her reason' and she was diagnosed as insane. By the end of 1842, some fifteen men and thirty women had also been removed to Växjö hospital diagnosed with 'theomania' and 'religious ecstasy'.[59]

There were differences of diagnostic opinion amongst the Swedish medical profession. One physician equated the outbreak to historic cases of chorea. Others thought it explicable by animal magnetism. Some of Lisa's friends, and some doctors, suspected initially that she was suffering from cereal convulsions. This was known as *Raphania*, a term which derived from the old Latin name for a wild radish that grew widely in arable fields. Linnæus noted it was prevalent in Sweden, particularly in barley crops. He deducted that its seeds were toxic and when they were ground with cereal grains and eaten as bread it caused convulsions not dissimilar to those attributed to Chorea. *Raphania* stuck as a name for such bouts of rural epidemic convulsions even though other eighteenth-century scientists subsequently proved the wild radish to be harmless. By the 1840s *Raphania* or cereal convulsions caused by contaminated wheat or rye had also been equated in medical terms with ergotism or the toxic 'gangrenous' properties of the ergot fungus that grew on rye. French scientists had been studying it since the late seventeenth century, and ergot had come to be used in formal medicine by the early nineteenth century. Retrospective ergot diagnoses were being made about former convulsion epidemics during the early nineteenth century, and ergot was also put forward as an explanation for the 1841 outbreak. But by now psychiatrists had their alternative moral diagnoses for what was going on in Sweden.[60] Sondén, who did not have first-hand observational experience of the outbreak and based his views solely on official reports, saw the similarity with St Vitus' Dance but considered it a case of epidemic insanity manifest as 'Religious Ecstasy'—a 'stormy and devastating whirlwind' that proliferated amongst the 'ignorant and superstitious'. But he believed there were also physical triggers such as bad diet. The last two harvests in the region had failed and bread was scarce, and there was significant alcoholism in the area. Then there was the pernicious influence of hellfire evangelical preachers. Samuel Hanbury Smith also attempted to place the 1841 epidemic in its 'appropriate nosological position'. 'A simple definition will save many words', he decided.[61] He was clear that the 'disease' was not chorea. Neither was it demonomania, as there was no supposed demonic possession. Neither was it theomania because both it and demonomania he considered to be chronic in character, in other words more permanent forms of insanity that were not contagious and often led to death rather than recovery. In the end, Smith sided with Sondén in classifying the Swedish convulsives as suffering from episodic 'Religious Ecstasy'. Similar debates re-emerged years later in 1858 when over a hundred children in Gagnef in northern Sweden claimed they had been abducted by witches and taken to diabolic sabbats.[62]

Over in America, the early 1840s saw the emergence of another new prophetic evangelical movement known as Millerism.[63] William Miller (1782–1849) was a Baptist preacher and prosperous farmer from New York. He became preoccupied with the Old Testament prophecies of Daniel after serving in the militia during the War of 1812 against the United Kingdom. According to his own account, he had prophesied in private during the early 1820s that the second coming of Christ would happen shortly before or between 1843 or 1844. He went public during the early 1830s, attracting a wide following drawn particularly from fellow Baptists as well as Methodists and Presbyterians. His popularity coincided with the proliferation of asylums, and because his millenarian message quickly went regional, then national, and then international thanks to the flourishing periodical and newspaper publishing industry, Miller became intrinsically associated with epidemic insanity. He noted in 1842, 'They have reported that I was insane, and had been in a mad-house seven years; if they had said a mad world fifty-seven years, I must have plead guilty to the charge.'[64] With Christ's no-show in 1844 the 'Great Disappointment' followed. But while many followers were disillusioned others maintained the faith that Miller's prophecy would still come true sooner rather than later. The bitter disillusionment and the continued ecstatic hope engendered by the postponement of the new Jerusalem was thought by psychiatrists to have generated a tidal wave of insanity that surged through the mid nineteenth century.

George Chandler (1806–1893), the experienced superintendent at the New Hampshire State Asylum for the Insane, which opened in 1842, wrote in his annual report for 1844 that the influence of 'Father Miller', and what he described as the 'popular delusion' arising from his prophecy, had led to a great increase in mental alienation over the previous year or two. Several of the Millerites in his asylum believed they were Jesus Christ, and one of them said after his recovery that he became insane 'from attending so closely to this one subject of investigating the truth of the Miller doctrine for so long a time. He had devoted his whole time for three months to reading his Bible, and attending the meetings.'[65] At the Bloomingdale Asylum,

Pliny Earle observed regarding Miller's doctrines, that 'in those sections of the country where they obtained the most extensive credence, the institutions for the insane became peopled with large numbers, the faculties of whose minds had been overthrown thereby'.[66] An appeal to the United States Senate in 1849–1850 in the name of the pioneering mental health advocate Dorothea Dix (1802–1887), deplored that insanity in the country was increasing at an advanced ratio in relation to the growth of the country's population, and noted that 'the Millerite delusions prepared large numbers for our hospitals'.[67] The notion that America had a big problem with theomaniacs and religious monomaniacs was broadcast abroad as well. In an 1847 review of American and British annual asylum reports for the French psychiatric journal, *Annales médico-psychologiques*, Bénédict Morel noted the influence of Millerism and observed that such 'miserable charlatans' played on timorous and impressionable people, 'In this country of extreme freedom', he continued, people could 'indulge without restraint their guilty eccentricities'.[68]

But the asylum reports do not bear out these claims of a tidal wave of Millerite insanity. When Chandler began to single out denominations from the general category of religious insanity, he recorded only three cases of Millerism and one of Swedenborgianism out of 151 patients. The annual report on the New York State Lunatic Asylum for 1845 reported 102 cases of religious anxiety out of 553 patients but only nineteen cases of Millerism.[69] Then between 1848 and 1849 the same asylum reported an increase to thirty-six cases of Millerism compared to, for example, twenty-four from blows on the head, and fifty-one due to excessive study.[70] It was hardly an epidemic, although the effects were quite long-lasting. New Hampshire State Asylum accepted four cases of Millerism between 1854 and 1855, and even a case as late as 1862.[71]

Similar claims of epidemic insanity were also made during the Ulster revival of 1859. This was an unusual revival in that there was no single charismatic leader or leaders inspiring the evangelical eruption. It drew in people from across the Northern Irish Protestant spectrum—Presbyterians, Anglicans, Baptists, Methodists, and Independents.[72] More to the point, it was one of the last major European evangelical episodes where the full range of historically familiar mass convulsions and fits played out in public spaces. In this respect, some twentieth-century historians referred to it, just as with the witch trials, as a late bout of 'mass hysteria'.[73] Things were much more complex of course.

The 'mad excesses' were diverse and affected hundreds of women and men of all ages. There was collective psalm-singing and prayer day and night, dancing, shaking, and shouting. Numerous revivalists claimed to be in trance, receiving divine visions, prophecies, and stigmata. Some acted as if they were possessed by the Devil and others claimed they were moved by divine spirits and departed souls. A blacksmith and lay preacher named Richard Weaver told crowds that his own brother was in Hell. The respected Ulster physician Henry Mac Cormac (1800–1886) was a highly critical eye-witness to the events, and a few years later likened what he saw to Constans' recently published report on the Morzine affair. He described the behaviour of one young woman he had treated, who had been unwell in mind but had fully recovered prior to 1859 but was now 'struck down' again at a revival meeting house:

> I never beheld a more frantic creature. Both shoe and stocking were flung off, and ere my arrival she had literally kicked everyone out of the house... I found her dancing on the summit of a boundary wall, which she had climbed with the agility of a cat. There was not a sacred name or formula, in her rantings and ravings, that she did not in turn recite, every now and then, even in her perilous position and amid her frantic springs, clapping her hands above he head and hoarsely shouting, "Hurrah for the revivals, hurrah for the revivals."[74]

Miracles, stories, and revelations were spread not only orally and via newspapers but also by a huge outpouring of printed and hand-written ephemera exalting the revival and spreading the message. 'Words of warning and incrimination, pasted on wood or cardboard, were hung out here and there', observed Mac Cormac, 'as they shook and rattled in the wind.'[75]

The Unitarians were the only Ulster Protestant denomination to express sustained religious criticism of the physical excesses of the revival. One of its mouthpieces, the *Northern Whig*, printed a series of reports and letters with titles such as 'Witchcraft and revivalism', 'Revivalism and insanity', and 'Death from the effects of "revivalism" '. There were other isolated voices of clerical criticism. The noted Anglican evangelist William M'Ilwaine, rector of St George's Church, Belfast, received a lot of vitriol from some sections of the evangelical community for his outspoken criticism of the revival. For him it was uncontrolled fanaticism on display and not evangelical piety.[76] When M'Ilwaine wrote a piece for the *Journal of Mental Science* in 1860 he stated with relief, 'the excitement is over; it has utterly collapsed'. He was convinced it had created a 'fearful' amount of insanity, though, in the dreaded form of theomania and other manifestations of insanity such as acute mania. He reckoned from reliable sources that at least fifty cases of such religious insanity had occurred in the last six months in his immediate neighbourhood. In three Ulster asylums there were thirty-three patients, five of them male, who been admitted as a result of the revival, and there were numerous others who could not be admitted due to overcrowding.[77] The Irish press on both sides of the argument bandied around asylum statistics to defend their respective positions as to the increase in religious insanity. These were then picked up and published in a couple of articles in *The Times*, one under the heading 'Progress of Irish Insanity', thereby airing the arguments at a national and international level. The controversy of the numbers rumbled on. Meanwhile at the end of 1859 an outlying outbreak of revivalism occurred in the Scottish fishing village of Ferryden. A girl fell into a trance, people cried out and fell down, some had the shakes, others felt their sins rising physically in their throats and choking them.[78]

Symptom or cause?

In Britain, the category of 'religious insanity' was defended in the fourth edition of Bucknill and Tuke's influential *Manual of Psychological Medicine* published in 1879. They calculated that 3 per cent of total asylum admissions were attributed to religious anxiety and excitement. They observed that although in many cases these were the *symptoms* of mental disorder, 'we cannot for a moment doubt that the form in which religion is but too frequently presented is a serious cause of insanity'.[79] But the pathologizing of religion raised thorny issues for those running asylums, as churches and religious organizations had long played a charitable role in caring for the insane. In both Protestant and Catholic countries, religious services were a common feature in the life of asylum patients, and sober religious reflection was considered by some psychiatrists to have therapeutic benefits. County asylums in Britain were required by law to have a chaplain. There were critical voices from within as well as without the psychiatric profession that argued there was no such thing as religious insanity at all; it was deemed a pernicious sectarian and political fabrication conjured up by the secularist wing of the medical profession. The right sort of religion was the cure and not the cause of insanity.

Some of the most vocal critics were American. In 1850, for instance, Frederick A. Packard (1794–1867), a religious educationalist and leading light of the American Sunday School Union, took to the pages of the *Princeton Review* to attack anonymously an article recently written by Forbes Benignus Winslow in his *Journal of Psychological Medicine*. 'There is no such thing as religious insanity', Packard stated in response. 'i.e. it cannot be said of religion, as it can be of grief, or disappointment, or chagrin, that it causes insanity'. He admitted that religious delusions had in many instances 'been the ostensible cause of insanity, as our hospital returns allege', but that 'revealed religion' was no more responsible than paroxysms of dipsomania.[80] But the usual sectarianism was on display. Packard dismissed Mormonism, for instance, as having no connection with religion and suggested any intelligent and respectable persons who joined it clearly had a predisposition to insanity.[81] Forbes Winslow responded waspishly to Packard's criticism. He did not know the author's identity, but he dismissed his views as those of an ignorant theologian intruding on medical matters that he was not trained to discuss: 'the vast field of modern psychology . . . is to him a sealed book'. He went on to accuse the author of being disingenuous, stating that his 'weary' article contained 'dangerous errors in it, which are not peculiar to the writer, but rather to his *class*'. Winslow ended with a swipe at the state of America psychiatry in general.[82] The editors of the *American Journal of Insanity*, who worked at the New York State Utica Asylum, hit back. They resented the 'many recent English critical notices on the works of Americans', and, tit-for-tat, suggested that Winslow should learn from Packard's article: 'he will find some ideas which appear scarcely to have occurred to him in *his* "search after religion" '.[83] They went on to put forward the term 'ir-religious insanity' as a replacement for 'religious insanity' to reinforce Packard's point.[84]

The debate *within* the British psychiatrist community was much more muted than this transatlantic storm in a teacup suggests, but there were still tensions between psychiatrists and churches. In 1870, William Lauder Lindsay (1829–1880), physician at the Murray Royal Institution for the Insane, Perth, vented his professional frustration with the Scottish clergy. He had been told by revivalists in the Highland glens that insanity was the fruit of sin and that it was impossible for religion to have anything other than a healthy effect on the mind. 'I have met with so much clerical and lay bigotry, prejudice, ignorance or error, on the whole subject of insanity either caused by religious excitement, or attended with delusions of a religious character', he complained. But this was not the worst of it, for Lindsay also claimed that his reports on the matter had been suppressed by the Institution's board.[85] In 1875 the British psychiatrist Lyttelton Forbes Winslow (1844–1913), the controversial son of Forbes Benignus Winslow, picked up the baton and gave a full-blooded defence of the category of 'religious insanity' before the Medical Society of London. For Winslow it was an organic disorder of the brain that struck religious zealots. Those who suffered from it had formerly led generally irreproachable lives but suicide was an almost inevitable conclusion. The debate that followed among the attendees was really rather telling. Dr Edward Sheppard thought that religious insanity was on the increase because religion, like alcohol, had been much adulterated, in this instance by revivalism. He knew the case of a butler who had recently attended an evangelical meeting and had ended up in Colney Hatch Asylum as a result. Dr Williams chipped in with his own anecdote about a young jockey whose head was so turned by revivalists and he had begun to learn the Bible by heart. Thankfully he was cured by the administration of bromide of potassium, which was widely used as a sedative and anticonvulsant. Dr Leared took a familiar tack, observing that he 'could not help thinking the Roman Catholic Church was much to be recommended; it told these weak people what to think and thus relieved them from much mental anxiety'.[86]

The cases of the poor butler and jockey noted by the good doctors were related to the recent visit to Britain by the American evangelists Dwight L. Moody (1837–1899) and Ira D. Sankey (1840–1908). They had teamed up in 1870 and developed a formidable revivalist roadshow. Moody had an indefatigable preaching style and displayed great salesmanship, while Sankey's gospel-singing, catchy hymns, and sacred songs added entertainment and excitement. Moody had already conducted three preaching tours in Britain and so there was considerable anticipation regarding the arrival of the double act.[87] The duo toured England and Scotland between 1873 and 1875 attracting much publicity. Despite the hundreds of thousands who attending their services and all the press coverage, good and bad, once they had left British shores the anticipated national revival did not materialize. But some fears were expressed that they had left a trail of insanity in their wake. After Sankey and Moody sang and preached to large crowds in Manchester in early 1875, the Salford Board of Guardians had to consider two cases of alleged insanity and attempted suicide. One was a married woman, aged forty-eight, who said that the services she attended tended to sooth rather than excite her. The other was a 27-year-old Sunday School teacher. She had been in ill health, but since attending four of the services she had incessantly sang a hymn sung by Sankey called 'Dare to be a Daniel', which was written by fellow revivalist Philip P. Bliss. To give a flavour, it began:

> Standing by a purpose true,
> heeding God's command,
> honour them, the faithful few!
> All hail to Daniel's band!
>
> Refrain:
> Dare to be a Daniel!
> Dare to stand alone!
> Dare to have a purpose firm!
> Dare to make it known!

The Board declined to make any diagnoses: 'the subject of predisposing causes was one for medical men'. The following month newspapers reported that there had been an unusual increase of people admitted to the dementia wards of the Liverpool Workhouse diagnosed with religious 'monomania.'[88]

Back in America, one critical publication complained that there had been many cases of religious mania resulting from Moody and Sankey, but they had not come to public attention because 'the unfortunate subjects have been hurried out of sight to close family care or some private lunatic asylum'.[89] Theodore Willis Fisher (1837–1914), who frequently appeared as a medical witness on mental disease, and had formerly been at the Boston Hospital for the Insane, reported in the *Boston Medical and Surgical Journal* on several cases of insanity concerning people who had visited the city's impressive Moody and Sankey Tabernacle, which was said to hold up to 6000 people. One was Miss B., aged thirty-seven, whose two uncles were formerly Millerites. She suffered from debility and bad teeth and after visiting the Tabernacle she caught a cold and neuralgia. Yet she had been much impressed by her experience of the Tabernacle services, and when she returned to her own evangelical church she became 'reconverted' and began singing Sankey's hymns constantly. 'Mania soon developed', diagnosed Fisher, with it manifesting itself in B.'s claim to be Christ and that she was going to do great things for her church and neighbourhood. She was taken to an asylum.[90]

For several reasons psychiatric concern about epidemic revivals began to wane in the years after the Ulster episode. For one, the nature of participation in mass evangelism was changing in the age of Music Hall

Figure 2 Ira David Sankey and Dwight L. Moody at one of their revival meetings. From *A Full History of the Wonderful Career of Moody and Sankey* (1876).
Credit: Wikimedia Commons

entertainment with its collective singalongs. The performative aspects took a decidedly modern form. As one American family periodical, *The Galaxy*, put it approvingly, 'they are not spasmodical and hysterical, like those of an elder day'.[91] More rigorous clinical research was also undermining the link between revivals and insanity. In England, George H. Savage (1842–1921), then assistant medical officer at Bethlem Hospital and later Lecturer in Mental Disease at Guys Hospital, conducted his own study in 1875, published in *The Lancet*, to 'see how far the recent religious revivals have caused or precipitated insanity'. There were only three such cases at Bethlem at the time that were clearly linked to Moody and Sankey meetings. One was a 35-year-old dressmaker, a Congregationalist, who had heard Moody and Sankey but did not seem affected much at first. Then she began to develop the delusion she lived in America and started to call herself 'Moody and Sankey', offering up prayers, singing, and preaching, though 'her oratory was nonsense'. After three months in Bethlem she was declared cured and discharged. While there were only three explicit cases, Savage admitted that there had been a serious increase in admissions of general cases over the previous four months that might have some link the 'moral commotion' caused by the revival. He concluded, however, 'my experience is that religious revivals do but small harm to the able-minded, but to those who are weak there is danger'.[92]

When Savage returned to the subject a decade later in his book on *Insanity and Allied Neuroses*, he re-confirmed his opinion that religion was rarely causal, but that waves of religious excitement could unhinge the minds of young nervous females. He did not mention Moody and Sankey again, but gave the more recent example of the growing popularity of the Salvation Army with its street-level crusade amongst the poor and its military-style uniforms.[93] He probably had in mind a much-reported item in the *British Medical Journal* for 1882 concerning a meeting of the St Saviour's Board of Guardians, Southwark, where a discussion took place as to whether the sudden 'alarming' increase of insanity in the workhouse union was due to the local influence of the Salvation Army. They were, at that moment, awaiting to remove one case of religious mania to the asylum. The editor of the *British Medical Journal* took what was by now the common line on evangelical influence, namely that the services would only have a detrimental influence on those 'foredoomed lunatics on the verge of the catastrophe of fate'. Besides, he continued, for every case of insanity caused by its 'religious revelries' the Salvation Army probably saved two people from such a fate through their conversion of alcoholics.[94] By the time of the Welsh Revival of 1904–1905, the connection between revival phenomena and insanity was still being suggested, particularly in the press, but by now new psychological and psychoanalytic explanations also swirled with the psychiatric and began to blow away the remaining associations with insanity. Talk of the subconscious and the subliminal replaced the old terminology of pathology.[95]

The late nineteenth and early twentieth centuries witnessed a surge of high-profile Marian visions, 'living saints', prophecies, and demonic possessions across Catholic Western Europe. The Belgian stigmatic Louise Lateau (1850–1883) was one such international *cause célèbre* adopted by German Catholics in particular, with cards depicting her divine, bloody wounds circulating widely as devotional objects.[96] Following the supposed apparition of the Virgin Mary to 14-year-old Bernadette Soubirous (1844–1879), in 1858 Lourdes grew to be one of the most importation pilgrimage sites in the world. The creation of the Lourdes Medical Bureau in 1884 to assess the many thousands of professed cures claimed by pilgrims to determine which were 'true' miracles blurred the lines between the medical and spiritual realms at a time when psychiatrists were offering 'scientific' hysteria diagnoses with great abandon. Meanwhile the Church's official French exorcist, the Jesuit Maximilien de Haza Radlitz (1831–1909), was busy exorcizing demons from women and men in Paris and around the provinces. A 30-year-old domestic servant of Auxerre named Désirée Léjeune (1846–1940) underwent forty or so exorcisms over three years.[97] The psychiatric question of symptom or cause was rendered redundant by the sheer weight of the continued social and cultural engagement with the miraculous and the providential.

Spiritualism shakes things up

The last gasp of the rancorous debate over revivalism coincided with the controversy over the link between spiritualism and insanity. Ghost-seeing had long been a matter of medical debate. A key issue was determining the boundary between the hallucinations and dreams of the sane who said they saw the spirits of the dead and hallucinations of ghosts that were symptomatic of incipient insanity.[98] But spiritualism was considered a 'craze' in its own right. When table rapping and table turning first emerged in America in 1848 and spread quickly across the globe, some conservative religious voices, both Catholic and Protestant, were quick to denounce it as necromancy. Stage magicians and others argued that the whole movement was based on nothing more than trickery and charlatanry. Some psychiatrists believed that spiritualism was another episode in the long tradition of contagious religious insanity, rooted in the recrudescence of old superstitions and wrought by ignorance and excessive religious excitement. Analogies were made with the witch trials and Salem, and by this time, of course, the trials had already been pathologized.[99] The profusion of mostly female mediums also naturally attracted the psychiatrists and perniciously reinforced the stereotype of the female hysteric at a time when the gendered nature of hysteria was being questioned in some quarters. In 1874, R. Frederic Marvin, Professor of Psychological Medicine and Medical Jurisprudence, coined the term 'mediomania' to describe the 'insanity of mediums', and a couple of decades later French psychiatrists worked on the theory that mediums exhibited symptoms similar to those of delirious asylum patients and that mediumship could lead to the disintegration of the nervous system.[100]

In several respects, spiritualism provided psychiatrists with a more problematic challenge than evangelical revivalism. Revivals and their physical manifestations had a long lineage that psychiatrists could define and categorize through historical analogy, and so feel confident about determining their cause. The participants in grassroots evangelism could also be associated by their generally modest social level with old-fashioned religious 'superstition'. But the early adherents and advocates of spiritualism were primarily educated and urban. Mediumship was practised in middle-class homes in contrast to the open-air acrobatics and chapel convulsions of revivals. The doctrine of spiritualism, furthermore, made a startling claim that deviated even further from benchmark 'rational religion'. When the early psychiatrists went about retrospectively diagnosing the past, the notion of being in dialogue with the spirits, let alone trying to contact them, was a sure sign of insanity. Yet here was a new intellectual movement in the mid nineteenth century, supported by eminent scientists and clergymen, based on talking to the dead! For this reason, the comparison with revivalist phenomena provided good ammunition for the evangelist movement. If the 'absurdities' of spiritualism believed in by educated middle-class people were not marks of insanity then how could the physical excitement of revivalists by classed as insane? The English physician and medical journalist Andrew Wynter (1819–1876), who specialized in treating wealthy private clients with mental health issues, was no evangelist, but found in the likes of the Shakers and their modern successors 'something really grand...compared with the miserable delusions educated members of the upper classes profess to believe in, to wit, mesmeric influences, table-turning, and spirit-rapping'.[101]

There were concerns in France as well. In 1862 Philippe Burlet, one of the medical students of Joseph Arthaud, the director of the l'Antiquaille hospital in Lyon, who we met earlier with regard to his investigation at Morzine, made considerable waves in the press with a much-referenced couple of articles and a booklet raising the fear that spiritualism was also generating a crisis of insanity across France.[102] The most influential of the French spiritualists, Allan Kardec (1804–1869), responded sarcastically uttering the saying, 'If you want to kill your dog you say it is rabid.' He did not doubt that some spiritualists, like the rest of the population, succumbed to mental illness, but he saw the label of insanity being cynically employed to undermine the spiritualist movement and his own branch known as *spirit-isme*, which embraced a broader world of spirits and the concept of reincarnation. Kardec believed in the power of the Devil and warned that some people who had all the appearance of insanity, and were diagnosed as such, were actually under the influence of evil spirits and not the diseased workings of their minds. This was not much different from the Catholic position on the matter.[103]

In American asylum reports only three religious denominations or movements were named as direct causes of insanity distinct from the generic category of religious insanity: Mormonism, Millerism, and Spiritualism— and the latter was clearly overtaking the former in the asylum statistics. In 1860 the Worcester Asylum (Massachusetts) reported ten cases of Millerism but twenty-five cases of Spiritualism. The Indiana Hospital for the Insane reported thirty-five cases where spirit-rapping was the cause of admission.[104] The American spiritualists were a much more influential and social and politically diverse bunch than the Millerites and they fought back effectively in public debate, questioning the statistics and pointing out hypocrisies. In 1854, for instance, the writing medium and socialist, Alfred Cridge, who lived in Ohio with his wife, the British-born suffragist Annie Denton Cridge (1825–1875), perused the Fifteenth Report of the Ohio State Lunatic Asylum to find that while eleven people had been admitted in relation to table rapping, thirty-eight had been admitted for religious excitement. Orthodox religion, therefore, was by a long stretch the greater cause of insanity, 'Yet nobody talks of suppressing orthodoxy on this account', he complained. Cridge had also talked to an asylum clerk who claimed that when patients arrived due to religious excitement their friends and family usually assigned other causes out of reluctance to offend their faith. In other words, there was a much larger hidden figure of orthodox religious insanity.[105] Around the same time, the American attorney, abolitionist, and spiritualist Joel Tiffany (1811–1893) combed through the statistics of as many asylum reports as he could get his hands on. His research showed that the number of patients entered as suffering from 'religious excitement' was ten times greater than those admitted because of spiritualism: 'The Pulpit and the Press are or ought to be aware of these facts; but neither does it suit *their* purposes to notice them.'[106]

Animosity between American spiritualists and psychiatry reached a peak in the mid 1870s due primarily to the publication of a book by Lyttleton Forbes Winslow with the blunt title, *Spiritualistic Madness* (1877). Many years later, he recalled that when it was published he 'had a hard battle to fight in consequence of my views'.[107] This was hardly surprising as the book contained the most outrageous claim that there were nearly 10,000 cases of insanity attributed to spiritualism in American asylums.[108] The total asylum population of America at the time was estimated to be around 30,000, so Winslow was basically saying that spiritualism was responsible for a third of all insanity in the United States. As the editor of *The Lancet* wrote, 'The assertion was so manifestly preposterous, and evinced so little acquaintance with the subject, that we did not deem it worthwhile to contradict it.'[109] But it upset a lot of others and much energy was spent on a new round of refutations and asylum statistics. The American physician Eugene Crowell (1817–1894) sallied forth to crunch the numbers to crush Winslow's claim. Crowell was an ardent spiritualist who also believed that those suffering from insanity could be cured by therapeutic communicating with departed friends through a medium.[110] He wrote to the medical superintendents of over eighty institutions for the insane asking for data on the number of patients admitted or under treatment during the past year, and the number of cases that were ascribed to religious excitement or spiritualism. Fifty-eight medical superintendents responded with relevant information, enabling Crowell to calculate that 412 people had been admitted to institutions for religious excitement but only fifty-nine cases were ascribed to Spiritualism.[111] It was an echo of the statistics from the mid 1850s. Forbes Winslow was plain wrong. He had put his finger in the air and made up the figure. Its baselessness helped further undermine the idea that spiritualism was a cause rather than a symptom of insanity.

Keeping it in the family

Morzine, Verzegnis, and spiritualism fitted the psychiatric models of epidemic insanity that had been developed from studying the annals of history. But what of supposed possessions that were not concerned with religion per se and spread only within a family group, affecting both young and old, males and females? More spiritual flea infestation than plague. Take the case of the Marcet family of Plédran, Brittany.[112] In the early summer of 1881, French newspapers reported on the extraordinary events taking place in a hamlet some four kilometres from the small town of Plédran in Brittany. This is where the seven young children of a poor farming family, the Marcets, exhibited strange contortions and supernatural behaviour. They would climb walls like monkeys, throw themselves down the well, and dance on top of the chimney like demons, shouting wildly. The neighbours and the local priest of Plédran came to the conclusion they were possessed.

The young Breton physician Jean Baratoux (1855–1956), who studied periodic ear bleeding in hysterics and would go on to be a leading ear, nose, and throat specialist, was in the area at the time and visited the Marcet family to gather evidence. The contagion began in February with the oldest daughter Marie Jeanne, aged fifteen, complaining of violent head pains and a feeling of sickness. Then her upper limbs became periodically powerless, she lost consciousness from time to time, and felt as though a ball was rising from her stomach to her throat. At times she would jerk spasmodically. Baratoux observed:

> It is very difficult to attempt to describe these singular movements. One time she would be crawling on the floor; another time she would be leaping about shaking her head. Her respiration was gasping, interrupted by piercing cries during inspiration. One moment she was tearing her clothes, the next grasping her throat as if something were choking her.

She also had visions and hallucinations, including seeing the Devil escorted by a troop of demons, and also separate visitations by her dead godfather and grandmother. Marie Jeanne's brother Pierre, aged eleven, soon began to suffer similar fits and sensations, and then the rest of the children became infected. Even the youngest, aged seven months, was said to have been afflicted, though Baratoux found nothing abnormal and observed the infant was merely entertained and animated by seeing her brothers and sisters perform their antics.

For Baratoux the Marcet children presented a rare example of Charcot's *grande hystérie*. He noted, for instance, that Marie Jeanne had pain in the ovarian region. But the outbreak had been provoked, he said, by ignorance and credulity amongst the local population, observing that 'their great and only, so to speak, diversion during the winter being the evening gathering, where each relates a tale of which fairies and wizards are the subject'. The priesthood was also to blame for fanning the flames with their talk of devils. The strict moral and medical treatment of the children rather than prayers and exorcism would soon cure them. But how did boys and girls supposedly become hysterical or insane at the same time? W. Herbert Packer, assistant medical officer at the English Salop County Asylum (Shropshire), suggested that it was a case of '*folie-à-deux*' and that 'it may, from a medico-legal point of view, assume considerable importance'.[113]

Folie à deux, 'insanity between two', was first proposed in an article written in 1877 by the influential psychiatrist and neurologist Charles Lasègue

(1816–1883), who specialized in delusions of persecution, and Jules Falret (1824–1902), who had made his name with a study on psychosis.[114] The two men recognized that under normal circumstances insanity was not contagious, otherwise asylums would obviously not be able to function. Attendants would be at risk of infection from their patients and their patients would be perpetually infecting each other. But under certain, exceptional pathological conditions, they postulated, delusions could spread from one person (often congenitally insane) to another ostensibly sane person (usually of low intelligence). The content of the delusion had to be familiar to and plausible within the circle of people amongst which it could spread. Moreover, they explained, 'it is necessary for both individuals to have lived a very close-knit existence in the same environment for a long period of time, sharing the same feelings, the same interests, the same apprehensions and the same hopes, and be completely isolated from any outside influences'. Family groups were, therefore, particularly susceptible to this contagion, and women would come to be more associated with the condition than men.[115]

The diagnosis of *folie à deux* was developed further by Evariste Marandon de Montyel (1851–1908), who would later shake up French psychiatry with his attack on the asylum system. He was, at the time, the head of the female section of Marseille asylum before becoming medical director of the Dijon asylum. In 1881 he published his ideas on the condition, based on his own observations and those of similar recorded cases.[116] He considered there were three types of *folie à deux*. First, there was *Folie imposée* where an insane person imposed his delusions on someone intellectually and morally weaker but who may not have previously exhibited any signs of insanity. De Montyel used the example of someone with religious insanity imposing his spiritual hallucinations on another. Then there was *folie simultanée*, when two people predisposed to hereditary insanity became insane at the same time under the influence of the same instigating cause. *Folie communiquée* described the transmission of hallucinations and delusions from one insane person to someone already hereditarily predisposed to insanity.

A year after de Montyel published his typology of communicated insanity, Paul-Alphonse Reverchon, a botanist and doctor at the Roche-Gandon asylum, Mayenne, and his medical assistant Dr Pagè, wrote up their observations of a case of bewitchment and spirit persecution that looked like *folie à famille*—in other words *folie à deux*.[117] In January 1882, two guards and two asylum assistants were ordered to a modest, well-run farm near the village of Andouillé to bring back to the asylum all the members of the Lochin family, namely the father Pierre and his wife, and their four children, Léon, Pierre, Jeanne, and Marie, all aged between twenty-five and thirty-one. They were terrified, looked ill and haggard, and were in a delirious state.

There was little evidence of hereditary insanity in their family history, though Jeanne had been diagnosed with the symptoms of hysteria for several years. They were no more or less assiduous in their religious devotion than their neighbours. For a year or more the family had experienced a loss of appetite. Something felt wrong. Several doctors in the vicinity had been consulted and all had prescribed tonics to revitalize their digestive systems, but to no beneficial effect. So, the Lochins came to believe themselves bewitched and called in a cunning-man named Moreau who spent two days with the family at the end of December. He was paid the handsome sum of sixty francs for his work. Not long after, though, Jeanne began to be tormented by noises around her bed, knocks on the door, and flashes of light and white flames. The other members of the family soon shared her hallucinations. They sweated profusely, stopped eating, had a burning thirst and a great constriction in the throat. They smelt sulphur and believed they were all possessed by the Devil. Visions of ghosts, black and white cats, and snakes plagued them. To rid themselves of the affliction they invoked the Blessed Virgin and the saints and adorned their home and themselves with images and statuettes for divine protection. But to no avail. On a sign from one of them, they would suddenly leave the farm in great terror and go running around the countryside half-dressed, sometimes together, sometimes in isolation. Then the Lochins became aggressive to their neighbours, smashed shop windows in Andouillé, and accused the locals of blowing dirt and bad smells down their throats. They shouted rude words, swore at people, and made threats against those who tried to approach them. They excited both fear and pity amongst their neighbours. The day the asylum officials came to take them to the asylum the local population flocked to see the spectacle. Once the family was safely within the asylum, Reverchon's first step was to have them all isolated from one another to try and break any contagious influence. They were all deemed fully cured within weeks and discharged and returned to their farm.

Reverchon and Pagè considered the confinement of an entire family for simultaneously showing symptoms of insanity too unusual not to be recorded in the annals of psychiatry, but they were unsure as to what category of insanity best explained the case. They were obviously well aware of the Morzine affair, but that was not a directly analogous example in various

respects; there was little religious 'hysteria' and both male and female members of the household exhibited the same symptoms. From their reading of
the recent literature, the case certainly had the characteristics of *folie à famille*
they suggested, but they were not convinced about this diagnosis on the
basis that there was no evidence of hereditary insanity in the Lochin family.
In the end, Reverchon and Pagè made a diagnosis on the basis of the physical rather than mental sufferings of the family—the soreness and dryness of
their throats, extreme thirst, hallucinations, nausea, and vomiting—and concluded that the temporary insanity was caused by poisoning, possibly from
the Solanaceae plant family, which includes deadly nightshade and jimson
weed or thorn apple. It was likely, they suggested, that such a toxic hallu-
cinogen was in the medicine provided by the cunning-man. Moreau was
subsequently prosecuted in April 1882, and during the trial it was stated that
the drink he gave the Lochins contained nothing more than absinthe and
calvados (a spirit made from cider). When challenged that he was not a doctor, Moreau replied, 'No, but I have a herbal book.' The cause of the Lochin's
behaviour remained a mystery.

This was not the end of the story. In 1886, Dr Lapointe, the new director
of the Roche-Gandon asylum, wrote an article published in the *Annales
Medico-Psychologiques* telling how the Lochins had all been brought back to
the asylum again in 1884.[118] In August that year mother Lochin became
more agitated than usual saying that she was being persecuted by two
witches and an evil spirit. Nothing could console her, and so she went on
pilgrimage with two of her children to the sanctuary of Our Lady at
Pontmain, some twenty-five miles away as the crow flies. This was a recently
established regional shrine inspired by a vision of the Virgin Mary during
the Franco-Prussian War of 1870–1871. She returned in a worse state. She had
hardly eaten for months and continued to say she was bewitched. The rest of
the family once again began to mimic the same symptoms. On 18 November
the family was brought back to the asylum and separated for treatment.

Lapointe read through the old newspaper reports of the original case and
mulled over the account by Reverchon. He began to doubt that the Lochins'
insanity was the result of hallucinogenic poisons. How could it repeat itself
so exactly two years later? The family told him that they had continued to
take spoonfulls of the absinthe concoction from time to time. Reverchon
sent Dr Pagè to visit the Lochin's farmhouse in Andouillé to find the
medicine prescribed by Moreau. Pagè's mission was a success. A botanist was
employed to identify the plant content of the potion. It turned out to be the

leaves and stems of wormwood (Artemisia absinthium), which has no hallucinogenic properties but was the basis for absinthe and used in medicine
as a tonic. Reverchon concluded, with reference to the Morzine affair, that
it was a rare family case of *hystéro-démonpathie* brought on by religious preoccupations. Pierre Lochin, furthermore, also had specific hallucinations,
such as seeing rats, mice, and snakes crawling over his body, which was
attributed to his excessive drinking. In January 1885, the six members of the
family were once again released and returned to their farm.

While Reverchon eventually plumped for an old, familiar diagnosis from
the mid nineteenth-century, *folie à deux* seemed a perfect fit for several contemporary cases of family murder that occurred in Ireland, and the diagnosis
was argued with great vigour by Oscar Woods (1848–1906), the medical
superintendent of the Killarney Asylum, Ireland.[119] Woods, who was from
Birr, County Offaly, graduated in medicine from University of Dublin. Like
numerous other budding psychiatrists, he began his studies in insanity at the
West Riding Asylum, Wakefield, England, before becoming assistant medical
officer at Warwick Asylum. The Lord Lieutenant of Ireland appointed him
superintendent at Killarney Asylum in 1875. He was still there in 1888 when
he gave details of a sensational case of *folie à deux* to the British Medical
Association in Glasgow and the Irish branch of the Medico-Psychological
Association in November, which was published a few months later in the
Journal of Mental Science.[120]

As Woods recounted, on 29 January 1888, Sergeant Crowe and three
other constables of the Royal Irish Constabulary were called to the house of
a farmer named Michael Doyle who lived in the hamlet of Gortboy, near
Beaufort, County Kerry. The family were shunned in the neighbourhood
because Michael's brother had previously prosecuted some local moon-
shiners. Michael had recently been attacked while riding home from
Killorglin as a consequence, and his horse was killed by a stone projectile.
On arrival at the farmstead on 29 January the constables from Beaufort
found a crowd of locals around the house including the parish priest, the
Rev. W. Neligan. On the ground lay the body of a 12-year-old boy, Patrick,
his head badly beaten, and the six members of the Doyle family half
undressed and in a state of 'raging madness'.[121] The whole family apart from
the two youngest, Dan and Denis, were swiftly taken to the Killarney District
Lunatic Asylum for a medical assessment and brought before two magistrates.
The father was considered to be of sound mind and was subsequently sent
to prison, but his wife Johanna and four of their children (Julia aged 24,

Michael aged 22, Mary aged 18, and Kate aged 15) were committed for insanity. After receiving and interviewing Johanna at the asylum, Oscar Woods wrote down in his private minute book her explanation of the tragic evening:

> On Saturday night at cock-crow, I took that fairy Patsy—he was not my son, he was a devil, a bad fairy. I could have no luck while he was in the house— carried him out of the house and threw him into the yard, and then got a hatchet and struck him three blows on the head. I then came back, and we all prayed and went to Heaven.

Mary would later corroborate this version of events, relating that she heard her mother say to Patsy, 'It is time for me to kill you, you young devil; I wonder if I have killed you enough now.' Mary was not shocked at hearing this as she had heard people say her brother was a fairy and she believed them.[122] Patrick had severe disabilities from birth, suffered from epilepsy and was deaf and mute. From the age of seven he could not walk or feed himself. In the medical language of the time he was described as an 'idiot' but in the minds of the family and neighbours he was a fairy changeling.

In early March, Michael senior, who had been released from prison early due to ill health, appeared before the Board of Governors of Killarney District Lunatic Asylum requesting that his children be returned to him. Woods said that none of them were fit to leave, and besides, as the Chairman explained, his children would be immediately arrested on leaving the asylum and be taken before a magistrate on the charge of murder. 'Would you wish to have your children be left out and be taken to Tralee Gaol?' Asked the Chairman. 'I suppose I would not, sir', replied Doyle.[123] By early July, Mary, Julia, Michael, and Kate were eventually deemed recovered from their insanity and were discharged from the asylum and brought before the Killarney magistrates. Julia remained in the asylum for another year or so. The asylum casebook noted on 1 December that she was 'becoming more demented'.[124] Meanwhile, Johanna was tried for murder at the Kerry Assizes and pleaded Not Guilty. After hearing all the evidence, it only took the jury twenty minutes to return a verdict of guilty but that she was under a fit of insanity at the time. She was sent to the Central Criminal Lunatic Asylum at Dundrum, County Dublin, where on admission she was described as a 'fierce wild Kerry peasant, scarcely able to speak English intelligibly'. Her husband began petitioning for her release in 1893, which eventually led to Johanna being transferred back to Killarney District Asylum, where her husband was able to visit her and she could converse with others in her native language.[125]

What was the cause of this supposed collective insanity? Woods looked into their family history and could not find any significant evidence of hereditary influence. Perhaps it was the goat meat? As in the Lochin case, poisoning as a trigger for contagious delusion was considered. At the coroner's inquest, Dr W.H. Dodd, who conducted the autopsy, noted that he had seen and smelt some putrid goat's meat on the kitchen table. It was green looking, and it was observed that 'if it was salted at all the pickle was very bad'.[126] Exhaustion might also have instigated the episode. The Family had been up all night the previous week minding a sow who was giving birth. Woods decided a range of external factors, along with a predilection for belief in the supernatural, was ultimately to blame for triggering the *folie à deux*: 'The strong superstitious ideas instilled into their ignorant minds by the old country women, acting on people whose bodily health was somewhat undermined by bad food and loss of rest, had much to say to the cause of the attack.'[127]

In 1888 Daniel Tuke surveyed the different types of *folie à deux*, using examples from the French literature, including the second episode of the Lochin saga, and British cases regarding which he had been personally consulted. One concerned a couple who had experimented with a *planchette* for communicating with the spirit world and came to believe evil spirits plagued their house. From this experience Tuke drew up some practical advice for avoiding situations conducive to one insane person infecting another. He discouraged, for example, a sister nursing an insane sister for a long time, particularly as he thought women were more prone to this contagion. 'Susceptible young women, and especially hysterical ones', were also to be discouraged from associating 'with persons having delusions, or even entertaining wild eccentric notions short of insane delusions'. The *planchette* couple refused to be separated, however, so in order to break the influence he gave them a course of medicine and ordered a spell at the seaside, which apparently eventually cured them.[128] As Tuke was writing, though, Charcot's hysteria appeared to answer the puzzle of how males and females, boys and girls, could all be caught up in the same suffocating family situations, and the Plédran case came to be widely cited as evidence in the new hysteria literature.[129]

★ ★ ★

Come the turn of the twentieth century there was no sense that the profusion of asylums and their medical staff were in any way curing the perceived ills of belief in the supernatural. We began with Thomas Bakewell's view that to *believe* in supernatural beings was rational but to think one was in some sort of *relationship* with them was a mark of insanity. Yet, a century on, many people of all ranks believed they regularly talked to the dead, that they were plagued by devils, persecuted by witches, and blessed with divine interventions. The fairies also held their own in some communities. The First World War, furthermore, heralded both a continuance and renewal of the supernatural across Protestant and Catholic cultures, further normalizing the experience of visions, apparitions, and providential interventions on the battlefields and on the home fronts.[130] It was a defeat for the great psychiatric project to advance a rational and sober religious outlook across the social spectrum. The belief in the supernatural proved to be just as modern as early modern. Yes, the psychiatrists proved that pathologies were clearly involved in the supernatural fears and ecstasies of some individuals, but the mental states of nations, religions, societies, and communities could not be reduced to culturally-defined and ever-shifting categories of insanity. In a sense, the early psychiatrists, however well-meant their goals, could not cope with the continuous and overwhelming evidence that the irrational and delusional was increasingly accepted as part of the ongoing human condition.

3

Madness in popular medicine

A thousand years removed from the kindly doctrine of the good Pinel.

(Arthur Mitchell, 1860)

So said Arthur Mitchell (1826–1909), historian, physician, and deputy lunacy commissioner for Scotland with reference to the popular cures for insanity he had found in the annals of his country. He wrote up his research in an article for the Society of the Antiquaries of Scotland, observing that 'superstition may be regarded as a disease' but it was one that was at least being eradicated by the efforts of the schoolmaster and only lingered in remote areas. The same sentiment was echoed a couple of decades later by psychiatrist Daniel Hack Tuke in his *History of the Insane*, where he sarcastically referred to the 'the popular and medical treatment of lunatics in the good old times in the British Isles'.[1] But how was insanity understood in the folk cultures of the past and, indeed, in the age of the asylum? The antiquarian psychiatrists were mostly interested in digging up gross cures to titillate rather than researching the vernacular understanding of the cause and nature of insanity. And, besides, were popular remedies really as bad and barbaric as the psychiatrists liked to make out?

The early psychiatrists wrestled with the sheer weight of evidence for long-held popular notions of madness that may seem nonsense today, but which had deep roots in the old orthodox medicine of the early modern era and beyond. The *physical* causes of madness, for instance, were recognized across the board. Everyone could easily accept from personal experience and lore that a kick in the head from a horse or other such cranial injuries could bring on madness. An analysis of sixty-six cases in which lay witnesses gave their opinion on the cause of madness from the London Old Bailey between the mid eighteenth and mid nineteenth century found that in forty-nine cases the given causes were physical, such as headwounds, fits, drink, fevers, accidents, or hereditary conditions.[2] The remaining cases reflected the popular link between moral or emotional trauma and mental sickness, with lay witnesses attributing the madness of defendants to the death of a family member, family distress, grief, love, and ill-treatment. The myriad emotional reasons for why people were committed to an asylum will be explored through the inner lives of asylum patients in the second half of this book. Most of this chapter is taken up with the notions that lie behind terms such as 'touched in the head', 'moon-struck', 'sun struck', 'possessed', and 'mad as a dog'. These suggested that madness was a result of uncontrollable external forces that affected both the minds and bodies of animals and humans equally. As we shall see, they were rooted in ancient medical theories and venerable notions of astrology, providence, sympathetic magic, and supernatural assault.

The use of 'madness' in the title and throughout this chapter is a deliberate shift in terms to explore these issues. To try and understand what people felt, feared, and diagnosed we need to ditch the term 'insanity' for the moment. It only came into medical usage in the eighteenth century and there is little evidence it became part of popular vocabulary until the twentieth century. No medical condition has generated so many popular expressions as madness and its symptoms. During the period covered by this book we find 'daft', 'distracted', 'troubled in mind', 'deranged', 'not right', 'simple', 'silly', 'flighty', 'out of sorts', 'unhinged', 'barmy', 'foolish', 'out of his mind', 'not in her senses', 'senseless', 'low in spirits', 'wandering in his mind', 'being out of his wits', 'crazed', 'void of reason', and 'not born right'. Some terms denoted a sense of deficiency or lack of control, and others the idea of being broken, such as 'cracked' or 'crack pot'. Then there were the metaphors and similes with animal behaviour, such as 'mad as a march hare', or as one trial witness said of a defendant in 1805, he was 'like a mad bullock'.[3] Some trades were proverbially considered prone, such as 'mad as a hatter' or 'mad as a weaver'. There were also various phrases and sayings, such as 'go to Bath and get your head shaved', or 'to have a bee in one's bonnet', or to be 'queer in one's attic'.[4]

The overarching term 'madness' was not the preserve of any profession or section of society, and until the psychiatric lexicon became established in the early nineteenth century, madness was, by and large, a term whose general meaning was understood in both orthodox and popular medicine,

and by physicians, sufferers, their families, and their neighbours.[5] Eighteenth
and early nineteenth-century court rooms were spaces where we can see
the exchange of this shared language, with judge, juries, doctors, and witnesses roughly understanding each other when describing the 'madness' of
a defendant. We also see it in pauper letters seeking medical relief payments
under the English Old Poor Law in the same period. The rhetoric of illness
was part of the language of negotiation with officialdom, with pauper
writers using phrases like 'deranged in his Intellect', 'state of Distraction',
and 'a sullen State'. As has been observed, this was not 'a function of imperfect medical knowledge', but rather a strategy to obtain medical acceptance
through the shared diagnostics of the visibly intense experience of mental
illness.[6] The growing influence of the psychiatric profession would break
this linguistic consensus with their new classifications and terminology—
and their rejection of the old terms. Indeed, one French commentator on
this shift bemoaned in 1839 that the 'words of the people are abandoned
today for words invented or introduced by scholars'.[7]

If we move away from the matter of language, though, and focus instead
on notions about the causes, symptoms, and cure of madness we find a
much more entangled history than is generally suggested in the mainstream
histories of medicine with their message of scientific progress. Medical historian Roy Porter once asserted that the discipline of psychiatry was 'shaped
from below'.[8] He was right. By 'popular medicine', then, I do not mean a
blunt binary division between official and unofficial, scientific and folkloric,
but rather a shared set of ideas that were deeply engrained in culture for
much of our period. We have few direct sources in which labourers and the
working classes explained in their own writing what they and their family,
friends, and neighbours understood by madness in relation to religion, philosophy, and the natural world. Physicians and folklorists were not particularly interested in asking either.[9] But we can attempt to excavate it from
medical literature, asylum records, court archives, and ethnographic sources.

Frightened mad

We are all familiar with the phrase 'frightened to death'. Today we normally
use it metaphorically, but in the past a sudden fright was widely thought to
be a significant cause of death, madness, and deformity.[10] It was a notion that
was accepted by the psychiatric profession right through the nineteenth

century. Esquirol counted forty-six cases of fright out of 1218 admitted to the Charenton and Salpetrière, and observed that 'many women, who were pregnant at various periods of the Revolution, have become the mothers of children, whom the slightest cause has rendered insane'. In mid nineteenth-century America, seventeen cases of fright out of 3390 patients were recorded at Taunton Hospital, Massachusetts, over a fifteen-year period. And, later on, at the Bristol Lunatic Asylum, England, twenty-eight patients were admitted for fright between 1861 and 1900.[11] It was also identified as a significant cause of 'puerperal madness', which was a widely recognized though disputed category of mania that afflicted women in childbirth.[12]

Records reveal a myriad causes for fright. Examples from an American asylum in the 1840s included a young woman who went insane with fright after lightning struck the ground near her, and another who went mad after someone fired a gun in her home when she thought she was alone.[13] Practical jokes gone tragically wrong were another source. In October 1822 Thomas Dowle, a 28-year-old farmer's son from near Chepstow, England, was brought to Bedlam. There was no evidence of insanity in his family, but he was crossing his father's fields one day when an acquaintance seeing him coming, and wishing to have a frolic, suddenly jumped out on him from behind a bush with a loud shout. He fainted, delirium followed, and then a state of complete madness: 'he tries to kick all who come near him, and even to bite them, with all the rabid fury of an enraged dog'.[14]

Fright from supernatural fears were also recorded. Some cases derived from pranks on people thought to be particularly 'superstitious' by their neighbours. In the Taunton Hospital, Massachusetts, there was a boy aged sixteen who had been chased one evening by someone dressed up in grave clothes like a corpse. The next day the boy was deranged. In another case a young man who was known for frequently expressing his fear of ghosts was the target of a prank by local boys. He was in the habit of sleeping with a revolver in easy reach, and so one day the boys replaced the bullets with blanks. At midnight he was awoken by a ghostly vision in his room. He grabbed his revolver and fired. The ghost made as if it had caught the bullet and then threw it back onto the man's bed. This happened repeatedly. The poor victim of the prank fainted with fear and shock and his condition swiftly gave way to 'melancholia with frenzy'. He was taken to the asylum and recovered after three months. One of the pranksters also succumbed to insanity out of remorse for his actions and was likewise removed to the asylum.[15] Then there were the cases of mistaken ghost sightings. In 1911 a healthy farm servant-girl of Coatbridge, Scotland, went to fetch water from the well one night when the farmer dressed in light-coloured clothing appeared and walked towards her. She thought it was a ghost and became so frightened she went temporarily blind. Her mind became so 'unhinged' that she had to be taken to the asylum.[16] Such cases served to underscore psychiatric concerns about the consequences of popular beliefs in the supernatural.

Fright was also widely thought to cause birth defects that led to children being classified as 'deaf', 'dumb', and 'idiots'. The records of the Earlswood National Asylum for Idiots in Redhill, Surrey, between 1861 and 1886, reveal that the most common *supposed* cause of ante-natal damage was, indeed, fright or anxiety during pregnancy. One woman, for instance, attributed her child's 'idiocy' to a 'flock of geese flying at her' when eight months pregnant. Another study of child asylum patients found numerous such examples too, including a couple of cases where mothers explained they had been frightened by monkeys at the zoo when pregnant.[17] Such beliefs had a long history. The notion that divine punishment for moral failings or diabolic influence led to birth defects and 'monstrous' children was a favourite topic in sectarian and popular literature during the seventeenth century. While this interpretation drained out of medical discourse during the eighteenth century, evangelical movements such as Wesleyan Methodism continued to preach the providential origin of some disability and deformity.[18] The notion lingered into the late nineteenth century in both Catholic and Protestant communities. The 1871 Irish Census, for instance, which asked people for explanations for the cause of the mental and physical disorders of those in the household, included dozens of cases of childhood deafness, muteness, and idiocy due to fright during pregnancy, as well as a few cases of divine punishment. The father of a man, aged forty, born deaf and dumb in Carlow County, explained to the census enumerator that 'the neighbours look upon it as a mark of God's anger on account of the father's habit of mocking a certain dumb man' and also because of the blasphemous expressions he had uttered about dumbness. A 60-year-old woman from Cavan, born deaf and mute, was likewise thought to have been afflicted due to her mother having mockingly mimicked a deaf mute while pregnant.[19]

The medical profession may have dismissed such supernatural explanations by the nineteenth century but the idea of maternal mental influence continued to be widely held.[20] There were two aspects to the debate. First, there was the venerable notion that a striking mental impression influenced the physical development of the foetus, which in some way, through deformity or bodily marks, mimicked or represented the maternal impression. One widespread belief, for instance, was that if a pregnant woman saw a hare her child would have a 'harelip'. Robert Burton, author of *The Anatomy of Melancholy*, mentioned the notion back in the early seventeenth century, and it was alive and well two centuries later. Of forty-five cases of cleft lip operated on by Frank Hastings Hamilton (1813–1886), an American Professor of Military Surgery, three were attributed by the mothers to having been frightened by seeing someone with a 'harelip', while another case concerned a woman who saw a rabbit during her fourth month of pregnancy.[21] The life of Joseph Merrick, the 'Elephant Man', provides the most famous and profound example of this belief. He explained in his autobiography that 'the deformity which I am now exhibiting was caused by my mother being frightened by an elephant'. While his self-diagnosis was taken by some as a sign of his feeble mental state, Merrick was, in fact, an intelligent man who simply believed in a form of causation that was still a matter of serious medical consideration as well as popular belief.

Adherents to the notion of imitative defects were particularly numerous in the American medical establishment, with examples reported by general practitioners and surgeons during the mid nineteenth century. We can turn, for instance, to a report in *The United States Medical Investigator* regarding a paper entitled 'A Case of Monstrosity' given to the Cook County Medical Society (Illinois) in 1867. During the ensuing discussion one Dr L. Dodge reported a case known to him of a pregnant woman who saw a man in a barnyard run a pitchfork through the head of a toad. When the child was born its left foot was shaped like a toad's head. A Dr Kendall chipped in to say that he observed a similar case twenty years before. A woman two-months' pregnant had been severely frightened by a monkey jumping on her shoulder. At four months she suffered a miscarriage and while the upper half of the foetus was perfectly normal the bottom half looked like a monkey—'tail and all'. When a Dr Wilbur asked another doctor whether he thought emotional influences affected the child *in utero*, he replied in the affirmative, but went on to qualify this by stating, 'I should very much dis-like, however, to admit it to my patients, sometimes.'[22] The distinguished American neurologist William Alexander Hammond stuck his neck out on the matter the following year. Doubtless many examples were false, many were exaggerations, and many were mere coincidence, he agreed, but there remained some that could not be rejected in this way: 'Where there is so universal belief in the existence of certain facts it may safely be assumed that there is some truth.'[23] The editors of *The Humboldt Medical Archives*, and others, were not convinced. Sure, they said, 'there is scarcely a midwife or old woman to be found, who cannot narrate a dozen cases corroborative of her belief', but why should any credence be given to such sources?[24]

It was another American doctor who did most to undermine the enduring edifice of maternal impressions and their physical and mental consequences. His name was George Jackson Fisher (1825–1893), one-time surgeon of Sing Sing prison, New York, and president of the New York State Medical Society. Fisher compiled a large body of evidence from the past and present and concluded that this 'popular error' problematically lingered 'in the present age in the minds of not a few'.[25] A key reason for this was that some medical men were reluctant to dismiss the sheer weight of anecdotal evidence that had accumulated over the centuries. He concluded with a degree of sarcasm: 'While I deny that the mother's mind has any power to produce physical changes in her offspring during gestation, I am free to admit the unlimited power of her imagination in the explanation of abnormalities *after* the period of gestation has terminated.'[26]

The second key debate, which proved more challenging to dismiss in the long run, was the idea that a strong emotion like a fright or shock injured the foetus and damaged it in mind or body, but without any imitative associations. The influential French physician and educationalist Édouard Séguin (1812–1880), who emigrated to America during the 1848 European revolutions, and specialized in the education of deaf-mutes and the physiology of idiocy, maintained in cautious terms that 'idiocy holds unknown though certain relations to maternal impressions as modificators of placental nutrition'.[27] It is no surprise, then, that references to fright as a cause of neo-natal disability continued to appear in asylum records into the early twentieth century.

Looking to the skies

'The changes in the weather, or atmosphere, have a very considerable influence', stated the late eighteenth-century asylum owner, Thomas Bakewell, 'and I recollect, hearing an observant keeper of a mad house, say, "We shall have a change of weather; I can tell by yonder people making such a noise this morning."'[28] In their search for scientific evidence rather than anecdote, physicians and early psychiatrists became enthusiastic meteorologists during the first half of the nineteenth century, logging rain patterns and moon cycles and plotting barometric fluctuations.[29] In the tropics, the idea of atmospheric influence on disease became particularly entrenched amongst late eighteenth and early nineteenth-century colonial physicians who drew upon indigenous understanding of the effects of the weather, the sun, and the moon that chimed with naval lore and early modern western medicine. These 'Lunacist' physicians considered that the sun and moon had a greater and more corruptive influence over nature in the hot tropics than in temperate climates. Their research, which was given added relevance during the 1817 cholera epidemic in British India, concerned proving that the moon cycles and atmospheric pressure had an influence over the severity and spread of fevers.[30]

The idea that the sun, the moon, and weather conditions affected temperament, and could turn the minds of people and animals, was also deeply embedded in European folklore as well as medical science. Thunderstorms, for instance, could cause fright but also disturb the mind more generally. An elderly woman was brought to an Oxford asylum in the mid nineteenth century for insanity apparently induced by thunder and lightning. Perpetually strong winds, such as the fierce *Mistral* that blows down the Rhone valley in southern France, and the *levante* winds in Spain, were legendary for making humans and livestock go mad. A dry, warm wind known in Central Europe as the *Föhn* was thought to cause *Föhnkrankheit* (Föhn's disease) which caused suicidal depression and other symptoms.[31] Generally, though, such winds were thought to cause temporary madness among those buffeted day after day, and there is little reference in the archives of people being treated in asylums and hospitals for wind-induced mental disorder. But the effects of the sun were of a different magnitude and seriousness.

Sunstroke, which was also known in medical literature as 'insolation' or by the French term '*coup de soleil*', had been thought a cause of madness as far back as antiquity, and the notion continued in popular belief and asylum literature throughout the nineteenth century. Esquirol noted sixteen cases of sunstroke out of the 710 cases he categorized as insanity arising from physical causes. Thirteen cases of sunstroke were dealt with at Bethlehem Hospital between 1846–1860, and at the Glasgow Royal 1 per cent of patients between 1862 and 1886 were recorded as having sunstroke or lived in hot climates.[32] As these statistics suggest, the problem was considered rare in northern Europe for obvious climatic reasons. Blistering hot weather, however brief, could bring on a rash of localized cases for asylums. This explains the six cases of sunstroke admitted to the Borough of Portsmouth Lunatic Asylum in 1884. *The Meteorological Office Monthly Weather Reports*, which began in 1884, stated that in July that year the weather was 'decidedly warm' with highs of thirty-one degrees in southern England, while August continued to be hot and sunny with temperatures climbing to thirty-three degrees in the south and southeast.[33] Agricultural labourers were particularly prone to sunstroke at these times of haymaking and harvesting. Alexander Morison (1779–1866), who had been physician at Bethlehem, Surrey Lunatic Asylum, and Hanwell Asylum, confirmed that this partly explained the reported spike in mania and madness during the summer months. In late August 1869, for instance, there were reports of a rash of deaths due to sunstroke, particularly among harvesters working in the fields. One was Thomas Choyce, aged forty, of Seagrave, Leicestershire. About two o'clock in the afternoon he suddenly became 'raging mad' and it took six men to hold him down and march him home. He died two hours later. A few years earlier an agricultural worker was brought to Warwick Asylum on the hottest day of autumn. While working in the fields sunstroke caused him to go mad. He believed his body was putrefying and that he had sold himself to the Devil.[34]

Morison also noted cases of soldiers 'being suddenly seized with madness' while being reviewed on the parade ground in the burning heat of the summer sun. Francis Skae of the Royal Edinburgh Asylum wrote one of the few early psychiatric papers devoted to the subject. The cases from his institution were also mostly soldiers who had become insane due to their exposure while on duty. The symptoms included mania, hallucinations, and delusions.[35] The other main sun-struck group were sailors, who were thought to be particularly prone to bouts of madness due to their confined environment, knocks on the head, alcoholism, and exposure to the sun.[36] In the 1750s William Battie, physician at St Luke's Hospital for Lunatics, London, noted that he knew a sailor 'who became raving mad in a moment while the sun beams darted perpendicularly upon his head'.[37] In 1828 Royal Navy Surgeon, James Mitchell (c. 1793–1858), wrote up his observations on the cases of *coup de soleil* he had seen and treated on his global voyages, which included several convict ship journeys to Australia. In 1815, while posted at Lake Champlain, Canada, he had seen numerous cases of marines seized with fury from sunstroke. He observed three kinds of the 'disease', and the one he associated with clinical insanity he termed chronic phrenitis (an old term for inflammation of the brain). It came on gradually and continued for a long time, and the victims usually expressed 'perversion of ideas' such as considering themselves the Saviour of the World or that they were a prophet for a new millennium. It was a disease he had only witnessed in hot climates. Mitchell said that in most such cases the patients were sent back to England to enjoy the 'bracing air', though in severe cases they had to be cared for in an asylum.[38]

The trouble with sunstroke-induced madness was that while it was considered curable, there was always the danger that it could revisit the patient years later. In 1881 a Sunderland police court heard the case of Edwin Wood who had turfed his wife and children into the street and was seen wandering around at midnight in an excited state. It transpired he was a ship's master who had gone insane some seven years before due to sunstroke and had spent most of the intervening years in Sedgefield Lunatic Asylum. Eleven weeks after he was released his insanity reoccurred much to the distress of his family. In 1898 a Kilmarnock mason was seen running naked and wild on the sands at Barassie on the southwest coast of Scotland. On being detained he said he had saved the lives of fifty men from a ship. He was certified insane and taken to Ayr District Asylum, where it came to light that he had been seized with sunstroke during his time as a soldier.[39]

Moon madness

The influence of the moon on human health was much discussed in the sixteenth and seventeenth centuries and was deeply influenced by the medical theories espoused by the Greco-Roman physician Galen (129–216), who set out the idea of bodily humours in writings which continued to underpin European medicine 1400 years later. There were four humours or fluids that dictated pain and health—black bile, yellow bile, blood, and phlegm. Imbalances of any of the four had negative effects on mind and body. Lunar control over the amount of phlegm in the brain was thought to trigger epilepsy and madness. Richard Mead's *Treatise Concerning the Influence of the Sun and Moon upon Human Bodies* proved an enduring defence of these views. Like most of his contemporary physicians, Mead (1673–1754) adhered to humoural theory and mixed it with entrenched folkloric notions, but he nevertheless professed he was presenting a cutting-edge scientific theory of solar and lunar influence on mental and physical health.[40] He was, after all, one of the first English public figures to look back with horror on the witch trials and decry the many lives destroyed: 'I most heartily rejoice, that I have lived to see all our laws relating to witchcraft entirely abolished.'[41] His enterprising re-packaging of familiar ideas certainly gave them longevity in the medical literature and thereby ensured that popular notions regarding natural astrology and mental health continued to have medical currency as the psychiatric profession developed. The French physician Pierre Foissac (1801–1886), for instance, well known internationally for his work on meteorological influences on health and hygiene, continued to draw uncritically upon examples of lunacy from antiquity and the works of Mead.[42]

One popular notion regarding lunacy was that sleeping in direct view of a full moon caused madness. This raises the question of who would be out sleeping in the open air on a moonlit night in the eighteenth and nineteenth centuries? Sailors mainly. In 1828, James Mitchell noted that he had heard of moonstruck sailors who, as a consequence of sleeping on deck in the full moon, had their mouths contorted awry and never again regained their normal facial appearance. 'Once, when at Java, a sailor was under my care for intermittent fever, apparently produced from sleeping on deck in the moon, attended with very anomalous symptoms, such as sudden swelling of the face, delirium, livid spots on the face and countenance', Mitchell recalled. 'The people and himself attributed it all (on my inquiries) to his sleeping in the moon.' Mitchell was sceptical in this instance, but he had seen and heard enough not to be completely dismissive of 'the superstitions of the sailors'.[43] But the main popular link between the moon and insanity concerned the waxing and waning influence of the moon during the monthly lunar cycle.

John Haslam, apothecary to Bethlem Hospital, observed in 1808 that when patients had been brought to the Hospital, especially those from the countryside, 'their friends have generally stated them to be worse at some particular change of the moon'. One such case was an excisemen admitted in 1787 who 'was said to have been furious and maniacal at the full and change of the moon for six months'. At the moon's change he accused his wife of stealing his money and tried to cut his own throat. Several decades later, the author of a book on 'lunatic life' similarly noted that he had repeatedly come across this strong belief expressed by the family and friends of those they had brought to the asylum—'urged too, with a great deal of earnestness and sincerity'.[44] Haslam wrote that some recovered lunatics had told him that the overseers or masters of the workhouses in which they had been kept had bound, chained, and flogged them after consulting almanacs regarding the phase of the moon.[45] The belief in the moon's influence on mind and body was so engrained in tradition and early modern medical thinking that the early psychiatrists felt bound to test the theory using their asylums and hospitals as laboratories. Haslam was one of the first to keep a rigorous register of the lunar cycles and patient behaviour. But, after two years, he found no evidence of a connection at all. The first half of the century saw further numerous endeavours to prove or disprove the effects of the moon on the welfare of asylum patients.[46]

One of the last of the ardent supporters for lunar influence in Britain was Matthew Allen (1783–1845). He started his medical career as an apothecary's assistant before becoming an apothecary to York Asylum in 1819. Like earlier madhouse keepers, he never seems to have obtained any higher formal medical training. His Doctor of Medicine degree from Aberdeen only required a fee, a certificate of medical competence, and two sponsors. He was a bit of a scoundrel in his early adult life, serving time in prison for debt, but this did not prevent him founding his own private asylum at High Beach, Epping Forest, in 1825. He developed a reputation for being a bit of a maverick, economic with the truth at times, but he was also praised for his compassionate and liberal treatment. He is known today as being the asylum keeper of the poet John Clare who was cared for at High Beach between 1837 and 1841.[47] In 1831 Allen published *Cases of Insanity*, in which he set out his views on the moon's impact on the weather—particularly on rainfall—and the evidence for the atmospheric and lunar influence on epidemic disease, the mind, and the body. With regard to the moon, he recognized it was difficult to measure its influence because its effect varied from person to person, but he did conclude that there was a 'lunar period of excitement'. He produced a table setting out the position of the moon at the time of death of thirty patients at the York Lunatic Asylum between 1820 and 1824 to prove the correlation that the new and full moon led to fatal levels of excitement. In 1845 the superintendent at the York Retreat and statistician, John Thurnham, re-assessed Allen's data in relation to a larger survey conducted at the Retreat and came to the opposite conclusion: the evidence of correlation was 'altogether doubtful'.[48]

Over in America, in 1845, Samuel B. Woodward (1787–1850), the superintendent at Worcester Lunatic Hospital, Massachusetts, one of the first public asylums in the country, conducted one of the last detailed asylum studies of the moon. He meticulously logged the stages of the moon in relation to paroxysms of excitement in 125 patients suffering from periodical insanity and also to 175 deaths that had occurred. He admitted his failure to find any clear correlation between insanity and lunar cycles, but he remained convinced that there was evidence that periodicity influenced human physiology, noting menstrual cycles and the cyclic fluctuation of fevers as examples. 'If these coincidences were observed only by the ignorant and superstitious', he thought, 'they might pass unnoticed as too intimately connected with preconceived notions and partial examinations of occurrences to establish and sustain what tradition has handed down as true ... but men of the greatest science and closest observation recognise such influence.' The study of lunar influence 'should be encouraged and examined', he stated, 'rather than ridiculed and rejected.'[49] But the tide was turning.

By 1862 the likes of the pious, popular literary and science periodical, *Good Words*, which was read by the fireside for the improvement of the middle-class household, could state matter-of-factly that 'the influence of the moon in insanity is now entirely discredited, but many cling to its influence on the weather'.[50] Yet when Forbes Benignus Winslow went over the evidence for lunar effects in his book *Light and Its Influence* (1867) he was very careful to tiptoe around the subject. In a chapter entitled 'On the alleged influence of the moon on the insane' he clearly did not want to dismiss such a deeply engrained notion. While making allowance for Mead's obsolete terminology and the state of knowledge in Mead's time, Winslow still believed his theories of lunar influence on disease contained 'germs of some great truths'.[51] He ended his chapter by confessing that he had never got around to making a systematic register of the lunar phases and the behaviour of the insane under his care, and instead deferred, once again, to the weight of anecdotal evidence and popular experience over clinical results. There was, he said, an 'intelligent' matron at his institution for insane ladies who was adamant that the patients were always more agitated at the full moon.[52]

The mid nineteenth century saw growing efforts to expunge the terminology of 'lunacy' and 'lunatic' once and for all from the asylum profession. In America, in 1855, Thomas Story Kirkbride (1809–1883), superintendent of the Pennsylvania Hospital for the Insane, wrote a guide to setting up a 'hospital for the insane' in which he observed that 'lunatic' and 'lunacy' were terms 'particularly objectionable from their very derivation, tending to give wrong impressions of the disease and to perpetuate popular errors'.[53] The same year a London meeting of The Association of Medical Officers of

Asylums and Hospitals for the Insane, chaired by the president John Thurnham, set out a policy to eradicate the terms in Britain:

> *Disuse of Obsolete Terms:–* That by Members of the Association such terms as 'lunatic' and 'lunatic asylum' be as far as possible disused, and that except for official or legal purposes the terms 'insane person' and 'asylum' or 'hospital for the insane' be substituted; and that generally all terms having an opprobrious origin or application in connection with the insane be disused and discouraged.[54]

This was an effective policy in terms of the naming and re-naming of institutions, and the phraseology of the reports they produced, but it took decades to expunge the terms from both the statute books and medical literature. In Britain, for instance, the Lunacy Act of 1890 helped keep the term, and, inadvertently, its old associations, alive and well in legal and popular language.[55]

Mad as a dog

Canine madness or rabies was also well known from antiquity. Galen was convinced it was caused by a toxic corrupted humour and other Roman physicians thought it a poison. The Roman naturalist Pliny the Elder considered that the source of the virus—as venom was also known—was a parasitic worm found under the tongues of dogs. He referred to this "worm' as the '*lytta*', which derived from the ancient Greek *lyssa* for 'fury' or madness' (the modern name for the rabies virus is lyssavirus). This supposed worm is in fact a natural fold of tissue under the tongue known as the frenulum that helps hold the tongue down. Humans have a less developed one. But thanks to Pliny and others the notion of the tongue worm became pervasive in medieval and early modern medicine. Various early modern authors on hydrophobia and veterinary disorders also constructed distinct classifications of madness in dogs based on symptoms such as sleepiness and a lack of interest in eating.[56] In 1686, the *Philosophical Transactions* of the Royal Society included 'An Account of the Diseases of Doggs' by the royal physician and Paracelsian Théodore Mayerne (1573–1655) in which he defined two forms of canine madness, the 'hot madness' during which they 'fly upon every thing and can hold out but 4 days', and the 'running madness' which included fits. Both were 'catched by the breath of *Dogs* being together as is the Plague among Men', and both were incurable.[57]

Richard Mead, like most early modern physicians, considered rabies a violent fever caused by poison, though, by the end of the eighteenth century, doctors were increasingly turning to the view that it was a spasmodic, nervous affliction. Whatever the cause, it was considered a major health problem because of its evident transmission from animals to humans through contact with saliva. Those humans bitten by rabid animals were considered to suffer from a condition known as hydropohobia, which literally means an irrational fear of water, but the condition was also thought to include a range of other physical and mental symptoms.[58]

The human symptoms were sometimes reckoned to mimic those of dogs, with some victims observed to go on all fours and bark and howl or to froth at the mouth. People feared that hydrophobics would also bite those around them to spread the malady. Up until the mid eighteenth century, medical and popular conceptions of rabid madness and its transmission remained rooted in long-held magical as well as medical notions of sympathy. The influence of the moon was one of the most enduring. Royal physician Daniel Peter Layard, in his *An Essay on the Bite of a Mad Dog* (1763), was quite convinced of the relationship between the onset of rabid fits and the position of the moon. One such case he reported as occurring in 1757 concerned a 22-year-old woman named Elizabeth Bryant. She was bitten on the third finger of her right hand by a mad turnspit dog. A few hours before the next full moon she began to feel pains in her finger, then a choking sensation and she could not bear the sight of water. Another young woman became 'a perfect maniac' thirty hours before a full moon.[59] As well as physical symptoms, Layard identified three stages of the progression of the malady towards madness. In the first, the victim suffered from frightful dreams. During the second phase these increased, along with trembling and convulsions. Then finally 'the patient is in the greatest fury; his madness increases with every exacerbation...yet in the whole course of his fury he continues in his senses'.[60] This self-awareness of the deterioration of one's mental state was remarked upon by others, and it was illustrated by a well-recorded American case from 1771. The patient was a farmer named William who exhibited all the initial signs set out by Layard. It was William who first diagnosed his own mental decline, rather than his doctor. One day he began to bark like a dog, and he was heard to exclaim, 'Oh dear! I believe I am going mad!'[61] Such cases would later provoke the question of whether someone who believed they were going mad was really mad rather than physically ill.

Examples of bestial imitation continued to be reported at coroners' inquests and in medical literature and newspapers right through the nineteenth century. There were even reports where those bitten by supposedly rabid felines would mew and hiss like a cat, lap at their food, and attempt to scratch people with their hands taking a claw-like shape. In 1874 it was reported in the press, for instance, that a mason from Sheffield had been bitten by a cat that had been bitten by a rabid dog. The man at once became convinced he was going to die and, overcome by a sense of futility, sold all his tools. He became 'quite mad' and would bark and jump about like a dog, and then behave like a cat, arching his back, spitting and hissing.[62] In other words, he exhibited the animalistic traits of the whole chain of transmission. This behaviour was thought more likely to afflict the poor, 'superstitious', and ignorant who were considered more prone to slip regressively into the bestial moral universe of the lower animal world.[63]

Some victims of hydrophobia found themselves in hospitals and workhouse infirmaries, but because of the old link with madness, some also ended up in asylums, even though by the early nineteenth century it was accepted that the convulsions and frenzy of the hydrophobe were usually brought on by *feverish* delirium and not *insane* delirium.[64] One such victim was John Lindsay, a 36-year-old weaver of Fern Gore, near Bury, Lancashire, who was brought to Manchester Lunatic Hospital in May 1794. He was perfectly rational but had an apprehension of danger and had developed an aversion to water, noise, and the proximity of people. He was described as having a melancholic temperament. Lindsay thought his disordered feelings were due to having been bitten by a mad dog twelve years earlier. He told his story to the doctors. Work had been hard to come by and he had been finding it increasingly difficult to look after his wife and children. He had applied to the Overseer of the Poor of the parish for help to pay his rent and avoid the seizure of his goods. But he received no help. He worked at his loom night and day until he was mentally and physically exhausted. And then his symptoms started. It was when he tried to drink a cup of balm tea, but could not, that he realized his illness, and exclaimed, 'Good God! It is all over with me!' He told his wife how he had been bitten by a dog that he had encountered as it was being chased along the highway by a crowd. He took himself to the Lunatic Hospital, where his condition worsened with spasms, convulsions, and retching. He had terrible visions of a black dog and after one such fit he died.[65] Surgeon Jacques Tenon (1724–1816), who knew well the Salpêtrière, complained shortly before he died that those bitten by

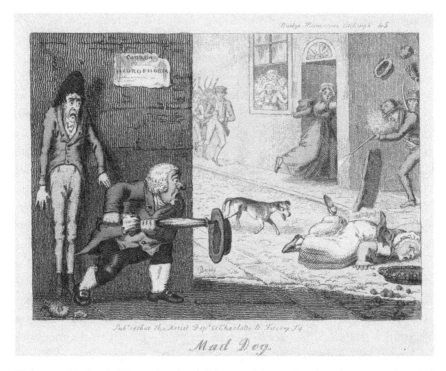

Figure 3 Hydrophobia panics. A mad dog on the run in a London street. Satirical etching by T.L. Busby, 1826.
Credit: Wellcome Collection

rabid dogs were still being kept in French hospitals along with those suffering from insanity, to the detriment of both groups of sufferers. Even in the 1850s the Warsaw lunatic asylum was taking in up to twenty or so people bitten by rabid dogs as part of a quarantine programme. Those suspected of having hydrophobia were contained in a special area of the asylum for forty days to see if their symptoms developed. This was considered a peculiar and unusual state of affairs by this time.[66]

Periodic waves of public concern about rabies epidemics ebbed and flowed over the centuries. One peak occurred in Britain in the summer of 1760 when the City of London instituted a two-month dog cull.[67] The action provoked a series of public debates regarding animal welfare, sanitation, and the confused understanding of the disease. As a correspondent to the *Gentleman's Magazine* observed at the time, 'The manner of knowing whether a dog be mad or no, somewhat resembles the ancient custom of trying witches.'[68] The popular fear of an ensuing epidemic of madness in humans was stoked by lurid stories reported in the press, such as *Lloyd's Evening Post*'s account of a 9-year-old girl in Wapping bitten by a puppy. She became raving mad, barked like a dog, and had to be tied to her bed.[69] Rumours and reports were exaggerated and invented in classic fashion. The Irish novelist Oliver Goldsmith (1728–1774) satirized the 'Epidemic Terror' of mad dogs in an essay. He related how his landlady had woken him up one morning to tell of a recent case of a mad dog in the countryside that had bitten a farmer. The farmer had gone mad and bitten one of his own brindled cows, which also started raving and foaming at the mouth. It reared up on its hind legs and barked like a dog and sometimes attempted to talk like the farmer. 'Upon examining the grounds of this story', Goldsmith continued, 'I found my landlady had it from one neighbour, who had it from another neighbour, who heard it from a very good authority.'[70]

During the 1760 scare, one correspondent wondered aloud whether the whole thing was a scam set up by quacks to boost sales of their rabies medicines. Again, in 1794, another correspondent to the *Gentleman's Magazine*, wrote that, 'there is great reason to believe that the dreadful cases, so frequently related in the public papers, originate from persons interested in patent medicines for the complaint'.[71] As well as those who suspected quacks were stoking public fears, there were puzzling elements to rabies epidemics that led some to believe the condition did not exist at all. If hydrophobics demonstrated a strong aversion to all liquids, for example, why did they not have an aversion to seeing their own urine? Were some of the symptoms a product of the mind and not the virus? There was much debate about its pathological mental status rather than its physical cause. The Irish physician Christopher Nugent (1698–1775) suggested, for instance, that hydrophobia was 'a species of *Mania*' with a 'certain Alienation of Mind'. Indeed, there was some debate into the nineteenth century as to whether hydrophobia could be caught without any contact with rabid animals or brought on by other factors, including fright and shock. The French physician Armand Trousseau (1801–1867) argued that there existed 'mental hydrophobia' where the symptoms were triggered by strong emotions after seeing someone else suffer from hydrophobia or hearing about alarming real cases.[72]

In 1809 Rotherhythe surgeon William Maryan wrote a radical and remarkable treatise about the received wisdom on rabies and hydrophobia. He was not the first to consider it was physiologically impossible for dogs to convey madness to men, but he went further by stating that hydrophobia was basically a medical chimera. According to Maryan, witchcraft was 'a disease, which may be considered coeval with hydrophobia', which 'did once exist over the whole of that now enlightened part of the world called Europe'.[73] Both were delusional mental afflictions along with hysteria and hypochondria. It was the fear of ensuing death and madness that generated the symptoms rather than any virus, but the mental shock could still kill and thereby reaffirm the fallacy to untrained minds.[74] Maryan was not drawing upon cutting-edge psychiatry to support his conclusion, but rather first- and second-hand patient evidence, observation, and the study of nature. The best way of treating those who thought they were going mad from the bite of a dog was to tell them straight that it was basically all in their mind, a fear, an apprehension, and if their fears could be allayed then they would be cured without any need for nostrums and lunatic hospitals. Maryan's treatise did not convince the medical establishment at the time let alone public opinion. The *Medical and Physical Journal* called his arguments ingenious but 'by no means satisfactory'. With regard to the witchcraft analogy, the reviewer went on to observe that witchcraft had disappeared with 'the improvement of human knowledge' but that hydrophobia had 'become daily more confirmed'.[75]

But could animals be insane in the first place let alone transmit their madness? It has already been observed that in popular medicine madness was believed to afflict animals in similar ways to humans. In 1870, Scottish doctor William Lauder Lindsay, physician to the Murray Royal Institution for the Insane, Perth, wrote an article on 'Madness in Animals' roundly criticizing veterinarians for their long and continued ignorance of animal psychology. Their view, he summed up, was that 'animals have not sound minds, and cannot, therefore possess unsound ones!'[76] This old notion had been soundly and comprehensively questioned by recent science. If animals experienced similar emotional states to humans, such as sorrow, joy, anger, gratitude, and fear, perhaps they also experience similar forms of insanity—other than the diseased rage of rabies? In 1839 the French physician Claude-Charles Pierquin (1798–1863) published a pioneering treatise on animal insanity in relation to humans that argued that they did. He thought that the only human form of insanity that was not mirrored in the animal kingdom was demonomania, which was a religious form of mania and animals were not susceptible to religion. Nevertheless, back in the bad old days of the witch trials, he complained, any animal exhibiting symptoms of mental alienation was considered possessed and so was unnecessarily destroyed.[77]

He also argued that the mass killing of animals suspected of having disease-induced insanity, without any attempt to cure them, had a general negative impact on human public morals as well. Despite his problematic assumptions about the witch trials, Pierquin was a pioneer in this field, and the likes of Charles Darwin, Lauder Lindsay, and early anthropologists took note of his ideas when exploring insanity in relation to animal and human emotions.[78]

A late series of popular scares regarding epidemic rabid madness occurred in Europe and America in 1874, and then again in Britain in 1877, leading to the proliferation of the term 'hydrophobia mania' in medical discourse and the press, which obviously echoed the already established term 'witchcraft mania'.[79] Lauder Lindsay blamed the 'evil influence of the Press' for whipping up a storm of credulity, cruelty, and superstition.[80] As to the reality, there were only 387 deaths attributed to hydrophobia in England and Wales during the panic years between 1866 and 1876.[81] In 1888, Philadelphia medic Charles W. Dulles looked at all the hydrophobia cases reported in the United States for the previous year. There were only fifteen. One case for every four million people. There was no proof any of the dogs were rabid, and in half the cases the 'victims' anticipated they would get hydrophobia before the symptoms actually kicked in.[82]

By the 1880s there were growing voices of scepticism that echoed the long-forgotten view of William Maryan. Symptoms such as fear of water and barking like a dog were increasingly being described as the 'vulgar errors' of popular credulity and out-of-date medical theory. Hydrophobia was a condition and not a disease at all. Those liable to spurious hydrophobia were 'naturally or morbidly timid, superstitious, illiterate persons in whom *delusional fear* is readily engendered'.[83] New comparisons with the witch trials began to appear. For Dulles all this was proof that hydrophobia was a self-induced condition. 'I do not despair of seeing the belief in hydrophobia follow the belief in witchcraft', Dulles observed, 'which once had the support of Church and the State, of the medical profession and the laity, but which now, thank God! Torments our fellow men no more.' The *American Lancet* headed its report on one of Dulles's talks, 'Hydrophobia, Like Witchcraft, an Ancient Superstition'.[84] Years later, in 1914, the American anti-vivisectionist Sarah N. Cleghorn wrote a piece for the *Journal of Zoöphily* entitled 'Witchcraft and Hydrophobia'. She also argued that the similarities between claims of hydrophobia in her day and the old witch trials were 'really startling'. History was repeating itself, she concluded. This time the victims were dogs, not humans.[85]

Fits

The expression having a 'fit of madness' was common enough in the eighteenth and nineteenth centuries. Fits were often thought the physical manifestation of some sort of mental or physical pathology but it is often unclear how people made sense of them. There was certainly a long-held, widespread recognition that there were different species of fits. The case-books of the seventeenth-century astrologer-physician Richard Napier contain numerous examples of clients or their families reporting fits that were emotional as well as physical in nature. They were described variously as quarrelling fits, mopish fits, sullen fits, talking fits, weeping fits, convulsive fits, and fits of uncontrollable laughter and rage. Some were simply described as 'strange fits' denoting, perhaps, an inexplicable and therefore supernatural cause.[86] The situation was not dissimilar 200 years later in popular discourse. One common diagnostic for defining fits was whether they were feverish or not. Those accompanied by a high temperature could be put down to disease such as ague (malaria) or external influence such as sunstroke. But fits without fever could have either emotional or supernatural origins. There was also a long-held belief that fits could *cause* temporary forms of insanity as well as being a symptom. This is most apparent in terms of contagious fits. William Falconer (1744–1824), physician at Bath General Hospital, recalled seeing what he described as 'hysterical' contagion spread before his eyes in a church in the spa town of Buxton sometime before 1791: 'in less than a minute, six persons were affected in a similar manner, some of whom had never been subject to such attacks, but were notwithstanding violently agitated and convulsed in body as well as mind'.[87]

In northern Scotland there was a fit known popularly as the 'leaping ague' or 'louping ague' that affected humans and sheep. The Rev. John Jamieson described it as a 'melancholy disorder' and noted that some put it down to a nervous condition while others said it was the effect of intestinal worms. It appeared to be hereditary and the fits were triggered by noises such as the clanging of tongs or the ringing of bells. The Rev. James Paton, describing conditions in Craig parish, Angus, in 1792, said there had been a few cases of epilepsy, lunacy, and louping ague, and described those seized with the latter as having 'all the appearance of madness'.[88] One of the last reported cases occurred between 1817 and 1818 and concerned a teenage girl who seems to have been afflicted after the shock of finding thieves in her house followed by the loss of a beloved sister.[89]

William Cullen had a correspondence with a Dr Farquison of Dundee regarding a case of 'louping ague' Farquison had witnessed in Forfar. Four or five families were infected, the victims ranging from girls as young as five to married women and also boys. He described seeing two girls succumb to the condition as follows:

> I was in the house, one of them was attacked with this disorder, and immediately fell upon her knees; with her head bent back betwixt her shoulders, her neck projecting outwards and vert turgid, her eyes not at all disordered nor fixed in this posture, she remained half a minute; after which she got up in great confusion, ran to a large table, leaped up to it at once, though three feet high; her tongue making a circle in her mouth and producing a confused, blubbering noise... When on the table, she tried to get off her shoes, after which she jumped three or four feet perpendicular for some minutes. By this time the other was seized in like manner, and went through the same operations. Both ran from the table to the head of the bed; from this to the couples and joist of the house. In short they performed most of the postures of Sadler's Wells.

The attacks lasted half an hour or more, during which time the girls were lucid and able to answer questions. Farquison was told that the pains began in the little finger of both hands and then spread to the head. Others described it beginning with a pain in the head and the lower back, which then led to convulsive fits that, as well as manifesting in leaping in the air, also included running almost unfeasibly fast until the patient was utterly exhausted.[90] Some also had the urge to hide things while in this state of excitation. 'Your Louping Ague is a singularity but not altogether unknown in physic', Cullen replied to Farquison, observing that similar symptoms had been recorded in France, Germany, and elsewhere. 'After all my conjecture', he concluded, 'I am disposed to think your Disease not a proper epidemic but to be spread by imitation only.'[91] Other eighteenth-century Scottish physicians likened it to chorea or St Vitus' Dance.[92]

Epileptics were often described as having 'fits of madness'. In both popular belief and medical understanding epilepsy or 'falling sickness' was not generally thought to be a category of madness in itself, but rather a related condition, a kindred affliction, and sometimes as a symptom of insanity.[93] It was generally understood as a distinct condition of fit, though outside of medical discourse it was rarely referred to as 'epilepsy'. As the Scottish physician Alexander Gordon noted in 1786 it had various vernacular names that distinguished it from fits in general. The parliamentary medical report on the Irish census of 1851, for instance, listed the popular English and Irish names for epilepsy encountered by the census enumerators and from other sources. It included 'falling sickness', 'the fits', 'the blessed sickness', 'the terrible disease', 'St Paul's disease', and 'earth sickness'.[94]

Medical definitions and opinions were broad. Critics of the Quakers and later Protestant evangelicals likened their ecstatic convulsions to a 'species of epilepsy' to consign the movements' followers to the realm of pathology.[95] William Cullen considered it a spasmodic condition without fever akin to St Vitus' Dance. John Haslam said that he had 'known madness alternate with epilepsy'. In his *Observations on the Religious Delusions of the Insane* (1841) Nathaniel Bingham explained, 'epilepsy combined with insanity is a form of madness most frightful and dangerous'. Then again, the British neurologist Marshall Hall (1790–1857) wrote in 1848 that he would like to expunge the term 'epilepsy' from all discourse as it was completely inadequate to define the range of convulsions attributed to it; and, besides, he complained, 'like the term insanity, it stamps the poor patient for ever, inflicting a stigma which is frequently most injurious'.[96] Indeed, when reading eighteenth- and nineteenth-century field reports of epilepsy or falling sickness, it often seems from the sources that it was the reporter that determined that the 'fits' observed were of an epileptic nature, rather than the diagnosis clearly deriving from popular nosology and idiom.

While there was a long and entrenched view that epilepsy was usually a hereditary condition or connected to hysteria in women, some physicians and the general population also continued to believe that external influences could cause or trigger epilepsy. The Dutch physician Herman Boerhaave (1668–1738) included shock at the sight of an epileptic fit as a cause, and this notion was still held into the nineteenth century. In a lecture given at King's College, London, in 1841, the physician Dr Thomas Watson observed that 'in this way the disease will now and then run through a boarding school; or through a ward in a hospital'. For this reason, John Haygarth had, a few decades earlier, refused to admit females suffering from 'hysterical' or epileptic fits into his Chester Infirmary because of the 'mischief' caused by such sympathetic contagion.[97]

The strongest popular link was between the moon and epilepsy. Mead and others of his period believed, for instance, that some epileptics had spots on their faces that resembled the dark patches on the moon. These would vary in colour and size according to lunar phases and so help predict the onset of seizures.[98] Although the Swiss physician Simon August Tissot

(1728–1787) rejected the influence of the moon on epileptic seizures in the first major treatise on epilepsy in 1770, the notion persisted for a long time.[99] The belief was too well engrained in popular medical cultures, and physicians and psychiatrists preferred to rely on Richard Mead rather than Tissot because he provided a wealth of anecdotal observation on the matter. Mead recounted his own experience, for instance, of some naval sailors in St Thomas's hospital who had contracted epilepsy 'by frights, either in sea-engagements, or in storms'. The moon's influence on their fits was so evident at the new and full moons that Mead 'often predicted the times of their fits with tolerable certainty'.[100] Over in America, in 1845, Samuel Woodward at Worcester Lunatic Hospital, Massachusetts, was still confident in stating that, 'epilepsy often occurs at nearly regular lunar periods'. His convictions were confirmed by many of the friends of his patients who 'say that this disease and the excitements of insanity occur most frequently at the new and full moon'.[101] The Italian psychiatrist and notorious criminologist Cesare Lombroso (1835–1909) was one of the last to persist with the theory. Amongst various medical roles in a long career, he was physician at the insane asylum in Pavia in the 1860s. Here he tested the usual correlations between lunar phases and epileptic attacks and concluded that epileptics had more attacks at the new and full moon and at the summer solstice, and that they were also more affected by barometric changes than people with insanities. Lombroso had a penchant for testing venerable popular notions about criminality and the mind to prove they held some truth. His racialist theories on craniology and crime, based on biological determinism, were inspired, in part, by outmoded theories of physiognomy and phrenology. His flawed patient surveys suggested to him, for example, that the old Italian belief that criminals could not blush was medically true.[102]

But opinion was beginning to turn decidedly during the 1850s. Jacques-Joseph Moreau (1804–1884), a student of Esquirol better known for his work on the mental effects of hashish in relation to insanity, comprehensively demolished the link between the moon and epilepsy in a prize-winning essay published in 1854. The belief was 'strongly accredited by the public', he observed, and his aim was to once and for all confirm whether it was nothing more than a venerable 'popular error'. He logged 42,637 epileptic attacks among 108 epileptic patients at the Bicêtre over five years. He found that the majority of seizures, 26,313 to be precise, occurred *between* the phases of the moon. From the same data he also discounted temperature and seasonal fluctuations as influences. The finding was reported in a few English-language medical journals.[103]

As asylum provision expanded during the mid nineteenth century many epileptics found themselves living for months or years behind their walls, and this, in itself, perpetuated the notion that they were also insane people. Of the first 1300 patients admitted to Somerset County Lunatic Asylum since it opened in 1848, some 145 (11 per cent) were epileptics. The asylum's physician, Robert Boyd, described most of them as suffering from one form of insanity or another, particularly mania, dementia, and idiocy.[104] Some of those described as epileptics were placed in asylums because of other symptoms of mental disorder, some because their seizures became unmanageable for their friends and families, and some because of fears that epilepsy would worsen to become incurable insanity. But during the later nineteenth century advances in medical knowledge led to growing doubts that it was appropriate for epileptics to be kept in asylums. In 1882, for instance, Northampton General Lunatic Asylum decided it would no longer accept epileptics.[105]

Supernatural agency

In 1830, the English physician and apothecary William Newnham (1790–1865) noted in his *Essay on Superstition*, 'I have been frequently told that such and such an epileptic individual was "*overseen*" '. 'Nor can we blame these results of superstition among the vulgar', he continued, 'while their superiors in intellect and acquirement continue to refer *similar* effects to mental agency.'[106] Newnham was convinced that all mental conditions were a product of physical effects in different parts of the body which then influenced the brain's nervous response. Thus, anxiety was ultimately a symptom of heart conditions, for example, and the liver caused melancholy and hypochondria. His medical opinion was wrong but his cultural observation was correct. 'Overseen' was a vernacular term for bewitchment, and in popular belief epilepsy, and those fits considered peculiar or strange, were widely considered an affliction caused by unseen malign forces. The girls described earlier by Dr Farquison in his letter to William Cullen as suffering from the louping ague intriguingly described their affliction as 'It', something which forced them to do their performance: they had to 'obey it'. It reminds me of the Irish family a century later who referred to the 'Thing' that possessed their son.

The language around such afflictions was more usually couched in terms of demoniacs, divine intervention, or bewitchment. One Norfolk folklorist recorded that local people believed epilepsy was considered a visitation from God and as a consequence they were very reluctant to touch a person during a fit so as not to interfere with the divine presence.[107] Such notions stemmed in part from the King James Bible, where in Matthew 17:15 it is told, 'there came to him a certain man, kneeling down to him, and saying, Lord, have mercy on my son: for he is lunatick, and sore vexed: for ofttimes he falleth into the fire, and oft into the water'. At a time when the Bible was taken literally in popular culture this passage reinforced the relationship between falling sickness and madness. There was also an ongoing theological debate about the nature of the 'demoniacs' referred to in the New Testament. Some scholars of the Bible were convinced that they had been truly possessed by the Devil, while others proposed they were merely sufferers of madness, epilepsy, and diseased imagination.[108] In the 1850s a couple of asylum chaplains continued to gnaw away at this old debate in the *Journal of Psychological Medicine*.[109] Contemporary cases of epilepsy also attracted such debate at the time. George Lukins the 'Yatton Demoniac' is the classic example. In the 1770s and 1780s this Somerset man suffered from 'fits' of an extraordinary kind, turning him into a minor celebrity. His case was widely reported but there was very little debate about Lukins being insane, though one commentator explained that he was driven 'mad' by his fits. Some doctors diagnosed him as an epileptic, others denounced him as an impostor, and there were those who believed he was possessed by devils. Locals suspected he was a victim of witchcraft.[110] In the Plymouth Dock possession case of 1820, the Methodist minister John Heaton accepted that 'there were occasionally some very strong symptoms' of epilepsy in John Evens' behaviour, but that 'nevertheless, there were others which fully distinguish his case from being merely epileptic'. To diagnose him as an epileptic, he said, 'is to give but a mere scrap of the truth of the case'.[111] As to Evens, he declared he was 'overlooked' and described the witch responsible. Heaton commented in response, 'asserting that he was bewitched, is not a sufficient proof of the fact: and it would be cruel to criminate a poor old woman without substantial evidence of guilt'.[112]

'A woman put this trouble into her', explained one patient in the Crichton Royal Hospital who suffered from epileptic fits.[113] This was in 1889, and by this time diabolic possession cases were few and far between in nineteenth-century Britain compared to the many such accusations of witchcraft. A detailed account of how such fits were understood in this respect was reported by the Reverend Isaac Nicholson in 1808 in a sermon admonishing his parishioners after some of them had badly beaten and scratched a woman named Ann Izzard, of Great Paxton, Cambridgeshire, for alleged witchcraft. In February 1808, a young woman named Alice Brown attempted to walk over the frozen River Ouse, when the ice broke and she fell into the freezing water. Her friend Fanny Amey helped her home, whereupon Alice was almost immediately 'seized with a strong epileptic fit'. Fanny, who had apparently suffered from epilepsy several months prior to this, then fell into similar sympathetic convulsions. Alice's fits continued periodically over the next couple of months. When Nicholson went to inquire of her condition on 5 April, he was shocked to hear her brother say, 'she is under an "ill tongue"'. This was affirmed by another man present, who said that this was 'as sure as you are alive sir'.[114] Were Alice and Fanny really suffering from epilepsy as we understand it today? We do not know. It is not really the point. What the example illustrates is how such 'fits' were diagnosed from multiple religious and cultural perspectives to which the psychiatrists added another layer of interpretation.

Kill or cure

Popular cures for the various forms of madness, epilepsy, and fits can be broadly categorized as either medical, religious, or magical, though the boundaries between them were porous in practice and people sometimes resorted to all three in their search for cure and relief from their conditions.

Medical cures were often based on remedies drawn from early modern herbals and books of physic, which, in turn, usually borrowed heavily from the works of the great physicians of ancient Greece and Rome. John Wesley's popular *Primitive Physic*, which went through many updated editions in America and Britain, drew from a range of contemporary works on medicine, which he presented as a self-help guide to healing body and mind. He included several cures for lunacy. These included drinking a decoction of the herb agrimony four times a day or a daily dose of an ounce of distilled vinegar. Or one could shave the lunatic's head and anoint it with the juice of boiled ground ivy mixed with sweet oil and white wine. This had to be done every other day for three weeks. A bit more challenging was binding the bruised leaves of ground ivy to the shaved head.[115] The many editions of Nicolas Culpeper's famous *Complete Herbal*, first published in the 1650s, continued to provide herbal remedies for madness based on ancient humoural theory. An edition printed in 1816 noted that the plant senna was good for melancholy, madness and falling sickness, and that eating whey 'wonderfully helps melancholy and madness coming of it'. Syrup of Apples, which also included borage and bugloss, 'purged choler and melancholy' and helped 'resist madness', while plantain juice mixed with rose oil applied to the temples and forehead was said to help 'lunatic and frantic persons very much'.[116] There were numerous other diverse herbal cures practised in local communities. In parts of North Wales *Peltigera canina* or dog lichen was dried, ground to a powder and mixed with black pepper. In the first half of the nineteenth century a popular female healer of canine madness in cattle who lived in Bridgend, Glamorgan, grew elecampane in her garden, which she mixed with milk, chicken feathers, and other secret herbs. Elecampane was recommended by Culpeper as good against poisons.[117]

Mustard plasters and poultices were used equally widely in veterinary medicine, folk cures, and in asylum medicine for a range of fits and madness. At an inquest in 1854 on the body of Harriett Smith, of North Curry, Somerset, it was heard how a local cunning-man, Edward Tucker, had treated her fits by prescribing a tea of sage, wormwood, and chalk, and a little ointment composed of lard, sage, wormwood, and jack-in-the-hedge (wild mustard) which she had to rub on the back of her ear. Her local general practitioner also separately prescribed a mustard plaster to be applied to the back of the neck.[118] In 1865 the *British Medical Journal* included a report on 'Application of Mustard in Insanity'. It was concerned with the experiments of one Dr Newington, who found the application of mustard as an irritant to the surface of the body was particularly effective in cases of mania. He thought that it drove blood from the brain thereby inducing sleep.[119]

Many people were no doubt tempted to try the numerous quack medicines vaunted in newspaper advertising columns. In 1819, for instance, one Job Orme, of High croft, Stoke-on-Trent, advertised in the press that he possessed a recipe that was an infallible cure for every branch of 'lunacy', and that he had thereby restored the reason of several people in his neighbourhood.[120] The well-known Morison's Pills flogged by the controversial quack James Morison and his British College of Health, were advertised as a universal cure-all that also encompassed illnesses of the mind. One advert from 1838 contained a statement by an Exeter surgeon named Richard Tothill that by prescribing Morison's Vegetable Universal Medicines he had cured of insanity a man named Samuel Crab who had spent time in a local asylum. In 1848 'Miss Pike's Powders' were widely advertised as 'a cure for

Epileptic, Hysteric, and every other description of Fits and Nervous Diseases'. Around the same time a 'Dr Anderson' was boasting of his 'Great Discovery' which permanently cured groundless fears, delusions, thoughts of suicide, epilepsy, and insanity generally. The periodic rabies scares also generated a lively market in such commercial quackery. One of the most lucrative nostrums in the late eighteenth century was William Hill's 'Ormskirk medicine'.[121] It was said in 1798 that it was still held infallible by people in northern and western England in particular, but it was also sold elsewhere through agents. It underwent a series of chemical tests by medical doctors and was found to contain powdered chalk, allum, Armenian bole, elecampane root, and anise oil. Around the same time another Lancashire nostrum for the bite of mad dogs, 'Colne medicine', was peddled by Elizabeth Shackleton (1726–1781), who was a member of the minor gentry and professed to distribute her medicine for a shilling a bottle as a philan-thropic act.[122] In the 1850s one sceptical surgeon observed that to list all the medicines applied to hydrophobia over the years 'would be tediously long' and that some of them were as useless and disgusting as the potions prepared by the witches in *Macbeth*.[123]

Through the eighteenth century, the medical fraternity devised various cold water showtsers or douches to cool the over-heated brains of maniacs and hydrophobes or to shock melancholics out of their lassitude—as well as to punish the disobedient patient or inmate.[124] John Wesley recommended more humble variants to cure raging madness: 'Set the patient with his head under a great water-fall, as long as his strength will bear: Or, pour water on his head out of a tea kettle.'[125] Sea bathing was also recommended by eighteenth-century doctors in an age when hydrotherapy and the seaside spa came into vogue in Britain and elsewhere. In 1775, for instance, a 25-year-old farmer who lived near Leicester was taken to be bathed in the sea at the next full moon after having been bitten by a rabid dog but before the hydrophobia had set in. He also drank some of the sea water as a purge. It did not help, and he was later taken to Leicester Infirmary.[126] At one point in the long saga of George Lukins' possession the parish authorities required him to be 'dipped in the sea' off Flat Holm island in the Bristol channel to cure his fits before they would pay him any more medical poor relief. The Cornish antiquarian, mineralogist, and folklorist Robert Hunt (1807–1887), writing in the 1860s, provided evidence that the plunging of the insane in the sea had continued to be practised until recently in the county. He said he was consulted by a woman of 'weak mind' who suffered from 'religious monomania' about whether electric treatment would help her. She felt she had 'lost her God' and wondered whether a sudden shock would effect a cure. To that end she planned that her husband and friends would take her to a rock on St Michael's Mount when the waters were flowing strongest and push her into the sea. Hunt never found out if she carried out this act but he had heard of several other instances where this cure for insanity had been carried out.[127]

Pinel considered the merits of the 'bath of surprise'—in other words the unexpected dousing of patients in cold water—and concluded that it was extremely dangerous and should only be tried as a very last resort, such as in cases of inveterate insanity or insanity complicated with epilepsy. As to bathing in general he concluded its value was yet to be ascertained.[128] But in the mid nineteenth century cold bathing gained new psychiatric currency under careful and often elaborate asylum conditions, and it was sometimes applied as an alternative to mechanical restraints. In 1842 James Freeman, physician to the Cheltenham Hydropathic Institution, observed that in Germany it had been used successfully to tranquillize violent mania. Forty years later the superintendent of the Central Kentucky Lunatic Asylum gave a round-up of current bathing and cold-water immersion practices in asylums across western Europe. Hot and cold plunge baths and Turkish bath treatments were clearly in fairly widespread use. At the German Siegburg Asylum, for instance, maniacs were treated with warm baths and melancholics with cold baths. But some patients clearly considered the cold treatment as a punishment rather than a cure. At one Staffordshire asylum two women complained of having been cold-bathed against their will.[129]

Up until around 1870 a family in South Wales known for their hydrophobia treatment instructed patients to bathe in the sea then walk home and take a dose of their famed herbal beer when the moon was either full or new.[130] Around the same time we find the last instances in Scotland. In 1868 John Sibbald, medical superintendent of Argyll and Bute Asylum, wrote in his annual report that a patient currently in the asylum had been taken out to sea by her relatives where she was thrown overboard and kept underwater until half-drowned to cure her madness.[131] Three years later a correspondent for the *Inverness Courier* wrote a widely-reprinted, eye-witness account of the ritual bathing that had recently taken place at Loch Naver in the north east of Scotland. Between midnight and one o'clock some fifty or so people brought their friends and family suffering from a range of conditions including 'lunacy' to the loch shoreline where they were stripped and immersed in the water three times. One woman 'raved in a distressing manner, repeating religious phrases, some of which were very earnest and pathetic. She prayed her guardians not to immerse her, saying that it was not a communion occasion.' Coins were then thrown into the loch as 'payment' to seal the ritual cure. The newspaper correspondent considered it an absurd 'superstition', commenting, 'I would have more faith in a shower-bath applied pretty freely and often to the head.'[132] The double standard inherent in such criticisms of popular cures at this time will not be lost on the reader, and it is noteworthy that the old folk custom of medical sea bathing for insanity died out while it was still a well-established asylum therapy.

One of the most puzzling traditions regarding the cure of hydrophobia sufferers was the notion that victims had to be killed by smothering. It was considered a particular problem in parts of France. The French physician François Boissier de Sauvages wrote a prize-winning dissertation on hydrophobia in which denounced the peasant practice of smothering incurable hydrophobes between two mattresses. He expressed the wish that harsh punishment would be meted out to those who practised such inhumanity.[133] In 1812 Doctor Fauchier of Lorgues, southern France, published an article on 'the cruel custom of smothering hydrophobes', which was praised as a laudable attempt to destroy the vestiges of barbaric 'superstition' that still survived in some areas. Twenty years later, P.-F. Saint-Georges Ransol, a doctor practising in western France complained that 'this barbarous custom of smothering the sick has not yet disappeared from the minds of the people of the Vendée. It is only too real.' For some Vendéens, he was sad to say, the hydrophobic was 'a monster in their eyes that must be promptly destroyed'. He had heard a report of a young man at Curzon who died of hydrophobia. People had said that his life must be cut short either by opium, bleeding, or smothering between feather beds. As late as 1838 the newspapers reported the supposed smothering of a hydrophobic women in the department of Aisne by two *gendarmes*.[134]

Concerns were also recorded across the Channel. In the 1870s, Thomas Michael Dolan, physician to the Halifax Fever Hospital, collated a series of Irish, Scottish, and English smothering reports he found in the periodical press from the 1720s to the 1860s.[135] Other cases can be found as well. Around 1795, for instance, Samuel Webb, a 33-year-old butler, was bitten by a mad dog. He went to a doctor who cleaned out the wound and cauterized it, and then he travelled to Ormskirk to obtain a dose of the famous cure directly from William Hill himself. But despite taking the famed elixir he got worse and with the progression of the typical symptoms he found himself in Lancashire Lunatic Asylum under the care of physician David Campbell. As Campbell later recalled, Webb got 'it into his head that persons in his situation were often put to death', and he then took a 'maniacal turn'. Webb feared that the doctor and his assistants planned to smother him and, as a consequence, they had to use force to give him further treatment. He died shortly after.[136] In 1871 a Unitarian minister named D. Berry, aged thirty-two, from Mossley, Greater Manchester, was bitten by his cat, which had been behaving peculiarly. Berry began to exhibit signs of sickness and anxiety and developed an aversion to drinking water. His sleep was deeply troubled and muscular spasms set in. He was treated by a local doctor with standard medicines. Berry did not seem at first to have any thoughts of having hydrophobia, and then it suddenly dawned on him. He told his doctor, 'this is the end of the cat; I know that I shall have to be smothered'.[137]

It is difficult to separate rumour, anecdote, and hearsay from fact when it comes to smothering, and a detailed study of criminal records would be required to ascertain the extent to which it really happened rather than relying on reportage, as any smothering would have ended end at the assizes as manslaughter or murder. One clear case, which, importantly, did not end in death, was reported at first-hand by the surgeon James Vaughan (1740–1813) at the Leicester Infirmary in the 1770s. The patient, 14-year-old Thomas Nourse, had been bitten by a mad foxhound. He had been bathed in the sea and had taken Ormskirk medicine. In the Infirmary Vaughan treated him with musk, opium, and mercury ointment. But there was no great improvement. Then one day Vaughan found half a dozen strong assistants confining Nourse tightly under his bedding. They 'had almost persuaded themselves, that the opinion universally received by the common people, of smothering such unfortunate objects, was not only justifiable but expedient'.[138] A rare, confirmed example of the practice being carried out was heard at the Longford Assizes, Ireland, in 1841. Michael and Henry Cordial were charged with murdering their brother William Cordial with the help of three other male relatives. In June the previous year William had been bitten by a rabid dog and had been taken to a reputed healer of hydrophobes in the region. The cure seemed to work, but in December William began to suffer all the tell-tale symptoms and within three days he 'became raging mad'. Local physician Dr Park Dobson was called in. He found William in a terrible state and frothing at the mouth. He bled him but this only brought on a violent paroxysm. William's brothers decided to put him out of his misery and smothered him to death between two mattresses. The jury returned a verdict of manslaughter and the five men were sentenced to one week in prison.[139]

It is clear that there was an engrained popular belief, sustained by press reports, that the authorities turned a blind eye to such killings and even tacitly sanctioned them. This popular conviction of official connivance was noted in Britain in 1828, while in America in 1860 a temperance advocate recalled that during his childhood he read about how hydrophobics in England were smothered between feather beds and the 'law justified the deed'.[140] Smotherings can be interpreted as mercy killings to end the suffering of the victims, but then why only for hydrophobia and not for other infectious diseases? Whether real or rumour such acts were also thought to serve as a means of preventing the spread of contagious madness. Smothering between mattresses reduced possible intimate and bloody contact with the infected compared to other methods of killing. There was also a sense that smothering was a ritualized form of *community* preservation from madness.

Now we come to cure by faith. Catholic priests had their trusted cure in the form of exorcism. A rare exorcism conducted by a Catholic priest in England in 1815 involved a young married woman who was described as having 'an extraordinary kind of mental complaint' that including raving and delirium. A local doctor concluded it was a terminal mental affliction but the woman and Peach were convinced she was possessed and so he exorcized her.[141] Most of the exorcisms conducted by the maverick Joseph-Xavier Tissot during the mid nineteenth century concerned sufferers of what doctors had diagnosed as epilepsy.[142] Protestant clergy were not allowed to conduct exorcisms but they had been known to resort to repeated and concerted prayer in rare cases of suspected possession concerning falling sickness. In his popular guide *Modern Domestic Medicine*, first published in 1826 with at least eleven further editions over the next few years, physician Thomas John Graham considered the healing power of prayer on epilepsy in particular. While he noted that ordinary prayer or the reading of prayers was unlikely to effect any cures, the exceptional, ardent clergyman could have remarkable success. The several examples he gave were, however, all from the seventeenth century and involved well-known Calvinists and a Welsh Nonconformist. Few Protestant clergy or ministers attempted such charismatic healing by the second half of the nineteenth century, but it did happen. In 1853, for instance, a 37-year-old Methodist began to have fits, and swore uncontrollably after hearing a fire and brimstone preacher.

He was convinced he was possessed, but his family had him removed to an asylum. During a day release from the institution he was prayed over intensely by several Methodist preachers and ministers. They failed to expel the Devil but felt they had weakened his power and relieved the man's suffering.[143]

In Catholic countries the saints had long played a major role in the healing of madness. In Brittany, up until the French Revolution, the cult of Saint-Jacut and his healing waters had long been associated with the curing of demoniacs and the insane. The strongest continuing traditions concerned the healing of epilepsy and canine madness. In France, for instance, epilepsy was popularly known as the *mal St Jean* after the legends of St John, which tell how he 'lost his head' after having it chopped off by King Herod, and how Herod was punished for this act by being afflicted with epilepsy. In the Low Countries, from medieval times to the present, St Cornelius was also particularly associated with epilepsy and gave his name to it. People came from other countries to shrines dedicated to him. A chapel dedicated to the saint in Soignes Forest, near Brussels, still bears the sign, 'St Cornelius, pope and martyr, patron against cramp, paralysis and epilepsy'.[144]

Saint Hubert was the saint most associated with canine madness. In 1812 medical student J. Camille Gorcy submitted an essay on hydrophobia based on his knowledge of patients in the department of la Meuse, in northern France. One of them was a woman aged thirty bitten by her own pet dog. She was diagnosed with delirium and melancholy. She barked like a dog and went into furious rages as the condition progressed. She would also repeatedly call upon St Hubert to save her.[145] Hubert, who was also considered the patron of hunters, had been associated with the cure of '*le rage*' since medieval times. He was the first bishop of Liège in the early eighth century but the legends surrounding him, like so many medieval saints, range far beyond verifiable history. The spirit of Saint Peter apparently visited him on his consecration and bestowed upon him a great power against evil spirits. His reputation for healing rabies was based on another a story that he cured a man who had been bitten by a mad dog. One of the enduring healing traditions associated with the saint is known as Saint Hubert's key. In practice this was often a piece of blessed iron or nail that was heated red hot and applied to the bite to cauterize the wound. During the nineteenth century the making of healing bread also continued. In 1833 a Belgian periodical noted that the 'bread of St Hubert', blessed by the church, was eaten by both humans and given to animals as a cure for rabies and hydrophobia. Later in the century it was reported that across Flanders on St Hubert's Day it was still customary for bakers to bring fresh batches of bread to the churches at half-past-four in the morning. After Mass the priests would bless the loaves, imbuing them with the power to prevent and cure hydrophobia, and the bakers would then deliver them to their customers.[146]

Across Belgium and northern France, those bearing the surname St Hubert, or who were believed to be descended from the saint, also accrued popular powers. One such family was the Lavernots, who lived in the Picard village of Nibas, during the nineteenth century. They were said to be descendants of the saint and several members of the family cured rabid animals and people bitten by them with their touch while mumbling a prayer. At one time the family also gave out small copper medals bearing the image of the saint for protection from hydrophobia. A local shepherd said in 1901 that he would rather go to the Lavernots than be cured at the Pasteur Institute where Louis Pasteur and Émile Roux had developed a vaccine for rabies in 1885.[147]

The holy healing tradition also continued into the modern era in Protestant countries, though with a less overt resort to pilgrimage and saint worship. In 1811 it was recorded that the parish church of St Edren's or Edeyrn's near Haverfordwest, Wales, had long drawn those suffering from hydrophobic madness:

> The Grass in the Church-yard is in great esteem, on account of its efficacy, and wonderful effect, in curing People, Cattle, Horses, Sheep, and Pigs, which had been bitten by *mad Dogs*. The people cut the grass with a knife, and eat it with bread and butter; the Cattle are turned in to graze; and no symptoms of madness have ever afterwards appeared, provided they would eat some quantity of the grass: but there have been instances when Horses and Sheep would not graze in the yard, and which died a short time afterwards. This account is attested by persons of veracity, resident in the neighbourhood. In the Chancel wall is a cavity, with a stone trough into which Persons put what they are pleased to pay for the grass: this is the perquisite of the Parish Clerk.[148]

The cure was still being taken several decades later. In the summer of 1848, a dog thought to be rabid attacked and bit several animals in the neighbourhood of Marloes, including an ass that grazed on a bit of roadside pasture. A child and his mother had to pass by the ass to get home and the ass attacked the boy. The mother fought off the raging ass and was badly bitten in the process. As a result, the following morning her neighbours took her the twelve or so miles to the churchyard of St Edren's to eat the grass.[149] Also in Wales we find St Tegla or St Thecla, who gave her name to epilepsy, as in St Tegla's 'evil' or 'disorder'. The healing well dedicated to her at Llandegla, Denbighshire, was widely resorted to for cure. During the early eighteenth century, sufferers apparently washed in the well water, walked around it three times while saying the Lord's prayer, and left an offering of a few pence and a live chicken in the church. In 1815 the Rev. Peter Roberts recorded the history of the well's epilepsy cure and noted that he had recently been informed that it was 'not yet wholly abolished'.[150]

Some holy wells were also used as water sources for cold water immersion, thereby merging religious and medical therapies. In 1602 the Cornish antiquarian Richard Carew (1555–1620) described the set-up at St Nun's Well in Cornwall, one of numerous 'bowssening' or dipping sites in the county for curing 'mad men'. The spring was controlled so that it filled up an artificial square pool. The 'franticke' patients stood on the edge of the wall with their backs to the pool and then they were pushed into the water and dunked several times until their fury dissipated. The patients were then taken to St Nun's Church and certain prayers or masses were said over them.[151] In 1865 Robert Hunt cited Carew's account of St Nun's Well and described it as the only holy well he was aware of in the region that had remained specifically associated with the cure of insanity. At the time of his writing, though, the well was largely abandoned and overgrown. A newspaper reported a few years later said it was known locally as the pixie's well, its old associations now forgotten in the locality.[152]

In Scotland there were two holy sites that had long been resorted to as a cure for madness and other ailments. One was St Fillan's Well in central-western Scotland where a holy pool had been venerated for centuries. The ritual was described in 1845. After sunset but before sunrise, patients took three stones from the bottom of the pool, thus ensuring their bodies were partly immersed, and then they walked three times around each of three cairns on the bank, and a stone was placed on each one. Next the patients were taken to the ruins of the nearby chapel and tied up and lain on their backs, where they were left until morning. Other variations on the same were recorded over the next few decades.[153] Around 1860, the Rev Stewart of Killin informed the Edinburgh Professor of Midwifery James Young Simpson (1811–1870) that one of the last such rituals at St Fillan's Well had taken place only a few years before, with the female patient being found in the morning sane and unbound. She said the spirit of a dead relative had visited her in the chapel and freed her ropes and mind. Simpson reflected on the matter: 'It was a system of treatment by mystery and terrorism that might have made some persons insane; and hence, perhaps, conversely, some insane person sane.'[154] When, in the early 1770s, Thomas Pennant visited the holy pool at Isle Maree, further up the western coast, he noted that the spring was 'of power unspeakable in cases of lunacy'. The guardians of the lunatic would leave some money, the lunatic would sip the spring water, and would then be dipped three times in the lake. This was to be repeated every day for several weeks. The last resort to Isle Maree for insanity appears to have been in the 1850s, around the same time as at St Fillan's. When Arthur Mitchell visited in 1863 he found the spring dried up and full of leaves.[155]

We come finally to magical cures in their various manifestations. They sometimes took the form of direct counter-magic spells with regard to witchcraft. Drawing blood from the witch suspected of causing fits, for instance, continued to be practised into the twentieth century. We saw one example of this earlier in the assault on Ann Izzard. Another example occurred in 1870. A 23-year-old agriculture labourer named Adam Lamb, of Corton Denham, Somerset, was prosecuted for assaulting a 39-year-old spinster named Mary Crees, who he accused of bewitching him. He suffered from periodic fits during which it took as many as six men to hold him down. In court he described how the fits had begun two years before. He 'was like a dead man for three hours. Sometimes I be obliged to be tied down. I could see her when she began it as plain as I can see this hat.' To break the spell he attempted to draw her blood—a widespread and violent means of counter witchcraft.[156] We do not know if he suffered from epilepsy or some other malady. Such courses of action were quite often advised by cunning-folk who also provided talismans, charms, and amulets to cure and protect people whose afflictions were natural and supernatural. I have come across very little evidence, though, that they offered to cure madness per se. The familiar symptoms would usually be couched in terms of supernatural influence, and therefore a supernatural cure combined with tonics and herbal remedies were prescribed.

At least up until the mid nineteenth century people in northern parts of Britain resorted to well-known healing objects. In Scotland an amulet made from a piece of ivory called Barbreck's bone was thought to be a powerful antidote against all forms of madness in Argyllshire. The afflicted person drunk the water in which it had been dipped. But by the 1830s it was sitting in the museum of the Society of Antiquities of Scotland.[157] In the Scottish Borders there was the Black Penny owned by a Mr Turnbull of Hadden, near Sprouston. Farmers would travel many miles to borrow it or carry away barrels of water in which it had been immersed. The Lockerby Penny was similarly much prized for curing madness in cattle. It was placed in a cleft stick and then used to swirl the water in a well at Lockerbie, which was then bottled and given to the mad livestock. When a rabies panic struck the area of Kirkwhelpington and Birtley, Northumberland, in Spring 1844, a voluntary subscription was got up to pay for a shipment of Lockerby water along with a worming programme for the dogs in the neighbourhood.[158] In Wales there was the renowned Llaethfaen Stone or Milkstone, which was still in demand into the second half of the nineteenth century. Bits were scraped off it and either ingested as a powder mixed with milk or rubbed into the animal bite. Its reputation was enhanced by the perception that despite hundreds of people taking scrapings it never seemed to dimmish in size.[159]

There was such a thing as a 'madstone' in America, which derived from the much older notion of snakestones that counteracted venom or poison. These were often bezoars, in other words the spherical, concreted hairballs found in the stomachs of ruminants across the world.[160] The terminological shift from snakestones to madstones in America was, in part, due to the nineteenth-century rabies scares we have already seen, and the notion that hydrophobia was caused by the venom transmitted by the bite of a mad dog. In the 1890s the *St Louis Republic* could list sixteen famous madstones in use across the country for the cure of hydrophobia and other ailments. The one owned by Turner Evans of Linn County in the Upper Mississippi River Valley had boiled so often in milk to give to hydrophobes that it was reported that it had become nearly unusable from wear and tear.[161]

Sympathetic magic, simply put, was the notion that like cures like. It was the basis of three old forms of medical treatment for hydrophobia that continued well into the nineteenth century. The first gave rise to the phrase 'hair of the dog'. The extent to which it was practised in the nineteenth century is difficult to assess but it was clearly widely known. The German physician Moritz Romberg (1795–1873), one of the early founders of neurology, recalled a case of hydrophobia that he had dealt with in 1820. A young boy was bitten while visiting a relative. A few of the dog's hairs were taken and placed on the wound, and at first it seemed to be effective but twenty-eight days later the familiar troubling symptoms began to occur.[162] In England, the Anglican nun and nurse Dorothy Wyndlow Pattison (1832–1878), better known as Sister Dora, dealt with numerous cases of dog bites amongst those brought to the hospitals in Walsall, Staffordshire, where she worked, but noted only one instance where she tended an out-patient who had dog hairs plastered on his or her wound.[163] Across the Atlantic, Virginia doctor William Townes Walker (1825–1898) recalled a female patient who came to him after her dog had gone mad and bitten her. She had followed the advice of friends and neighbours and placed hairs from the dog on her wound. Walker was of the opinion that hydrophobia was largely in the mind, a form of Lyssophobia—the irrational fear of going insane. As a consequence, he reassured the woman that hair of the dog was, indeed, an efficacious cure and she had done right. He encouraged her to continue the treatment along with the topical application of a salve and lotion he provided. She later reported with great delight that the dog had not gone mad and consequently neither had she.[164]

When Townes Walker talked to his rabid patient he advised her firmly that the hair of the dog would only work if the dog was still alive, and that there was no virtue in the hair of a dead dog. This was a compassionate strategy to ensure our second piece of sympathetic magic was not enacted, for the killing of rabid dogs as a cure was far more widespread than the hair of the dog. Once the canine had sunk its teeth into human flesh an invisible link, or what one newspaper described as 'some mystic tie', was forged between mad dog and victim, rather like that between a witch and those she or he had bewitched.[165] The sympathy was so binding that if the offending dog was not rabid at the time but went mad later, those bitten in the past would likewise develop hydrophobic symptoms. But if the dog was destroyed, its death would break the link and the madness would not spread. Lauder Lindsay described it as a 'mischievous superstition' not only because it was a false idea but because it destroyed the chance of clinically testing whether the offending animal was really rabid or not. It was described elsewhere as 'among the stupid popular ideas prevailing at the present time'.[166]

The belief was brought up repeatedly in British magistrates' courts during the late nineteenth century as people took advantage of the Dogs Act of 1871, which made local authorities responsible for destroying dangerous and rabid dogs or making sure they were under proper control. In one case heard before the Worship Street Police Court, London, in 1884, the magistrate, Mr Bushby, considered a man's request for a summons against the owner of a dog that had recently bitten him. The applicant told the court that he feared he would be afflicted with hydrophobia if the dog was not destroyed, and that his doctor had advised that the dog should be killed. Bushby was shocked by this and replied, 'What! Why, the doctor who so advised you must be a goose.'[167] When, in 1898, another London magistrate, Mr D'Eyncourt, heard a similar request from a woman whose child had been bitten, he asked 'Do you think that if the dog is killed it will prevent your child from having hydrophobia?' When she replied 'Yes', D'Eyncourt told her off. 'That is a common superstition', he warned. When a Lancashire magistrate refused to issue an order to destroy a suspected rabid dog but advised the owner to destroy it anyway, he made it clear to the court that 'it must not be understood that he believed the stupid rubbish that the death of the dog assisted the healing of the wound and prevented the person bitten from going mad'.[168]

The ingestion of body parts has a long history in European medicine, and so it is no surprise that we find elements of such cures in relation to madness and epilepsy.[169] One example was the eating of a rabid dog's liver, raw or broiled, for the cure of hydrophobia. Robert James noted in his *Treatise on Canine Madness* (1760) that, 'many people have even eat[en] the liver of a mad dog by way of medicine'. Daniel Layard thought this the most dangerous and absurd of popular cures. 'Every author, now a days', he stated, 'judiciously pronounces, that such a distempered liver is neither good for food or physic.'[170] But the cure continued to be practised decades later. Anyone reading the entry for 'canine madness' in the 1807 edition of *The Complete Farmer: Or, a General Dictionary of Husbandry* would have read that 'even the liver of the mad dog himself has often been taken as a remedy, without communicating the disease'. It was such old literary sources, perhaps, that inspired the family of Elizabeth Walters to try it in 1866. Elizabeth, aged five, lived in the village of Bradwell, Buckinghamshire. She had been bitten by a supposedly rabid dog and the dog had been quickly killed and buried. To prevent her from getting hydrophobia the parents asked a neighbour, Sarah Mackness, to dig up the dog and obtain some of its liver. She brought it to the Walters' house where the mother cut off a piece weighing about an ounce and a half, put it on a fork, and frizzled it before the fire until it had shrivelled up. This she gave to Elizabeth with a piece of bread and some tea. Elizabeth died nevertheless, and at the inquest it was heard that one of her uncles had escaped getting hydrophobia after similarly eating a bit of the liver of a mad dog that bit him. On that occasion the offending dog had been drowned, and the body fetched out of the water nine days later to obtain the liver and effect the cure.[171]

While the examples of smothering and liver eating are obviously shocking they were exceptional and rare events, and the over-riding impression is that some venerable popular cures informed and mirrored early psychiatric treatments. Herbalism, immersion, patent medicines, and religious remedies were the norm in popular medicine, and one suspects that, until the experimental application of electricity by asylum staff, the friends and families of most asylum patients would not have been shocked by the therapies they experienced. Even the physical restraint of seriously ill people was practised both inside and outside the asylum.

★ ★ ★

In Western Ireland there was a popular tradition that *Gleann-na-nGealt* near Tralee, Kerry, was a great healing place for the insane. In English it was known as the 'Valley of the Mad' and people would come to its springs to drink the waters and eat the watercress growing around the margins. When Daniel Hack Tuke asked Oscar Woods about it in the 1870s or early 1880s, Woods told him that the 'superstition' about the glen, and resort to it, had nearly died out since the Kilkenny asylum had opened in 1852. Over and again through this chapter we have seen how such venerable popular remedies and explanations for madness fizzled out during the mid nineteenth century. It is likely the rise of the asylum was responsible in part for this general decline. The asylum became an essential aspect *of* popular medicine, one amongst several alternatives for the care and cure of the mentally ill. Research on rural Irish asylums confirms, for instance, that the asylum became integrated into the strategies of the poor for dealing with unsocial behaviour and were looked upon as necessary and benevolent compared to the stigmatized workhouse.[172] The perspicacious author of an article on the 'Curability of Insanity' published in the *British Medical Journal* identified this trend in 1871: 'The general practitioner has tried his hand; the local panacea has had its turn; spiritual advice, or exorcism, or quackery, has done its worse; the healing power of time has been invoked: all these have failed, and then the asylum is resorted to as a desperate expedient, a forlorn hope.'[173] But the growth of asylums increasingly rendered folk medical options redundant as the state provided a low cost, hands-on alternative at a time when it was also intervening directly in the improvement of health and sanitation from village to city. I suspect that by the turn of the century the resort to the asylum had become less the last option and increasingly the first choice in popular culture when it came to mental illness, no matter whether it was thought natural or supernatural in origin. But the age of the asylum as popular medicine would prove relatively short lived and the advent of psychiatric drugs and the institutional acceptance of psychotherapy in the mid twentieth century would herald a whole new era of treatment— and new popular concerns about the role of the state and the medical profession in 'policing' mental health.

4

The mad, the bad, and the supernatural in court

The proverbial differences of medical men are exceeded by those of the lawyers.[1]

(Physician Edward Sieveking discussing monomania in 1889)

It was not only in the asylums that people and their supernatural beliefs were assessed and analysed for signs of insanity. The criminal and civil courts became controversial battlefields where legal minds clashed with the upstart psychiatrists over language, symptoms, and diagnoses. The outcome of these battles determined the fate of defendants, whether they were to be executed, imprisoned, or relieved of their money. Beliefs were on trial as well as people. So too was the fundamental concept of free will—the view that everyone was ultimately responsible for their actions and thus subject to the full force of the law in both criminal and civil cases.[2]

The length of trials increased during the eighteenth century. In Britain, this was partly a result of an act of 1702 that allowed indicted felons to call defence witnesses. The role of medical testimony became more influential and consequently more of a focus for courtroom contention. Juries were increasingly confronted with defendants or their lawyers making pleas of diminished responsibility. Poverty, drink, and madness were commonly cited in mitigation. This destabilized the fundamental legal principle of *mens rea* (guilty mind), in other words that the *intention* to commit a crime had to be proven as well as the proof of the actual criminal act. The question was increasingly being posed in court as to the extent to which a crime was the result of an aberration of the mind, an irrational compulsion induced by drink, a loss of reason due to injury, or a moment of temporary insanity.

Perhaps some supernatural inspiration was involved. Whatever the excuse, the implication was that the impulse or compulsion to commit the crime was beyond the control of the criminal and therefore he or she was not fully responsible. These issues continued to challenge the courts into the nineteenth century, and the influence of expert psychiatric witnesses raised fundamental issues about the nature of rational or irrational beliefs that juries had to grapple with in cultural as well as legal terms. In the civil courts too, the advent of Spiritualism generated a new set of questions about supernatural influences over the free will of those making wills. But before the rise of modern psychiatry transformed the nature of medical jurisprudence, jurors, judges, and lawyers had to negotiate and ultimately dismiss the thorny issue of satanic instigation. In other words, the notion that one of the Devil's disruptive strategies was to render people *non compos mentis*, to force them 'out of their senses' and thereby lead them into crime.

The Devil made me do it

Did the criminal under satanic influence really have a guilty mind? Or did the guilty mind invent the Devil? The idea that the Devil stalked the country promoting mischief in people's minds continued to be held quite widely in eighteenth- and early nineteenth-century Britain, including amongst Anglican clergymen and many nonconformist ministers. It was also a notion commonly represented in ballads and other forms of popular literature. Legal rubric, furthermore, continued to perpetuate the notion.[3] In swearing in witnesses, magistrates and judges held out the prospect of the Devil for those who swore falsely on oath. Until well into the nineteenth century, coroners' verdicts and indictments in cases of murder, rape, treason, and other felonies contained the statement that the defendant committed his or her crime 'maliciously, feloniously, not having the fear of God before his eyes, but being moved and seduced by the instigation of the devil'. So, nearly a century after witchcraft was decriminalized, the diabolic origin of crime was still being cited in indictments for capital offences. How to interpret the longevity of the Devil in criminal law? Maybe the wording was just one of those odd survivals like the failure to decriminalize witchcraft in Ireland until 1821. The author of a booklet on libel law, published in 1785, commented that, with regard to the phrase 'being moved by the instigation of the devil', 'a very little consideration will convince any impartial man that this is mere sophistry. Every man sees that that phrase just mentioned, and others of that sort, are mere words of course.' It contained no 'essential words' that aggravated the charge—there was no Devil in the detail.[4] But the Devil was very real to those in the dock.

Three types of diabolic strategy can be detected from criminal confessions in the eighteenth and early nineteenth centuries: temptation, compulsion, and possession. Satanic *temptation* was sometimes described in terms of the Devil having put the idea of committing a crime 'in their heads' as well as acting as an accessory.[5] Several thieves, for example, claimed that the Evil One had guided them to the goods they were after. When, in March 1741, Sarah Palson was caught stealing gold rings from the house of Mary Leach she said, 'the Devil guided her to them'. The following year, William Edwards, when accused of stealing some money, 'said the Devil told him where the Money was, and that the Devil bid him do it'.[6] Criminals' own narratives, as recorded in the published confessions collected by the Ordinary or chaplain of London's Newgate prison, sometimes suggest that their first perception of satanic influence occurred just prior to committing a crime. Consider, for example, the Ordinary's account of George Cock, executed in 1748, in which it was recorded how, 'In his Way to Spittlefields one Day not thinking of any Mischief, of a sudden the Devil and his own wicked Heart contrived another Scheme'.[7] Even in such instances, however, it is likely that criminals constructed a narrative of cause and culpability after the event as a means of rationalizing their actions and assuaging guilt, particularly so, perhaps, if they were first-time offenders rather than recidivists.

While claims of satanic *temptation* were usually cited in theft cases, satanic *compulsion* was generally pleaded in cases of murder and infanticide. The criminal discourse emphasized the terrible insistence of the Devil. He did not stop at implanting a sudden sinful thought or impulse but drove the criminal mad with his iniquitous urges and commands. At the trial in 1812 of the wife murderer John Chaplin, one witness recalled a conversation with Chaplin in which he stated, 'I am going to dispose of my goods; I said, what is the matter; he said, oh, the devil has got me, he is coming for me.' After Chaplin's initial attempt to murder his wife a witness deposed how, 'In the afternoon I went up into his room; he was lying on the bed; he appeared in a very wild deranged state; I asked him how he could attempt such a wild act upon his wife; he said the devils were tempting him night and day until he made away with her; he must do it. He said by so doing he should save the life of thousands.'[8] Cases of suicide, or self-murder as it was described at

the time, were also sometimes ascribed to the Devil's compulsion. A sample
of thirty-one, seventeenth-century petitions to the Vicar General of London
for the Christian burial of suicides revealed two cases where the act was said
to be committed at the instigation of the Devil. It was a crime that could
not be understood in terms of obvious human impulses such as greed,
covetousness, or violence, and it was considered a deliberate damnation of
the soul.[9]

The temporary physical *possession* of the criminal-to-be by the Devil was
often expressed in terms of the Devil being 'in' them rather than just playing
with their minds. This was a common idiom also expressed, as we shall see
in a later chapter, by those suffering from mental illness in nineteenth-
century asylums. When, in 1759, a Worcestershire victualler and labourer
named Richard Durham confessed to having stolen a bag of his master's
wheat, he said, 'He thinks the devil was in him' when he did it. Asked why
she had stolen some clothing in February 1730, Hannah Burridge replied,
'because the Devil was in me, and is now'.[10] Robert Wid, a farmer of
Troutsdale, North Yorkshire, who was tried in 1817 for stealing some sheep
grazing on the moors that belonged to Thomas Sawdon, talked of being
'entered'. When Sawdon got wind of the theft, he and his servant tracked
Wid down and after a brief struggle subdued him. The repentant Wid apolo-
gized and said, 'he had no need for the sheep, that he had more of his own
than he had meat for, and that he thought the devil had entered into him,
for, seeing the sheep running backwards and forwards along the road side,
he could not pass them by without attempting to steal them'.[11] The
term 'possession' was also used. When Henry Fielding asked Anne Fox in
December 1752 why she had pawned some goods she had stolen, she replied
'she believed the Devil possessed her'. The thief William Beeson explained
to the constable who arrested him in 1745 that 'he believed the devil was in
him, or the devil possessed him'. On being charged in 1772 for stealing
several gold and silver items Christopher Curd 'said he was sorry for it, he
could not help it, the Devil possessed him'.[12]

Some such claims of physical possession or entry were likely used in a
metaphorical sense, of course, but there is ample evidence that people
believed the Devil readily had his way with sinners in whatever physical
way he desired.

In the most extreme examples of diabolic persecution, expressed in terms
of irresistible compulsion and possession, we find more frequent reference
to the physical presence of the Devil.[13] In 1714 the wife murderer Richard

Chapman, when asked why he had killed his wife, 'said the Devil lay under the Bed, and bid him do it'. Witnesses came forward to say he was *Non compos mentis* and he was acquitted. In 1731 a gentleman named Edward Stafford was also found *Non compos mentis*. Much evidence was brought as to his 'lunacy', including his complaints of being tormented by devils. He was plagued by constant noises in his head and believed the Devil was in his lodgings and there were devils in his closet, and he fired pistols to drive them away. He told the owner of a coffee-house he frequented that 'he would thrust his Sword into Witches if he found them, and if he found the Devil he would chain him down'. When a constable and watchman approached a raving, homicidal sailor named Isaac Foy in 1815 he was 'crying out murder! saying he was in hell, and the devils were tormenting him'. He went on to claim that the Devil, thieves and spirits were in the ship 'and that they had been tearing his heart out. That the devil had been running after him through the ship, and wanted to put him on a spit and roast him; he said he had killed one man, and wounded all the rest.'[14] As some of these cases suggest, one reason for the greater emphasis on the presence of a physical Devil in murder trials is that it bolstered pleas of insanity more effectively than claims of moral diabolic inspiration.

Some criminals, no doubt, resorted to claims of diabolic intervention as a legal strategy as well as a personal rationalization of intrusive thoughts and compulsive actions. Popular crime reports in publications such as the Old Bailey Sessions Papers, ballads, crime pamphlets, and newspapers could also have served as 'instructional manuals in the arts of evasion'. Insanity, along with drink and poverty, became increasingly prominent in narratives of excuse, and, as a consequence, defendants, their friends and families, and increasingly defence lawyers, deliberately attempted to 'broaden the definitions of mental incapacity'.[15] While poverty and drunkenness were not recognized as mitigating states, suggesting that they could induce bouts of mental aberration appealed to the growing medico-legal sensitivity towards the concept of temporary or partial insanity. Satanic instigation could also be inserted into this narrative framework by suggesting that the Devil interceded by taking advantage of poverty and drunkenness, thereby setting up a two-tier mitigation plea. The Ordinary's account of the thief and murderer William Descent, for example, recorded that the latter thought 'nothing could have prompted [him] to it but the Rage of strong Drink, and the Devil taking Advantage of it'. Likewise, the horse thief Robert Radwell 'said he was much in Liquor, and short of Money, and therefore was tempted by the Devil to commit this rash action'.[16] Once again, we have to consider, of course, at what point in the judicial process such narratives were introduced. The above examples were statements uttered after conviction, and in the *Proceedings* of both men's trials there is no mention of the Devil. Faced with death and the divergent paths to Heaven and Hell these were, presumably, mitigation pleas directed to the mercy of God rather than the mercy of the courts. In the majority of theft cases, furthermore, the offenders did not make their appeal of satanic inspiration in the formal legal arena of the court but rather when first confronted by their victims or at the moment of arrest. This suggests that the narrative of satanic instigation was deemed more likely to be effective in appealing to the compassion of victims, who were usually neighbours, employers, tradespeople, and constables, than the sensibilities of jurors.

Despite the continued emphasis on satanic inspiration in certain judicial and religious discourses, with the exception of the insanity defence in murder trials, the resort to the Devil in mitigation did not prove effective. In Scotland satanic influence pleas seem to have ceased by the early 1780s, though they continued to be heard sporadically in English courts for several decades longer.[17] Ultimately the principles of free will outweighed the Devil's influence. In theft cases at least, juries seemed to concur with the view of the Rev. Gillespy, curate of Blisworth, Northamptonshire, who, in his *Disquisition upon the Criminal Laws*, argued that the exercise of people's mental and corporal powers 'must convince us of the freedom, both of our wills and actions'. 'We are free, rational, and consequently accountable creatures', he asserted: 'In vain therefore do men plead an irresistible fate in extenuation of their crimes.'[18] Even those who were outspoken in their belief that the Devil stalked the land sowing mischief and misery also forcefully propounded the same message. The Rev. John Prince asserted that despite being a 'subtle, powerful Spirit', the Devil 'can't compel you to any Thing against your will. The Advantage he gains over you, at any Time, is chiefly from your own Consent.'[19] The Shrewsbury vicar and schoolmaster Thomas Humphries warned criminals, 'do not lay the fault on the weakness of your nature, or the strength of temptation. This is only the devil's stratagem to make you deceive yourselves. For, when you come to see it fairly, you will be forced to own, that it is your own fault; and that you deserve to suffer the sad consequences.'[20] At least one criminal agreed. On being arrested in 1758 for theft, Samuel Cordwell said he did it under the influence of 'drinking and the temptation of the Devil; but he took all the blame upon himself, he thought it would never be found out'.[21]

The Devil gives way to delusion

The trial of James Hadfield for treason in 1800 marked a new turn for the insanity plea at a time when talk of satanic instigation was receding in the courts. Hadfield, a Dragoon Sergeant who had received a bad head injury during military service, had millenarian convictions. Inspired by a minor London prophet named Bannister Truelock, he believed that by killing King George III he would hasten the Second Coming of Christ. On 15 May 1800 he fired at the king during the playing of the national anthem in the Theatre Royal, Drury Lane. Hadfield was acquitted on the grounds of insanity and died in Bethlem in 1841.[22] As the Attorney General, Lord Kenyon, explained to the jury at Hadfield's trial, in the eyes of the law there had to be evidence of 'absolute madness' so that it was clear to the jury that the defendant had no idea of the consequences of his actions. In practice this usually meant the physical manifestations of insanity in terms of fits or violent raving. While witnesses testified that Hadfield had moments when his appearance was 'much like a mad man's', and his head wounds were accepted as one possible cause of these aberrations, he generally functioned normally and continued to hold down his job. Hadfield was defended by one of the finest legal minds of the time, Thomas Erskine (1750–1823). Erskine's cleverness was to focus on Hadfield's delusions and suggest to the jury that his client's insanity lay *inside* his head. As Erskine put it, God had been pleased to attack his client's mind 'in its citadel, filling it with delusions which had no foundation in the actual state of things'.[23] His 'disease', according to Erskine, began when he conceived that the world was coming to an end, and the insanity of Truelock 'mixing itself with that of Hadfield, tended only to confuse his mind more and more'. He would ramble confusedly about the vileness of the Virgin Mary and called Christ a 'damned bastard' and a thief. He said he communicated with God, and that he had been instructed to build a home near White Conduit House, which was a popular green leisure space for Londoners. He and Truelock would live together there, Truelock as the Devil and he as God.[24] So the evidence lay, in part, on the supernatural content of his delusions, which were deemed sufficiently deviant in religious terms.

The Hadfield trial led directly to parliament passing the Criminal Lunatics Act the same year, which introduced the formal verdict of 'not guilty on the ground of insanity' and put in place procedures for the indefinite detention of those so sentenced. Before this, the likes of Hadfield were simply let free to the care of family or guardians. It has been argued, however, that the trial and acquittal was the result of Erskine's legal brilliance, rather than representing a breakthrough in medical jurisprudence regarding insanity. That would happen several decades later.[25] But the trial did cement the concept of partial insanity in case law. In other words, that a crime could be plotted and committed in an insane state and yet the criminal could function rationally in other respects.

In English and Scottish Common Law judges were meant to instruct juries on legal matters but they were not meant to advise them on what decision they should make. In reality their egos, scepticism, frustration, and arrogance led some judges to try and steer the jury as to the alleged insanity of defendants. Sometimes this was based on nothing more than their personal opinion, but sometimes their interventions were well meant in terms of their superior understanding when it came to the state of medical knowledge and case law.[26] The Dublin-born judge William Johnson (1760–1845) is a good example. He was appointed to the bench in 1817 despite the stigma of being the brother of the disgraced judge Robert Johnson, who was found guilty of libel in 1804 (Erskine acted on behalf of one of the plaintiffs). William was considered an able lawyer but was described as having a 'rough and overbearing demeanour'. More to the point, Johnson's father was a Dublin apothecary, once described as a 'hard-praying Protestant'.[27] I introduce him here because he presided over a fascinating case that grappled with the relationship between faith, crime, and insanity at a moment when the psychiatrists were only just starting to get a foothold in the court room and religious politics was flaring up in Ireland.[28]

In 1824 Father John Carroll, Curate of Ballymore, Wexford, described as a tall man with marked and regular features that denoted 'nothing of the fanatic, or the maniac', was tried for murder along with five other accomplices.[29] He had become curate of Ballymore in 1819 after several years as curate for the parish of Kilrush. Locals testified that he was considered a good, pious man who could work miracles. One witness even said that Carroll was 'considered by the people to possess superior power to other Priests'.[30]

On the evening of 9 July, Carroll embarked on a terrifying and violent tour of exorcism around the neighbourhood of Killinick in the southeast of

Ireland. First on the itinerary was the house of Henry Neale, who was dangerously ill with apoplexy, which was a term to describe a usually fatal loss of consciousness such as from a stroke. Carroll declared Neale was possessed with devils and jumped on him several times as he lay in bed, while ordering those around to pray fervently. One of the bystanders, Peggy Danby, was so shocked by what she saw that she 'fell to the ground in hysterics'. Carroll leapt off Neale's bed and shook Danby violently calling on Jesus to expel the evil spirits from her as well. He jumped on her body thereby breaking several ribs. Blood poured out of her mouth which other present took to be a sign of the devils' escape. He then marched towards the bridge of Assaily some 400 yards further, followed by dozens of spectators. He arrived at the home of Robert Moran, whose wife was ill and was also thought to be possessed by this plague of devils. He struck her violently, stamped his foot, and spat two or three times at her, shouting, 'Jesus, Jesus, Jesus! Father, Father, Father, assist me!' He then spoke some words in Latin and demanded the devils 'Begone!'

His final stop was at the home of the local nail maker, Thomas Sinnott, where he began his version of an exorcism which bore no relation to any sanctioned orthodox rite. Before an audience of dozens crowded in and around the cottage, which included Sinnott family members, neighbours, and the priest's sisters, Carroll went to the bedside of Sinnott's 3-year-old daughter Catharine who was troubled with fits. Catharine was doused in salt and water and then placed under a tub on the bed. Carroll jumped up and down on the tub before sitting on it for over three hours. The poor infant cried out, 'Mammy! Mammy! Save me!' But Carroll was deaf to her pleas, believing that it was the Devil speaking. He said in a loud voice at one point, 'bury him Jesus in the depth of the Red Sea!' While he sat on the tub Carroll whistled a hornpipe to pass the time. A passage was kept through the attending crowd to facilitate the eventual escape of the Devil from Catharine's body. Around four in the morning the tub was removed and Catharine was found lying dead. Her father took her lifeless body in his arms and sat on the bed with the priest. Everyone knelt down and prayed. Thomas asked what he should do. Carroll replied that he should resign himself to the will of God. Then he rode home.

An inquest was held on 12 July, and then, on 4 August, Carroll and five male parishioners who aided him during the exorcism, James Devereux, Nicholas Wickham, Patrick Parel, Nicholas Corrish, and Walter Scallan, were brought to trial at Wexford Crown Court charged with wilful murder.

In his opening remarks, Mr Driscoll, King's Council, told the jury that 'it is, indeed, so novel a case, that there is not a parallel to be found for it in the annals of British History'.[31] Several witnesses were cross-examined, and when Thomas Sinnott was questioned and asked why he did not query Carroll's conduct when he found his daughter dead, he replied, 'I did not, as I thought he would return and bring the child to life again.' When asked to clarify if he thought the priest could bring the dead back to life, he answered, 'It was my opinion that he could.'[32]

It was clear that the prosecution, defence, and the judge were all of the determined opinion that Carroll was insane. Witnesses to the event were repeatedly asked if they considered the priest was mad. William Furlong, for instance, a relative of the Sinnotts through his wife, said he sent for one Father Keeffe, Father Walter Rowe, who was the parish priest at Tagoat, and Father Aedan Ennis (1756–1840) the parish priest at Mayglass, to come and take Carroll away, 'as I thought he was mad, but the messenger, I believe, did not go'.[33] A Doctor Renwick visited Carroll the morning after the tragedy and found him

> so insane that he was obliged to put him under restraint. He did not put him in a strait waistcoat; bled him profusely in the temporal artery; Mr. Carroll removed the dressings, and witness was therefore obliged to place handcuffs upon him; he was raving, and speaking very incoherently, particularly about the devils which he had driven out of people.

The key witness was a Wexford physician named Devereux who had known Carroll well for some fourteen years and had been treating him professionally for the last three years. For much of the time he had known Carroll he thought him an exemplary and pious clergyman. Then, around three years ago, he began to exhibit the signs of incipient insanity. He expressed no delusions at the time, but rather he had 'an impaired memory, a vacancy of mind, a confusion of ideas, and a determination of blood to the head'. Then, about two months before the events of 9 July, his condition seemed to deteriorate. 'He was, in fact', said Devereux, 'what medical men call having a predisposition to insanity.' Devereux treated him with medicine but Carroll ceased taking it, and that, concluded the physician, explained the intensification of the insanity and the disaster that ensued. Devereux had met Carroll by chance during the exorcism rampage: 'I saw him in the gripe of a ditch by the road side, with his hat off, and his coat covered with dust, and a number of people about him; he had then the appearance of being deranged.'[34]

In his address to the jury, Judge Johnson explained that if they were of opinion that Carroll was of sound mind when the act was committed, they must find him guilty of murder; if the contrary, they must acquit him. Indeed, his Lordship said it would be monstrous, in his opinion, to come to any other decision, but that the prisoner, at the perpetration of this act, was deprived of reason. He then went on to give an outline of the trial of James Hadfield by way of example. Johnson did not mention the religious aspects of the Hadfield case, but he concluded that the evidence was similar to that heard by his jury. Johnson also told them that they had heard 'the positive testimony of a medical gentleman, who had for years professionally engaged in attending upon him [Carroll]'. The jury obliged. They found the five accomplices 'Not Guilty' and that 'the said John Carroll has been acquitted by us of the said offence, on account of the said insanity'.

Carroll spent the next few years in Richmond District Lunatic Asylum, Dublin. In October 1832 he requested permission to say Mass on Sundays and days of precept in the chapel of the House of Industry, which was adjacent to the asylum. Sometime that year he was apparently declared cured of 'lunacy' by the asylum physician and it was ordered that he be transferred to the newly opened Carlow District Lunatic Asylum. Once there, he sent regular letters to the Lieutenant Colonel Sir William Gosset, Under Secretary for Ireland, with requests for various permissions. On 14 May 1833, for instance, he wrote to say he was grateful for having been allowed to hear Mass and also asked for a yearly grocery allowance including the purchase of tobacco and snuff. The last we hear, in December that year, he made a request to be moved to Swift's Hospital (St Patrick's Hospital, Dublin).[35]

The notion that fervent belief in religious or supernatural powers could be a mark of insanity was suggested during the trial but it was clearly a tricky issue for the defence and prosecution in the context of Catholic belief and the popular influence of the Catholic clergy under British rule. The judge referred to such belief as 'fanaticism' and, confronting Carroll about his power to exorcize devils, he declared, 'that you were the victim of delusion I hope and admit'. But the fact that so many locals believed completely in Carroll's miraculous powers, and participated one way another in his exorcism rampage, was problematic because if Carroll's conviction of his own extraordinary ordained powers was proof of insanity then what about the mental state of all the locals? The judge concluded that a rational being, like *himself*, could not comprehend how the Catholic 'lower orders' could believe that priests could perform miracles, which was not the same as implying *they* were all insane. To his mind they were merely fanatics and blasphemers. Despite the considerable media coverage of the trial, and Mr Driscoll's claim that it was an unparalleled case in British history, the case was quietly 'forgotten' and made no impact on British and Irish medical jurisprudence.

Eccentric or insane?

Criminal and civil cases involving what were deemed irrational or peculiar notions at this period, like those of Hadfield and Carroll, struggled with the issue of eccentricity. Was eccentricity normal? And where did eccentricity end and insanity begin? There was a cultural as well as a medical angle to the question. French commentators looked upon England as a country of 'half mad' eccentrics. The view was well encapsulated by a character in one of the novels of Honoré Balzac (1799–1850), who explained, 'you are perhaps unaware that in English society there are many madmen who are not incarcerated and who are termed eccentrics'. But, as the same character argued, one had to be rich to be defined an English eccentric. If a London cobbler exhibited the same behaviour he would end up incarcerated as dangerously insane.[36] There was a core of truth in the observation, yet eccentricity amongst the poor was also celebrated in English ballads and newspapers of the period, with various peddlers, tramps, workhouse inmates, and self-styled prophets being affectionately portrayed as harmless working-class 'characters' and 'oddities' who added colour to local life.[37]

In the 1880s Henry Maudsley rather blithely stated that, 'all insane persons are necessarily eccentric, but not all eccentric persons are insane'.[38] This was not much use to the jurist and, indeed the need to determine the boundary had been debated without much resolution for sixty years. In the late 1820s, the English physician Robert Gooch (1784–1830) attempted to set out several categories of eccentricity that were not pathological states. He admitted, however, that from his own observation there were individuals whose disproportionately high opinion of themselves was deemed merely eccentric by others, but which he diagnosed as 'slumbering undeveloped madness'. Around the same time, John Conolly (1794–1866), Professor of Medicine at the University of London, suggested that there were two types of eccentricity—one where the departure from norms and customs was 'plainly repugnant to reason' and the other where it was 'apparently reasonable'. All eccentricity was a departure from sound *judgement*, however, and he admitted that there were cases where the boundary line between eccentricity and madness 'seem to bid defiance to definition'.[39]

It is understandable then, that this was a fraught issue from the early years of medical jurisprudence. James Cowles Prichard was one of the few to confront the matter. The eccentric may be an absolute pest to society, said Prichard, but impossible to interfere with legally. For such behaviour to become a medical or legal matter, the eccentricity must assume a threat to the individual, or to his or her family and wider society. This could apply, for example, to those who persistently complained of being bewitched and threatened their neighbours. The issue came to the fore in the trial for murder of John Howison in Edinburgh in 1831. His fate rested partly on whether a preoccupation with witches and other obsessive 'superstitious' habits constituted an eccentricity or insanity. As one of the medical experts for the prosecution, Alexander Watson (1799–1879), Surgeon to the Royal Infirmary, observed, 'for such a case as this, the law of the country has not yet made any provision'.[40]

Howison, aged forty-five, was clearly a strange, morose character who made a living as a hawker. Neighbours called him a 'daft creature'. He was described as 'miserably superstitious' and fearful of persecution by witches. He put salt around his bed and his head and carried folded paper charms in his clothes, without which he said he would have been long dead. As further protection he carried a Bible around his wrist and neck. He also exhibited other eccentric behaviour such as eating his meat raw, and regularly pricking himself with pins and needles to draw blood, which he would then suck. He attempted to join the Quakers. On one occasion he was seen at the local meeting-house early in the morning, kneeling and invoking the Virgin Mary. He drew blood from himself and smeared it on the doorway. Then, in the autumn of 1831, he disappeared from his lodgings and apparently tramped the countryside in northern England and Scotland. One day he turned up in the village of Cramond, now in the northwest of Edinburgh, asking for alms. He entered into the cottage of a widow named Martha Geddes. A short time later he was seen fleeing the house and Geddes was found dead, her head split open with a spade. Howison was arrested the next morning but denied all knowledge of the murder or even of having been in Cramond.

The prosecution called upon Thomas Spens, physician at the Morningside Lunatic Asylum, and physician Alexander Watson. Spens had interviewed

Howison at length several times since his arrest and found no signs of insanity or idiocy, though he admitted there were forms of insanity that could not be detected through conversation alone. Watson, who subsequently published his own account of the case, interviewed Howison twice and considered him to be 'of low or weak intellect' but sane. Both he and Spens were ready to agree that Howison had exhibited signs of insanity in the past but not during or after the crime. There was mention that Howison had apparently had a fever during his weeks in England, but Watson found that 'no correct account' could be obtained of its nature.[41]

The defence was supported by a more stellar line up, including lecturer in medicine John Mackintosh, John Scott, a physician in practice since 1818 who had made a particular study of insanity, and the star witness William Pulteney Alison (1790–1859), Professor of Medical Jurisprudence and a leading social reformer. It was Alison who reflected most on Howison's 'superstitions' during the trial. He thought there was evidence that Howison was of unsound mind prior to the murder. 'Putting papers about his head, and sowing salt about his clothes to protect them from witches', he told the court, were 'among the acts which makes witness doubt his [Howison's] sanity.' Under cross-examination he wondered whether Howison thought Geddes was a witch and said he did not think it sane to commit a murder with a Bible tied around the wrist. But in addressing the jury, the Solicitor General, who fulfilled the role of presiding judge under Scottish law in this instance, was quite clear, 'all the peculiarities which have been sworn to only amounted to eccentricity of character. The prisoner's belief in witches was no proof of insanity.' He went on to observe that in the north of Scotland one in ten men entertained the same belief, and that 'the greatest man of the last century, Dr Samuel Johnson, believed as firmly in the existence of witches as any of the Jury or Court did in the immortality of the soul'.[42] The jury found Howison guilty, and he was executed.

A couple of years after the trial the advocate James Simpson (1781–1853) re-assessed all the evidence, including material that emerged during the campaign for Howison's clemency plea, and concluded that the 'wretched man was not a responsible agent'.[43] 'The ground upon which Howison's plea of insanity failed, no doubt, was that he did not prove insanity *enough*', he suggested with frustration, and that, at the most, the defence had only proved what the Scottish judge and legal scholar Baron Hume (1757–1838) held insufficient in mitigation, 'namely eccentricity, a crazy or irregular temper'. John Cowles Prichard shared Simpson's conclusion. Having read his extensive review of the evidence Prichard was in absolutely no doubt that Howison was out of his senses at the time, arguing that 'his case constitutes a very characteristic case of moral insanity'. Howison's conviction, therefore, was considered a tragic miscarriage of justice due to judicial ignorance of the new, cutting-edge psychiatric diagnoses.[44] But times were changing and the new generation of psychiatrists would come to challenge the authority of the judges.

The age of the experts

University Chairs in Forensic Medicine proliferated during the early nineteenth century and from the 1820s handbooks and treatises of medical jurisprudence began to proliferate in France, Germany, and Britain.[45] Two landmark books were published in England in 1844. One was *Principles of Forensic Medicine* by William Augustus Guy (1810–1885), Professor of Forensic Medicine at King's College London, and the other was the *Manual of Medical Jurisprudence* by Guy's great rival the toxicologist Alfred Swaine Taylor (1806–1880). These two works helped cement in British and American medical jurisprudence the four main distinct forms of insanity originally proposed by Esquirol: mania, monomania, dementia, and idiocy. The Bachelor of Medicine examinations at London University, for instance, included the following examination paper in the 1850s:

> What are the circumstances, medical and legal, to be observed in signing a certificate for the confinement of a person who is of unsound mind? How would you test the existence of unsoundness of mind? Describe the special characters of mania, monomania, dementia, and idiocy.[46]

It was hoped that the four categories would provide better diagnostic certainty and more legal precision in criminal cases. Swaine Taylor cautioned medical jurists, though, not to fall into the error of pronouncing a defendant of sound mind because the symptoms of alleged insanity did not clearly fall into one of the four categories.[47]

Taylor and Guy were regular stars in the witness box during sensational murder trials, but it was local asylum superintendents who were most frequently called to proffer their expertise on the psychiatric state of defendants, although general practitioners and prison medical officers also often gave testimony.[48] While there was a debate as to whether courts should employ impartial medical experts to assess the evidence for insanity, in Britain they were appointed either by the defence or the prosecution to suit their arguments. But the discourse on insanity in the court room, and in professional forensic medicine, proved to be substantially different in nature to that found in psychiatry journals and annual asylum reports.[49] The ever-shifting sands of psychiatric debate and terminology clashed with the necessity for stable legal definitions. At the Southern Counties Asylum in Dumfries, for instance, Lauder Lindsay subdivided monomania into the following forms: religious; joyous/sad; superstitious; of fear; homicidal; suspicious; proud; of discontent. He was careful to point out that no patient exhibited solely a pure form of any such category but rather a complex mix of mental and physical conditions in different forms and degrees. As David Skae observed in 1863, 'I venture to say there are no two asylum reports published in the empire in which the same rules and distinctions are rigidly observed in tabulating the forms of insanity under treatment.'[50] Contrast this with the fact that Guy was fundamentally critical of the term 'insanity' itself. It had become divorced from legal applicability by its increasingly precise meaning at the hands of the new asylum psychiatrists. He concluded that 'insanity' did not 'include all possible deviations from the sound and healthy condition of the mind'. In its precision it was, ironically, too blunt an instrument for effective jurisprudence. Swaine Taylor also decided that it was 'impossible in medical jurisprudence, to give any consistent definition of insanity. A medical witness who ventures upon a definition, will generally find himself involved in numerous inconsistencies.' He gave the example of a trial in 1839 where a medical man was reluctant to sign the certificate for the confinement of an alleged 'lunatic', because the term 'unsound mind' was used. If it had referred to 'insanity' instead, he said he would have had no problem signing it.[51] Confusion and contradiction abounded.

The main flashpoint in court between experts and judges concerned the diagnosis of monomania. Whereas the symptoms of idiocy, mania, and dementia were generally observable to the untrained eye and based on longstanding lay understanding, monomania was often deemed only detectable by the medical expert. In several high-profile murder trials part of the contention, in this regard, concerned the pathology of the belief in the supernatural. The eminent German psychiatrist Wilhelm Griesinger (1817–1868) reflected on the matter:

two individuals may say and do the same thing; for example, they may express their belief in witchcraft, or the fear of being eternally lost; the intelligent observer would declare the one to be healthy and the other to be insane. This judgement is come to by a consideration of all the accompanying circumstances, and from a knowledge gained by experience of the various forms of insanity and their accompanying phenomena.[52]

While the tensions between judges and medical experts have already been noted, the jury also had to make sense of what they were being told by psychiatrists in language and terms that they may have only heard of for the first time when uttered in court.[53]

Juridical acceptance of monomania in Western Europe was in part due to the influence of Étienne-Jean Georget (1795–1828), who studied under both Pinel and Esquirol. Georget, who came from a poor farming family and who contributed much to early psychiatry before dying young of tuberculosis, argued vigorously that monomania was grounds for a defendant to be considered *non compos mentis*. In France this set up a clash with the upholders of the Napoleonic law code and its strict sense of criminal responsibility. The issue was discussed and increasingly contested in a number of trials in the 1850s, including that of Claude Feuillet for poisoning his wife and baby to death in 1852.[54] Feuillet was an industrious 36-year-old farmer and a skilful craftsman. Around the age of twenty he began to suffer epileptic attacks. Believing he was bewitched, he consulted a cunning-man who told him the stunning news that he could only be completely cured if he changed sex. Feuillet began to wear women's clothes, first in private and then in public, to hasten his cure. He even inquired of a local doctor whether he could have his sexual organs removed, and also consulted Dr César Chiara, who would later investigate events at Morzine, about whether he could stop his beard from growing. At the end of 1850 Feuillet married the daughter of a man named Roux who had convinced him that marriage would break the spell over him. But in March 1852 both wife and baby died of arsenic and mercury poisoning. Feuillet denied the crime but faced trial for murder. Three doctors were called to assess his mental state. One of them was the psychiatrist and expert on medical jurisprudence, Horace-Honoré Tavernier (1811–1894) of Lyon. He had recently been involved as a medical witness in the high-profile Jobard murder trial. In his report on Jobard he had concluded that he was in such a state of dementia and homicidal monomania when he committed the murder of Anaïs Ricard that Jobard could not be held responsible for the act, and that he should be committed to an asylum for the rest of his life.[55] His report on Feuillet, written with his fellow doctors, was similar. They concluded that, at the time he went to the doctors requesting castration and beard removal, Feuillet was suffering from lypemania, but otherwise he was perfectly sane in his daily actions. But they could not say for sure that he committed the crime because of monomaniacal belief in his bewitchment and his need for a sex change, or because of other motives. The court sentenced Feuillet to life in prison with hard labour rather than a lifetime in an asylum.

By the 1860s, French judicial concerns with monomania were rebounding back on the psychiatrists' own asylum practice, and it was being rejected in medical diagnoses as outmoded and unfit for purpose. The delusions, deliria, and hallucinations that were often diagnostic of monomania were increasingly being problematized. It was fiendishly difficult to claim categorically that they were physiological or mental in origin, marks of insanity or signs of somatic conditions at the time of a criminal act.[56] Monomania began to disappear from asylum reports, admissions records, and casebooks. An analysis of the Salpêtrière admissions registers, for instance, shows that 'monomania' had vanished as a diagnostic category by 1870.[57] Psychiatrist Charles-Auguste Bihorel, writing in that year, declared, 'We can no longer depend upon the classifications of Pinel and Esquirol.'[58] In Germany, where the discipline of psychiatry was led by academics and developed primarily within the setting of university medical clinics rather than the asylum system, the concept of monomania never became such a battleground concept. In the year of German unification a new law code of 1871 established that accused criminals could not be punished if expert medical witnesses could prove that they did not have free will when committing the alleged crime. Defendants could be observed for up to six weeks in a public asylum to draw up a psychiatric dossier before sentencing.[59]

In Britain and America monomania continued to be used and debated in asylum literature and in the court room for several decades after it had been expunged from French jurisprudence. This was in part due to nation-based legal histories and judicial developments. In England, for instance, the books by Guy and Swaine Taylor were published shortly after the creation of the M'Naghten Rules. These were formulated as a consequence of the trial of Daniel M'Naghten for attempting to shoot the Prime Minister Robert Peel. The defence argued that M'Naghten was insane at the time and suffering the delusion that he was persecuted by the police. Several high-profile medical experts, including Forbes Benignus Winslow, were called by the defence. The jury was convinced by the defence case and gave a verdict of 'Not Guilty' on the grounds of insanity. Due to the public uproar arising from the decision a panel of judges was commissioned to look into the matter. They concluded that to establish a defence of insanity it must be proven that the defendant suffered from a disease of the mind to the extent that they did 'not to know the nature and quality of the act he was doing; or if he did know it, that he did not know he was doing what was wrong'. The Rules made it very difficult to conduct a defence on the grounds of monomania but this did not stop legal teams and medical witnesses attempting to put the case for monomania before judge and jury over the next few decades with varying degrees of success.

In 1856 the trial of William Dove for killing his wife was in all the papers.[60] Although it was clear he was culpable and had been slowly but surely poisoning his wife with strychnine, a case for insanity was constructed and easily paid for by his wealthy Leeds family. The main medical witness for the defence was Caleb Williams (1798–1871), a long-time medical attendant at the Retreat Lunatic Asylum at York, who testified: 'I consider his powers of mind during the fatal week were probably influenced by his notions regarding supernatural agency, and that consequently he was the object of delusion.' This referred to Dove's relations with a cunning-man named James Harrison, the Wizard of the South Market, who provided a magic charm for William's farm, divined the identity of a thief for him, and predicted the death of both his wife and father. Homicidal monomania was brought up as a defence, but the psychiatric experts were divided on the matter, leading the judge, Baron George William Wilshere Bramwell (1808–1892), to exclaim witheringly, 'Experts in madness! Mad doctors! Gentlemen, I will read you the evidence of these medical witnesses—these "experts in madness."—And if you can make sane evidence out of what they say, do so: but I confess it's more than I can do.' The insanity plea was dismissed by the jury and Dove was executed at York. The plea of homicidal monomania was successful a few years later, however, in the case of Adelaide Cole who murdered her 15-month-old son in 1862. Cole believed she was haunted by evil spirits and told her physician, John Rogers, 'that she saw the spirits murder the child before her eyes'.[61]

An attempt was made to introduce 'religious monomania' in the defence of murderer Constance Kent. In 1860, at the age of sixteen, Kent killed her infant step-brother in 1860 and hid the corpse down the servants' outside privy.[62] The case, known as the Road Hill House Murder, was a national sensation. Years passed without the killer being identified. Kent entered a convent in Dinan, France, and then returned to England where she became a resident at the St Mary's Home for Penitents. Then, in 1865, she confessed to the murder during confession with Anglo-Catholic clergyman, Arthur Wagner, and told him she intended to give herself up to the police, which she did. The defence of homicidal monomania was floated, but before the trial, friends of Kent apparently tried to convince her to put in a plea of 'Not Guilty' as her lawyer would then argue that her confession to Wagner was produced in a state of religious monomania. As one periodical reported at the time, the trial threatened to raise 'the old dispute'.[63] But Kent was not to be convinced and entered a plea of guilty.

Witchcraft was at the heart of a monomania defence in 1871. John F. Dawe Bird was a 23-year-old farmer, son of Esau Bird, a substantial farmer of 126 acres at Batcombe, Dorset. The Dorchester prison admission register described John as being 5 foot 9 inches, quite tall for the time, with brown hair and dark grey eyes, and a ruddy complexion with a scar behind the left ear. He had suffered from being 'hag-ridden' three times, or what we now know in medical terms as sleep paralysis, during which he had hallucinations of an elderly woman named Charlotte Griffin coming to his bedroom to torment him.[64] On 4 March he found Griffin in one of the cottages of his father's labourers, and in a rage beat her badly with a stick. Realizing he was in serious trouble, Bird fled and headed for Portsmouth where he was caught attempting to board the *Abyssinia* destined for New York. He was brought back and the case was initially heard at Cerne Abbas Petty sessions, where Bird said, 'this will be a lesson to me. I will never beat her any more whether she hag-rids me or not. I used to see her come into my bedroom window as plain as I see you now. I should not have beat her so much.'

Bird was subsequently tried at the summer assizes for grievous bodily harm. His defence lawyer Mr Collins attempted to argue that Bird was a monomaniac. Esau testified that his son had 'never been strong in his mind' and two years earlier he had had an abscess in his head. He fell ill in a hay field one day as a consequence, suffered a long, low fever, and was 'never correct in his mind afterwards'. This was the venerable defence strategy of proving a physical origin for the alleged insanity. Mr John Good, the surgeon of the Dorset County Prison was called and described Bird as 'a simple, weak-minded monomaniac'. Dr John Clapcott, who had attended Bird during his illness, was also of the same opinion. The judge asked Good,

'What do you mean by monomaniac?' To which he replied, 'He was suffering from a certain delusion, my lord.' The judge was having none of it: 'there was no pretence for saying that prisoner did not know right from wrong, and he should treat him as a sane person who had committed a very cruel act'. The jury found Bird guilty and he was sentenced to six months' hard labour. After his release, he married a young widow in 1873 and by 1881 he was running a large farm in Romford, Essex, though his fortunes subsequently waned.[65]

The last major British criminal trial in which the issue of witchcraft monomania was debated occurred in 1875. On the evening of 15 September the peace of the small village of Long Compton, Warwickshire, was shattered by a murder. As 45-year-old labourer James Hayward returned home from harvesting in the fields with his pitchfork over his shoulder, he encountered his next-door neighbour, a 79-year-old woman named Ann Tennant, wife of a shoemaker, who had stepped out of her cottage to buy a loaf of bread from the local shop. On seeing her on the road, Hayward stabbed her in the legs with his pitchfork and knocked her over. Tennant cried out, 'Oh dear!' several times. He was about to strike her again when he was stopped by farmer John Taylor. As Taylor later recalled, Hayward 'swore that he would kill all the damned witches in Long Compton, sixteen of them. I held him till Police Constable Simpson came and took him into custody. The prisoner has delusions about witches.' Tennant was carried home and died three hours later. When Police constable John Simpson came to arrest Hayward he told him, 'I must lock you up for I think that you have killed that poor old woman.' Hayward replied, 'It is no odds about it. I hope she will die. There are fifteen more of them in the village that I will serve the same. I will kill them all.' He had clearly been drinking and had been out in the harvest fields but said he could do no work because she had bewitched him.[66]

Hayward was tried for murder at the Warwick Assizes that December.[67] A reporter from the *Stratford Herald* described him as 'evidently a very simple-minded and superstitious man. He is about 5 feet 4 inches in height, with a low receding forehead, and an almost "idiotic" expression of countenance, his awkwardness being increased by his great deafness.' When asked in court how he pleaded, Hayward said, 'I be sorry I hurt the woman, but she tormented me for a long time in witchcraft.' He pleaded 'Not Guilty'. Mr Buzzard was then appointed by the court to defend him. As the outcome of the trial was clearly going to depend on whether Hayward was diagnosed insane or not, Mr Dugdale for the prosecution informed the court regarding the law on insane delusions and how far persons suffering from them were liable. Each witness made some comment or gave their opinion on Hayward's state of mind and behaviour. Local lad, John Henry Ivens, aged fifteen, said that the boys of the village looked upon Hayward as a madman. Ann's husband, John Tennant, who had lived next door to Hayward for thirty years, also said that when the defendant got drunk 'he ran about like a madman'. He and his parents were always talking about witches, and about twelve months previously he had also accused Ann Tennant's daughter Elizabeth Hughes of being a witch. Elizabeth then gave evidence that Hayward frequently talked about witches, 'but the villagers never took any notice of him as they thought he was a "wild" man'. Police constable John Simpson presented a different picture, saying that he considered that Hayward was a generally quiet peaceable man whose father and mother both went to chapel. Hayward's general practitioner, George Hutchinson, said he used to prescribe medicines for him and he seemed sane enough when they talked about the weather, crops, and other subjects. Hutchinson attributed Hayward's strange manner to his deafness.

Two medical witnesses were called by the defence. First up was the long-time superintendent at Warwick Asylum, Henry Parsey (1821–1884), who visited Hayward in jail on 21 and 24 September and once more shortly before the trial.[68] Parsey found him to be of 'feeble mind' and noted that he took 'quite a childish interest in the notes which were taken at the interviews'. Although Hayward was aware he was in trouble, he did not seem to realize the life and death gravity of the situation. He had been reading the Bible in gaol and pointed out to Parsey the passage in Leviticus 20: 'A man also or woman that hath a familiar spirit, or that is a wizard, shall surely be put to death: they shall stone them with stones: their blood shall be upon them.' Hayward believed he had done his Christian duty. Parsey gave it as his opinion that Hayward in many instances could exercise his mental faculties normally, even if he was preoccupied with the delusional idea of witchcraft. He was of sufficiently sound mind to understand the proceedings at his trial. As a consequence, Parsey told the court that he would not certify that the prisoner should be removed to an asylum before sentencing because he thought 'justice would be defeated'. He would, however, have no hesitation to sign a certificate after the trial had taken place. The second medical witness, Mr John Robert Nunn, surgeon at the Warwick County Prison, had talked to Hayward and found that the prisoner felt he could not control his actions because he was bewitched. Under cross-examination Nunn concluded, 'I do not consider that he had sufficient brain power, under a sudden impulse, to control his actions. He would not consider an action wrong in the same light as a sane person.' Parsey supported Nunn's evidence with regard to 'sudden impulse', noting an example from his own experience at the asylum where a patient was complaining to him about a warder and suddenly attempted to kill him. It was only a day or two after that the patient realized what he had done and was penitent and distressed about it.

The judge was none other than the belligerent Baron Bramwell, who had presided over the trial of William Dove. In between, he had also overseen another case of witch-scratching. In June 1862, an ex-soldier and collar maker, Charles Tilbrook, aged twenty-seven, born and brought up in Shudy Camps, Cambridgeshire, was charged with wounding his grandmother Mary King with intent to murder at the Central Criminal Court. Tilbrook shared lodgings at 31 Charles Street, Westminster, with his grandparents, and one day entered Mary's room and slashed her forehead with a knife or razor and then beat her with a stick. 'I merely intended to draw some of her blood', he told the court, 'and that is the fact of the matter. If she does not work at devilish arts, or witchcraft, I am willing to forfeit my life for hers.' Mary King testified in court and said that her grandson was 'strange in mind—people have said that he is out of his senses'. A plea of insanity was not raised at all on Tilbrook's behalf, though. Bramwell, perhaps with the Dove trial in mind, informed the jury of the laws on the matter of insanity and criminal responsibility, and told them that it was now up to them as to whether Tilbrook knew what he was doing and knew what the consequences would be for his act. The jury took only seconds to find him 'Guilty', Bramwell concurred, and Tilbrook was given a life sentence.[69]

Bramwell became something of a bogey figure in the psychiatric community as he routinely critiqued and dismissed medical expert witnesses and scoffed at the notion of moral insanity. He did not always have his way with the jury, though.[70] In one instance the Shrewsbury surgeon Francis Whitwell wrote to the British Medical Journal to complain of Bramwell's behaviour in court. Whitwell had recently appeared as an expert witness at a murder trial. The defendant was an epileptic, and Whitwell explained to the judge the nature of 'epileptic mania'. Bramwell roundly discredited his statements on the matter and recommended the defendant be hanged. The jury, however, found the defendant 'Not Guilty' on the ground of insanity.[71] Back to Hayward's trial, and Judge Bramwell asked Nunn:

'Supposing anyone had stopped him [Hayward] as he was crossing the road to her and said, "Now, mind, you will be hung if you kill that woman." Do you think he would have attacked her?'

Nunn: 'I do.'

Bramwell: 'I don't'.

In his final address to the jury, Buzzard contended that Hayward was completely under the influence of his delusion 'and therefore not accountable for his actions'. Bramwell complimented Buzzard on his able defence but did not accept the medical argument that Hayward was under the influence of an irresistible sudden impulse and advised the jury that the evidence suggested clear intent to murder. But it took only a few moments for the jury to decide 'Not Guilty on the ground of insanity'. In response, the thwarted Bramwell hoped that something could be done to instruct the people of the village of the foolishness of the belief in witchcraft, and he wondered, acidly, whether the jury might say anything which might have a good effect to that end. The jury made no comment, and the Court adjourned for lunch. Hayward was taken to Broadmoor Criminal Lunatic Asylum on 28 January 1876 to live out the rest of his life. He was one of eleven men admitted that year who had been charged with murder, and he died there fourteen years later in June 1890 from chronic abscesses and dropsy at the age of fifty-nine.[72]

Two years after the Hayward trial, British forensic specialists William Bathurst Woodman and Charles Meymott Tidy continued to defend the category of monomania in their *Handy-book of Forensic Medicine* (1877). 'Whether law-makers or law administrators like it or not', they asserted, 'it is perfectly certain that there is such a thing as monomania.'[73] But the language of monomania started to fall out of use in jurisprudence, though the concept was retained in terms of the diagnosis of 'temporary insanity', which was commonly employed by coroners when bringing suicide verdicts, and was also put forward in some murder trials concerning claims of being under the control of mesmerists and hypnotists. But Juries found 'temporary insanity' equally challenging to comprehend as monomania when it came to criminal trials. In 1891, for instance, William Burns was charged with the attempted murder of his wife. He claimed he was under the influence of mesmerism at the time. The defence argued the case for Burns' temporary insanity due to this belief, but the jury rejected it and instead gave the verdict 'Guilty but Insane'. In other words, Burns general insanity was proven but not the concept of temporary insanity.[74] The related notion of 'irresistible impulse' was equally discredited, with Thomas Stevenson, lecturer on medical jurisprudence, writing in the early 1880s that this doctrine 'and the theory of impulsive insanity have been strained to such a degree as to create in the public mind a distrust of medical evidence'.[75] It was, in essence, a reformulation of the old 'Devil made me do it' defence, and proved equally ineffectual.

Wills and witches

In 1852 the editor of the *American Journal of Insanity* noted how frequently asylum superintendents were called as witnesses in criminal prosecutions, but he could only hazard a guess that they also had 'their full share of subpoenas in civil cases'.[76] To ensure the profession was kept abreast of developments it was decided that henceforth the journal would also report on significant civil as well as criminal trials. Most of the psychiatric discussion occurred in probate cases involving contested wills. The main issue was proof of 'testamentary capacity'—was a person making or changing a will (the testator or testatrix) of sufficiently sound mind at the time? If it could be proven in court that he or she was not, then the will could be annulled. Will disputes were sometimes heard at bench trials that did not have juries and in such instances the expert medical witnesses called by both sides directed their evidence to the presiding judge or bench of judges. But as we shall see, though, decisions were usually determined more by case law than fresh clinical evidence presented in court—and some of the most influential cases in Britain and America involved belief in the supernatural. Because America followed English Common Law, albeit with variations from state to state, a case in either country could set a legal precedent on both sides of the Atlantic.

The rise of the expert medical witness ruffled as many feathers in the civil courts as it did in the criminal courts. Indeed, in the English case of *Waring v Waring* (1848) judicial resistance to psychiatric theory and diagnoses led to a major new principle in probate law that caused much controversy and legal dissatisfaction.[77] The case concerned an 'eccentric' elderly lady who disinherited her brother because she was under the delusion that he had become a Roman Catholic, a faith she detested. The presiding judge was Lord Henry Brougham (1778–1868), an eminent statesman and powerful advocate for law reform. He had no truck with the concept of monomania or partial insanity and took the position that the mind was one and indivisible: one was either insane or not insane, though he did accept that the insane did not always appear or act like they were insane. So, if a testator or testatrix clearly exhibited delusions before and after the making of his or her will then it could be presumed that they were *non compos mentis* during its execution.[78] Brougham's ruling was never accepted in Scottish courts, however, and it was also widely rejected in America where partial insanity was more generally recognized in jurisprudence.[79]

It should come as no surprise that a testator's or testatrix's belief in witchcraft was seized upon as compelling evidence of testamentary incapacity in numerous American probate cases. What is most interesting is how lawyers attempted to counter such claims with what can be called the 'historic witch-believers defence'. You will see what I mean by examining the much-cited case of *Leech vs Leech* heard before the Court of Common Pleas (which had a jury), Philadelphia County, Pennsylvania.[80] It was the first civil case reported by the *American Journal of Insanity* in 1852. Charles Leech died at the age of eighty-three having never married. He had a natural son, however, whom he cut out of his will along with his brother's children, bequeathing the entirety of his estate to another family of his acquaintance. He later wrote another will, though, leaving everything to his son. Numerous witnesses were called on both sides with respect to Leech's mental state. The evidence relied heavily on the fact that Leech believed in witchcraft and had a delusion that somebody wanted to poison him. This was one of the very last cases heard by the well-respected judge Edward King (1794–1873) before his retirement from the judiciary. He had served twenty-seven years as judge for the Pennsylvania Court of Common Pleas, and he took the opportunity to reflect at length on the implications of the case, thereby ensuring its place in future case law on the matter.

King made the point that 'the will of a maniac is good—if made in a lucid interval', which obviously contradicted *Waring v Waring*. With regard to the belief in witchcraft, he was quite clear that such 'eccentricities of conduct' and 'absurd notions' did not invalidate a will if the content of the will had no explicit connection with those opinions or conduct. In other words, there was nothing in Leech's will that was provably related to his belief in witches. King then went on, crucially, to put Leech's idiosyncratic personal beliefs in historical context. Leech was born before the American

Revolution, King observed, a time not so distant from the age of the witch trials, and so his early impressions were formed when 'the belief in witches and witchcraft, still lingered among persons of a much higher social position, and of much better education than himself'. So, in short, the belief in witchcraft could be held as reasonable relative to the time in which it was expressed.[81]

A few years later, the case of *Addington vs Wilson* (1854) followed a similar pattern. This dispute concerned the will of the deceased Francis Stephen, an Indiana farmer and prudent businessman who had lived unhappily with his wife and five children. By the time he had come to make his will his wife had died (an event that he greeted with unconcealed joy) and several of his children had left him due to domestic tensions. He cut those children out of his will, and it was they who instigated the legal proceedings to have it overturned after their father's death. The claim that Stephen was insane at the time of making his will rested principally on his belief in witchcraft. He accused his wife and some of his daughters of being witches and said that 'at her death she [his wife] had left her witch-sticks to her children'.[82] The lawyer defending the will accepted that a monomaniacal belief in witchcraft, or Millerism, could render a person unable to undertake the ordinary transactions of life, but, he argued, this was clearly not the case with Stephen. And then came the 'historic witch-believers defence'. At the time of the witch trials, he said, 'one of the ablest and purest of the judges that have graced the English Bench', namely Lord Chief Justice Hale (1609–1676), had sentenced people to death for the crime of witchcraft. So, if Stephen was insane then *ergo* Hale was insane, and no one past or present considered the great English jurist to have been anything other than of perfect intellect and reason. Once again, the will was upheld. In the 1888 dispute over the will of the witchcraft-believing Eliza Ann Vedder, the lawyer defending the will similarly referred to the 'hundreds more of the greatest and soundest minds which ever existed on earth' who believed in witches, and picked out Martin Luther and John Wesley as examples.[83] If famous historic witch believers were not convincing enough then lawyers could always refer to the King James Bible as an authority on the reality of witches in the distant past—just as people like James Hayward did to justify their abuse of suspected witches in the present. Indeed, if the same arguments had been transposed to the criminal court the lawyers would have been dangerously close to being apologists for egregious offences against innocent people in the name of a belief in supernatural influence.

The issue of witchcraft beliefs for civil courts was of sufficient currency in the 1880s for the eminent American lawyer James Schouler (1839–1920) to include a section on the matter in his *Treatise on the Law of Wills*. He was categorical, based on case law, including the examples mentioned above, that 'the will of one who believes in witchcraft, magic, ghosts, and spectral influences, whether supernatural or only mysterious, is not on that sole account void'.[84] The 'historic witch-believers defence' became rather redundant as the belief in witchcraft became normalized. We can see this prevailing view playing out in *Schildknecht v. Rompf* (1887), heard before the Kentucky Court of Appeals. The will of Conrad Rompf was contested by one of his daughters, Juliana Schildnecht. Rompf had been born into abject poverty in Wetteraukreis, Hessen, Germany, in 1825. We find him and his young family living in Llanelly, Wales, in the 1851 census, where Juliana was born, and then he emigrated with his family to America, settling in Louisville, Kentucky, where he founded a successful restaurant business. Through hard work and business acumen he amassed an estate worth up to $20,000. He died in August 1885 and in his will he left his estate to his wife with the power to divide it up between their numerous children after his death, save for Juliana and a son named George, who were bequeathed only $500 each. At the time of writing his will, Conrad and his wife refused to accept Juliana's marriage to fellow German immigrant Conrad Schildknecht, who was two years older than Conrad, and who they claimed was a bigamist. Juliana contested the will on three counts. First, on the grounds of her father's want of mental capacity; second, her mother's undue influence; and third, that her father held an insane delusion that she was a witch. Both Conrad Rompf and his wife had long been convinced that his mother Elisabetha Klippel practised witchcraft, and when she went to stay with Juliana they suspected she had recruited her to her evil magical arts. It was proven in court, however, that this suspicion had only arisen in Conrad's mind after he had made his will, and, besides, the judge instructed that a belief in witchcraft did not justify the assumption that he was insane.[85]

By the time of the Rompf dispute, a hugely influential piece of English case law was also becoming established as a precedent on both sides of the Atlantic. *Banks v Goodfellow* (1870) concerned John Banks of Keswick, Cumbria, the son of a pencil manufacturer, who died in 1865 aged fifty-three of 'Epilepsy, Insanity and Coma'.[86] He left a number of properties worth around £2000 to his niece, Margaret Banks Goodfellow. The pair had lived together for a time, but she died of consumption in 1867 at the age of twenty. As she was under the age of majority the will was contested by relatives. John clearly suffered from mental illness throughout his adult life. In 1841 he was committed to the private Dunston Lunatic Asylum for a time. He had taken an extreme dislike to a Keswick grocer named Featherstonhaugh Alexander. After the latter's death aged fifty in 1860, Banks began to complain that the dead man followed him about and tried to 'fash' or bother him. Banks' landlady testified that she thought him 'a mad man' who suffered from fits and memory loss, and amongst his strange behaviour, she said, was that 'he used to talk about imps, and say the devil was in his head'. Another of Banks' landladies said that she caught him one night in the chimney. He told her he was trying to catch the Devil. On another occasion he claimed he had killed the Devil with a cream jug.[87] Local boys called him 'crazy John'.

In defence of the will, the lawyer admitted Banks was subject to fits and delusions but resorted to the 'historic witch believers defence', stating that Martin Luther believed in a physical Devil and referred to the legend that Luther had even thrown an inkwell at his Satanic Majesty. More concrete evidence was given, however, namely that Banks was able to manage his business affairs and perfectly knew the extent of his property. Why would he not be able to make his will on a rational basis? Chief Justice Cockburn concluded that the real question was not whether Banks had a mental disorder, indeed, he recognized there was plenty of evidence for his 'general insanity', but whether 'the testator was of [a] sound mind, so as to be capable of making a will'. In other words, a testator could be insane and yet still have testamentary capacity, and on that basis the Banks' will was upheld, the Brougham ruling finally consigned to the bin, and Anglo-American civil case law on the matter enshrined for the next century and a half.[88] The ruling recognized, in effect, what asylum superintendents had been saying from long observation: that many patients diagnosed as insane could be just as lucid, knowing, devious, or conscientious in their everyday lives as those considered mentally healthy.

Of spirits and undue influence

When, in the 1860s, the legal author and judge Isaac Fletcher Redfield (1804–1876) reflected on Edward King's summing-up in *Leech v Leech*, he made a telling remark about recent developments regarding the supernatural.

Rather than refer to the history of witchcraft before the American Revolution, he suggested King 'might have found a readier apology for the "absurd notion" of the testator, in the extensive belief, which now prevails, in the preternatural pretentions of modern spiritualism'.[89] The point was well made, but probate cases concerning the belief in spiritualism were quite different conceptually as well as in terms of the social dynamics involved. In cases concerning witchcraft disputes, living relatives and neighbours, people with rights and free will, were accused of having supernatural powers to cause harm to others. With spiritualism the issue concerned relations with purely spiritual entities whose existence and sentience were a matter of vigorous scientific and cultural debate at the time. Then there was the influence of a third-party—the medium and her relationship with the testator. Mediums joined physicians, lawyers, and clergymen amongst those professionals most suspected of having undue influence over people making their wills.

Spiritualism probate cases usually involved large sums of money and the scale of the trials was sometimes quite remarkable. In the case of Morris Keeler, a prosperous farmer of Moravia, New York State, who died aged eighty-two in May 1886, nearly 100 witnesses were examined at length. Much evidence was given as to Keeler's belief in spiritualism and many anecdotes were given of how he thought they were constantly around, guiding him in his daily labours, gossiping with him, and giving advice. The witnesses included three local physicians who knew him, two of whom had provided certificates that he was of sound mind. Two medical experts on insanity were also called to testify. One was the highly respected Theodore Dimon (1816–1889), Medical Superintendent of the New York State Asylum for Insane Criminals, and the other the psychiatrist Carlos Frederick MacDonald (1845–1926), who would shortly become Professor of Mental Diseases at the Bellevue Hospital Medical College.[90]

By the late nineteenth century, civil case law on spiritualism had become principally concerned with the issue of 'undue influence' rather than insanity per se, though the two were sometimes entwined by plaintiffs' lawyers and had to be teased apart in court.[91] The case of *Thompson v Hawks* (1883), heard before the Indiana Circuit Court, is a good example. John Thompson died in 1877, aged seventy-six, leaving his entire estate to a long-standing family friend Amanda E. Hawks, the wife of a shoemaker, thereby depriving his only child, George Thompson, who was the plaintiff. Hawks had practised as a spiritualist medium for some years, and John Thompson would visit her regularly as she said she could train him to be a medium as well. He came to believe he was in communication with his ex-wives through Hawks' mediumship. There was bad blood between Thompson and his son at the time, and the spirits of his ex-wives repeatedly urged him to ignore him in his will and to 'do well by' Mrs Hawks. He duly did. The plaintiff's lawyer noted that John Thompson had a sister and a niece confined to insane asylums and gave numerous examples of his eccentricities. Others testified, however, that they thought him completely sane. The ruling on the case rested on the basis that a belief in spiritualism was not *ipso facto* an insane delusion, but that a dominating, monomaniacal belief in it offered potential for 'undue influence'. In other words, it was not Thompson's beliefs that rendered him incapable but the influence over him of the medium Hawks due to his beliefs:

> a belief in Spiritualism may justify the setting aside of a will, when it is shown that the testator, through fear, dread or reverence of the spirit with which he believed himself to be in communication, allowed his will and judgement to be overpowered, and in disposing of his property followed implicitly the directions which he believed the spirits gave him.[92]

The ruling in the similar case of *Middleditch v Williams* (1889) was one of the most influential on the matter. It concerned the will of William H. Livingston who died in Newark, New Jersey, in February 1888.[93] His wife had died a couple of years earlier and since then he had lived with his young daughter and his mother-in-law, Marie C. Williams. Livingston began to consult a spirit medium residing in Forty-Sixth Street, New York, and came to be convinced that he was in contact with his deceased wife. His wife's spirit apparently, communicating through the medium, urged him repeatedly to make his will and leave all his estate to her mother Marie, which is what he did. Marie also attended some of the séances. The case was heard by Judge Van Vleet, who clearly suspected that Marie and the medium had conspired to dupe Livingston, but neither were called to give evidence. In light of this lack of testamentary evidence for undue influence, the court upheld the will on the ruling that a belief in having communication with spirits of the dead was not an insane delusion. George Helm Yeaman (1829–1908), politician, lecturer on constitutional law, and president of the Medico-Legal Society of New York, found the Middleditch ruling troubling. He believed that if the rule gained precedence, it would encourage unscrupulous, avaricious mediums: 'How many other families are yet to be victimised in the same way?'[94]

Yeaman also highlighted a profound metaphysical issue that the courts were very reluctant to address. If it was tacitly accepted in law that the spirits of the dead could or did communicate with the living, then would the law have to recognize that not only mediums but also the spirit world could exercise undue influence? Yeaman noted sarcastically that the Constitution did not yet provide for spirit-voting in law, and likewise the statutes did not recognize spirit will-making. 'Let them devise their own property, if they have any, and send their wills in for probate when they die', he suggested; 'though their dying might shake the faith of some who now consult them.'[95] Lawyer Ardemus Stewart was one of the few others to give thought to this thorny matter in 1892. Up to that point, he noted, the question of whether the spirits alone, and not the medium, could be determined as having undue influence on a testator had never yet been raised properly. 'It has been either tacitly or expressly assumed that it is in all respects similar to that of human beings', observed Stewart, 'to be treated by the same rules and regarded as mere advice, or as undue influence, according to the relation of the medium to the testator.' [96]

There was a more serious legal issue underpinning these musings because decisions made about the nature of spiritualism in the civil courts were essentially in contradiction to those made in the criminal courts. The point was first raised by Isaac Redfield in response to the probate case of *Robinson v Adams* (1874), heard before the Supreme Judicial Court of Maine. The case concerned the will of the late Mary W. Green, of Topsham, who had made provisions in her will following advice from her husband's spirit. She also believed her son-in-law was controlled by devils and had supernatural influence over his wife, and so she left him out of her will. Redfield observed that if Mrs Green had killed her son-in-law on the advice of the spirits there would not be the slightest doubt that a jury would consider her insane. So why was she not treated as insane when it came to deciding her probate?[97] Ardemus Stewart made a similar point when he questioned why, when, criminal law was pretty clear that mediums taking money for communicating with spirits were guilty of either fraud or false pretences, the civil courts did not think the criminality of mediumship an issue in probate decisions. 'The fact that a different view is taken by the two branches of the judiciary is an anomaly, and one that ought to be corrected', he stated. The only way to correct this situation was for the civil courts to adopt the sceptical position of the criminal law and set aside any will that was drawn up under the supposed influence of spiritualist communications as an instance of fraud.[98] And there is evidence that probate disputes in the early twentieth century focussed more on the issue of fraudulency, nudging out the hazier legal status of 'undue influence' let alone the issue of insanity.[99]

★   ★   ★

Some sixty years or so after psychiatrists entered centre stage in the civil and criminal courts their lasting influence on jurisprudence was decidedly mixed, at least in terms of how supernatural beliefs were considered to influence human behaviour and free will. Juries and judges had to unpick what sorts of supernatural notions and convictions were irrational in relation to societal norms at any given period. Faced with lawyerly casuistry, a psychiatric language that was alien to many jurors, and a judiciary that liked to deal with simple certainties about human behaviour, it is not surprising that a rather different picture of mental pathology emerged from verdicts. The debates and decisions coming out of the courts, and the inconsistencies between civil and criminal case law, fogged the clarity of the psychiatrists' vision of societal progress across the centuries. The dominant educated view was that the greater the distance in time from the witch trials the more the witch believer could be categorized as of unsound mind. As we have seen, though, some lawyers tried to normalize the belief in witchcraft. The timeline of intellectual progress was scrambled. If a seventeenth-century judge and a nineteenth-century labourer believed the same thing then there 'was nothing to see here, move along'. Both lawyer and labourer could also hold up the Bible as support for their convictions. Legal decisions over spiritualism further shifted the normal time paradigm. The greater the distance from the table-rapping days of the early 1850s the less easy it was to consider spiritualists insane in a legal sense because of the movement's increasing embrace by intellectual and religious adherents. By the twentieth century, Spiritualism had become so well established as a *faith*, and not just as a personal belief and practice, that it became fiendishly difficult to argue its belief system should be pathologized in contrast to the other diverse religious denominations that were followed by people of all social classes, cultures, and education.[100]

By the early twentieth century the rule of 'common sense' dominated in the courts. The medical experts needed to be heard but juries and benches exercised their judgement within the compass of their own general knowledge. This did not mean that insanity defences were rarely accepted. Between 1910 and 1919, for instance, thirty-two percent of convicted murderers in England were found 'guilty but insane'.[101] But the attempt by many early psychiatrists to locate supernatural beliefs within the realm of the pathological gained little traction. The supernatural and superstition could be found reasonable without being rational, and belief in them was culturally relative rather than medically or historically determined. Whether devils, witches, and spirits were delusions, caused by insanity or not, became largely irrelevant in legal terms.

PART II

Inner lives

Introduction

It is possible to write the history of a period from the delusions of the patients admitted into asylums.

(Thomas Aitken, Superintendent of the Inverness District Lunatic Asylum, 1868)

Thomas Aitken was inspired to write the statement above after reading Esquirol's suggestion in 1816 that he could compile a full history of the French Revolution from the fears and delusions of his patients alone. There were numerous French asylum patients who claimed they were the Emperor Napoleon, for instance, some of whom hanged around imperial residences before being hauled away by the police. Esquirol never got round to writing such a history, but the sentiment was prescient.[1] Recent psychiatric and ethnographic research has shown how hallucinations, whether pathological or not, are profoundly shaped by the cultural worlds that different people share at any given period.[2] The second half of this book is not about me attempting to retrospectively diagnose people with the hindsight of another century of neuroscience, though. The ensuing chapters are concerned with exploring why some patients in English and Scottish asylums believed what they did in relation to the times in which they lived. It also aims to normalize the varied supernatural beliefs expressed by patients. Yes, the confused and jumbled beliefs, delusions, and hallucinations of some patients were the unique product of individual pathologies, but many were shaped by broad societal concerns and cultural motifs. I do not want these people to be just statistics and anonymous. Patient names and appropriate personal details are provided where possible. I try to trace them in other records, just as I would any other person I seek to understand when studying the past. The attempt to capture the 'voices of the poor' from the records has long been an aim of social historians, using criminal, welfare, parish, and newspaper archives. We catch valuable glimpses of the everyday life, beliefs, and emotions of ordinary people from such documents, but few sources take us so deep into the intimate and collective psychical realms of the nineteenth and early twentieth centuries as the asylum records. They provide a unique path into popular mentalities, into inner lives steeped in the ideas and imagery of folklore and faith which helped people make sense of the ever-changing world around them.[3]

Reading the records

Despite the sensational, fictional portrayal of insane people dragged off to a Gothically dark asylum against their will (which did happen for a few), the process was mundane, highly bureaucratic, and time consuming.[4] Most of the asylum records used in this half of the book date from the 1870s onward by which time the process of admission was set in law by the Lunatic Asylums Act (1853) and subsequent amendment legislation for England and Wales, while the separate legal processes in Ireland and Scotland were similar in nature.[5] Two types of official document were required for someone to be admitted to a private or public asylum. One was the Certificate of Insanity. For private patients two Certificates were required based on personal examinations by two physicians, surgeons, or apothecaries who were not related or professionally involved with each other, and they had to be conducted within seven days prior to admission. Information was also garnered from third parties who knew the patient. For pauper patients only one such Certificate was required, signed by a physician or Poor Law medical officer.

A survey of Certificates for Buckinghamshire County Pauper Lunatic Asylum reveals that some 56 per cent of men and 68 per cent of women were described as exhibiting delusions.[6] The problem for the asylum superintendents was that general practitioners, Poor Law officers, and the families of the certified were obviously rarely trained in the discipline of psychiatry and often failed to argue convincingly why the delusions were caused by insanity. In the 1859 annual report for the Derbyshire County Pauper Lunatic Asylum, the superintendent complained bitterly about how badly Certificates were being completed and the lack of sufficient information they provided. He and the asylum clerk were wasting a lot of time in further correspondence. They did not want to turn any patient away at the door, and 'yet by receiving him into the Asylum upon such imperfect Certificates your Physician incurs great legal peril'. Similar concerns were expressed a year later by John Bucknill at the Devon County Asylum. It was causing him a lot of bother. Sometimes the Certificates contained too much information irrelevant to the diagnosis of insanity. Bucknill gave the sardonic example that if a man said he was the Emperor of China there was no need for the doctors 'to state that he wore a chintz dressing gown of a willow plate pattern'. Sometimes not enough care was given as to whether the information on the Certificate distinguished between hard evidence of insane actions and delusions, and beliefs and behaviour that may have been the product of mere eccentricity. The Commissioners in Lunacy advised that it was insufficient to merely state the existence of a delusion; the general practitioners had to describe its nature. Bucknill advised that they state clearly, 'I know [it] to be a delusion', though this was unnecessary when the delusion was self-evidently pathological. Bucknill gave the example of a Certificate that he had received which stated clearly that the patient believed, 'that the devil comes through the roof of the building, and catches him by the throat, and pulls him about'.[7]

A document known as a Reception Order was also needed for admission to an asylum. It required basic information about the person who was considered to be of 'unsound mind', such as whether they were subject to epilepsy or suicidal. A statement on the 'supposed cause' and 'factors indicating insanity' were essential. For private admissions the Order was usually completed by the nearest relative.[8] The procedure for paupers was rather different again. First the medical officer for the district had to be informed, and then he had to notify the poor law Relieving Officer or Overseers of the Poor. The Relieving Officer then had to notify the local magistrate within three days to deal with the case. Normally the patient would then be brought before the magistrate or bench of magistrates, but if that was not possible then the order could be completed by a clergyman in conjunction with the Relieving Officer in the home of the patient or some other suitable place. Information on the alleged insanity was often based on the evidence and experiences of the family, but also sometimes on the word of friends, neighbours, and employers of the patient. As with Certificates there were also complaints about the quality of information provided in the Orders. As Lyttleton S. Winslow remarked in his *Manual of Lunacy* (1874), the most important statement was the 'supposed cause', but 'great difficulty often exists in obtaining any information on this point from the patient's friends; the answer given to the question is, that no cause can be assigned, or that the cause is known. It rarely happens that a distinct cause cannot be discovered, although the friends object to mention it in the statement.'[9] The 1890 Lunacy Law Amendment Act tightened the process with clergymen and poor law officers no longer able to sign off documents. The Reception Orders can provide insight into lay opinion, and the phrasing 'supposed' suggests that whatever was reported was not to be taken as a medically supported diagnosis. A study of Orders for the Hampshire County Lunatic Asylum shows, for instance, that lay informants tended to emphasize personal histories, self-harm, and unacceptable 'mad' or violent behaviour, noting specific threats and incidents, rather than aligning evidence with recognized categories such as mania, melancholia, or monomania.[10]

Much of the evidence in the ensuing chapters comes from casebooks. It was only with the Lunacy Act of 1845 that casebooks became compulsory in English and Welsh asylums, while in nineteenth-century Scotland there was a similar process of recording despite the lack of statutory requirements.[11] Details from the Reception Orders and Certificates were usually copied onto the first couple of pages of a patient's notes and then updates were added as to his or her progress or lack of it, their physical condition, and the continuation or disappearance of the delusions recorded on admittance. Sometimes the treatment or type of drugs that had been administered are mentioned. Such details might run on for several pages depending on the length of stay, the type of mental illness, and the assiduousness of the assistant medical officers who kept them updated. Occasionally other materials such as newspaper clippings, photographs, or letters were included along with the case notes. For this book, casebooks have been searched extensively for the Scottish Crichton Royal Hospital, Dumfries, and four northern English asylums, namely, Manchester's Prestwich Asylum, South Yorkshire Asylum in Sheffield, Lancaster Moor Asylum, and Parkside Asylum in Macclesfield.[12] Examples have also been drawn from published case notes by asylum superintendents and more limited archive searches in other asylum casebooks. This has brought together the experience of several thousand individuals from the mid nineteenth to the early twentieth centuries. Newspapers, court records, and the censuses have also been used to provide further details for select cases.

These documents admittedly provide little of the direct voice of the patients themselves. Everything was mediated by officialdom. The case notes were not written for historians or medical posterity but were produced primarily for immediate administrative purposes to prove that good practice was evident in the care of the insane.[13] The idiom and language of the patients comes through in glimpses, though. Patient swearing and foul language were rarely recorded verbatim, for example, but some medical assistants would occasionally mention dialect words, expressions, and phrases and put them in quote marks.

Those documents written by patients also have their interpretative challenges. Published autobiographical accounts of the experience of mental illness in the period certainly provide insights, though they were usually written after recovery, and can be prone to retrospective revision and dramatic license. They rarely represent the voices of pauper patients either.[14] Over the ensuing chapters we will come across a few examples of letters written by patients in which they explain their ideas and emotions.[15] Letters to and from patients survive in small numbers because they were often intercepted, vetted, and sometimes vetoed by superintendents, and while a few were inserted into casebooks most of those retained do not survive as they were dismissed as merely 'insane literature'. One such letter written to her doctor by a patient in the Hampshire County Lunatic Asylum who claimed she had a 'call from God', was described, for instance, as 'incoherent and unintelligible & entirely on the subject of religion'.[16] Those that do survive were quite often letters written to asylum staff. Superintendents would sometimes reproduce them in their research articles printed in psychiatric journals and in their manuals and textbooks as illustrative of certain aspects of insanity.

Life in the asylum

Much has been written on the workings of the asylum and asylum life, and so I give only a brief overview here to ensure that perceptions of asylums as stereotypically terrible places governed by cruel, sinister medical staff are challenged. Abuses obviously took place, just as we have seen in care homes today, and examples of cynicism and harshness toward patients can be found, but asylums could be places of compassion and sensitivity, with staff driven by the earnest desire to help patients and improve the wellbeing of society. The idea of being locked up for life was also wide of the mark, though high-profile notorious cases concerning the elite in society are well known. It has been estimated from various private and public asylum studies that across the nineteenth century some 40–60 per cent of patients stayed less than twelve months, and that by the end of the century that turnover accelerated with two-thirds of patients spending less than two years.[17] Every individual's experience was different of course. Many stayed for only a few weeks before being deemed recovered, some had repeat short-term stays over years, while a small percentage spent decades and died in the asylum. Some were in such an advanced state of physical as well as mental illness that they perished within months of admission despite good care. In cases involving delusions, being diagnosed as 'recovered', and therefore released, did not necessarily mean a patient had renounced the beliefs and convictions that led them to be admitted in the first place, only that their behaviour and health had ameliorated sufficiently that they were deemed fit to return to their families and communities. The beliefs expressed by patients at any point were not necessarily fixed, and delusions could change, evolve, intensify, or disappear during a stay in the asylum and after.

As to the staff who interacted with the patients on a daily basis, the medical superintendent, who was in overall charge of running the asylum, was supported by one or more assistant medical officers who constantly monitored the health of patients, administered therapies and drugs, filled in the casebooks, and managed the visits of the relations and friends of patients. Then there was a matron and assistant matron in charge of the nurses, and an army of male and female attendants who kept order and discipline on the wards night and day, served food, reported patient behaviour to the doctors, and supervised patients in the workshops, on the farm, and during leisure activities. Sympathy and watchfulness were considered ideal qualities for nurses and attendants.[18] Cooks, kitchen maids, house servants, laundresses, and craftsmen made up the rest of the support workforce. Each asylum also had a chaplain, usually non-resident, to minister to patients' spiritual needs.

The daily life of patients was governed by the various activities put in place to improve patient health and to police behaviour. Keeping the mind and body active was considered the best treatment. The more the patient was occupied with positive or productive occupation the less time they had for morbid introspection. Many pauper asylums had their own farms to provide both fresh food but also outdoor manual occupation. For male patients there were numerous craft activities from bookbinding to carpentry that also had an economic value for the asylum, while female patients were employed in needlework, cleaning, and cooking, contributing to the upkeep of the institution. Regular indoor and outdoor leisure activities were organized throughout the year, from sports events to patient orchestras and picnics, and even day trips.

Beyond the simple therapeutic effects of work, play, and diet, there were a range of medical treatments that attracted debate and criticism at the time. We saw in a previous chapter that the practice of cold and warm bathing was not without its controversies. Phlebotomy or bleeding was also practised on patients. With its origins in humoural theory, this had been a widespread practice for the cure of fevers and inflammations up until the mid nineteenth century. As Bucknill and Tuke put it, though, 'we have never used the lancet in the treatment of Insanity'.[19] In other words, they did not cut arteries and veins to cause blood loss. Instead, the application of leeches to the temples continued as an asylum practice to remove blood, as did the old practice of cupping to the nape of the neck. This involved applying a glass vessel and creating a vacuum within it, thereby expanding the blood vessels and drawing blood to the cupped area.

The most controversial aspect of asylum therapy concerned the use of drugs. Opiates had long been administered. The commercial production of morphine began in the 1820s, and with the invention of the hypodermic syringe in the 1850s it became widely used in asylum medicine, though there was much debate about its efficacy on different types of insanity. Other drugs from plant extracts, such as hyoscyamus or henbane, were considered by some asylum doctors as milder but safer narcotics. Digitalis and cannabis were used as sedatives. Ergot, with its lysergic acid content, continued to be prescribed by some for treating mania, as was conium or hemlock. One wonders whether such psychoactive drugs enhanced the hallucinatory supernatural experiences of some patients. It is ironic that the likes of henbane and hemlock were cited in early modern texts as constituents in witches' supposed flying unguents. Then came the artificial compounds. From the 1860s, bromide of potassium was used widely as a sedative, relaxant, and anti-epileptic in asylum medicine, with Clouston describing it as 'at the very head of the list of neurotic drugs'.[20] It was a white crystalline salt that dissolved easily in water for administering to patients. Around the same time chloral hydrate was also becoming a widespread asylum sedative and anti-anxiolytic. Then there were the usual purgatives, emetics, and tonics used for easing general physical conditions.

Letters of complaint from patients and their families were not unusual. Some were based on delusions of being poisoned or persecuted by asylum staff, for example, while others involved genuine issues about treatment. The dark side of asylum care mostly concerned aspects of coercion and control, such as the use of restraints, both chemical and physical. Though little talked about in psychiatric literature, straightjackets were widely employed to restrain extremely violent or self-harming patients, though their application was usually only recommended for a few hours at a time. Force feeding was also practised on patients who obdurately refused to eat, though as John Bucknill observed of his practice at the Devon County Asylum, for every patient force-fed by a tube there were twenty who would not or could not eat who were fed by a spoon, pap-boat, or other less invasive means.[21] Bucknill and Tuke made the observation regarding the use of drugs that, 'it may not always be easy to draw a line of strict demarcation between the medical treatment of the insane, and measures adopted for their discipline and control'.[22] They had in mind the use of tartrate of antimony or tartar emetic, for instance, which caused nausea and thereby suppressed violent behaviour. Patent medicines based on it were used in working class households to 'quieten' violent drunken husbands. By the end of the century there were growing complaints from some psychiatrists that the much-lauded demise of mechanical restraints in asylums had been replaced with the equally problematic use of chemical restraints in the form of sedatives.[23]

★   ★   ★

We now move from the mundanity of asylum life to the fantastical. The asylum has often been researched as a political, economic, and administrative institution, and has been framed by some as an instrument of authoritarianism and social control. Over the ensuing chapters the asylum will be cast in a different light, as an extraordinary cultural space where under one roof prophets, messiahs, the bewitched, and the haunted, wrestled with angels, devils, imps, and witches. It was a place filled with talk of infernal machines, unseen agents, and sinister electrical forces. The asylum as a place of enchantment was full of anguish and extasy, terror and enlightenment. Whether seriously ill and deluded, or sane and lucid in their beliefs and imaginings, patients' experiences were rooted in the mental worlds of wider society. We must not think of their voices as the collective delusions of the madhouse but as representative of the myriad individual fears, anxieties, and expressions of a country undergoing extraordinary transformations. To glimpse their thoughts is to be privileged with a unique insight into history. Let us now open the door into their inner lives.

5

Between Heaven and Hell

She says she has frequently seen angels & they have beckoned to her. She
has also seen imps & Jesus Christ.

(Case notes of Mary Ann Anleyark, Prestwich Asylum)[1]

A survey of recent studies of nineteenth-century asylums shows that
cases involving religious convictions constituted no more than ten
percent or so of 'moral causes' of insanity in our period, which was significantly lower than cases attributed to alcoholism, for example. As a total of
the asylum population that figure drops several percentage points. So, religion was a small but not insignificant preoccupation.[2] But such statistics tell
us very little really and saying anything concrete about the relationship
between specific religions and insanity is fraught with problems. We saw
that earlier in the book. The religious notions and beliefs expressed by individual asylum patients were sometimes idiosyncratic and based on personal
experiences, fears, and preoccupations. Just because some casebooks stated
the official faith of their patients tells us nothing about their private religious influences. Someone recorded as Church of England could have been
attending Spiritualist seances. A patient listed as a Methodist could have
been inspired by evangelical revival meetings. A Catholic might have been
experiencing profound doubts about his or her faith. We just do not know.
Some asylums did not list religious affiliation at all for long periods; all the
more reason not to try and extrapolate much from patient statistics. What
we can do is to try and make sense of what patients believed and said rather
than what the official documentation stated simply about their faith. Once
you have read hundreds of casebook notes it is clear that the individual
hallucinations, delusions, anxieties, and dreams of asylum patients often

reflected the social and religious environment at the time as well as deep-seated fears of salvation and damnation. Broad differences between the theologies of Catholicism and Protestantism reveal themselves in some respects, but both faiths were undergoing change, adaptation, and expansion in the age of the asylum.

The relationship between religion and culture is never static, and the period from the late eighteenth to the early twentieth century in Britain saw a flourishing of religious diversity and reformulation.[3] Nonconformist churches and chapels proliferated. New evangelical movements, such as Primitive Methodism and the Christadelphians, preached the message of a providential world in which miracles still occurred and the Devil was an ever-present threat to the sinner. Prophets raised their heads every now and again and local and national evangelical revivals cropped up across the period, demonstrating the growing influence of American Protestantism on this side of the Atlantic. A so-called 'Crisis of Faith' in the Anglican Church led to soul-searching about the material and spiritual nature of devotion as church attendance dwindled slowly but surely. The move towards Catholic emancipation, culminating in the Roman Catholic Relief Act of 1829, boosted the profile and influence of Catholicism. It is not surprising, then, that the 1851 Census of Religious Worship revealed a religious environment markedly different from a century before, albeit one overwhelmingly Christian—though over fifty synagogues were also recorded.

Following the Irish Famine, huge numbers of Irish immigrants settled in towns across the northwest, swelling the already large number of pauper lunatics in the region, which during the second half of the century was second only in number to those in the old populous county of Middlesex. By 1874 over a quarter of the patients at Prestwich Asylum, Manchester, were Irish, including many recent arrivals. A decade later, Lancaster Asylum was reporting the same ratio amongst its patients.[4] The medical superin- tendent at Rainhill Asylum observed in his annual report for 1870 that with a large second generation of Irish in Liverpool growing up, Irish admissions to the asylum did not reflect fully the Irishness of its patient population, many of whom were 'essentially Irish in everything but their accidental birthplace'.[5] Not all first- and second-generation Irish immigrants were Catholics, of course, but most were. Look more widely and other develop- ments emerge during the second half of the century. There was a growing middle-class interest in Eastern religions and mystical traditions, particularly Hinduism and Buddhism, which was expressed in the foundation of the

Theosophical movement created by Russian immigrant Helena Blavatsky in the 1870s. Britain became one of its main centres, and by the early twentieth century it had a membership of over 20,000 worldwide. In the same period Spiritualism became an organized religion and not just a mediumistic practice. By 1914 there were around 145 worshipping spiritualist groups in the Spiritualist National Union, and the Union did not represent all such communities of faith.[6] Most such societies did not have their own churches until the 1920s, so they would hold their Sunday worship in rented halls and other venues.

The age of the asylum also coincided with what has been described as the 'feminization' of both Catholicism and Protestantism in western Europe, with women playing a more substantial organizational and leadership role. The extent of this shift is more nuanced than it has sometimes been argued, but there was a large increase in the number of convents, sisters, and female religious communities in Catholic Europe, while grassroots evangelical Protestant revivals and organizations, such as the Salvation Army, provided environments in which women preachers and instructors could establish themselves and act as role models.[7] The extent to which these broad, gender developments in religious cultures is mirrored in the beliefs of women patients is difficult to calibrate but what the casebooks do reveal is that numerous poor Catholic and Protestant women assumed for themselves a sense of religious empowerment and entitlement that adds a new perspective on women's religious identity in the period.

Dealing with the religious

Before we delve into the inner lives of asylum patients and their intimate thoughts, there are a few general issues to consider regarding the way in which British asylum superintendents treated and understood those in their care who expressed deep, emotional religious convictions. William G. Davies, the chaplain at the Joint Counties Lunatic Asylum, Abergavenny, was far from being a lone voice when he observed in his first annual report of 1854 that when patients were insane on a religious point there was no point trying to dispel their delusions. Attempting to do so 'may be hurtful rather than otherwise' by over-exciting the patient, he said.[8] Henry Maudsley agreed. Contradicting their claims or arguing against them was futile, he thought, 'their faces then flush, their eyes sparkle, they become passionately energetic and denunciatory and perhaps actually incoherent in their language, and it may be some time before they forgive the offence done to their dignity'. Besides, the more articulate could respond with clever arguments, such as one patient who believed he was Jesus Christ. When told that this was impossible because Christ was in Heaven, he replied 'Heaven is wherever I am'.[9] Despite their lofty pretensions and divine proclamations, W. Bevan Lewis at the West Riding Asylum observed that such religious 'monomaniacs' were usually easy to deal with, 'requiring only tact upon the part of the nurse to transform them into most useful and willing helping hands at various employments'. He wrote with some dry amusement that, at the time of his writing, there was in the West Riding Asylum a self-proclaimed patriarch and delegate of God working in the asylum's bookbinder's shop, the Empress of the biblical Mount Hermon trimming patients' bonnets in the workroom, and the 'Saviour of Mankind' taking an active role in the domestic arrangements of her ward.[10]

Although there had long been an assumed connection between religion and epilepsy, and early psychiatrists played their game of retrospectively diagnosing famous religious leaders from the past as epileptics, it was during the second half of the nineteenth century that concerted studies of asylum patients across Europe led to what was thought to be firm clinical evidence for the nature of the relationship. The Italian psychiatrist Enrico Toselli studied the religious delirium and trance-like states experienced by his epileptic patients during which they said they received divine orders from God or the Virgin. We will shortly see various examples of this from England and Scotland. Adolph Kühn at the Moringen House of Correction, Germany, closely observed several such patients and suggested that their bouts of religious hallucination were a substitute for ordinary epileptic attacks. James Howden, Superintendent at the Montrose Royal Lunatic Asylum, wrote an article on the subject in which he clarified that there were no forms of religious insanity peculiar to epileptics, but that their 'craving for sympathy' manifested itself particularly in delusions of religious succour and communication.[11] By the mid 1880s, Maudsley felt absolutely confident to conclude that epileptics were particularly prone to religious delusions. 'Very dangerous beings too they sometimes are in consequences of their hallucinations', he stated. He gave the example of an epileptic labourer who worked at Chatham Dockyards who killed a fellow worker. The crime seemed motiveless, but while in the criminal lunatic asylum he said that he had received the Holy Ghost at the time, and that 'it came to him like a flash of light and that his own eyes had been take out, and other eyes, like balls of fire, substituted for them'.[12] Research on the manifestation of religious experiences during epileptic episodes continues today, though the issue remains contentious.[13] There was nothing in the hallucinations, delusions or convictions of the patient notes I have seen that was exclusive epileptic in nature, and I make no connection.

A final observation concerns the borderland between dreams and hallucinations. This was a considerable area of debate in early psychiatry that impacted significantly on notions of religious insanity. Some argued that hallucinations in a waking condition and those in dream states were essentially the same. In the 1840s Alexandre Brière de Boismont and others set about destroying this notion, for, as Boismont said, 'If this be admitted, the result would be that none would escape insanity, since those whom it would spare during the day would be attacked in the night.' He gave the example of ghosts. Seeing ghosts in dreams rarely caused any excitement or surprise, whereas they did in waking apparitions. Boismont accepted, though, that dreams could be pathological and precede bouts of mental alienation, while hallucinations during sleep could provide 'valuable' information about the nature of an individual's insanity. Maurice Macario elaborated on this aspect, suggesting that different types of insanity shaped the type of dreams, so the dreams of the melancholic were sad and depressing and those of the religious monomaniac were exciting.[14] Another key observation made by various psychiatrists was that dreams merged with waking hallucinations in the insane, and, crucially, the patient was unable to separate at all the two delusionary states.[15] John Thompson Dickson, medical superintendent at St. Luke's Hospital, provided a notional religious example from his experience:

> If a person has a dream in which the impression, that it is the Divine will that he shall throw his children out of the window, becomes imprinted upon his brain, he is not necessarily mad; his reasoning power on waking may be sufficient to correct the impression, and as long as this is so he is sane. If, on the other hand, he cannot correct the impression but proceeds to commit the homicide in consequence of a belief in a Divine authority for the act, he cannot be considered other than mad.[16]

These were the general views of the profession until the advent of psychoanalysis reconfigured how dreams were to be understood.

What is most important to note here is that some of our asylum patients were perfectly clear that their divine communications and revelations occurred in their dreams as distinct from waking delusions. The patients knew they were dreaming but ascribed agency and meaning to their dreams. William Bradshaw, aged twenty-three, admitted to South Yorkshire Asylum with mania and epilepsy, was subject to excited fits but he saw Jesus Christ only in his dreams. John McNee, forty-one, believed that God controlled his life through his dreams.[17] Other dreams were taken as premonitions. The records for Ann Wolf note, 'Says that God comes to her in a vision to warn her when there is danger... Says she is warned in her dreams if her children are about to do anything wrong.'[18] A woman aged twenty-seven in the Somerset County Asylum, who had no family history of insanity, 'dreamt that the world was about to come to an end; next day there was a thunder storm; she believed her dream was about being fulfilled, and she became at once insane and violent; said her soul was lost, and prayed fervently'. She recovered after eighteen months but sadly had a relapse seven years later. In Prestwich Aslyum Margaret Bartlett had a similar experience, telling a medical attendant that 'she knew her soul was lost by dreams... [she] weeps over the loss of her soul'.[19] Shift focus from psychiatric debate to cultural experience, and such notions fitted a normalized way of understanding the meanings of the mind in *every night* experience rather than everyday experience. Dream premonitions of murders were vibrant in popular culture, cheap dream interpretation books sold in their tens of thousands, spiritualist literature frequently reported on recent examples of prophetic dreams, and mystical and evangelical groups promoted the notion of divine inspiration through dreams.[20]

Religious persecution

Fears of religious conspiracies had long fuelled popular concerns about the enemy within. The Gordon Riots in London in 1780 stand out as a good example of English suspicion of Catholics, with a riotous orgy of destruction destroying the homes and places of worship of the capital's Catholic population. In nineteenth-century France old conspiracy theories about the secret activities of the Jesuits flourished and were imbibed across the social spectrum. They were portrayed as a quasi-secret fraternity operating outside of official state and church authority. Fears of their unseen agency were quite evident in the French asylum population.[21] While Jesuit conspiracy theories also circulated in Britain, and scheming Jesuits were represented in villainous terms in popular fiction, I have not come across any examples from English asylum case books.[22] There were, though, a few fears expressed of being forcibly converted to Catholicism. In 1908, for example, Caroline Furby told a doctor at Prestwich Asylum that the Virgin Mary was plotting along with an asylum attendant named Roche to convert her to Catholicism, and at Lancaster Moor Sarah Ann Bourke, whose religion was listed as Church of England, claimed she was 'haunted by Catholic priests'. Mary Ann O'Neill, twenty-nine, complained in 1910 that 'Roman Catholics' had covered her body with electric wires by means of which they controlled her every actions.[23] But, in Britain, concerns of mystical conspiracy and coercion were mostly focused on the Freemasons and Spiritualists.

By the second half of the nineteenth century Freemasonry had become woven into the fabric of urban civic society in Britain with membership drawn from the aristocracy and middle classes. A few of its members were certainly interested in the esoteric and were practicing occultists, but otherwise Freemasonry was, by and large, a sober fraternity of male professionals who officiated at foundation ceremonies for churches, chapels, and civic buildings.[24] Yet there had always been an element of suspicion about their secrecy that could lead, in extreme cases, to diagnoses of monomania. James Cowles Prichard, writing in 1835, knew a university professor who was sane in all respects other than his conviction that all the Freemasons had entered into a league against him.[25] During the mid nineteenth century vocal attacks on Freemasonry as an unseen hand, and enemy within, were mostly from the Catholic Church in Ireland. On 26 December 1871, for instance, a co-ordinated series of talks were arranged in Catholic chapels across Limerick, which were described by the *Belfast Weekly News* as a 'crusade against Freemasonry'. Speakers preached that Freemasonry was an 'institution devised by Satan, and doing day-to-day Satan's work'.[26] It may have been the influence of such pulpit harangues linking Freemasonry with devilish works that led to Helen Shaw being taken to the Crichton Hospital in 1876. Her medical certificate stated that she was convinced 'three men are trying to make a freemason out of her and that she often sees them on the tree at the back door and that they use the Black Art and throw imps at her, which produce peculiar sensations on her body as if she were squeezed or pricked with pins'.[27] During the second half of the nineteenth century the Papal invective really stepped up a gear. Pope Pius IX and Pope Leo XIII clocked up over 2000 denunciations in their papers and speeches.[28] Public consciousness of these Church accusations really penetrated when, in 1884, Leo XIII produced an Encyclical letter denouncing Freemasonry which was reported in the British press. It stood accused of promoting the denial of God that ultimately led to Communism, Socialism, and social subversion. All bishops were required to unmask Freemasonry in all its aspects.[29] There followed a flourishing of anti-masonic organizations, literature, and international congresses that influenced perceptions beyond the Catholic world.

The 1890s saw lurid accusations emerge in France that the satanic nature of the Freemasons was not just metaphorical. The claims originated with a journalist who wrote under the name Léo Taxil. He claimed to have evidence that Freemasons worshipped the Devil in rituals and pacts. It was all a toxic hoax to mock the Church, however, but served to further cement suspicions of conspiracy. The cases from the English and Scottish asylums from the 1880s do not suggest that persecutorial concerns regarding the Freemasons were influenced much by such satanic associations, though, and were, instead, jumbled with other religious delusions. A 21-year-old Jewish clerk and art student from Manchester believed Christ had revealed many things to him in 1893 but also worried that his semen had been removed by means of freemasonry. In 1908 Alfred Liddell, a 45-year-old Manchester accountant and Baptist, was also worried: 'he speaks in a very incoherent manner about Freemasonry, Druidism, the government & Manchester Corporation...he says by the aid of the "Mystic Light" he is able to see further into things than other people'. Charles Purdy, aged twenty-five, believed in 1884 that the Freemasons were trying to poison him 'to prevent him disclosing secrets revealed by God to him'.[30]

Patients felt threatened by spiritualists in two main ways. One was the spiritualist as unseen agent and the other was Spiritualism as the faceless conspiratorial organization. The two were sometimes mixed up in patients' paranoia. In 1877 Walter Wild, aged twenty-five, thought he was under the influence of three spiritualists who made him so ill he was 'a living corpse'. Amelia Collins, aged twenty-six, believed in 1883 that somebody was trying to 'make a spiritualist of her' and this had also caused her heart disease, while several decades later Annie Smith, thirty-eight, felt impelled by spiritualism to slash her own throat.[31] A 49-year-old servant woman diagnosed with mania in the Royal Edinburgh Asylum wrote in a letter about the 'Torturer of Spiritualism' who tormented her every minute of the day: 'If I am not taken out soon I will be found dead with the Tortures of Spiritualism...God help Me I am a Poor Persecuted Woman by Brutes of Men.'[32] Cinnamon May, a migrant from Belfast, and a Presbyterian, came to believe in 1882 that all the 'working class in Barrow' were collectively using spiritualism to persecute him. They caused him to have a sore back and bowels, and more disturbingly caused his semen to be brought up into his neck. A couple of patients were also convinced they were being continually followed around by malign Spiritualists.[33]

Bibles and books

There was a huge commercial boom in cheap Bibles during the nineteenth century providing copies for the burgeoning working classes, affordable luxury editions for the expanding middle class, and pocket ones for missionary work across the globe. Never before had the Bible been so freely available and at such low cost. By mid century some four million copies were being printed each year in Britain. Cheap illustrated editions gave a new reality to Bible stories. *Cassell's Illustrated Family Bible*, which sold in large numbers, contained over 900 illustrations, and was produced in a range of paper qualities and instalments, with forty-page sections in their own wrappers costing as little as six pence. As well as the commercial market in Bibles, national organizations such as the Bible Society and Society for Promoting Christian Knowledge made strenuous efforts to distribute cheap, mass-produced Bibles at home and abroad, while numerous smaller initiatives such as the Biblewomen's movement set up in the 1860s paid working-class women to sell Bibles to the London urban poor through subscriptions.[34] Behind all this was the evangelical mission to ensure the poor could be responsible for their own salvation through Bible contemplation. Many Bibles went unread of course, and some were used for ungodly purposes such as folk divination, but some people evidently drew such deep spiritual inspiration from both text and image that it shaped their psychical engagement with the external world in troubling ways for themselves, family, and acquaintances.

The view was widespread in the psychiatric profession that over-zealous or excessive reading of the Bible and other religious texts was unhealthy and symptomatic of mental health issues. It is no surprise, then, that the issue cropped up fairly regularly in admission records and case books. In Montrose Asylum, in 1871, we find an epileptic handloom weaver who was much given to Bible reading. A disease of the wrist joints had meant he was unable to work looms anymore, and he had then taken to what were described as 'over-officious missionary efforts in his native village'. He was a public nuisance in other words. It was for this reason he had been certified and admitted to the asylum. While a patient, he spent all of his time reading the Bible, apart from when he was walking and eating, and could repeat most of the Old Testament by rote. In a letter to friends, expressing hopes of his release to continue his missionary work, he explained, 'what my work has been every day is to have been reading at the Bible, which I like to make as the man of my counsel and as the rule of my life. I have no more to say.' A year earlier at the Middlesex County Lunatic Asylum a sober and steady labourer was observed to sit up late at night reading the Bible and religious books, thereby depriving him of 'rest and proper sustenance'. He said he could influence the course of the sun and the motions of the stars and planets.[35] The case notes for Elizabeth Crackston, aged forty-one, similarly remark that, 'she begged much for the Bible & was noticed to read it a long time before going to bed. When spoken to she at once began to quote verses speaking rapidly & disconnectedly about having seen "the light" "God being light". She stated that she had seen this light frequently specially during the night.'[36]

Religious reading materials were readily available in asylum chapels, and Bibles were lent out to patients under the supervision of attendants. In the early decades of the Suffolk Lunatic Asylum the medical superintendent John Kirkman (1829–1876) even ensured that a Bible and Prayer Book were regularly placed at the bed head of every patient that could read.[37] Although obsessive Bible reading was linked with insanity, the therapeutic benefits of moderate religious contemplation, were generally thought to far outweigh the triggering effect it caused in some patients suffering from mania and melancholy. Besides, access to Bibles and religious books could be policed if necessary. The case notes for Janet Baird Strathearn, who fancied she heard God and the angels speaking to her, noted that she 'spends all her time in reading the bible when she can get it'. Annual reports sometimes indicate a high rate of attrition in terms of patients' treatment of Bibles and Prayer books. Some of the damage was wear and tear due to constant usage, but Bibles could also come in for more curious abuse. William Ellithorne, admitted to the Lancaster Moor Asylum in 1872, said his parson had told him 'to lick the leaves of the Bible and eat one every day and that would teach him the right way'.[38]

The Bible was more than a devotional text. It was also a talisman and it was carried as a protection from harm—as the experience of the First World War amply showed.[39] The asylum casebooks also reveal other ways in which people *used* as well as read the Bible. For some it was an active divine instrument—a message board from the heavens. John Killeen, aged fifteen, a Roman Catholic, said 'he has had an interview with Christ, who wrote certain words on his Bible telling him as to his mother's address'.[40] John Ormston saw references to himself in the Book of Revelation and spoke to God who answered him. He explained to a medical attendant, 'from what I read in the bible, I thought the floor was bent for me, it came to me, it is gold'. People looked for signs as to their problems and anxieties. Elizabeth McCormick, an Anglican, explained that 'she has learned from the Bible that her husband, her child & herself are under a spell'. The Wesleyan James Preston, aged thirty, was much anguished that he was a lost sinner because the Bible told him so. Others held up the Bible as the ultimate defence for their unsociable behaviour. Another Wesleyan in Prestwich Asylum, Samuel Wood, forty-two, was gripped with religious fervour, constantly quoting scripture and singing hymns. He defended his every action by quotation from the Bible, including the foul language and threats he directed against his wife and children.[41] The Bible also provided people with the proof that they were privileged with the power of prophecy.

Prophets, revelations, and the Second Coming

The British surgeon Thomas Inman (1820–1876), who was also an amateur scholar of ancient religion and myth, observed in his study of Old Testament prophets, 'there is scarcely a lunatic asylum in Great Britain where such prophets do not abound; and scarcely a county in which there are no others of a similar stamp, whose insanity is yet not sufficient to warrant their removal from home'.[42] We find several self-proclaimed prophets, all Protestants, passing through the doors of Lancaster Moor Asylum from the 1870s to the early 1900s. There is brief mention in 1872 that John Rimmer, twenty-nine, 'thinks he has the power of prophecying', and in 1901 Wesleyan Joseph Smith Gorrill, a currier and farmer aged sixty-seven, 'considers himself a prophet; is excitable & shows symptoms of religious mania'. Gorrill had a long history of periodic insanity and violence which had led to a least two court cases in the 1870s.[43] Robert McCready, twenty-five, admitted to Lancaster Moor Asylum in 1879 for the delusion of believing he was a prophet, explained how 'about 3 months ago God began to reveal himself to him. When he went through the streets the people vanished and the shops closed like the day of judgement. God revealed himself by a voice in the top of his head.' In the same asylum there were those who identified with specific Biblical prophets, such as Henry Riley who believed he was Jeremiah from the Old Testament and Robert Rockliffe, aged twenty-four, who declared he was 'the rod of Jesse & the prophet spoken of in Isaiah' and that he had received six visions.[44] The rod or root of Jesse was a biblical metaphor for the coming Messiah born of King David's family line, Jesse being King David's father. Many more such cases could be found from other asylums. One of the members of the Select Committee on Lunatics in 1859 recalled visiting one asylum and asking an educated patient, a lawyer, why he was not attending religious worship. The man replied dismissively that there was no reason why he should because he was *the* prophet Amos, the first of the Biblical prophets to write down their divine messages.[45]

While some claimed they were biblical prophets there were many who were merely convinced that they had been chosen to undertake divine missions. Some jobs were the hum-drum tasks of evangelism. After paying visits to Hell and then Heaven, Robert Ball, thirty-four, was told by God that his task was to preach the Gospel. In Parkside Asylum in 1907, Hannah Newton, Church of England, experienced 'a divine feeling' coming over her one day, 'so she had to preach a sermon to the inmates of the ward—it was not her voice but the voice of God that spoke'.[46] Margaret Joynt, a domestic servant from Pendleton, aged twenty-one, 'saw a vision in which God told her she was the "Comforter" & she believes that God has given her a wonderful voice to comfort people & to earn money'. On another occasion she told asylum staff that God had given her 'a mission to unveal [sic] the Bible & that she has the star of Bethlehem in her eye'. Joynt was a member of the Catholic Apostolic Church founded in the 1830s by the ejected Church of Scotland minister Edward Irving (1792–1834). He and his followers preached that the age of miracles never ceased since the days of the New Testament and that prophecy was an integral aspect of faith. It is no wonder, then, that Joynt fully believed in her divine mission. She was released from Prestwich asylum in 1904 but a few weeks later she killed herself by drinking carbolic acid. The verdict was suicide whilst insane.[47] Other missions were personal and idiosyncratic. Irishman William Henry Conroy, a labourer and former soldier in the King's Own Regiment, believed Christ had sent him to South Yorkshire Asylum for a mysterious special purpose, which he said he had already accomplished. In the same asylum, 62-year-old hawker William Anyan, diagnosed with mania and epilepsy, said he was on a special mission from God to save England. Robert Carruthers had a vision from God and was instructed to catch 'Dynamitards', a recently-coined term for political terrorists. The case notes for Peter Knight, aged thirty-one, report that 'he had special knowledge from God to add to the Bible & had a revelation of a new country to be peopled by white people with twice the knowledge we have in this country'.[48]

Another distinct category of belief was that God had bestowed special divine powers upon people for a specific purpose. These were no mere messengers but were commanded to execute God's will. The power could be directed in retributive ways. Margaret Ann Twaddle, aged thirty-nine, a long-term patient at the Royal Crichton Hospital, suffering from 'Religious Excitement', 'stated that she was elected to destroy all who did not belong to the Established Church of Scotland, and used to pray and invoke the aid of Heaven against all whom she called unbelievers'.[49] A patient in the West Riding Asylum, a former prison warder in his late thirties, considered that he had been appointed by God to denounce all evil-doers—who were mainly doctors to his mind, and the worst of them all was the asylum superintendent William Bevan-Lewis. He sent him a sketch of a coffin accompanied by the words 'Behold they doom', and in 1887 he wrote the following letter addressed to all Englishmen:

I, an English-born subject, J.O., born in the County of Yorkshire, near Huddersfield, Do hereby solemnly declare in the name of 'God', the Almighty, the Supreme and Invisible Spirit, and pronounce through His Almighty authority, His damnable curses and judgements upon you, and your supposed and so-called Gracious Sovereign and all her subjects, both spiritual and temporal, for this my incarceration in this Asylum or any other.

J. O., late of Halifax.[50]

A servant named Euphemia Paterson, aged twenty-four, had more prosaic personal aims, believing 'that God gave her power from on high to attack the old woman in the poorhouse'. Then there was global control and command authority. Edward Robinson believed that through God he could control the weather, while another young man, William Somersgill, claimed God had enabled and commanded him to raise the dead.[51]

One of the strongest themes in terms of divine purpose concerned the imminence of the Second Coming of Christ when the Saviour will return and build a new kingdom on earth, the living and dead will be judged, and a small elect will enjoy a new millennium of divine peace. Although the Second Coming is indicated in different parts of the Old Testament and

Gospels it is most explicit in the final book of the New Testament—
Revelation. This relates the extraordinary vision of a prophet named John
that graphically describes the nature of the Apocalypse wrought by the
antichrist and his minions and the coming of the new millennium. While
not all early Protestants accepted or placed importance on the Book of
Revelation, and there were and are numerous theological disagreements
regarding the nature of the Second Coming, millenarianism became a central tenet of numerous evangelical denominations and the Book of
Revelation the inspiration behind such early nineteenth-century prophets
as Joanna Southcott and Richard Brothers (1757–1824). We saw in Chapter 3
how it was also central to the James Hadfield affair. The preoccupation with
the Second Coming was alive and well in Britain during the second half of
the century as well with the establishment of millenarian denominations
such as the Catholic Apostolic Church and the Christadelphians. Seventh
Day Adventists were also setting up churches in Britain the 1880s, and the
Watch Tower Society (Jehovah's Witnesses) was beginning to gain a foothold.
The latter end of the century saw the growing influence of what is known
as premillennialism, in other words the idea that the Second Coming and
the rapture of the faithful would occur before the Apocalypse. This was an
enticing vision of imminent paradise without the horrors of the antichrist
and the playing out of the Book of Revelation on the horizon. It was a
message promoted by the likes of Sankey and Moody. As one historian puts
it, 'Now an ethereal heaven of golden gates, bells, harps, and peaceful
deliverance from the world's trials were all back in vogue.' We shall hear
more of those golden gates shortly. By the time of the First World War, which
provoked a new boom in millenarian preoccupations, anticipation of the
Second Coming was a well-established aspect of popular religious culture.[52]

Patients of all denominations and not just evangelicals expressed millenarian preoccupations. Thomas Lawton, whose religion was recorded as
Church of England, explained in 1892 that 'now is the second coming' and
wanted to see the Queen about it. In 1898, Unitarian Fanny MacDonald
also claimed 'the end of the world is coming'.[53] A year earlier, Bertha
Fielding, a 45-year-old Roman Catholic who called herself 'Mother Eve'
and the 'third person in the Trinity', said that 'the millennium is coming in
9 years & that she has found the secret out before them'. She also explained
that 'the world is destroyed in every 2000 years and that the millennium
comes when she is annoyed'. John Byers, a Wesleyan, was convinced in 1880
that the new millennium would begin before the year was out and that God

had appointed him to herald its arrival. But he was despondent and feared divine wrath 'because God has given him a work to do in which he had failed viz. the introduction of the millennium and salvation of the human race'.[54] A female patient in the Middlesex County Asylum was much more confident in her pursuit of the same mission. The arrival of Christ was to take place within days and she had been commissioned to proclaim his descent to earth. 'These poor people', she confided to a visitor, referring to her fellow patients, 'think that I am here on the same account as themselves, when I am only here to prepare the way for the second coming.'[55]

It is useful to pause for a moment and consider a couple of nineteenth-century prophets who also assumed divinity but who did not end up in an asylum. George Ord was one such character who lived in Preston, near Stockton-on-Tees. Described as a monomaniac on matters of religion, he believed he was the Messiah and called himself the great 'I AM', 'Shilloh', and the 'Prince of Peace'. Ord tramped the countryside spreading his message, and was a regular at the markets of Darlington, Sunderland, and Stockton, preaching and selling the religious tracts and broadsides he had written. When Joanna Southcott visited Stockton for several weeks in 1803 to drum up new followers, Ord sought an interview with her. As one might suspect when two such divine beings collided, things did not go well. Ord wanted to convert her to his cause, 'but I could not persuade her I was the only true Branch. She called me a vile impostor, and laying violent hands on me she scratched my face.' Many years later, the local printer, bookseller, and poet Henry Heavisides (1791–1870) met Ord and asked him if he ever got any converts from his endless preaching:

> 'Oh Yes!' he replied, 'lots of converts', and handing a book to me, which he pulled out of his pocket, he said, 'You will find all their names registered in this book!' On looking over the names I found them of the most laughable and fictitious character, such as Tommy Swillpot, Abraham Likes-a-drop, David Funnychap, and so on. 'And where did you obtain these names?' I enquired. To which he answered with the greatest simplicity, 'At the public houses where I've called to sell my books.'[56]

A few decades later, in 1874, a failed attempt was made to have prophetess Mary Girling (1827–1886) placed in the asylum. She had begun preaching in Methodist chapels before attracting her own millenarian following after she received several visitations from Jesus between 1858 and 1864 who intimated that his second coming was imminent. She toured the villages and towns of Suffolk spreading her message before leaving her husband and children and heading for London. She set up camp under a railway arch near Walworth Road in South London, and her followers were known as the Walworth Jumpers due to the ecstatic convulsions they experienced during Girling's preaching. In 1873 she and a small band of followers, numbering some 160 or so, moved from London to create a self-sufficient commune in Hordle in the New Forest. In December 1874 they were briefly evicted for defaulting on mortgage payments. The local general practitioner and Poor Law Union medical officer, Dr Adams, took advantage of the situation to draw up and sign a certificate of lunacy regarding Girling. As a result, on 18 December she was brought before three magistrates and two doctors to assess her alleged insanity. According to her own account, Adams 'told her she practised mesmerism upon her people, making them dance and putting them through much suffering; and she answered that she had no such power, but that if she had she would certainly exercise it on Dr. Adams. She said it was the Word of God and the Spirit of God that made them dance.'[57] The magistrates decided there were insufficient grounds to have her placed in an asylum and she was returned to her commune. As one periodical observed, 'Mrs Girling would certainly seem to be in some respect what most people would call crazy, although magistrates were probably right in thinking that there were no sufficient grounds for shutting her up.'[58]

So how did Ord and Girling evade the asylums when numerous other self-proclaimed prophets ended up behind their doors? It was not necessarily anything to do with the nature of the prophecies espoused or the level of perceived self-delusion involved, but rather a matter of behaviour and social relations. For one, neither Ord or Girling were considered violent or 'maniacal' in appearance, speech, or action. Both had families they abandoned when they began their vagabond preaching lives, so the usual ties of domesticity that enabled the successful drawing up of certificates of insanity and reception orders was rendered more challenging. Then there was the relationship between celebrity and eccentricity. Garnering a following like Girling or at least local and regional acceptance, like Ord, protected such prophets from proactive members of authority from intervening successfully.

Assuming divinity

Several Jewish asylum patients assumed the identities of key figures from the Torah. In Birmingham Asylum in 1853 a hawker named Abraham Hyam called himself King Abraham and said that his mother had visited him at night to tell him that if he did not go to Bristol she 'would send Rebecca out of the grave to fetch him'. A German Jewish shopwoman in Rainhill Asylum proclaimed herself King of Israel, and when placed in a padded cell declared that it was her palace.[59] Quite a few patients of all denominations were like the Wesleyan, William Rowland, who was admitted to Bootham Park Asylum for mania in 1847 because of his conviction that 'he is God and can rule the world'. But the most potent fantasy was the conviction of being the returning Messiah. Alfred Bridgwater, fifty-five, was admitted to South Yorkshire Asylum in 1905 for grandiose delusions following his wife's death. He said he was the second son of God and was going to save the world. He also said he owned millions of pounds.[60] A patient at the Royal Edinburgh Asylum explained in a letter his role in the coming Apocalypse:

> My own name is to be changed to the Holy and sacred one of Israel Jesu Christ, the Second son of God the Father to reign for thousands of years in the New World that will appear out of the debris of the Earth when after 115 years or more or less shall have expired after it has been burned up & purified from all filth & uncleaness by a fervent fiery heart & by deluges of the boundless & mighty waters of the Oceans that occupy so large a portion of this fair earth.[61]

Maudsley described the habits of an asylum patient he knew who believed himself the Saviour and cut an imposing figure in the institution. He was always meticulously dressed and grew a long white beard. Although he seldom spoke, he answered questions politely and never expressed insane ideas of his own accord. One time his wife requested that he be released and two eminent physicians were sent to examine him. They could find no evidence of insanity and recommended his discharge. But this was not allowed. The reason he was sent to the asylum in the first place was because he had struck a cab horse on the head with an axe. He did this in order to be prosecuted in court, thereby providing him with a public platform to proclaim his divinity and messianic purpose.[62] So in this instance believing one was Christ was not a sign of insanity but acting on that belief in a violent manner was considered as such. This case reminds us that there were some messiahs who had violent tendencies along with their delusional omnipotence and desire to save humankind. One of Alexander Morison's cases was a 40-year-old labourer who believed he was the Saviour and caused much harm and nuisance by beating people up under the delusion they were possessed by devils and that he had to pummel the evil out of their bodies.[63]

Thomas Bouskill Hodgson, aged thirty, who believed he was the second son of God and the brother of Jesus, was described as having a wild and violent manner, and 'said that if he cut his own throat he would be shedding Holy blood'. He also believed his house was built of holy bricks and mortar and, as a consequence, everything in it was holy.[64]

Female prophets also assumed messianic divinity. Joanna Southcott claimed she was giving birth to the coming Christ at the age of sixty-four. Ann Lee, the leader of the Shakers, believed she was the female embodiment of the Messiah, and Mary Girling came to believe she was 'the God-mother and Saviour'. It is no surprise, then, that we find women with similar convictions in the asylum records. Mary Lord, aged thirty-eight, who spent a few years in Parkside Asylum, stated that she *was* Jesus Christ and resented being called by any other name. One of the medical attendants wrote wryly in her case notes that she was still 'quite willing to scrub the floor nevertheless'. A 42-year-old patient in the West Riding Asylum also said she felt that she was Jesus Christ and read scriptural passages about the Messiah as referring to herself. She declared she loved everybody in the world and had a sweet, gentle disposition, though she was in the unfortunate habit of regularly standing at the window in the evening singing loudly 'Hold the fort, for I am coming' in shrill tones. This was a popular song by the American revivalist Philip Paul Bliss, who collaborated with Moody and Sankey. A 33-year-old domestic servant in the Royal Edinburgh Asylum, diagnosed with mania, wrote in a letter: 'I am the Goddess of Heaven in my own right made into a woman to atone for sin...God says he has to obey me in heaven.'[65] One wonders whether she conflated the Virgin and Eve, and conceptualized her own feminine sense of divinity.

The role of the 'Bride of Christ' clearly caught the imagination. Mary Carson's Certificate stated that she 'fancies herself to be the wife of Jesus Christ. Has a divine mission to fulfil. Her children are of divine origin.' Mary Shepherd, in South Yorkshire Asylum, also believed that she was to be the 'Bride of Christ' at his second coming. Margaret Irvine, a 47-year-old Presbyterian, believed one of the asylum doctors to be the Lamb of God. 'She came to me a few days ago demanding sexual rights, under the delusion that I am the Lamb of God & she is the Lamb's Bride', he wrote in her case notes. 'She told me that when the marriage is consummated the millennium will commence.'[66] The Bride of Christ or the Lamb's wife were not literally the Saviour's spouse, of course, but metaphors for the Christian church. Both terms were used in Revelation with reference to the New Jerusalem. Revelation 20:2 states, 'And I John saw the holy city, new Jerusalem, coming down from God out of heaven, prepared as a bride adorned for her husband', and a few verses later, 'And there came unto me one of the seven angels which had the seven vials full of the seven last plagues, and talked with me, saying, Come hither, I will shew thee the bride, the Lamb's wife.' The fact that these women took the term literally and self-identified as the wife of the new Messiah indicates less about their diagnosed insanity and more about the wider Bible literalism we find in popular religion of the period. We also see this with regard to Biblical reference to witches, as in Exodus 22:18, which states, 'Thou shalt not suffer a witch to live', and the figure of the Woman of Endor in Samuel 28 who supposedly conjured up the spirit of the prophet Samuel for King Saul on the eve of battle. She was not called a 'witch' in the King James Bible but was popularly known as such and widely referred to in this way in sermons. When nineteenth-century clergymen upbraided their parishioners for believing in witches, the parishioners would reply, 'they are in the Bible'. The clergyman would then argue, as others had done for centuries, that the term 'witch' in the Bible was a mistranslation of the ancient Greek for diviners and had nothing to do with the witches of popular concern. But the argument was usually to no avail. One such exchange with a farmer concluded with him 'being apparently "convinced against his will," and, therefore, "of the same opinion still." '[67]

Henry Maudsley observed in 1863 that amongst Catholic patients it was not unusual to find women who claimed they were the Virgin Mary.[68] The casebooks reveal a more complex picture. Women of all ages and Christian denominations could identify with her as a holy and venerated woman and also as a mother figure. In a sample of eight women who claimed they were the Virgin Mary in Lancaster Moor between 1865 and 1911, four were Church of England, two were Roman Catholic, and two Methodists. Assuming the role of the Virgin clearly gave some of these patients a sense of validatory status and empowerment similar to the many female patients who had delusions they were the queen or other members of the royal family. At Colney Hatch asylum, a patient named Edith, categorized as suffering from 'religious mania', was described as 'very grandiose and exalted and believes that she is the Virgin Mary and that the archangel has visited her and greeted her with "Hail, Mary, full of grace" '. She also professed that she 'could feel the Holy Child leave her womb'.[69] Twenty-four-year-old Maude Greaves stated she was the 'second virgin since the Virgin Mary and that

she is going to give birth to a second saviour'.[70] One of the patients in the
Suffolk Lunatic Asylum in the 1850s who thought she was the Virgin Mary
'braided and dressed her hair with all the attractiveness of juvenile vanity'.
When asked why she gave so much care and attention to her hair she
replied that first, as the Virgin, she 'had no right to be matronly in appearance', and second, 'her head felt hot and she wanted the hair off'.[71] There
were also those who bestowed such divinity on their loved ones. Edward
Isaac Hewitt, a 43-year-old Anglican, believed his mother was the Virgin
Mary, while Thomas McDonnell, a Catholic, said he was St Joseph and that
his wife was the Virgin and his son the Saviour.[72]

Saints and angels

The veneration of the Virgin Mary was integral to popular Catholic liturgy,
and we can certainly find expressions of it amongst Irish Catholic migrants
who spent time in British asylums. But the late nineteenth century also
heralded a major remaking of the Virgin Mary as a central saint in English
Catholicism, with representations of her flourishing in art as well as in
devotional manuals and sermons. Her renascent role as the 'Queen of
Heaven' in the public consciousness can also be seen in relation to the
country having a long-serving female monarch as well as the growing influence of the women's emancipation movement.[73] While communications
with God and Christ were quite often aural in nature, the long Catholic
tradition of Marian *visions* seems to have clearly influenced patient notions
of their experience of her. While some Marian apparitions at this period
ended up with the founding of such famous international pilgrim sites as
Lourdes and Knock, the asylums confirm that the vast majority remained
personal, idiosyncratic narratives. Mary Leigh, a 31-year-old Catholic
diagnosed with religious melancholia, recounted how she saw a man whom
she thought was the Devil. She ran away from him and while fleeing
came across 'the blessed Virgin who saved her'. Elizabeth Todd, thirty-three,
believed that 'the blessed virgin appeared to her in a dream & told her that
her daughter was poisoning her & that after her death, she (the daughter)
would poison herself'.[74] No doubt the perceived incongruity of such
experiences with the formulaic encounters of female Marian visions promoted by the Catholic Church at the local level helped determine whether

people were considered insane or had been truly gifted the miracle of her divine presence. In 1892, Mary Lavery, a 26-year-old Catholic in Prestwich Asylum, thought she saw the Virgin Mary at Manchester's London Road Station.[75] It was highly unlikely that anyone would take Mary seriously as a consequence. Even though there was no reason why the Virgin should not appear at an urban railway station, tradition dictated that 'true' Marian visions occurred in either rural locations or in religious buildings.

Although visions of and intimacy with the Virgin have long been represented as a predominantly female Catholic spiritual relationship, there were young and middle-aged Catholic men in England's asylums who had clearly developed strong emotional bonds with the Virgin Mary in their inner lives. One wonders whether she acted as a mother figure for lonely male migrants. There were three such Roman Catholics in Lancaster Moor Asylum. Thomas Carey, aged nineteen, 1883, whom the census confirms was a bricklayer born in Dublin, fancied he saw the Virgin Mary and had attempted to climb through the window to worship her. Henry Smith, thirty-one, said the Virgin Mary came to his bedside every night and talked to him.[76] Thomas Kelly, aged thirty-five, believed in 1886 that

> an angel spoke to him at night & told him that his soul was saved: also that he met two men on the road who he believes were heavenly messengers to him: also that he has seen 'our Blessed Lady' herself on the altar...Is excessively attentive to his religious duties: said that the Virgin Mary appeared to him at night & told him to go away from house: that he has the bleeding Heart of Jesus at the back of his head.[77]

In Prestwich Asylum in 1893 we find another Irish Catholic, the 39-year-old Joseph John Gallagher, who talked incessantly about the Virgin Mary and claimed to have seen the Holy Ghost. While in the asylum he explained that he had 'the Virgin Mary one side of the bed and the Devil on other', and asked 'the Virgin Mary for advice and he acts on what he imagines she says'.[78]

Catholic asylum patients also had extensive relations with the wider world of the saints. In 1884 Francis Murphy, thirty-five, constantly muttered and prayed to the saints and spoke of nothing else. He refuses to eat and said he was eternally lost. Before his admittance to Lancaster Moor he had knelt on the ground in front of a tram-car and started praying. Emma Darlington, a 24-year-old Catholic who suffered from various religious delusions, was convinced she had seen and conversed with the saints. Margaret Regan also said that the saints in Heaven regularly talked to her and that St Anthony and St Philomena were going to pray for her.[79] Devotion to the virgin Philomena, the patron saint of babies and youth, began to spread through France and Italy during the mid nineteenth century following the 'discovery' of her bones in 1802. Her veneration was very much a grass-roots movement, and she became a popular figure in Ireland and amongst Catholic migrants around the world by the early twentieth century.

Angelic apparitions were common to patients of all Christian faiths. In most cases they were nocturnal visions that appeared as people lay in their beds at night. Some said they heard the angels singing or playing music to them. They were frequently described as 'flying about', sometimes around the asylum wards. Harry Price, aged sixteen, reported that they smiled when they looked at him. Seventy-year-old Ann Walker, who was diagnosed with mania, said that angels in chariots drawn by four horses came into her bedroom at night.[80] They could also appear outdoors. In 1882 we find one Hugh Mills in Parkside Asylum due to his angelic visions. His admission notes reveal that he answered most questions quite rationally, but that he

> talks willingly about a delusion he has to the effect that several weeks ago he worked near Liverpool with some other men, and a number of angels with wings and dressed in long robes. These angels and men he says, were working under the direction of God. In whom they were engaged in turning several fields into a flower garden. He says he several times saw the angels fly away and return.[81]

These angelic visitations were usually welcome and comforting, but the Devil also had his angels that came to pester and torment. Maria Casey complained in 1904 that both black and white angels followed her about and she would insist on going outside to meet them. Margaret Calligan, aged thirty-nine, was very despondent and depressed in 1888 and required force-feeding with a tube. She prayed to the Virgin for the sinful life she had led and confessed to having 'followed a dissipated career for which she says she now feels repentance'. She saw angels hovering around her and could hear their voices. It was they who told her not to eat. While in the asylum, though, the visitations took a more sinister turn. They were 'now all black and the other day she was annoyed by them asking her to set off for Alderley. They bothered her a long time and she had a hard struggle to refuse.'[82] Another Catholic, John Mason, aged fifty, was in a similar frame of mind. He said he was haunted by the devil and his angels. They caused him to have all sorts of disease owing to his previous 'wicked' life. He had sent so often for the priest that the clergyman ended up refusing to respond to his requests.[83]

Visions of Heaven

When people looked to the skies some saw more than just the clouds or the sun and moon. Isabella Lowther, aged fifty-four, was looking out of a train window one day when 'she saw the heavens assume a blood red colour . . . and at the same time saw angelic forms'. The Baptist James Jones saw instead 'a beautiful halo from Christ passing in the clouds', while Margaret Matthews saw a circle of light in the sky when she prayed. Thirty-one-year-old Harry Nuttall fancied 'he sees his sister Lucy in the clouds with wings on', in other words she had been transformed into a heavenly angel after death. Alexander Fletcher Walker, diagnosed with mania and epilepsy, said he had looked up into the night sky one time and saw 'Heaven appear to him as a star'. When widow Catherine Jack did likewise she thought she saw the star of Bethlehem.[84] Mary Lord, who believed she was Christ at one time, said that God 'shewed her in the sky a laid out body with an angel standing by'. While these experiences were considered symptomatic of insanity, move on a few years to the First World War and people claiming to have seen prophetic visions in the sky were taken seriously and their experiences reported in the newspapers as a matter for national consideration.[85]

Coming back to the issue of religious literalism, several patients talked of possessing or seeing a ladder to Heaven. Ada Tomkinson, aged thirty-six, told a medical attendant at Prestwich Asylum that 'she had a new ladder to heaven revealed to her & that she saw the Virgin & Jesus Christ coming down it'. On another occasion, he reported that 'she admits "climbing a high ladder" & "thought it would lead her by faith" '. But she was prevented by a witch who sent a flash of fire that blinded her. She drew a crude sketch of her vision with rays of light streaming from Heaven, which was inserted into her case notes.[86] This 'ladder' refers, of course, to Jacob's dream recounted in the Book of Genesis, that he saw 'a ladder set up on the earth, and the top of it reached to heaven; and behold the angels of God ascending and descending on it'. This image of a ladder between Heaven and earth, sometimes represented as stairs or as beams of light, had been widely represented in popular art, including an engraving in Cassell's Illustrated Family Bible, as well as in folk song, hymns, and carols. A widely published version of the hymn 'Jacob's Ladder' contained the verses:

> This ladder is long, it is strong and well-made,
> Has stood hundreds of years and is not yet decayed;
> Many millions have climbed it and reached Sion's hill,
> And thousands by faith are climbing it still.
>
> Come let us ascend: all may climb it who will;
> For the Angels of Jacob are guarding it still:
> And remember each step, that by faith we pass o'er,
> Some Prophet or Martyr hath trod it before.[87]

Sarah Ann Bentley, suffering from mania, thought she had seen Heaven with its golden gates, and the similarly diagnosed Rose Sykes said she visited the Gate of Heaven where she shook hands with her father, mother, brothers, and sisters but did not pass through.[88] The Golden or Pearly Gates of Heaven were another symbol of ascent widely represented in art, sermons, and literature, and particularly in expressions of evangelicalism. References appear in several of the popular songs written by Ira Sankey and performed at Sankey and Moody revival meetings. In the 'Ninety and Nine', for instance, there is the line 'Far off from the gates of gold', while the song 'The Gate Aint for Me' begins:

> There is a gate that stands ajar,
> And through its portals gleaming,
> A radiance from the cross afar,
> The Saviour's love revealing.

One Salvation Army song was based around the repeated refrain, 'I'm pressing towards the golden gates.'[89]

Some of those convinced they had fully ascended and passed beyond the gates provided detailed accounts of what they saw. From the visions of several patients in Montrose Royal Lunatic Asylum we can see how they were shaped by their earthly experiences. A 13-year-old boy who believed he was the biblical Adam, described Heaven to the superintendent, James Howden. The boy had grown up in Canada and had been sent home to Scotland to live with his grandfather who taught him to read the Bible. It was clear to Howden that the boy's description of Heaven was the landscape and scenery of the Canada he had left behind.[90] A 47-year-old epileptic gardener, who claimed his soul had visited Heaven, described it as:

> A glorious country, abounding with the most beautiful trees, shrubs, and flowers, the trees were loaded with the most luscious fruit, and the fields

waved with the most luxuriant crops. Everything grew spontaneously, the ground needed neither digging nor tilling, nor the crops sowing, and the trees needed no pruning.[91]

This man's paradise was free of the back-breaking grind of cultivation and garden maintenance: it was a Heaven conjured up by a worn-out labourer. A shoemaker from Caithness wrote to his wife of his own experience. He generally spoke rationally and intelligently but was fully convinced that he had visited Heaven, though things were not quite what they seemed:

> A person said, 'Would you undertake to go through the flames that Shadrach, Meshech, and Abednego went through?' I then thought that I was caught up by the hair of my head, and brought through the air to a beautiful country, which was surrounded by beautiful green grass parks, and those parks were full of young lambs, and lo! And behold I saw them…I then asked the person supposed to be in my company, where was God. His reply was in Heaven. I then said this was Heaven. He then said that this was only a kitchen to Heaven, and none can enter into Heaven but those that are pure and perfect.[92]

While some patients claimed to have visited or received visions of Hell, their case notes are disappointingly lacking in detail compared to those who described Heaven. Convictions of proximity to the Inferno were a little more evocative. Kate McDonald, a long-term patient in Lancaster Moor, explained in 1892 that 'she had a vision of a man in flames who spoke to her with her father's voice, said I am burning in hell, and another voice said let this be a warning to you'.[93] A woman admitted to Dundee Asylum who believed God had forsaken her said she could hear 'the killed in Hell panting', while Mary Degnan said her stepson had died and gone to Hell, but 'she saw his shadow & got him out of hell, & put him in heaven'.[94]

Dealing with the Devil

Some suicidal patients explained their impulsion in terms of a divine order. Florence Blanche Boyce, who was brought to Parkside Asylum in 1905, had attempted to throw herself through her bedroom window 'because she said the Lord told her her time had come'. In 1876 Henry Hartley tried to cut his throat under the awful delusion that the Lord had told him he would be tortured and gibbetted on Beacon Hill, Halifax. Executed criminals had been hung in chains on the hill during the eighteenth century but the practice had ended back in 1832, so Hartley was evidently influenced by local histories and legends.[95] Writing in the early 1870s John Thompson Dickson of St Luke's Hospital observed that, 'melancholic patients, and especially suicidal ones, are often remarkably well versed in Holy Writ, and not only quote it in everything they say but also attempt to prove the truth of their assertations regarding themselves, by the standard of their own interpretation of the Bible'.[96] But for people of all denominations the Devil was more often the terrible, tempting voice urging self-destruction. As we saw in Chapter Four, during the eighteenth and early nineteenth centuries criminals had sometimes blamed their crimes on the influence of the Evil One as a mitigating plea, and the notion that the Devil was the promoter of self-murder was still engrained in popular belief at the other end of the century. To give just a couple of examples, in 1883 Jane Shepherd, in South Yorkshire Asylum, admitted that she cut her throat 'because the tempter told her to do so', and Thomas Bann confided in 1878 that he 'does not know what he was doing when he cut his throat but that the Devil prompted him'.[97] But what sort of Devil did such patients believe in?

There were two main ways people conceived of the Devil. There was the religious Devil whose physical presence was restricted to his place in Hell but who acted as an invisible, spiritual tempter on earth urging people to suicide and implanting sinful thoughts. The writings and preaching of the Salvation Army were full of allusions to waging war against this ever-present Devil and his agency. William Booth (1829–1912), the Methodist preacher and co-founder of the Salvation Army, described the profession of prostitute as the 'ever-new embodiment of the old fable of the sale of the soul to the Devil', and referred to the slums as the 'heart of the Devil's country'. 'To the dwellers in decent homes who occupy cushioned pews in fashionable churches', he observed, 'there is something strange and quaint in the language they hear read from the Bible, language which habitually refers to the Devil as an actual personality.'[98] For some, the rise of spiritualism was another gateway for the Devil with mediums fooled into communications with Him when they thought they were contacting the dead. Then there was the physical Devil of folklore, widespread across Europe during the nineteenth century, who was known by such names as 'Old Nick' or 'Old Lad', a malevolent trickster or mysterious gentleman who could occasionally be outwitted, and who roamed abroad at night scaring the unwary or drunk. This Devil walked among men and women, perhaps giving himself away by a glimpse of hooves under his long coat. The two types of Devil were not mutually exclusive. Indeed, the mundane nature of the folkloric Devil had long provided a receptive cultural medium for the evangelical message that he was an ever-present tormentor and sower of sin.[99]

The old iconic image of the Devil was imprinted on minds young and old. In Lancaster Moor in 1881, John Thomas Gass, twenty-two, spoke with intense seriousness and in a whisper that he had 'seen the devil with horns & tail, enveloped in flames, [who] disappeared in a flash of lightning'. His hallucinations seem to have been instigated three years before, when, while employed as telegraph clerk, he received an electric shock during a thunderstorm. Mary Ann Marsden, twenty-eight, diagnosed with melancholia, believed that the Devil had got hold of her and said that she was afraid of the 'bad man with horns'. Mary Fishleigh fancied she had seen the Devil and explained that he was 'brown, has horns + hoofs + big eyes', and that he wanted to 'do her out'. A woman in the Somerset County Asylum said she saw Satan in her home and burned her hand while trying to escape up the chimney.[100] As in numerous local legends he was also encountered physically outdoors while going about one's daily business. Henry Morton, aged twenty-eight, believed in 1884 that he had met the Devil on the road while he was out of the asylum.[101] The incriminating smell of brimstone or sulphur when he was near was reported by several patients. William Carter, twenty-seven, suffered from hallucinations about devils and said 'his mother's breath smells of fire + brimstone', an allusion perhaps to the description in Revelation Chapter 9 of the fire, smoke and brimstone that poured forth from lion-headed beasts that annihilated a third of men. Mary Bruckshaw said she could smell sulphur when the Devil was in her, and a woman in Bothwell Asylum said she smelt sulphur and heard the clanking of chains. Elizabeth Broadbent, forty-two, who was fearfully depressed and wracked with guilt about her sins, said 'she can taste sulphur in her mouth which she says comes from hell'.[102] The old folkloric motif of the Devil appearing in the form of an animal is also evident. Robert Marshall, aged forty-five, had hallucinations about the Devil in the form of a cat, but the diabolic association with black dogs was more widespread in popular belief. The case notes for Ann Sweenie state that she 'thinks she has sold herself to the devil who comes as a black dog'. In Prestwich Asylum John Henry Kirk, aged forty, who saw devils about him, told one of the medical attendants that a big black dog followed him about.[103] Reference to the 'black dog' as a metaphor for depression was popularized by Winston Churchill with regard to his own battle with mental illness, and 'black dog' has been co-opted into modern psychiatric language, but, as these examples confirm, the association has much deeper folkloric roots.[104]

As well as being followed by a black dog, John Henry Kirk, mentioned above, also said he saw 'little fellows like Imps & about 8 or 9 inches high'. Indeed, patients suffering from delusions of diabolic persecution quite often talked about such imps around them. These were not the familiars of early modern witch trials, though, but another species of spirit from Hell or from the Catholic realm of Purgatory. They crowded about the patients in an annoying fashion. Around 1870, one of the patients in Middlesex County Lunatic Asylum had sleepless nights and said he saw imps flitting in the air. The husband of Mary Ann Connor, a 35-year-old Catholic, explained that she jumped up in the middle of the night and ran downstairs in her night clothes, declaring that there were devils and imps behind the walls and in the cellar 'which are wanting to get hold of her'. Alice Butterworth heard imps and spirits talking together, and her case notes for the 10 November 1891 state that she 'kicked some imps off her bed last night'. Thomas King, thirty-one, believed he had been in purgatory and come back again, and was now constantly hunted by imps.[105] Sixty-year-old John Ratcliffe, an Anglican, wrestled with imps in both mind and body. He said they carried him off over the countryside every night and so he determined to 'dissolve' them. As he explained to one of his medical attendants, 'he dissolves them by shutting his eyes when the Devils, which are quite black, fall down like bits of dirt'. But the devils would then 'revive themselves by spitting each other out of their mouths as spiritual matter'. Thankfully all this torment was relieved by periodic visitations from the Lord and his angels, 'and a most entrancing sight it is', said Ratcliffe with satisfaction.[106]

These references to hellish imps are curious. The term appears rarely before the mid seventeenth century and mostly in relation to witches' familiars, and there was no substantive folklore about 'imps' per se other than when folklorists attempted to lump them in with a whole host of fairy types.[107] Neither was the term used much in published sermons and other religious literature. There are a few folklore references to witchy imps from around the early twentieth century, but the patients' imps were not given names, were not associated with witches, and they had their own diabolic agency. Searches through newspaper court reports, though, reveal several references to imps in radical religious contexts and also as a term of religious denunciation by both Catholics and Protestants. A curious prosecution took place in 1855, for instance, concerning a sect of Southcottians living in Kings

Row, Walworth, London. One of its members was the notorious if now forgotten Charles William Twort, author of *The Vision of Judgment; Or, the Return of Joanna from her Trance* (1829). For a year the sect had processed through the streets on Sunday evenings, accompanied by fife and drums and bearing large Union Jack flags, asking people to sign a petition against the Devil. Anyone who refused was denounced as 'imps of Satan'.[108] Three years earlier another prosecution concerned a visit to Limerick by two London missionaries of the Evangelical Alliance. They were mobbed by the Catholic locals and denounced as 'imps of the devil'.[109] So, perhaps the language of imps used by the asylum patients was inspired more by evangelical idiom than folk tradition.

The term 'pact' rarely appears in asylum records, People, well men basically, did write pacts with their blood during the eighteenth and nineteenth centuries. The most sensational example is the Methodist murderer William Dove whom we heard about in Chapter Four. While in jail awaiting trial, he wrote a letter to the Devil in blood offering his soul in return for getting him off. This was brought up in his defence as a sign of his insanity.[110] But there is no sign in the casebooks that any of the patients had attempted such a formal agreement of any sort or sealed such a pact through supposed sexual relations. Yet the long-held concept of *selling* one's soul to the Devil comes through strongly amongst the notions entertained by asylum patients of all Christian denominations. In Lancaster Moor Asylum both Mary Pollard, a 36-year-old Anglican, and Roseann Roberts, a 34-year-old Roman Catholic, stated they had 'sold' themselves to the Devil in 1869 and 1879 respectively. Elizabeth Nuttall, a 27-year-old Congregationalist, was diagnosed with melancholic religious delusions and was convinced that she had sold herself to the Devil for 1000 years.[111]

For both men and women the language of 'selling' themselves was framed in spiritual terms of having given themselves up to Satan through their sinfulness or loss of faith. Nathaniel Bingham noted the case of a labourer's wife from Dorset who had been suffering from 'insane melancholy' for two months. She believed she had 'sold' herself to the Devil and the reason she gave was that she had received 'the Sacrament unworthily after being a frequent communicant for many years'.[112] Some half a century later, the case notes for Francis Turner, a 54-year-old Catholic, state that 'she has sold herself to the Devil & that nobody must go near her because of her sins. Requested me to keep away from her so that she might utter some dreadful curses. After speaking a few words suddenly stamps her foot, screams & says the Devil has her again.' Around the same time, another Catholic, 28-year-old Mary Gleason believed 'a certain Catholic Priest to have sold himself to the devil for her special benefit'.[113] The idea of the Devil as the great tempter also comes through in a couple of cases where patients were upset and confused because they heard voices telling them that they had sold themselves to the Devil.[114]

It is no surprise that we also find convictions of being diabolically possessed amongst the religious fears and torments expressed in asylum casebooks. A study of patients in three asylums in York between 1880 and 1884 found that satanic possession was evident in 11 per cent of women suffering from delusions, but that there were no cases amongst the men.[115] This is clearly just a matter of a limited sample size for numerous cases of both men and women claiming to be possessed can be found in other asylums during the second half of the nineteenth century. In South Yorkshire Asylum in the early 1890s there was George Lyles, who 'has the delusion that he has the devil in his inside', and Walter Wood, aged forty-four, who was extremely depressed and said he was 'possessed of the Devil & that spirits are about him'.[116] While we saw a few high-profile cases of diabolic possession in earlier chapters, mostly from the eighteenth and early nineteenth centuries, the asylum records suggest that claims of possession either by patients themselves or by their families, guardians, and neighbours were more prevalent than we might think. In Scotland, for instance, where the certified insane (often those classified as 'idiots') were sometimes boarded-out lodgers, we find a couple of disturbing cases from the mid nineteenth century. In 1867 one such boarded-out patient was found restrained by a straightjacket and strap binding her ankles together. It transpired that the woman paid to look after her while her guardian was out at work believed she was possessed by a devil and so needed to be restrained for safety. When, earlier that decade, Mitchell visited a 16-year-old congenital 'idiot' cared for by his elderly parents, the mother asked, 'Do you not think, sir, that he is possessed of a devil?' The poor young man was living in filthy conditions, and ate grass, cinders, and faeces, so Mitchell had him removed to the asylum for his own good.[117]

In some self-diagnosed cases the notion of being physically possessed was akin to having sold oneself to the Devil in that they had given 'him' entry through their sinfulness, rather than having been forcibly and violently possessed in stereotypical terms. Such patients were passive and depressed, resigned to their fate. Henry Hunt admitted in 1873 that the Devil has 'hold of him' and that his soul was lost. He told a medical officer that he was going to Hell, but as the officer noted, 'he seems very happy under the circumstances'.[118] For others we find the exhibition of physical torment, though none of the cases were 'classic' in the sense of speaking in foreign tongues or spewing sharp objects as recorded during the witch trials. Victims of supposed possession in the past were usually female and young but not so our asylum patients. Margaret Lightfoot, aged forty-nine, believed that she had been transformed into a dog by Satan and her children changed into other animals, and she would have uncontrollable outbursts during which she was extremely noisy. Susan Good, sixty, was taken to Parkside Asylum in 1889, because she was 'singing, shouting and making great noise, which she said was because of the Devil which possesses her'.[119] The possession of Edward Prince was a more extraordinary affair. He told a doctor that, 'if I would only wait a few minutes I should see a devil come out of his throat...the head of a dog, horns of a sheep & ears of a cow'. He was tormented, furthermore, by a devil in the shape of a dog due to his unpardonable sins, while the Devil also made him abuse himself. On 4 June 1908 a medical officer wrote, 'says he has the Devil in his inside. He can breathe fire & brimstone from his mouth. Makes a hissing noise & says that is the Devil coming out.'[120]

When Joseph Parry, aged forty-four, said 'he felt a devil inside him, scraping him', it is likely he was suffering real physical pain.[121] This is what the Scottish psychiatrist Thomas Clouston described as 'visceral melancholia', and he had treated numerous sufferers who complained of such abdominal pains and a sinking feeling in the stomach. These sensations became the source of such patient delusions as being poisoned or that they had cats, mice, serpents, or rats inside them. This sometimes led to refusal to eat and drink and the not unusual belief that they had no stomach at all. One of Clouston's patients was a woman who had long believed the Devil was inside her, and when he examined the exact area where she said the Devil was located he found a terminal cancerous tumour.[122] The sensations of pregnancy and childbirth could also potentially engender diabolic thoughts, which were sometimes ascribed to puerperal insanity at the time. When Ann Elizabeth Kingston, aged forty-one, said 'that she feels as if an evil spirit was in her impelling her to do outrageous things', the cause was put down to her pregnancy (at a late age).[123] Elizabeth Stoner, aged nineteen, in South Yorkshire Asylum, would spell on her fingers 'Baby is a Devil', while a woman in Bothwell Asylum, who, at the age of twenty-eight had already given birth to five babies, and complained of a pain in her throat and on her left side, said the Devil had full possession of her.[124]

Frederick Walker Mott (1853–1926), who studied the pain symptoms and delusions of syphilis patients at the Claybury Lunatic Asylum, made the distinction that such people were actually suffering from an *illusion* rather than a *delusion* because the pain was very real and patients' way of making sense of it was to see it as an aggressive attack by external agents—in this case the Devil, but as we shall see later, also in terms of witchcraft and the malign use of electricity. The pains formed a realistic basis for the illusions around which the patient's 'whole psychical existence may centre'.[125] John Thompson Dickson found a rather ingenious cure for one patient suffering from visceral melancholy, whose physical condition generated the conviction she was possessed, by medically 'removing' the devil:

> In endeavouring to quiet her in a paroxysm of excitement I injected some solution of morphia into her right arm; she told me the next day that I had taken the devil out of that arm, so I suggested his extraction from the other, which a similar injection accomplished.[126]

Several patients talked of long, traumatic struggles with the Devil to try and prevent him from taking possession of them. From 1872 to 1873 William Butcher, a 37-year-old Anglican, was continually wrestling Satan for his life, so much so that he had no time for work. It was a battle to the death. He would go to the church, fasten the pew door, and lie 'down under the seat for fear the devil would take him'. It was while resident in the asylum that the Devil finally got his way. On 22 July 1873 his case notes report: 'says the devil has him, and he is burned first in one part of his body, and then in another, and feels a hot and sulphur taste in his mouth'.[127] In 1908 a certifying doctor went to see Joseph Hadfield, a 43-year-old Wesleyan labourer, who complained he 'had a buzzing noise in his head which was caused by the "Old Lad" meaning Satan'. He found him 'fighting & struggling face downwards on the floor, shouting at the top of his voice. He afterwards told me that the devil had told him he was lost & that he had been fighting him. He also asked us to kill him before night & then he would be dragged into heaven.' Hadfield's mother explained later that her son had told her that he and his late wife 'were on the Throne in Heaven & that he was afraid that Satan would pull him back'.[128]

Such mental struggles could obviously lead to assault and potential murder when an individual became identified with the aggressing Devil. On 16 September 1883 a 22-year-old sheep-shears cutler named William Simpson, who lived with his mother, stepfather, and brother in Sherrington

Road, Ecclesall Bierlow, Sheffield, was seen pacing up and down the churchyard of St Mary's. He was in an exited state, muttering to himself, and brandishing a club. When he was confronted by a churchgoer Simpson declared that the parson of the church was the Devil and a murderer, and that God had sent him to kill him. He had been stamping the ground with his feet saying he had got the Devil on the ground and was crushing him. He then hit the man on the head and ran through the gathered crowd and down Bramall Lane with some fifty people in hot pursuit. They caught up with him and took him to the local police station. Police Sergeant Walsh sent for Simpson's parents who were then charged with escorting him home. But on the way Simpson escaped and rushed into a house, and much to the alarm of its occupants, started banging on the table with his hat shouting that the Devil was after him. Walsh found and grabbed him and ensured he returned home without further incident. Local surgeon and dermatologist, Dale James (1850–1902), was sent for and certified that Simpson was insane. He was admitted to South Yorkshire Asylum the following day. Although the admissions record does not give a cause of insanity, the *Sheffield Daily Telegraph* headed its report of the incident as a case of religious monomania. Simpson was an abstainer and had recently been reading religious literature 'to excess'. He was deemed recovered and discharged after only five weeks in the asylum.[129]

★ ★ ★

Oral history interviews with elderly working class residents in Southwark, London, which captured childhood family life in the late nineteenth and early twentieth centuries, showed that their abiding memories of religious teaching was of Bible stories, hymn singing, images of biblical scenes found in book illustrations, brightly coloured cheap prints, and the magic lantern shows often put on in Sunday schools. The theological messages that sunk in were simple: the love of God, personal salvation, punishment of the wicked, and the existence of Hell and Heaven.[130] We can see this exact baseline of themes in the religious lives of our asylum patients, but the way they were expressed often did not follow the official line of the various churches and denominations. Assuming biblical identities, professing divine communications, talking to angels, journeying to Heaven and Hell, and encountering the physical Devil, were not the sort of faith experiences generally promoted from the pulpit. The beliefs of the asylum patients suggest a rich, shared folk religion of the imagination that often transcended the doctrinal and liturgical differences of diverse Christian faiths. This is not surprising, perhaps, when Catholics and Protestants inter-married and some people, particularly in urban areas, engaged with multiple denominations. Oral histories conducted in the industrial towns of Lancaster, Barrow, and Preston in Northwest England revealed a fascinating 'pick and mix' attitude to religious institutions, with some people attending the events, services, and activities of multiple churches and religious organizations out of need for charity, curiosity, and leisure.[131]

Sectarian divisions remained significant in major cities, of course, but such mixing and exposure may have fed the heterodox inner religious lives that we see in the beliefs of asylum patients. There is clearly a strong vein of evangelical influence, which says more, perhaps, about the attraction of religion as entertainment and emotional stimulation than it does about actual conversion at the time. It fits with what the author of the Southwark study described as 'undenominational popular religion' and what has also been called 'diffuse Christianity' in the literature. Through the asylum records we see how people wrestled with their religious identity—whether, atheist, lukewarm, or committed. Their spiritual journeys were a very personal matter based on self-assessment of character, emotional relationships with others, and the vibrancy of the religious imagination, but they often played out against the backdrop of the migrant experience and the adaptation to urban-industrial life. The fundamental concerns over salvation and damnation remained largely unchanged and, whether the product of mental illness or not, the preoccupations of the asylum patients reveal the agonizing, uplifting, and conflicted role of faith in everyday life.

6

Encounters with witches, spirits, and fairies

Fairies speak to her in the night.

(Case notes of Cath Norris, Prestwich Asylum)[1]

County asylum superintendents recognized, somewhat reluctantly, that encounters with the supernatural were a part of rural and urban life for many people in the communities they served. It challenged their ideas of societal progress that among the farmers, tradesmen, factory workers, servants, miners, and labourers there were those who clung to what they described as 'superstitious' beliefs. As Thomas Aitken, superintendent of the Inverness District Lunatic Asylum wrote in his third annual report of 1867, the 'influence of ancient superstitions' in determining the nature of patients' delusions had been 'frequently verified since the opening of the Asylum'.[2] But the term 'superstition' covered a multitude of popular beliefs and practices that were being collected by early folklorists up and down the country at the same time, ranging from folk cures to divination rituals, love charms to protective magic. For the early folklorists such matters were quaint survivals of ancient belief systems and rituals that were rapidly disappearing in the face of the inexorable advance of modernity. In this respect they shared the same mindset as many early psychologists. While the demise of such 'superstitions' was mostly considered inevitable and right, for the folklorists there was an added wistful, romantic regret about a passing world and hence the urge to record for posterity. Folklorists of the late nineteenth century thought that the people of industrial-urban Britain had already shed such relics of custom and tradition decades earlier and so they ignored the towns and cities and headed into the deep countryside to record what they believed were the last remnants of an archaic past. The asylum records show how wrong they were and represent a largely untapped archive of the supernatural.[3]

At the core of the debate over religious insanity was the generally agreed view that religious faith was intrinsically good and right, but no one was arguing that 'superstition' had any positive effects on mental health. A few superintendents decided to create their own typologies of the insane to distinguish such beliefs from folk religion. Robert Boyd (1808–1883), the first medical superintendent at the Somerset County Asylum for Insane Paupers, created the category of 'superstition' in his annual statistical accounts on the causes of insanity. In the asylum's *Fifth Report* for 1852, for instance, we find one female admitted whose 'exciting causes' were 'superstition', compared to three patients admitted for 'religious excitement' and one for 'fright'. In the *Thirteenth Report* there were two people admitted for 'superstition' compared to forty-one for 'religious excitement'.[4] By the time Boyd came to write up the accumulated statistical analyses of his patients a decade later, he had ditched the category of 'superstition' and replaced it with the more precise 'belief in witchcraft' and 'fright and witchcraft' as causes. Between 1848 and the late 1860s he ascribed four cases of mania to the belief in witchcraft out of 792 mania patients, eight cases of witchcraft belief amongst eighty-eight monomaniacs, and fourteen cases of 'fright and witchcraft' out of 600 sufferers of melancholia.[5] Over at the Worcester City and County Pauper Lunatic Asylum, opened in 1852, the medical superintendent, James Sherlock (1827–1881), listed in his first annual report one patient under the category of 'monomania of witchcraft' and four under 'monomania of superstition'. In his second report he recorded one further case of monomania of witchcraft and one of superstition. After this, the reports and casebooks drop the category of 'monomania of witchcraft', though that of 'superstition' continued to appear occasionally in the case books until the early 1880s.[6]

A few examples of idiosyncratic 'superstition' crop up in the beliefs and concerns of asylum patients. The case notes for 29-year-old Robert Hadfield record that, 'he says he was engaged to his cousin & she has given him a love charm which has upset his nerves', and Elizabeth Alice Turner, thirty-one, said she had a talismanic tin canister which she rubbed to reveal the secrets of the future.[7] But the vast majority of cases that come under the category of 'superstition', whether officially adopted or not by asylum superintendents, concerned witches, ghosts, spirits, and fairies. In other words, the belief that there were supernatural beings out there who, for various reasons, interfered with the human world for good and ill.

From accusation to asylum

Some superintendents clearly identified witchcraft as a specific issue. I have not come across any asylums using the term 'monomania of ghosts'. Witchcraft was still a vibrant concern for many across the century. Newspapers repeatedly decried the continuation of such 'gross superstition' and folklorists recorded many legends about the nefarious activities of witches.[8] There was also undoubtedly a regional aspect to the social and cultural importance of witchcraft in everyday life at the time. It is not surprising that Robert Boyd at the Somerset County Asylum was concerned with witchcraft, for instance, because my own research amply demonstrates the strength of belief in the county. There were at least twenty-six court cases concerning the abuse of and assault on accused witches in nineteenth-century Somerset. As late as 1916 a 52-year-old Somerset farmer shot dead his neighbour believing him to be a witch. The farmer was sentenced to life in Broadmoor criminal asylum. Similar detailed research shows little evidence of the same level of concern in some other counties, and so I would expect to see less representation in the asylums there.[9] But only a tiny percentage of those people who made accusations of witchcraft believed they were bewitched, or beat-up suspected witches were certified insane and taken to the asylum. They would have needed a vast new asylum-building programme to house all the witch believers otherwise. So why did a small minority end up being treated as insane?

A few people were committed to criminal asylums following homicidal assaults on suspected witches. We saw the case of James Hayward in Chapter 4, and we can trace the journey from crime to certification and treatment from the tragic example of a Scottish murderer. Tucked away in tiny print in a published table of the 1858 returns of the visiting physician and resident surgeon of the Department for Criminal Lunatics at Perth General Prison, there is an entry for a female inmate named E.L. It reads: 'Had hallucinations, and was liable to violent paroxysms of mania; murdered her mother under the delusion that she was a witch.'[10] As other records reveal, the woman E.L. was a domestic servant named Euphemia Lees, who was described at the time as having an 'irreproachable character'. In June 1845, aged thirty-four, she was living with her 82-year-old mother, also named Euphemia, in Over Haugh Street, Galashiels. Neighbours said that the younger Euphemia was subject to fits of melancholy and lowness of spirits and would periodically fly into paroxysms of rage. One evening she pounced on her mother as she lay in bed, breaking several ribs, and thrust her hand down her throat to suffocate her. When some of the neighbours living in the same tenement came to see what was going on, they found the old woman dead and soaked in blood due to a ruptured blood vessel. Euphemia was singing 'Highland Laddie' at the top of her voice, and when asked why she had killed her mother, she replied, 'I have killed the Devil; had I not done so I would have been in hell tomorrow.' These words, said the press reports, 'at once indicated her insanity'.[11]

She was tried for murder before the High Court of Justiciary sitting at Jedburgh on 18 September 1845. The defence argued she was of unsound mind and unfit for trial. The Galashiels surgeon, George M'Dougall, was called as a witness. He had attended Euphemia professionally for some eleven years and had seen her numerous times in Selkirk jail while she awaited trial. In his opinion, although she was not in a state of dementia, her 'reasoning faculties' were very weak. In the past he had treated her for what he described as violent 'fits of mania'. Thomas Anderson, surgeon to Selkirk Prison, gave it as his opinion that she was 'insane' and incapable of understanding the nature of her trial. The presiding judge, Lord Mackenzie, ruled that this was sufficient evidence of her insanity and so a bar was put her trial.[12]

After a short time in Selkirk Prison, the jailer's wife escorted Euphemia to the Royal Lunatic Asylum in Glasgow. On admission she said that all her siblings were stout and healthy except for herself, and she described how her periodic fits had begun fourteen years earlier. They started with pains down her left side and then delirium. On the evening of the tragedy, she explained, one of these paroxysms of delusion came on and she thought that she was surrounded by evil spirits. In February and March 1846 her case notes say she was quiet, healthy in body, and free from excitement since admission. She talked often of her mother's death and shed tears but would then immediately laugh and change the subject. Euphemia said she wished she had been brought to the asylum years before as then her mother would still be alive, and she complained repeatedly that her brothers should never have left her alone with her mother knowing that she had terrible fits.

Over the ensuing months she continued to be well behaved, industrious, and free from delusions.[13] She stayed until December 1846 and spent her remaining years of life in the Criminal Lunatics ward at Perth General Prison.

In a number of cases, family members and neighbours sought to certify witch believers over concerns for potential violence and murder. The Lancaster Moor admissions record for 62-year-old Joseph Roberts includes the following account by the certificating doctor:

> When I first visited him, he had an axe in his hand waving it about and was frightening a number of children who was collected about the house. He made several rambling statements to me about losing various articles from his houses and places he had visited during the week. He said for two months he was bewitched. His neighbours are in bodily fear of him. He told his daughter the devil was in the house.[14]

Sixteen years later, in 1904, Thirston Newton, aged nineteen, a Lancaster iron driller and son of an engine boiler minder, was brought to the same institution because he declared he was bewitched and had become 'a terror to his neighbours'. He would struggle violently to escape into the streets and then just ran 'like a hunted animal'. Two years later he was dead. In 1908 a warehouse packer from Bolton named Albert William Sydney Bailey, aged twenty-three, became convinced that a young lady who lived opposite, with whom he was madly in love, had bewitched him. As his admission statement records, 'He says that if this young lady's parents thwart him he would tear them to pieces... The parents of the above young lady go in fear of him.'[15]

Mary Smith, of Curry Rivel, was brought to the Somerset County Asylum in 1883 after threatening to kill her neighbour who she accused of bewitching herself and her children. William, her husband, an agricultural labourer, had recently left her. The census for 1881 shows she was left looking after a son and four young daughters. The girls screamed all night and so Mary kept the light on all the time. The witch also sent pains into her limbs. She was suicidal. She went to see the famed Taunton cunning-man Billy Brewer who gave her some drops which made her much worse. She was described as looking weak on admission to the County Asylum in July, 'slightly melancholic, brightening at times'. Over the next seven years the medical assistants wrote over and again in her case notes, 'no change', 'much the same', 'no better', 'no improvement', 'delusions persist', 'as deluded & abusive as ever'. Her physical health in no way deteriorated, though.

There was no evident physiological cause for her monomania. She was just absolutely certain she was bewitched by her neighbour. In May 1890 she was transferred to Gloucester County Asylum. Seven years later there was still no improvement.[16]

Mary was not alone. Several other patients were committed because of the onset of severe depression and suicidal tendances triggered by their conviction that they were bewitched. Their families and relatives sometimes struggled to cope. The mother of Mary Dunn clearly found her daughter's moroseness and delusions too much in 1910 and had her admitted to Prestwich asylum. Mary believed a man had cast an evil spell over her, and as a result her mother complained that she could not even get her to leave the house anymore.[17] The table of causes in the annual report for the Devon County Lunatic Asylum for 1871 lists two men admitted due to 'superstition'. One of them was a 51-year-old shoemaker named James Carslake, who lived in Sidbury with his wife Clara, a lace maker, and their three daughters, Emily, Ann, and Ellen. James was admitted on 8 February and discharged as cured on 6 June 1871. The reason for his committal appears in the local newspapers under the heading 'Sad Case of Superstition'. It told how one of his daughters had for a long time suffered from a throat disease that caused her to emit a hiccupping noise that sounded like the chuckle of a hen. The suspicion was that she had been bewitched. The tragic thing was that his wife came to be suspected of being the witch responsible. He had perhaps been told so by a cunning-person. We do not know. But this terrible thought played badly on his mind. He kept to his bed for several days, and then without warning got up one morning, dressed himself, went to an orchard and tried to hang himself from a tree. He was cut down and taken to the asylum.[18] We catch other glimpses in the asylum records of such tensions between married couples. Ann Doyle, thirty-three, fancied in 1874 that her husband was possessed by the Devil and had the power to bewitch her. Elizabeth Hill, forty-five, also believed her husband was bewitching her 'by something he puts under the pillow & in the fire'. Michael Deakers, who lived in Prestwich, got married in his forties but just two years later he was suffering from the conviction that his wife had bewitched him, stating that 'he sees her day & night & she claws his eyes'.[19]

The employer-worker relationship crops up several times as another cause of stress and anxiety. Robert Green, forty-three, was 'very suspicious in manner' and said he had 'been witched thro' his employer & his daughter'.[20] Most of the workplace cases were concerned with women in domestic

Figure 4 Seven vignettes of people suffering from different types of mental illness from the Devon County Asylum. The woman at the top of the page believed she was bewitched. Lithograph by W. Spread and J. Reed, 1858.

Credit: Wellcome Collection

service. In 1891 two women in their mid thirties were admitted to Prestwich
Asylum with such suspicions. One was Henrietta Yule, a 33-year-old sewing
machinist at a Manchester stocking factory, who told a medical assistant that
'her mistress charmed her by tying the legs & eyes of animals together—this
affected her sight and voice'. The case notes for the other, Mary Jane Royle,
wife of a cotton spinner, record on 25 October 1891: 'She is very delusional
accusing her mistress of bewitching her', and again on 15 November, 'complains of her mistress still bewitching her'.[21] Two years later, Ellen Jane Kelly,
aged twenty-three, complained that her 'late mistress instigated a man—a
fortune teller—to work a charm on her. He did so and put the Devil on her
& caused her great pain in her inside for 6 months. She says her mistress
denies it but she heard her mistress tell another woman about it & heard
every word she said most distinctly.' In 1905 a charwoman named Catherine
Layton, thirty-six, similarly claimed to have been 'bewitched' by her mistress: 'On admission she was much excited & noisily exclaimed that she had
been bewitched & pierced in the eyes by the woman she lived with. She
repeats this story today & adds that she was grumbled at & begrudged by
this woman... Is nervous & frightened.'[22]

The casebooks provide a rare window into the continuance of witchcraft
suspicions and accusations in dense, industrial-urban neighbourhoods into
the early twentieth century. While folklorists tramped around the countryside looking for titbits, hundreds of thousands of rural folk were migrating
to industrial-urban towns and cities, bringing their beliefs with them.
Several cases from Prestwich Asylum provide insights. The Asylum was officially opened in 1851 as the Lancashire County Mental Hospital to cater for
the rapidly expanding population of Greater Manchester, becoming one of
the largest asylums in Europe by the end of the century. Many of the patients
that passed through it would have lived in the urban slums and dense back-
to-back terraced housing of Manchester and Salford. Health and sanitation
had improved by the 1890s when our witchcraft believers were living there,
but the quality of housing and over-crowding were still severe problems.
The *Seventeenth Annual Report on the Health of Salford* for 1885 reported sadly
that 'a large proportion of the people are still living under circumstances
little conducive to health, either of mind or body'.[23] One resident who lived
in the poor slum area of Storey Street, was Emily Wogden, aged thirty, wife
of a pantographer at a local calico printworks. She was brought to Prestwich
Asylum in 1894 suffering from the delusion that a neighbour had thrown a
spell over her and cursed her. She was in an excitable state and could not

sleep for thinking about. She told the staff that she was bewitched, and that 'a woman cursed her & that she felt a peculiar change come over her'. Over the next few months she was distraught and depressed as she thought she would never get better due to the curse. She became overwhelmed with feelings of persecution, believing that the Devil was tempting her, that she was possessed by evil spirits and her soul was lost. 'Oh save my soul or I die', she cried. She died in the asylum in 1902.[24]

Anxiety about what was happening the other side of the tenement or apartment wall, suspicions about the strange smells and sounds emanating thorough the floors and ceilings, could become all consuming. When patients said they continually heard voices from next door they were not necessarily hallucinating. Soundproofing and privacy were appalling in the dense housing of the time. An article published in 1856 on spousal abuse in working-class areas sets the scene well:

> The screams of his wife or paramour cannot be stifled in the close alley or teaming courtyard where he dwells. His home is perhaps a single room in a house where half a dozen families are herded together. Every sound is heard through the thin, dilapidated partition-walls. A score of witnesses are ever ready.[25]

Aural hallucinations merged with the half-heard conversations, arguments, snoring, and whispers of unseen neighbours—so close yet hidden behind flimsy walls. John Gilmore, a 46-year-old melancholic in Prestwich Asylum was one who heard voices and was 'convinced they proceed from next door neighbours who bewitch him'. He had various 'enemies' and was always hearing their voices annoying him. Elizabeth Nield believed her neighbours put a spell on her, spied on her, and had the power of controlling her actions and reading her thoughts. The next-door neighbours of Mary Hopwood came through the walls to bewitch her in 1896, and when questioned whether she really saw them, she said 'Yes'. She also accused them of burning a substance, 'some sort of mess which makes her drop off to sleep'.[26]

Asylum records tell us about the physical behaviour of those who considered themselves bewitched, and their apparently abnormal convictions and fears, but less so about what their relatives, friends, and neighbours *really* thought. Evidence given in certificates and reception orders was directed at ensuring the asylum took their family members or friends and so generally conformed to the norms of medical proof of insanity. One superintendent complained that friends and family 'sometimes purposely practice deception' in this respect. But here and there we get a glimpse that some people believed that the insane behaviour of their loved ones was actually caused by witchcraft and that the asylum was a surreptitious way of getting official treatment for a supernatural ailment. Henry Parsey, superintendent at Warwick Asylum, observed in 1875 that 'the relatives of patients at the asylum have come to me and asserted that those confined were bewitched and not insane'.[27] The medical superintendent at the Suffolk Lunatic Asylum, John Kirkman, had a long-term patient who bore the scars of small shot from a shotgun in the head and neck. The man had been admitted around 1842 and before admittance was described as a 'continual terror' to the neighbourhood due to his behaviour. It subsequently came out that some of his neighbours considered that he was bewitched. One night they got him into a barn and fired at him with a shotgun to dispossess him of the evil spirit put into him by a witch. The local magistracy got wind of what happened and had the man certified for his own good.[28]

The certification process was not without its problems when it came to such matters of shared communal belief involving witchcraft. John Charles Bucknill, when medical superintendent at the Devon County Asylum, complained of the lack of thought general practitioners put into their justifications on the certificates and orders. He urged them to take time to distinguish between true delusions born of insanity and the mere opinions of family and friends influenced by 'ignorance, superstition, or any other intellectual haze'. He gave the belief in witchcraft as a perfect example. He had often seen the belief in witches stated on certificates, but he was aware that it was still prevalent among the general population of the county. And, on this point, he gave an example that had clearly caught his interest more than usual. It concerned an old woman who was admitted on the basis that her certificate stated as fact 'that she imagines she is constantly surrounded by robbers, and that her house has been partially pulled down by them'.

> In common with the certifying medical man, I at first thought that these were delusions, but I subsequently ascertained that they were no such thing. The poor old woman had been the witch of her district, and she had been surrounded by a gang of superstitious brutes, each of whom had stabbed her, under the belief that by drawing blood from her they deprived her of her supernatural power over themselves. Three of these stabs were sufficiently serious to leave cicatrices which the poor old creature will carry to her grave.... A hut also she had built with her own hands upon a common, which had been pulled down, and thus both her apparent delusions had a sufficient foundation in fact.

While conducting a body inspection at the asylum they found among her ragged clothing a sum of over £30 which she had earned as a cunning-woman. Bucknill soon had her discharged and was delighted to return the money. He kept an ear open as to her wellbeing and found out that she had moved from her tumbledown home due to the scheming of the overseer of the poor and that she had set up her magical practice afresh in another parish.[29]

The threat of removal to the asylum could also silence complaints about witches. In September 1904 an inquest over the death of a 17-month-old child in Scarborough gave a verdict of death by convulsions from rickets due to improper feeding and 'want of attention'. The child was one of five of Francis James Cooper, a corporation cartman, and his wife Sarah, who lived at 5 Ewart Street. Sarah had told people, including her doctor, that the child had been bewitched by a neighbour who had a grudge against her. She complained to the police surgeon Dr Hutton that shadows and buzzing noises haunted their house, and that other children were also bewitched. During the inquest she explained that the witch next door, named Marshall, had threatened 'she would bewitch it by boiling eggs and smashing 'em'. A prosecution was subsequently brought by the National Society for the Prevention of Cruelty to Children, which had been founded in 1884. The husband produced a certificate for the magistrates from a Dr Megginson that stated his wife was suffering from hallucinations of sight and hearing, and also mental depression. The magistrates adjourned the case and gave the couple two weeks to improve their house and the children's living conditions.[30] When it was suggested that she be medically assessed regarding the state of her mind, her views suddenly changed and there was no more talk of witchcraft. 'The threat that she might be sent to an asylum had had something to do with it', thought the press. She was now pronounced perfectly sane by medical men, and she was accused of making up the hallucinations to absolve her responsibility. She was sentenced to three months' hard labour, and her husband to one month, for neglecting their children.[31]

Witchery in the asylum

The superintendents and their assistants who wrote the medical notes in case books were sometimes sensitive to the dialect and idiom of their patients, quoting terms and passages of speech. The admission information for Mary Smith in the Somerset County Pauper Asylum noted her phrase that her neighbours had 'imagined her' and explained it was her 'term for witchcraftery'.[32] While most patients in the asylums appear to have used the widespread phrase 'bewitched', across the country there were, indeed, a variety of dialect terms to describe the act of witchcraft, such as 'ill-wished', 'overlooked', and 'betookted' in the West Country.[33] Ellen Ormrod, aged forty-two, said in 1910 that she had been 'witchcrafted'. It was done, she claimed, when she was in domestic service in Bury. She also talked of an evil spirit being 'put upon her' by having her fortune told with playing cards. We also find the language of being 'charmed' in a negative sense, as distinct from the venerable popular tradition of 'charming' or curing natural ailments by simple oral and written healing charms. Mary Mullen, admitted to Lancaster Moor in 1886 as 'maniacal, noisy, excitable, violent', was convinced that 'people put charms on her'.[34] Henrietta Yule, who was originally from Gloucester, talked of being 'charmed' in terms of bewitchment. 'One woman has so charmed her with quicksilver & blood as to nearly take her life away', and she talked about people 'charming her voice away' so that she some-times lost the power to speak for several hours.[35] In Scotland, Mary Ann Conway at the Crichton talked of the 'black art' being practised on her.[36]

In some instances the suspicion of witchcraft or bewitchment was only alluded to or implied in such phrases as being 'tormented' or 'worked on'. The notes for Arthur Dowsett, in South Yorkshire Asylum, observe for example: 'He is quiet & orderly & manageable. In conversation he rambles on religious topics & is evidently deluded against his neighbours whom he accuses of tormenting him. Says they are very ungodly & that they mocked him.'[37]

The deliberate avoidance of reference to witches and witchcraft was not unusual. It was a way of expressing one's fears to those outside their usual discourse without making explicit that witchcraft was believed in, thereby protecting the believer from potential scorn or mockery. Consider a mar-ried farmer who was admitted to the Warwick Asylum in May 1881 due to his wife's and brother's concern over his melancholic mindset. Nothing was apparently said about the cause of his mental troubles by his family. Following admission, he refused to say much about what troubled him and he did 'not readily answer questions'. They knew he suffered from 'many delusions' and he talked vaguely of enemies and losses on the farm. After a couple of weeks, though, he finally opened up and said he was convinced his cowman had bewitched his cows.[38]

Sometimes the asylum records remain silent when we know from other sources that a patient suffered from fears of witchcraft, curses, or magic. This is well illustrated by the medical notes for Ritty Littlewood, who was admitted to the West Riding Pauper Lunatic Asylum on 20 July 1857. She was twenty-six, single, a member of the Church of England, and her occupation was listed as 'housework'. Although unmarried she had had two young children. No other relatives had a record of insanity. The admission records stated she talked incoherently and that she had manifold delusions including that she was about to be hung. They explain how she 'tears her face and body when at liberty and wishes to hang herself'. Her features were described as follows:

Temperament: lymphatic

Colour of hair: dark

Eyes: Brown

Pulse: feeble

Tongue: Clean

Skin: Cool

Expression of face silly – Appetite pretty good – Bowels regular. Gets out of bed and walks about her room.

Over the ensuing month her progress is briefly reported on in her case notes. On 1 December a medical assistant wrote, 'the mental state of Ritty is in a much more satisfactory condition than it has been for some time. Instead of "clawing" every one who enters the ward, and inflicting no end of nonsense on them—she has now lapsed into a state of quietude and talks rationally.' Then, on 20 January, it was noted that her 'catamenia [menstrual discharges] have appeared for the first time since admission...She is quiet and rational.' She was deemed recovered and discharged on 15 February 1858. There was nothing in her case records at all to suggest what Ritty had been through before her admission, and why she was in such a terrible mental state that she had to be brought to the asylum—except that is for a newspaper clipping inserted into her file. This recorded her dealings with a despicable cunning-man named Isaac Rushworth and the ensuing criminal trial. He had sold her magical charms against witchcraft, then coerced her into sex as part of her cure, and when she subsequently became pregnant he made her abort the foetus. Following the verdict she suffered a terrible fit and tried to gouge her face and neck with her fingernails. Two days later she was taken to the asylum.[39] There were, no doubt, numerous people in asylums whose mental health was influenced by such experiences and concerns but we will never know because they never became a matter for the courts.

Suspicions and delusions of being bewitched sometimes translocated to their new institutional environment. Twenty-eight-year-old Thomas Mullieu thought that poison was being put in his breakfast at Lancaster Moor and that some of the other patients had bewitched him, while at Prestwich Asylum, the medical assistant observed that Agnes Ogden, aged twenty-four, a cotton winder from Accrington, 'pointed out an inmate who was capable of bewitching'.[40] The staff also came under suspicion and accusation. As well as thinking her husband bewitched her at home, once Ann Doyle was in Lancaster Moor, she began to express great concern about her regular medical assistant. She thinks 'I will bewitch her & sometimes poison her', he wrote in her case notes, and 'she is constantly wishing to change to another bedroom in order to keep clear of witchcraft'.[41] In the same asylum a few years later, Mary Ann Scanlan, aged twenty-five, said the superintendent was 'a minister of the devil' and accused the nurse, Mary Smeaton, of putting 'a spell on her'. Mary tore Smeaton's dress and tried to bite her.[42] Donald MacDonald, a patient in the Inverness District Asylum, wrote letters to the superintendent Thomas Aitken in 1868 accusing him and the other medical officers of tormenting him with witchcraft. In one letter he queried why he was being kept in the asylum, or as he described it 'this cruel house', as there was nothing wrong with him and he was just as intelligent and wise as Aitken:

> Mr. Aitken God will try you how you are using me with witchcraft to my private parts me out of my judgement and straking my brain out of my head with torture...for you did put trouble on me that will never leave me. I can give my oath upon the Bible this is the bad house to me for you could woman me with witchcraft to my privates. Good Christian people would not be trying such things to their fellow creature.[43]

There was also witchery in the workhouse insane wards. John Clendinning (1798–1848), senior physician to St Marylebone Workhouse Infirmary, noted in 1842 that years earlier the house surgeon had kept an official register of the illusions and visions of the inmates on the insanity ward. 'It contained some curious matter', said Clendinning. 'Witchcraft frequently recurred in it, but, of course, amongst various other dreams.' He went on to remark that witchcraft was 'a common fancy of this class of wrong-heads, or a common form of what is now called monomania'. He recalled a 57-year-old woman whose mind was perfectly clear and healthy except that she was preoccupied with the belief that she had been bewitched by some-body during her time in the workhouse. 'I listened to her story gravely', he said, 'not attempting to dispute with her about it, as I knew I might add to her excitement materially by doing so, and that I should certainly not suc-ceed in undeceiving her.' He cupped the nape of her neck, gave her a draft of the laxative senna and mild emetics, and applied cold compresses to her head. After two days of such treatment she said she had no more trouble from the witch.[44] Several decades later, Mary Ann Jackson, aged forty-five, in Lancaster Moor, felt miserable and fearful, claiming she was 'bewitched and fancies it was someone at the Stockport Workhouse'. Jane Goldsworth, aged forty, was also brought to the same asylum in part because she fancied she was bewitched, along with all the other people in the workhouse, by the 'influence of an old woman'.[45]

During the mid nineteenth century the Lunacy Commissioners only considered workhouses appropriate places for the keeping of the certified insane if there was no prospect of cure. Most such people were those cat-egorized as 'idiots' or 'imbeciles'. In other words, it was deemed there was no point spending extra money on their long-term treatment in an asylum. The reality was rather more complex, with cure rates quite respectable in some workhouse insane wards, and as pressure grew on asylum capacity it became not unusual for those deemed curable to spend some time in the workhouse before being removed to the county pauper asylum.[46] In 1869, for example, the Commissioners in Lunacy heard the case of a young woman suffering from acute mania in Stepney workhouse. She told the police that she had been bewitched by her mother, and when they declined to do anything about the matter she bought some rat poison and intended to put it in a pasty for the family dinner. She was caught just in time and taken to the workhouse, where she spent months waiting for an asylum bed to become available.[47] Life in the workhouse was certainly not of a standard with the pauper asylums and overcrowding was a problem. It is no surprise that the experience, whether in the insane wards or the main areas, worked its way into narratives of persecution and bred witchcraft suspicions.

Feeling bewitched

Sometimes there was a clear bodily source of pain that doctors were unable to cure. We know from other sources that internal cancers, for instance, were attributed to witchcraft. Mary Jane Royle, aged thirty-five, wife of a cotton spinner, said that the effect of her being bewitched 'was that she felt a working in her womb as if all her inside was coming out'.[48] But it was more often described by asylum patients in terms of a disordered mind—a persistent, unsettling feeling or sensation or a depressive state. Esther Dearden, aged twenty-seven, said she felt 'queer'. John Nichols, thirty-two, diagnosed as suffering from mania, was dull, confused, and somewhat sullen, and explained that his bewitchment made 'all his nerves go & that he does not know what he is doing'. Manchester patient Thomas Payne, in his sixties, used a northern dialect term to express a similar feeling: 'says his brain is mithered & that it has been done by witchcraft', and also that 'he has had his brains made stupid'.[49] Philip Dorkin in the South Yorkshire Asylum was diagnosed with congenital imbecility, but he talked much about being bewitched as a boy and admitted to 'getting very low at times'. Such mental disturbance could also involve troubled sleep patterns. Bridget Ryans complained in 1884 that 'everyone was persecuting her & influencing the minds of her children against her'. Someone had a spell over her, she said, and that person was constantly sending her to sleep.[50] Lancastrian Sarah Jane Lonsdale, a 29-year-old cotton rover, believed she and others, including her ward nurse, Miss Smith, were bewitched. She did not sleep at night and was continually hunting about the beds for witches. Aural hallucinations were not uncommon. Mary Mitchell, aged fifty-two, said that someone was bewitching her and that they read bad books to her when there is no one there. Mary Ramsden, also in her fifties, was diagnosed as suffering from mania with aural hallucinations because she believed she was bewitched and that she could 'hear voices with sinister designs on her'.[51]

If they were willing to talk about their fears and suspicions, then those with clear, fixed convictions that they had been bewitched sometimes named the individuals they suspected. Samuel Nickling, a 37-year-old coal miner, was adamant in 1891 'that one William Evans has bewitched him & that he sees shadows at night & hears voices'. In 1882 Maria Nixon, fifty-two, said that she has been bewitched by a man named Gibsy. More often the relationship with the alleged persecutor is mentioned. Ann Jones fancied in 1867 that her landlady has bewitched her, 'and threatened to kill her for having done so'.[52] As we know from court cases concerning witchcraft accusations in the period, neighbours were the most common focus of suspicion.[53] Sixty-nine-year-old Mary Ann Higginbotham, a private patient in Parkside 1901, was annoyed by occult offensive smells and claimed she was bewitched by two neighbours, and more curiously that a young man had thrown his 'stink' over her in Church. A case of bad body odour or olfactory magic?[54] For some patients suffering from severe delusions of unseen agency, though, witches were a faceless army of evil beings, the kin of myriad spirits and devils that tormented them and caused their endless suffering. Mary Ann England, aged thirty-four, diagnosed in 1901 with melancholia, said she was 'lost' and had been turned out of heaven, and 'that the devil & witches want her'. She was miserable and frightened, and she had attempted to strangle herself since admission to South Yorkshire Asylum. The widow Jane Stalker was brought to the Crichton Hospital in 1894 due to 'delusions of witchcraft', and the casebook records that 'she complains still of witches, spirits, &C annoying her' and that she spoke to imaginary people talking to her from beneath the bed.[55] Mary Ann Bower believed she flew up in the clouds where she saw several witches flying about her. These witches were not identifiable individuals but a collective horde that whispered poisonous thoughts and haunted homes. Mary Henderson talked of 'witches hunting her' and she said she was among 'bad people' and 'living witches'.[56] A labourer's wife admitted to Warwick Asylum in 1867 told the medical attendants that, 'the witches used to come and make "a lumber" on the roof of their house at night', and that it was often so bad that she and her family were driven out of the house for hours by the noise. In 1879, Sarah Driver Kershaw, forty-four, who became a long-term patient in Lancaster Moor Asylum, would sit up late at night watching for witches. She said they had been brought to a house opposite hers by gipsies and that the witches sent children to annoy her.[57] Sometimes patients would just complain of a vague malign force they described as 'witchcraft' without talking about witches per se. Selina Whittaker was described as looking 'upon everything as a mystery which requires explanation & believes she is under the influence of witchcraft... She believes that all her life she has been under the influence of witchcraft.' John Livesey imagined in 1879 that 'some one is constantly blowing witchcraft in his face, that voices are talking to him through the wall, that he is being constantly drugged &c.... He rambled about at night and imagined one of his children had been changed into a devil.'[58]

Without going into retrospective diagnoses there is an obvious boundary between patients who had a determined belief that they were bewitched by specific individuals but were otherwise mentally healthy, and those whose concerns about witchcraft were bundled up with a range of other unconnected and confused delusions and hallucinations, such as those of grandeur, unseen agency, and persecution, which were indicative of pathology. Sarah Ann Wain, who was admitted to Prestwich Asylum in 1906, imagined she was the heiress to a large property. She said people hidden in the walls interfered with her at night, and talked 'volubly, violently & excitedly about witchcraft', asserting that 'various recently deceased people have been hastened to their end by sorcery'.[59] In the Devon Lunatic Asylum we find a 30-year-old woman whose mental health had collapsed after giving birth to an illegitimate child. Emaciated and anaemic, she believed she was tormented by witches who compelled her to make noises like dogs and cats and the crowing of cockerels. She also violently beat her belly as she thought an old woman was shut up inside her and was convinced all the people around her were murderers. Another woman in the same institution, who had suffered the loss of a son and the seduction of her daughter, said she was under the power of witches who whispered into her ear that her family were to be burned. She was suicidal and said her family was dead and their letters to her were forged.[60] Henry Glover, thirty-two, was also suffering from a host of fears and anxieties in 1910. He described how 'witchcraft has been put all through him by a 7th daughter who is a witch', but this was all bundled up with ideas that 'the mistress of the house has been chained to a coal scuttle by this witch', and that God had told him to protect her. Once in the asylum he explained that the seventh daughter had bewitched him by taking a chain from this mysterious scuttle. He warned of bloodshed in consequence, as he had given his life up to redeem her, but she was now in the asylum and he heard her talking to him.[61]

In a handful of cases the usual patient concerns over witchcraft were inverted in the sense that they feared *they* were witches or were convinced that other people thought they were. All such patients were women. Lyttelton Forbes Winslow had a patient, aged thirty-one, whom he described as suffering from 'demonomania', who told him that she was a wicked witch. She was in a state of continual nervous excitement and believed she was possessed by a devil and would go to hell. She jumped in and out of bed at night groaning and talking incessantly. In 1883 we find Alice Bentley, aged thirty-nine, in Lancaster Moor in part because she was under the impression she had bewitched a man 'so that he will never work again'.[62] The doctors considered she was delusional, but maybe she had actually carried out a spell on the man. People at the time did perform a range of rituals of harmful magic for love and revenge. Ellen Hutchinson's anxieties derived in part from the belief that 'the neighbours complain that she has dealings in witchcraft'. In 1904 Isabella Fender, aged seventy-six, saw visions around her bed making faces at her and calling her a witch, while Mary Ann Burgess, fifty, heard 'voices in the air which tell her she is to be burnt for a witch'.[63] This last example is intriguing from another perspective. Witches were hanged in England, but Mary Ann had come to believe in the common misconception that they were burned as on the continent or in Scotland (after being strangled).

Haunted by spirits

Many patients mentioned visitations from 'spirits', but it is not always clear from their descriptions and the notes of the medical assistants what type of spirits they were talking about. Some were considered benign but most were evil or at least troublesome. Some spirits were likely references to angels, devils, fairies, and imps, and some were the souls of the dead. We know from other sources that witches were also accused of sending 'spirits' to plague people. This vagueness sometimes represents the looseness and interchangeability of popular references to the diverse spirit world. In the Doyle case, discussed in Chapter 2, we can see the slippage between terms in action. Johanna Doyle referred to the malign presence in her son variously as a fairy, a devil, and a 'dirty filthy thing'. Her husband also said his wife referred to 'some bad angel in the house'.[64]

Sometimes the use of the term 'spirit' probably reflected the fact that patients were not sure what the entities were other than that they were not human but looked like people. A patient in the Inverness District Lunatic Asylum known as Malcolm the Piper, stated that 'a spirit lies on him here and that it is like the person of a man and "draws" and tries to fright people'. Kate Phillips, forty, a devout Roman Catholic, said her room was full of spirits and they called her cottage a church. She described them to the medical staff as 'live spirits like people'. She saw her husband among them. They talked to her and gave her their names and said they came from Runcorn.[65] A middle-aged Irish Protestant patient provided a detailed account of his dealings with such spirits. Early on in his illness he had seen ghosts on several occasions, usually naked men with knives, but their voices grew weaker, and they eventually disappeared. But subsequently he was surrounded by good and bad spirits that dictated his life. The evil ones caused all diseases and prevented him from writing his magnum opus on the history of the world before the Flood, while the good ones cured his rheumatic pains and bad eyesight and would enable him to live for ever. He explained to the superintendent:

> I determined to get rid of them by force of will, and have done so largely, although some are left, which I hear principally in the ticking of clocks and the creaking of my boots in walking…Some of these evil spirits I have captured by pressing down my pencil and quickly folding up the paper. I have thus caught a bottleful, and have in a bottle the veritable Satan.

While the evil spirits were explicitly understood as being the Devil's spawn, he did not seem to couch the good spirits in religious terms at all. They were not described as angels or ghosts. As the superintendent explained, the man was completely sane other than his spirit beliefs, and 'he has some reason for every possible objection to his theory, and argues tolerably well upon his absurd premises'.[66]

Talk of 'spirits' was obviously also influenced by the rise of Spiritualism as a language as well as a mediumistic and religious practice. The spiritualistic dead were conceived differently to the old tradition of ghosts and ghost seeing.[67] Indeed, the creed of Spiritualism held that people did not actually die but instead 'passed over' to the 'other world'. Life continued but in a spiritual form in a different realm. These spirits were conceived, therefore, as having more agency and more intimacy than traditional ghosts, which is why, as we saw in Chapter 4, the issue became a legal matter in probate cases. The asylum records also show they could be considered controlling and possessing. Mary Briggs, thirty-five, diagnosed with mania, believed she was being manipulated by a dead spirit, while John James Whalley, forty, thought he was under 'the influence of a spiritualist who puts a spirit into his body & causes him to act strangely'. Sometimes it made him 'walk as if he were drunk, at another time it made him walk as if he were sober'. In 1909, James Arnold Butterworth, twenty-seven, believed he was under the control of a spirit medium and that the spirits had given him a secret by which he would succeed in business but which he had to guard till death.[68]

Spiritualism was also predicated on the idea that humans could proactively contact those who had 'passed over' rather than being passive recipients of their communications. In 1871 James Troughton mimicked the table rapping communications of the mediums. He would 'knock on the floor and ask what he is to do endeavouring to speak to people who have been dead & waiting some time for a reply. Whatever they say he is to do. He says he must do it.' Ellen Royle, in Parkside Asylum in 1899, sang hymns and would implore the spirits of departed friends to come to her. Attending seances might also unleash a gateway to the other world that was not necessarily wanted. Sarah Iveson, a 37-year-old Unitarian admitted to Prestwich Asylum, attended several Spiritualist services and complained that 'as a result, spirits visit her night & day'. Alice Middleton, thirty-five, whose religion was listed as 'Spiritualist', consequently developed numerous con-victions about the other world, including that she was much persecuted by the spirits and that they were 'always with her & they should not be because they upset the system'.[69] Perhaps the 'system' was that the boundaries between both worlds were clear and that it was not expected for the spirits to intrude without being called upon by mediums.

The belief in *ghosts*, or the souls of the dead returned to earth, was wide-spread across the social spectrum in both urban and rural environments and remained relatively unchanged by Spiritualist conceptions. The ghosts of folk belief were based on long-held notions regarding purposeful and pur-poseless visitations. Apart from a few ritual magicians who attempted to conjure up or communicate with the dead, ghosts appeared unbidden and were often considered frightful encounters, particularly if they were uniden-tifiable. Purposeful ghosts would return to see justice done, such as to iden-tify the location of a murder or the guilt of a murderer, or to console a loved one, and then retire. Purposeless ghosts sought no interaction with the living but played out their own spectral personal tragedies as a memorial, whether battlefield ghosts, suicides lingering at the pools where they drowned, or the ghosts of gibbeted criminals.[70] Ghostly apparitions, as distinct from séance manifestations, were the topic of numerous works of popular fiction at the time and were represented on film in early cinematography.

Those who talked about seeing ghosts shared a clear set of motifs for what they saw and experienced which had deep roots in tradition but were also being represented in new media forms. The colour of ghosts is a good example. If people did not recognize the identity of a dead person and so were unable to deduce they had seen a ghost then their confirmation was due to the whiteness of the vision they saw at night. The case notes for Nancy Scott, aged twenty-eight, report that she 'rambles about having seen a white ghost', while those for Teresa Dillon, aged twenty, similarly states she 'sees ghosts, a white thing appeared to her last night'. A young domestic servant named Sarah Alice Wheelton, who said her nervousness and apprehensiveness was due to loneliness, saw ghosts and explained that 'she sees a white figure about the house at night'.[71] By contrast, the colour of indeterminate spirits was rarely described in terms of their colour. In popular tradition ghosts mostly haunted places. Annie Shepperd, aged thirty-two, believed with evident fear and sadness that 'every house she has ever lived in is haunted'. Catherine Power, in Prestwick Asylum, was quite clear in 1907 that she would not go back to her house 'because she said there was a dog & a ghost in the garden'. And ghosts also haunted asylums of course. Lydia Wilson told staff in Lancaster Moor that she had seen numerous ghosts and spirits in the place, and Sarah Wells told the night watch in Crichton Hospital that she saw ghosts come into her room.[72] But, like the Devil, fairies, and witches, ghosts also haunted *people* as well as places; they followed them about from home to workhouse to asylum. Many patient experiences consisted of intimate audio-visual encounters rather than shared sightings that accrued around place-based legends of hauntings. Mary Faulkner, a 43-year-old Catholic, is a good example. She said she 'has visions in the night & she is always thinking about dead people, she sees dead people coming about her at night... says she hears voices + sees visions of departed souls'.[73]

In most cases asylum patients said they knew the identity of their ghostly visitors. While Alice Holland, a 38-year-old Primitive Methodist, believed that the spirits of dead neighbours came to her bedside to converse with her, the vast majority of identifiable ghosts were close family members. Bridget Ward, forty, said that the spirit of her dead sister in the form of a bird visited her and cursed her. This was all mixed up with visitations from the Holy Ghost who showed her pictures of the Creation.[74] Those under the age of fifty often reported seeing their mothers and fathers. Ann Frankland told her medical attendant that 'she often sees her father's ghost' and Rosina Campbell in the Crichton Hospital said she 'sees her dead mother'.[75] The case notes for Mary Booth, aged thirty-one, in South Yorkshire Asylum, explained: 'Melancholia. She is quiet, dull, with difficulty is induced to speak, admits having said she has seen her mother (who has been dead six years) dressed in her shawl.' In the same institution, Phoebe Hornsworth, aged forty, was similarly diagnosed, and was recorded as saying, 'she saw her mother (who has been dead 8 years) standing at her side'.[76] It was not only daughters who said such things. Thomas Melling, aged thirty, in Lancaster Moor, talked of being visited by his mother's ghost, as did James McGuinness in Prestwich Asylum. He suffered from depression and told how 'his mother comes from heaven & stops with him every night'.[77]

As a couple of the above cases suggest, the medical staff who wrote down case notes regarding ghostly visions seem to have been interested in recording the length of time between the patient experience of haunting and the death of the family member who was believed to have visited from beyond the grave. It suggests that they were trying to assess the correlation between the pathology of grief over time. Grief was and is a powerful cause of mental distress as well as pathology, and numerous twentieth-century studies of bereavement confirm that it is common enough for those grieving to feel or see their deceased loved ones around them. Some conceived these experiences as comforting dreams but others were clear that the dead had briefly returned to them for real. Interviews with elderly women in Manchester conducted in the 1980s show that most of them were quite explicit that they had 'plainly' seen the dead person.[78]

With regard to the asylum patients, the bereavement was sometimes recent and had evidently affected the immediate mental health of the surviving husband or wife. Charles Turner, aged sixty-four, whose wife had died only two or three weeks before his admittance to the asylum, said he continued to see her in his room.[79] After the wife of a patient at Claybury Asylum committed suicide he said that she had come to visit and talk to him in the asylum. For several months after, he had the delusion that he had opened her coffin and found it empty.[80] Most patients saw the spirits of their loved ones many years after they had been buried, suggesting that visitations were mostly embedded in recurring and comforting emotional memories of the distant past. The case notes for Eliza Wiggleworth, aged fifty-two, record that she 'thinks she sees her husband who has been dead 14 yrs', while those for Jane Reeves, forty-five, note that 'she says that she has just seen her father, who has been dead 20 years'.[81] Some were one-off or occasional visitations but others were regular and part of an ongoing, intimate relationship with the dead. William Adams, aged sixty-eight, saw and heard his wife every night even though she had been dead many years, while in 1869, Matilda Slater, a 40-year-old Methodist, was frequently visited by her dead mother's ghost.[82] The sighting of child ghosts is rare in the annals of British hauntings, yet common in other parts of northern Europe and Ireland. At a time when infant mortality was very high compared to today this is somewhat surprising. It has been estimated, conservatively, that across the nineteenth century the infant death rate in England was

153 per thousand compared to around five per thousand today.[83] That is not to say that the grief of mothers was not manifested in occult experiences. Maria Nelson, admitted to an asylum in 1876 at the age of twenty-nine, said that 'all her dead children appear alive to her when she falls asleep'. The Prestwich Asylum case notes for Alice Briggs, aged forty-nine, recorded that she 'fancies she can see & hear her dead children'. Neither of these brief accounts mention that Maria and Alice thought they were visited by ghosts, though, and these appearances may have been conceived as intimate visions rather than actual visitations of the dead.[84]

Ghosts were generally reported as being silent in folklore and historical accounts, using gestures to make their point—if they had a point at all in returning to or lingering on earth.[85] The ghosts of asylum patients were quite talkative by contrast. Numerous patients said they maintained regular conversations with their loved ones. Henry Tonge, aged thirty-four, conversed 'with his mother + father as if they were beside him both having been dead years ago', while Owen Jones, forty-six, gave the medical assistants at Prestwich Asylum 'a detailed description of a visit his deceased wife paid him last night, stating how she was dressed & what they said to each other'. In the same institution Thomas Jenkins explained how he constantly saw and talked to his dead wife and child.[86] The desire to be reunited with loved ones was strong for a few. Annie Bloom, aged thirty-five, said she had seen her dead mother beckoning to her, while Charles Russell Beresford, sixty-six, whose wife had died a while before, 'says he sees his wife at night & talks with her but cannot feel her & is wishful to join her'.[87]

But not all ghosts were welcome. A 78-year-old patient admitted to the St Marylebone Infirmary in 1842 assured the senior physician John Clendinning that 'for a long time the spirit of some person that is dead has lain on her, and caused her sharp pain in every part of her body, so that she suffers torture from it'. Although she was a Protestant, she was adamant that only a Roman Catholic priest could release her from the oppressive spirit. The notion that only a Catholic exorcism would work has been recorded elsewhere in the annals of English folklore of the period.[88] In 1878, Hartley Allison, a 23-year-old cotton weaver, and a member of the Free Gospel Church, one of numerous small evangelical churches in Lancashire that had Methodist affiliations, complained that 'the dead folk would not leave him alone', and one day clambered over a cemetery wall saying he was 'going to raise the dead'.[89] If some ghosts reflected the flaws, faults, and crimes of their corporal human lives then it is not surprising that their appearance was also sometimes traumatic and unwanted. Elizabeth Williams said in 1894 that 'her father haunts her & tries to take liberties with her', and Elizabeth Tomlinson, thirty-three, heard 'voices at night threatening to kill her, thinks those voices proceed from her dead sister-in-law'.[90] Sometimes it was the past misdeeds of the patient that led to their being tormented. John Rostron in Lancaster Moor Asylum in 1885 suffered the classic guilt-ridden haunting we find across centuries past. He talked of having killed a man and now his ghost returned to haunt him night and day.[91] In other sources I have found examples of people making the threat to kill themselves solely to come back and haunt someone, and so it is no surprise to find the same vow in the asylum records. In 1881 Ann Lundie said that 'she will drown herself, taste poison, or cut her throat, & that her ghost will haunt her husband'.[92] It was not just the mere presence of the dead that was unwelcome but what they said. We do not know what he apparently told her, but 28-year-old Sarah E. Taylor was most upset by the appearance of her dead father who came to have words with her. The purpose of Mary Hair's husband was quite clear, though. At the age of fifty-two she had been a widow for eleven years. His spirit visited her nightly between ten and eleven o'clock, but only appeared once every three months thankfully, because by look and word he upbraided her every time for her former conduct.[93]

Fairies on the mind

Beliefs and legends about fairies continued to circulate around the country, though 'lingering' was a common adjective to describe their status in folk-lore. It was observed in 1867, for instance, that in northern Staffordshire the belief in fairies 'still lingers with some here', and folklorist Thomas Sternberg noted the same of Northamptonshire in 1851, but he qualified this by stating that it was 'almost within the memory of persons still living'.[94] People continued to associate certain places in the landscape with them and referred to 'fairy rings' and 'fairy loaves' in popular and local idiom, but there are very few concrete examples in England during the second half of the nineteenth century of people claiming to have interacted with the fairies, such as leaving out gifts for them, blaming illnesses on 'fairy shot', or believing their babies were replaced with fairy changelings. This decline was noted at the time, with numerous comments that the advent of the railways with their noise and disruption, the locomotions of 'progress', chased the fairies away.

As most of our asylums are in the north of England, it is also worth noting that there are no references to boggart lore in the patient records. Boggarts were shape-shifting, ghostly or demon-like spirits that haunted specific locations in the rural landscapes of Lancashire and Yorkshire.[95] It is possible, though, that some patients had boggarts in mind when they talked of indeterminate spirits, as discussed earlier. Encounters with boggarts were traditionally brief, disturbing experiences at night in isolated places, which obviously had the potential to lead to fright-inspired insanity, but they were not like the complex, ambivalent, and intimate human-fairy relations that we know fed real anxieties and concerns.

Belief in personal fairy relations amongst our asylum patients mostly concerned the Scottish and the Irish. Two women admitted to Montrose Asylum in 1855 claimed they had been 'visited by fairies', and in Lancaster Moor in 1898 Patrick Lynch, aged thirty-four, Irish born and bred, 'said he had fairies in his pocket'.[96] The records also show that by the early twentieth century the fairy-believers were not some elderly rump clinging on to the largely discarded traditions of their childhood. They were men and women aged from nineteen to seventy, and of different religious persuasions. Fairy belief was cultural not denominational and so we find both Protestants and Catholics sharing the same set of ideas.

Most of the patients were female though, and it has been observed how in official contexts, such as in criminal courts, Irish men were reluctant to express fairy faith due to it being unmasculine and considered a trait of female 'superstition'.[97] Most fairy doctors, who professed power from the fairies and also powers to deal with fairies, were also women.

Ethnographic fieldwork and oral histories confirm that fairy belief and the belief in the possibility of meeting the fairies were still quite widespread amongst Presbyterians and Catholics in the Highlands of Scotland during the early decades of the twentieth century.[98]

The rural Irish, in particular, continued to have an intense and personal relationship with the fairy realm in our period. This is most graphically evident from the belief that the fairies afflicted children and supplanted their own for human infants.[99] It was even a subject of note in the Irish census reports for 1841, which required householders to record not only those present in the house on census night, but also those who had died while residing with the family during the last ten years, including the cause of death. The report's authors explained that fairies were blamed for causing 'Tabes Mesenterica', which was a childhood wasting disease causing inflammation of the lymphatic glands and general atrophy. It was variously referred to as 'back gone' or 'fairy stricken', or as one householder explained of his child, 'the fairies tuck him away'. One of the recorded cures in the census was to put the affected infant on a spade or shovel and place it in the blast of a whirl wind with the hope that the fairies would take back the fairy child.[100] We saw a tragic example of fairy changeling beliefs in action in Chapter 2 with the case of the Doyle family in 1888. Seven years later the notorious Clonmel burning took place in County Tipperary. On this occasion 28-year-old Bridget Cleary, the wife of a cooper named Michael Cleary, was burned to death by family members who believed they were burning out the fairy that they had been told had taken possession of her body. Michael Cleary was found guilty of manslaughter and sentenced to twenty years penal servitude. He was released on petition in 1910 and emigrated to Canada. Several others involved in the burning were also given lesser prisons sentences.[101] I mention the case here because, unlike the Doyle affair, no insanity pleas were made on behalf of the defendants. Any case for insanity was probably considered indefensible because Michael Cleary and his accomplices exhibited no signs that they were unaware of the crime they had committed. They had secretly buried Bridget's body soon after her death and tried to spread the rumour that she had suddenly disappeared.[102]

Irish fairy belief was much more diverse than just the notion of changelings. Being fairy 'struck' was thought to be the cause of strokes, heart attacks, and insanity, and Bronze Age arrowheads found in the fields were considered evidence of the fairy arrows responsible. The Irish folklorist G.H. Kinahan wrote in 1881 that he personally knew a young man who suddenly went insane and was eventually taken to the asylum. The man's brother-in-law, who had looked after him, believed the affliction had been caused by being fairy struck, and during his worst moments had told his brother-in-law that he saw the fairies dancing around him and throwing their darts at him.[103] People also intimately shared the landscape with the fairies, with the hundreds of raths or prehistoric circular defensive settlements that dot the Irish countryside being associated with fairy dwellings. Shortly after the Clonmel trial, and in response to it, Leland L. Duncan set out to interview locals in the parish of Kiltubbrid, County Leitrim, about the fairies. He asked them 'Who are the fairies?' They all told him the same thing, 'They are the fallen angels.' When Edith Balfour toured western Ireland in the early twentieth century she talked to a priest who said he never discouraged his parishioners' belief in the fairies. 'They are quite sound on the doctrine of the Trinity and the Blessed Virgin', he said of his flock, 'and it is all a way into the unseen.'[104]

Fairies evidently played on the mind as well as in the Highland glens of Scotland and the raths of Ireland. Asylum patients' views on fairies reflected centuries-old folklore, which allowed that fairies could be human-sized or diminutive, that they could shape-shift, and wore distinctive clothing, often said to be green but not always.[105] In 1891, patient Cath Norris, a 39-year-old Wesleyan Methodist, who was noted to have 'delusions of fairies visiting her', 'says they are little people of a blue or light colour'. A 60-year-old hawker in the Fife and Kinross District Asylum said he saw 'wee folk, two or three feet high with brown dresses on, who could change shape and disappear into the wall'.[106] The fairies were ambiguous figures who were capable of good as well as harm. In 1885, Dinah Nicholson, a Scottish widow in Crichton Hospital, said that 'there are fairies which hover around her head and tell her to do things sometimes right & sometimes wrong'.[107] For some, the fairies were part of the general supernatural persecutorial horde along with witches, devils, imps, and spirits. Elizabeth Murphy, a 63-year-old Roman Catholic in Lancaster Moor asylum, complained in 1887 'that fairies annoy her and pull her cap'. Two years later, Jane Stitt, a Scottish-born Protestant woman aged fifty-five, similarly said she was 'annoyed by fairies, dogs & beasts creeping up the wall at night'. In 1895, Ellen Turner, a 48-year-old Catholic, protested that she had been trying to banish the fairies from her house.[108] For several other patients the fairies, as in wider Irish and Scottish folklore of the time, were beings that had to be accommodated rather than banished. They seemed like domestic companions to Anne Flannagan, a 70-year-old Catholic who, in 1885, said, 'she sees fairies and talks to them as they are dancing on the ceiling'. Around the same time another Lancashire woman of likely Irish extraction, though of Wesleyan religion, Sarah Farrel, described how there were fairies in her room who kindly swept the chimney for her.[109] Keeping good relations with them was generally transactional, so it was best to leave them gifts or show appreciation. A long-term elderly patient in Lancaster asylum, Ellen Crowley, believed the fairies visited her at night and she left food and snuff for them. In 1903, James Conway, a 25-year-old Catholic patient in Prestwick Asylum, believed the house he had lived in 'was haunted by fairies who kept constantly annoying & irritating him'. But in an attempt to appease them, he also explained that the walls of his house had been filled with 'peace offerings to the fairies the King & Queen of whom he knows very well by sight'.[110]

As well as the general characteristics of the fairies we also glimpse some fascinating references to the notion of fairy society and human interactions with their realm. James Conway mentioned the King and Queen of fairies, which reflected the long-standing notion that fairyland had its own royalty with princes and princesses. The fairy love of festive gatherings, and the human fear of being seduced into the fairy realm by their song and dance, was a common motif in Irish folklore. One folklorist observed in the 1880s: 'the fairies are passionately fond of music; it is therefore dangerous for a young girl to sing when she is alone by the lake, for the spirits will draw her down to them to sing to them in the fairy palace under the waves, and her people will see her no more'.[111] This concern was reflected in the worries of Scots woman Margaret Cathey, who said she was 'afraid to dance amongst fairies'. In 1892 Irish-born Helen Dolan, aged fifty-three and living in Glasgow, believed her house was infested with fairies who were 'anxious to make her join their company'. While in the asylum it was noted that she 'still believes in fairies but resents people talking to her about them'. Anne Lancaster, a 19-year-old Catholic in Prestwich, also had concerns, stating that 'she doesn't want to be a fairy'.[112] The idea of being fairy-led, that is being deliberately led astray and disoriented while traversing a familiar landscape, is suggested in the statements of Dinah Nicholson, who went walk-about from Crichton Hospital and explained to the medical officers afterwards that the fairies 'had witched her & made her walk on'.[113]

★ ★ ★

During the nineteenth and early twentieth centuries a world with witches, spirits, and fairies clearly seemed reasonable to many, and the asylum records provide a unique glimpse of how they were encountered in urban industrial environments as well as in the countryside tramped by the early folklorists. Belief in the various supernatural entities was difficult to separate out, furthermore, from the supernaturalism of popular religion, despite attempts by asylum psychiatrists to create boundaries of belief pathology. For some patients the interaction with supernatural beings and witches was grounded in the everyday experiences of misfortune, grief, and social relations. For others it was an expression of a mental other world inspired by the motifs and narratives of folk tales and legends, made real in the imagination and melded with the experience of mundane life. A study of the casebooks of the Santa Maria della Pietà insane asylum in Rome reveals a similar picture of patients living in a 'folkloric universe' and guided by fairy-tale morality and motifs.[114] While this blurring of mental experiences was sometimes the product of illness, it was also a state of mind that shaped the creative worlds of artists, fantasy and science fiction writers, and cinematographers at the time. The borders of the folkloric universe also proved remarkably adaptable to change, as we shall now see regarding the encounter with technology in everyday life.

7

Making sense of science
and technology

Talks about telephones, the devil & flying machines.
(Case notes of Dorothy Moseley, Lancaster Moor)[1]

In his *The Subconscious Self and its Relation to Education and Health*, published in 1897, the American pathologist and psychologist, Louis Waldstein (1853–1915), stated: 'the hallucinations of the insane to-day contain nothing alluding to the telephone, the phonograph, and other recent innovations, but those of twenty years hence may be full of wire messages from paradise or flash lights from hell'. Waldstein's prediction was way off target. Asylums across Europe and America had already been dealing with such patient delusions for years. Indeed, a review of the book in the *Journal of Mental Science* noted this failing as a flaw in Waldstein's arguments. It was often a matter of months not decades between the advent of new technologies and their appearance in patient case notes. A study of three York Asylum casebooks from the 1880s, for instance, found that 14 per cent of delusions concerned recent technologies or scientific developments such as telephones, electric lighting, and the London Underground.[2] Waldstein's mistake was to adhere to theory and ignore the evidence. By the time he was writing his book he had embraced the recent psychoanalytic theory of the subconscious, and so he postulated that adult experiences of street lighting and other technologies were unlikely to enter the deep subconscious: 'it is not generally the intensity of the first impressions which makes them thus permanent and of such influence in later life, but it is their repetition in the early life of an impressionable person'.[3] They would have to wait for the young generation to grow up to see the psychological toll on society.

Bethlem Superintendent George Savage was on the ground and knew what he was talking about when he explained in 1884:'with the development of any new instrument which becomes popularly known, there is always a free use of the discovery made by the insane'.[4] When it came to such 'technology insanity' it is difficult to discern any significant differences according to age, gender, class, or religion. Everyone was confronted with the same cognitive challenge when faced with new invisible power sources, mechanical innovations, electrical communications, and the replication of humanity through captured image and voice. Before they personally used the appliances of science they might have read about them in newspapers and magazines, attended a popular science lecture, or peered at strange electrical goods in shop windows. The press was full of talk of technological 'wonders' and 'miracles', thereby conflating the language of modern science with the supernatural.[5] Most people embraced such wonders immediately and unquestioningly, even if they did not know how they worked. The garbled popular understanding of science of the average man or woman on the street or in the pub was a matter of gentle mockery in the press. A magazine vignette from 1905 imagined a conversation between two men in a pub where one man explained to the other the essence of life before Adam and Eve from a science lecture he had just attended:

> This yer radium, Charlie, is reely life. On'y life is raely a jelly, what you find in the sea. So this jelly is radium, you see, on'y they can't find the jelly, an radium is scarce, so they invented electricity. And there's radium in electricity, if they could on'y find the way to get it out. But there ain't no jelly in it—see?[6]

But some people were initially confused, suspicious, and disorientated and tried to make sense of technology within the language and framework of magic and the supernatural. The asylum records suggest, though, that while techno anxieties were intense they were also usually fleeting. Familiarity soon allayed fears, although those with severe mental health issues would move on to fixate on some new subject of unseen agency or object of scientific terror. Societies and communities all over the world have experienced the same when first encountering the likes of cameras, cars, planes, and telephones.[7]

The rise of the machine

Mechanical innovation is a constant in human history and prehistory, from the harnessing of waterpower in the earliest civilisations to the engineering feats of antiquity, from the Antikythera astrological mechanism to the eighteenth-century pocket watch. We know very little of the initial popular interpretation of such wonders in the distant past, and how they played on the mind, provoked personal fantasies, or induced fears of unseen agency. But nineteenth-century industrialization provides some such insights.[8] In 1919 the Viennese psychoanalyst Victor Tausk (1879–1919) coined the term the 'influencing machine' to describe the persecutorial, technological delusions he encountered among sufferers of dementia praecox (schizophrenia). Patients usually had only a vague notion of the exact construction of the machines but talked of levers, springs, wheels, wires, batteries, and such like.[9] In 1890, Agnes McMuldroch complained that 'springs have been placed inside her and that they work upon her'. Her cough was due to springs in her chest and her trembling was caused by 'trembling springs'. A few years later, a Dublin post office employee stated: 'I am an automatic lunatic; I can sing, dance, or do anything through the wires that are acting on me.' He complained of being tormented by electrical instruments that he called 'tykes' and 'spankers'.[10] We will see plenty more such examples later.

A striking early instance of the influencing machine arose from the imagination of a patient in Bethlem, a London tea-broker named James Tilly Matthews (1770–1815).[11] In 1810 John Haslam, the Bethlem apothecary, published a detailed account of Matthews' persecutorial delusions based, in part, on Matthews' own manuscript account of his concerns. Matthews believed that he was in an invisible correspondence with a gang of spies and criminals via what he called 'brain sayings', which were a form of magnetic thought power.[12] The spies had built a sophisticated 'pneumatic machine' or 'air loom', the size of a large room, in a place not far from Bethlem. Mathews was a skilled draftsman and even produced a detailed illustration of the loom and its workers in action. They used it to torment him with rays in a variety of ways that he explained in great detail, describing them variously as foot-curving, lethargy-making, spark-exploding, knee-nailing, burning out, eye-screwing, sight-stopping, roof-stringing, vital-tearing, and fibre-ripping. Most remarkable was lobster-cracking. Matthews explained:

in that dreadful operation by them termed lobster-cracking, I always found it necessary to open my mouth somewhat sooner than I began to take in breath: I found great relief by so doing, and always imagined, that as soon as the lever was at the lowest, (by which time I had nearly let go my breath) the elasticity of the fluid about me made it recoil from the forcible suction of the loom.[13]

We can clearly trace an age of anxiety regarding technology from the development of the railways onward, which just so happened to coincide with the expansion of the asylum and what was described at the time as the 'frightful' increase of insanity. During the mid century the press reported concerns that a worrying number of apparently sane men were suddenly being struck down with violent mania while travelling, thereby endangering female passengers and even leading to murder. Various medical studies on both sides of the Atlantic were conducted to look into the health effects of rail travel. As the *St Louis Medical and Surgical Journal* explained, one issue was whether the sudden and abrupt vibrations of the carriages, and the rapid passage of objects from looking out the window, had 'a tendency to derange function and alter structure'. Medical opinion suggested that rail travel could trigger already latent mental illnesses.[14] There was actually very little evidence that the railways per se caused a wave of mental health problems, but the railway engine clearly played on the minds of some. A patient in St Luke's Hospital believed himself to be a steam engine and would mimic one in motion, while in 1890, Isabella Gilchrist in the Crichton Hospital was certain that machines worked upon her and that there was a railway train in her body.[15] A couple of engine drivers were suspicious of their steam-powered steeds. In 1876 John Oldfield was convinced there were devils in the engine he drove, while a few decades later, engine driver, Henry Beauland, said he was subject to 'brain storms' after receiving shocks while driving his engine which left him in a dazed condition and spoiled his memory.[16]

The language and notion of an indeterminate 'infernal machine' cropped up repeatedly through the century, though rarely attributed directly to the Devil despite the hellish allusion. Haslam used the term with reference to Matthews' accounts of the air loom. At the other end of the century, James Buckley, a patient in Lancaster Moor, claimed there were 'infernal machines' under the weather cock of the local church, which were to be used to blow up the railways. A female patient at Guy's Hospital who believed she had seen Jesus was also convinced there was an 'infernal machine' underneath her.[17] A 33-year-old servant in the Royal Edinburgh Asylum used slightly different language, complaining in a letter that she was 'followed by two torturers with some awful machine attached to me which is drawing the soul out of me'.[18] Patients often had hallucinations of mechanical noises. One woman explained how she heard whirring, rolling of wheels, and peculiar clattering before then hearing voices state, 'now we will put on the machine . . . now we will give it to her'.[19] By the end of the century these infernal machines were mostly associated with electricity, wires, and batteries, and, as we shall see, the mysterious, ill-defined conception of these machines gave way to concrete forms in the shape of telephones, phonographs, X-ray machines, and the cinematograph.

Mental science

Initial fears about machines were mostly about how they caused loss of will, took possession the body, or were tools of unseen agents. Similar concerns were also expressed with regard to mental sciences. James Tilly Matthews' infernal machine was, in part, a product of his intense interest in mesmerism. Half a century later, mesmeric influence was still playing on the minds of many. In an autobiographical account of asylum life by a patient in Morningside Asylum in the early 1850s the author observed that he found amongst his fellow patients a general delusion of mysterious unseen forces including mesmerism, electricity, and spiritualism.[20] This is hardly surprising as debates about the medical use of mesmerism, and also whether mesmeric power was electrical in nature, swirled around periodical literature in Britain through the 1840s and 1850s.[21] Regional newspapers printed curious examples of mesmeric influence and carried reports of lectures on the subject held in local towns. These, in turn, attracted indignant letters to the editor from advocates and critics. In December 1843, for instance, newspapers reported how a young lady of Newcastle who had been mesmerized kept falling into involuntary sleep for up to five hours because the mesmeric influence had not been 'properly destroyed'.[22] As to the application of mesmerism in asylums, much controversy was generated in 1852 by the opinions of James George Davey (1813–1895) who had recently returned from his role as medical superintendent at the colonial Lunatic Asylum in Sri Lanka to take up the job of resident medical officer at Colney Hatch Lunatic Asylum. He was an ardent believer in both phrenology and mesmerism and was interviewed by a lunacy commission on the matter.

Davey claimed to have cured several people of insanity by mesmerism in Sri Lanka, and when the commissioner asked him whether he thought any man who did not believe in mesmerism could be classified as of unsound mind, he replied carefully, 'He either does not think sufficiently, or is prejudiced.'[23]

General notions of mesmerism as a manipulative occult power were widespread in popular culture long after mesmerism had been roundly rejected by most of the medical and scientific community. Writing in 1883, Clouston described electricity and mesmerism as the two commonest expressions of unseen agency among asylum patients.[24] Patients saw mesmerism as a personal, targeted force rather than some vague occult threat. They usually accused a specific person of having applied the mesmeric influence. Some complained they had completely lost their will and were being bodily controlled. In 1886, James Needham, aged twenty-nine, was convinced that 'some one is able to influence him & make him do anything'—including not turning up for work as it happened. Thomas Holstein, forty-six, said on admission in 1883 that 'he had been driven here by the power of mesmerism practised on him by a certain clergyman', while a medical attendant wrote of patient James Haughton in 1893, 'He believes he is altogether under the influence of a man he calls Mr Penny who by "mesmeric" & "magnetic" means is driving him to do what otherwise he would not.'[25] Twenty-two-year-old hospital nurse and patient Agnes Caird Finnie was convinced that her own patients were 'clever thought-readers and mesmerists, who "think through her brain", and make her do anything they wish'. Some were, like Finnie, preoccupied that their minds were being read. William Cale in Lancaster Moor believed his 'landlady mesmerized him when he was asleep and became aware of all he had ever done'.[26] There were also those who felt they were being physically abused due to mesmeric influence itself or when involuntarily placed under a mesmeric trance. Ann Durkin, thirty-nine, when admitted to Lancaster Moor in 1899, rambled at length how a Dr Oswald Wraith had 'mesmerised & caused her acute torture of body & mind'. This was almost certainly the surgeon and physician of the same name who had his practice in the town of Darwen, Lancashire. Maude Lander, twenty-three, believed that she had been mesmerized by a schoolmaster the previous Christmas and had 'felt wrong in the head ever since'.[27]

Irish psychiatrist Conolly Norman (1853–1908) became the target of such suspicions. The patient concerned was a 20-year-old woman who had recently been removed from a convent reformatory to a Dublin workhouse where her mental illness became apparent. She claimed to have visions of and communications with the Virgin Mary as well as having suspicions of mesmeric persecution. She reported overhearing one of the medical officers planning with a couple of nurses about how to mesmerize her. Then, in early 1903, she began to accuse Norman of 'influencing' her by mesmeric means. He made her 'stupid' when he passed by. One day she turned around and saw him thrust his hand in the tail-pocket of his coat. After this she suddenly experienced a sharp pain in the back of her chest whenever she saw him. As he passed her by on another occasion he asked her, 'How was the pain?' And pointed towards her heart with his finger. She did not reply at the time, but later said that his pointing at her had caused great pain in her heart, and she had fainted three times the following night. She fell ill whenever she saw him from then on and suffered pains in her heart and all over her body as if she was being pricked with pins. Sometimes she felt 'something like a reel winding up in her chest'. His mesmeric power was such that, even from his own house half a mile from the asylum, he could deprive her of the ability to speak, and when she tried to utter words she said 'he winds up this reel and prevents her'. When asked how Norman had gained such influence over her, she explained:

> He asked somebody to get my handwriting. I wrote a letter to a girl who is a friend of mine. They got it and gave it to him and once he had my writing and my signature he could influence me by that as he wished, and it was from this it all came—all that followed, I mean. I was then in his power. He could do what he liked when he had my signature to work on.[28]

It is no surprise that during the late nineteenth and early twentieth century some patients also said they were persecuted by or under the control of hypnotists. Before the 1880s the terms 'hypnotist' and 'hypnotism' were not engrained in popular language, but they would become synonymous with the mesmerist and mesmerism as fears regarding hypnotism spread through popular culture during the 1880s and 1890s thanks to lurid newspaper stories, disapproving pamphlets, popular fiction, public lectures, and theatre hall entertainment.[29] George Du Maurier's best-selling novel *Trilby* (1895), first serialized in 1894, had a considerable impact on the popular consciousness in this respect. The story concerned the eponymous hero, Trilby O'Ferrall, who was half-Irish and worked as an artist's model and laundress in Paris. She was hypnotized by a musician named Svengali into becoming a hugely successful singer despite her being tone deaf, thanks to her abilities being unleashed when under hypnotic trance.[30] It was a huge transatlantic success and was turned into plays and stage vignettes, as well as inspiring a range of 'Trilbyana' merchandise from ice creams to sausages.[31] The satirical magazine *Punch* made much play with the sensation, stating in one item that 'Trilby Mania Grows Apace'.[32] Concerns over real-life Svengalis with diabolic criminal motives spread further due to reports in the international press of cases like the Czynski trial in Germany in 1894. The victim was Baroness Hedwig von Zedlitz and the predator, Czynski, a magnetic healer and hypnotist who had set up a clinic in Dresden the previous year. He was accused of various crimes including the alleged sexual assault of the Baroness while in a hypnotic state. Such was the concern that in 1892 the Belgian government even outlawed the public demonstrations of hypnotism.[33]

Despite the concerns over sexual predation by male hypnotists, men and women were equally prone to hypnosis fears, with asylum patients accusing their neighbours and family members of hypnotizing them in the same terms as mesmerism and magnetism. In 1888, Jemima Colville, a 31-year-old patient in the Royal Crichton, talked 'incoherently about hypnotism, magnetism, electro-biology, and says she is prevented from getting the magnet by which she could cure herself'.[34] For some, the hypnotist's gaze was essentially the evil eye in another guise. In 1904, Dora Emily Hanmer, fifty, said she had 'been hypnotized & has "been under the spell for 18 months"'. A 36-year-old barber, George Graham Bonnaud, attributed all his misfortunes to hypnotism. He told the asylum staff that 'some girl in Oldham has hypnotized him, read his thoughts + practically ruined him. He says she came to his eye, caught his glance + hypnotized him. All this has been done to favour another hairdresser in Oldham'.[35] The idea of having no free will was also expressed, with Jemima Colville believing that hypnotists 'control her actions' while Bonnaud stated that others had 'influenced him for evil & taken his will away'.

During the 1890s some British asylum superintendents were trying out hypnosis on their patients. George Robertson, Senior Assistant Physician at the Morningside Asylum in Edinburgh was one. He had recently studied the technique under Charcot and had also visited Bernheim at Nancy. Back at Morningside Asylum he found it very difficult to hypnotize insane patients, however, and thought that it was probably due to the 'steady and unexcitable Scotch brain' in contrast with the 'functional hysterical disorders so common in Paris'. He did report some success in allaying hypochondriacal notions that had previously prevented him from treating some patients with medicine.[36] But Robertson also noted the influence of 'highly sensational newspaper accounts' and the 'dramatic exhibitions of public performers' on 'ignorant and superstitious people'. In this respect, he warned of the dangers of using hypnosis on the insane:

> In an asylum, if extensively used, it may increase and strengthen the delusions about hypnotism, and about unseen agencies in general, and we have had one case here who, when she learnt that I made use of hypnotism, although not with her, imaged that all her delusions were confirmed, and became very difficult to manage, if not positively dangerous. This objection, however, may just as legitimately be urged against the use of the battery for electro-therapeutics, or against the introduction of the electric light and telephones in our modern institutions.[37]

Electrickery

The invention of the Leyden Jar in the 1740s, which produced electrical sparks, led to a boom in medical experimentation with electric shocks at a time when animal magnetism was also gaining influence. In the 1809 edition of his *Traité médico-philosophique*, Pinel had already encountered patients suffering from electrical delusions. He observed a widow in the Salpêtrière who was convinced that someone was persecuting her invisibly with electricity or spells. He talked of another woman, perhaps the same, who had heard about electricity and had read something about physics, who thought her enemies could send electric currents in the air to harm her at great distances.[38] This patient was clearly well-educated but most people would have been largely ignorant of electricity until the mid nineteenth century. But the vogue for mesmerism, and its high profile in popular literature, laid firm foundations for the public understanding of and concerns about electricity in the second half of the century. The already establish notion that invisible, magnetic fluidic forces could affect mind and body meant that electricity could be explained to people using similar, familiar language. It is not surprising that some patients saw the two powers as synonymous. John Edmondson, aged twenty, who spent a few months in Lancaster Moor in 1872 said 'he was mesmerized or electrified by the people in the mill where he worked causing him to have griping and cramps in the belly and confusion in the head'.[39] Around four years later, over in the West Riding

Asylum, a 56-year-old commercial clerk, named T.S., wrote a letter in light of recent pseudo-scientific ideas in which he attempted to explain the nature of the mysterious forces and voices that tormented him terribly:

> Dear Sir, I beg you will read the following without prejudice...My first wife's sister's husband, who resides forty miles south of London, is the inventor of an electro-animal-magnetic machine, and other inventions, made, I suppose, somewhat similar to a camera obscura, or camera lucida, both of which or all are fixed at Leeds or Wortley...Five or six persons whom I know by their voices (but there are many others I don't know) can see and hear all that transpires in the district...they can also tell (after having applied the electro-magnet to his head) what any person is thinking, and he is compelled and cannot avoid hearing all they say. It is impossible that mesmerism or electro-biology may be combined. The mind of the individual operated upon is affected through a material living agent, it may be through a material fluid—call it electric, call it odic, call it what you will, which has the power of traversing space, and passing obstacles, so that the material effect is communicated one to another. No man or woman's life is safe that they have any ill feeling or hatred towards.

There was much more besides, and he ended his letter, 'Don't imagine I am insane because I write this from a lunatic asylum.'[40]

We have encountered hallucinatory communications many times with regard to spirits, devils, and divine beings, and new technologies provided another avenue for delusional patients to make sense of the messages conjured up by their brains. The electric telegraph acted as the first such gateway. If a patient believed they were 'wired up' then it is not surprising that they also thought they could be subject to unwanted messaging from a distance. In 1867, Margaret Crosbie, aged fifty-five, suffered from various hallucinations, including 'that she is visited nightly by lovers, who communicate with her through telegraph wires'. Richard Hardaker, diagnosed with mania, had many delusions of suspicion, including that the telegraph wires 'whisper to him'.[41]

The advent of the electric telegraph coincided with the rise of spiritualism, and many were struck by the similarities between the morse code tapping across the ocean and the table rappings of spirits from the other world. An early American spiritualist periodical was entitled the *Spiritual Telegraph*, and in England the short-lived *Yorkshire Spiritual Telegraph* was also founded in 1855. There was excited speculation that this spiritual telegraph could supersede its cable cousin. 'There will soon come a Fulton or a Morse, who will put this ghost-power into harness', said writer and magazine editor

Figure 5 Electric Times. The power of electricity merged with the supernatural. A large vehicle (Phoebus's cart), on which is an electrical generator, being pulled along by winged horses with light bulbs on their heads. Wood engraving by Swain, 1881, after J. Tenniel.

Credit: Wellcome Collection

Nathaniel Parker Willis, 'and it will follow Steam and Electricity in doing' man's work for him.'[42] It is no wonder that people believed that the other world utilized the telegraph wires to communicate with them. In 1872, Edward Banks was exultant when claiming he could 'telegraph to the spirits and all the deities', while John Statters, forty, believed his sister was dead and that he was using her spirit as a telegraph wire.[43] William Murray Forbes, aged thirty-two, was very excited by such communication possibilities in 1879. On his admission he said he had been a medium for three weeks, and the doctors observed he 'appeared to be listening to sounds at a distance which he said were the voices of a policeman, a man being murdered and a band of people and a spiritualist meeting at Lancaster'.[44] God was naturally also thought to take advantage of the new technology. In the early 1890s Arthur Francis Ashcroft said that 'God & other invisible beings convene & telegraph to him & he has to obey their commands or be punished by them', while Robert James Haynes, said that he was 'a Spiritualist and by means of a system of telegraphy has communications with God'.[45]

The spread of the telegraph and spiritualism also fuelled popular interest in telepathy during the late nineteenth century. Psychical researcher Eleanor Sidgwick (1845–1936) wrote at the time that telepathy 'had now become a catchword of the man in the street, who used it like "electricity" to explain anything mysterious'.[46] Some scientists and spiritualists had high hopes that electricity would not only explain but also develop the power of telepathic communication. If messages could be transmitted along wires perhaps voices, smells, tastes, and thoughts from both the mundane and spiritual realm could also be communicated. A patient in the West Riding Asylum explained that the voices he heard were not sounds in reality but 'thoughts conveyed by electricity'.[47] In 1900, a 32-year-old ex-soldier who had served with the Royal Field Artillery, and had been sun struck three times in India, explained his views of the people who communicated with him: 'They can read every thought that is in my head. I believe that this system of telegraphy, the system of communicating with one another, is at work in the Transvaal. The Boers have this power, and are able to read our despatches at great distance.' On another occasion he explained, 'If I am reading a paper they can read it at the same time. It is said to be some system of wireless telegraphy, but I think it is a trick. I'm certain it is human voices.'[48]

By the end of the century, electricity had overtaken mesmerism as the main bogey of unseen agency. The idea of the electrical body, however vaguely understood or misunderstood, became engrained in the popular consciousness. Electricity was a life force and so the body could be energized or sapped by its application: it could be life giving and life threatening. Electrical engineers and medical men were using the same technology, and as electricity coursed through humans the link between electrical machines and the electrical body became wired together in the popular as well as the medical mind. Words such as 'battery', 'current', 'wired', 'energy', 'shock', and 'spark' developed wider meanings in common speech.[49] It was not only the body that was affected. The environment was being electrified and this, in turn, presented new health anxieties about invisible external forces.

Electric trams, which in some places replaced existing horse-drawn ones, proliferated in the towns of northwest England in the first few years of the twentieth century, with the Lancaster Corporation Tramways opening its operation in 1903. A year later, a patient in the local asylum named James Cork, aged thirty-four, constantly rambled about having electricity in him and claimed he had 'been injured by electricity from a tram-car' and 'was set on fire by the force of the shock'. In the same institution five years later

John Thomas Aspden, thirty-nine, said that he had been charged with electricity through riding on the trams, and that he had lost his speech due to it. He also talked of electricity in the air that annoyed him. Over in Ireland, in 1904, W.R. Dawson, medical superintendent at Farnham House Asylum, Dublin, related the case of a 43-year-old farmer, a heavy drinker and sufferer of piles for many years, who was admitted after showing signs of insanity. He had an operation to remove the piles but soon after developed delusions of electrical interference that Dawson put down to his concerns over the advent of electric trams.[50] The Dublin tramway had been fully converted from horse-drawn to electric power three years earlier.

It is not surprising that the places which contained the mysterious, electrical generation and transmission equipment also attracted suspicion. The first central electric power station was built for the town of Godalming, Surrey, in 1881, and they began to proliferate by the end of the century. In Lancaster Moor Asylum, Elizabeth Forster complained in 1909 that she was being 'played upon' by some invisible force at the control of 'an unprincipled operative at the electric generating station'.[51] The following year, William Moores, aged forty-eight, was tormented by a electricity testing station across the street from where he lived, which he blamed for his wife's miscarriage and the pains in his limbs and head. These were new pieces of equipment installed in boroughs that enabled engineers to test and measure electrical leakage from the central generating stations. An example of a testing station was exhibited at the Crystal Palace Electrical Exhibition in 1892.[52] But it was the proliferation and pervasiveness of wires that most troubled people's minds.

First came the telegraph wires that criss-crossed the landscape and the urban skyline. While people soon became familiar with the concept of the electric telegraph, the wires were considered an unwelcome intrusion by some and another means for spreading invisible malign forces. In 1889, the case notes for Henry Staples, fifty-nine, report that he 'Fancies telegraph wires are over his head. That messages are being sent to people as to his character.' A year later, 56-year-old Glaswegian Janet Sneddon complained amongst other delusions that there was 'a wire connecting her with the post office'. The Post Office had the monopoly on domestic telegraphic communications at the time. Mary Teresa Billington complained that 'wires follow her in the street & pull her bonnet off'.[53] In 1887, Johnson Short, a tanner aged forty-six, was convinced he was being affected by wires from the Atlantic Cable, which had been laid across the ocean some twenty years earlier, and that the cable actually ran through his bedroom. Mary Meade was convinced in 1896 that men were constantly digging in her cellars laying down telegraph wires. Even in 1910, William Pepphard was dismal and miserable because he suffered from telegraphy that made him feel 'dense'. The world's telegraphs, he stated, were 'most annoying to working people' and 'should be driven out of the country'.[54] As with Janet Sneddon, some had delusions that not only their homes but also their bodies were wired up to the telegraph. In Glasgow, in 1884, Laura Harding, twenty-six, was under the impression 'that she has heart disease caused by a telegraph wire being attached to her', while in 1899, John Simpkin was convinced that he was continually being electrified by telegraph wires that were wound round his body.[55]

Then, with the rise of domestic electric lighting and electrical appliances, the plague of wires spread from the streets and into the intimate spaces of the home. In 1908, Louisa Betsy Fleming, the 41-year-old wife of a Barrow dock worker, was much concerned that her house 'was underwired & surrounded by wires charging it [with] electricity'. She was released from Lancaster Moor after a few months. Two years later, factory labourer John Thomas McMullen, had delusions that his house was full of electrical wires that were charging him with electricity. Mathew Richardson, diagnosed with mania caused by influenza, 'thinks that his neighbours had an electric machine in the house next his own & that there was a fine wire going through the wall into his house & in this manner was affected by the electricity'.[56]

The spread of domestic electricity supply was slow and by the end of the nineteenth century the electrical home was largely the preserve of the upper class and the urban middle classes. While gas was increasingly being piped into working-class homes, the masses still lit their dwellings with fires, candles, and oil and kerosene lamps. There was initially quite a lot of popular concern about the idea of domestic electrification, fuelled by reports of deaths in factories and among engineers working at substations and central stations. Widespread reporting on the introduction of the electric chair in America in the 1890s did not help calm anxieties.[57] But among the asylum patients accidental electrocution was not the issue. It is unlikely any of them had electricity. Their language was that of agency, of sinister influence, of feeling beleaguered and beset with strange sensations rather than fear of untimely death by dodgy wiring. This is not surprising really. It was the very fact that electricity was not a utilitarian reality but an abstract notion, something familiar but out of reach, something read about but not seen, that made it a source of worry.

Power and persecution

A few young men had Frankenstein-like ambitions of harnessing electricity to render them divinely omnipotent. In 1899, William Pickton, aged thirty-one, believed he was not only a prophet but also controlled the electricity of the world and could use it to 'strike people dead & raise them again'. That same year, Hubert Carnall, aged seventeen, admitted to South Yorkshire Asylum for mania, claimed he had invented electric machinery for all sorts of imaginary purposes, including raising people from the dead. For patient Joseph Brindle electricity was clearly a divine source of power and he believed that God had put electricity into his body to inspire him to reform the world.[58] For Selina Wild, aged sixty-six, however, such divine electrification was a punishment and not a gift. She said God had charged her with electricity so that 'anyone who touched her will be electrified', and, in her own view, this burden caused her to suffer from her diagnosed mania.[59]

Most patients preoccupied with electricity were victims. They considered it a malign rather than divine power that was exploited by evil adversaries. In the case notes for Benjamin Harrison the medical attendant described in 1909 how 'with a face of agony he says he has been electrocuted, that electrical appliances are being used upon him: He knows the man who is doing this but will not divulge his name: On being pressed to tell more he becomes restless & walks about shedding tears. Is depressed & confused: He can speak of nothing but his persecution.'[60] Patients mostly accused their neighbours, believing the invisible force could easily be sent through the walls, floors, and ceilings to do its malign work. In 1896 Sarah Bintley complained 'that her neighbours filled her house with electricity to punish her'. William Ebenezer Jackson, thirty-eight, was placed in the asylum in 1885 due to 'strong delusions' that his neighbours, a family named Biescoe, sent electricity into him. He complained that it caused his watch to turn three hours in one go, gave him pains in the head, and made 'the oil boil out on his scalp'. He vowed vengeance on them. Blanche Amelia Baler, thirty-four, who was diagnosed as suffering from mania, suspected that electricity had been sent through the wall from the next house which caused her body to swell and then go down again. But she was unable to give any reason why such a thing was being done to her.[61] So concerned was Eliza Jane Lawford, that when the certifying doctor paid a visit before her admission, he found a workman there busy taking up the floorboards to find the electric machine she believed tormented her. She also said 'that someone got into the next house (an empty one) & touched a spring in the wall, & made her bed vibrate at night, with other similar delusions'. Annie Topping complained that her neighbours had put electric wires through holes in the wall to fill her head with electricity. She called upon a policeman to make the neighbours behave, and even visited her general practitioner at five o'clock one morning requesting that he 'remove the electricity from her head'.[62] Electric power was also blamed for delusional experiences of forced aerial transportation. Conolly Norman treated an elderly male drunkard who described being transported through space at night. He explained how 'electrical parties' would lift him up in his bed and carry him to-and-fro through the air before bringing him back down again. A 36-year-old woman also had delusions that an electric machine transported her through the air. From the experiences of these patients, Norman endorsed the view of the French expert on hallucinations, Jules Séglas (1856–1939), that such physical hallucinations of the 'muscular sense' helped explain the old notion that witches rode through the air on broomsticks and the like.[63]

From a patient perspective these suspicions of unseen agency, hateful neighbours, and invisible powers, often sound similar to the notions about and language regarding witchcraft. Take one of the syphilitic patients at Claybury Asylum, a single, 35-year-old clerk from Plymouth: 'female enemies follow him about; they work the electricity on him; the whole thing is going on owing to a jealous woman, who had followed him from Plymouth to Homerton, thence to Claybury'.[64] It is no surprise, then, that a few patients explicitly mentioned fear of witches in relation to electric torment. Amongst the delusions of Isabella Yates in 1904 was that her relatives were putting electricity and witchcraft into her in order to get her money, and 'that someone has been paid to practice witchcraft & use infernal machines on her & can see electricity coming out of her arms & legs'.[65] Jane Stalker in the Royal Crichton also had 'delusions of witchcraft', and complained that witches annoyed her, and that people 'constantly speak to her & torment her with electrical shocks'.[66] Maria Hall, a 22-year-old domestic servant in the Buckinghamshire Pauper Asylum, burned some wooden boxes that she thought contained wires that were 'bewitching her'. In South Yorkshire Asylum we find a 64-year-old street hawker named

William McLean, suffering from mania, who believed he was continually influenced by electricity and annoyed by what he curiously referred to as 'British Sorcerers', though this could be explained by the fact that McLean seems to have been brought up in Canada.[67]

Many patients were specifically preoccupied with batteries. From the early nineteenth century three alternative types of battery had been developed. The oldest type, Leyden jars, continued to be used, particularly for educational demonstration and entertainment, and we can perhaps see their influence on the imaginations of two women in Lancaster Moor Asylum. One complained that electricity had been 'put upon her' by her husband and medical staff at the workhouse. In November 1908 she said 'a ball of electricity burst above her head & the electric current has entered her brain'. Two years earlier, Gertrude Gordon, thirty, said 'she has been filled with electricity...lying on a pillow charged with it, that it leaves her at night in the shape of small golden balls'.[68] Their conceptualization of electricity as balls presumably derived from having seen the brass wires with small brass balls coming out of the tops of Leyden jars. The electric current visibly leapt between the balls when connected together.[69] Then there was the faradic battery, named after scientist Michael Faraday (1791–1867), which provided individual, alternating current. The French neurologist, Guillaume Duchenne, used such a battery in the 1860s to stimulate the facial muscles of his patients. But it was the galvanic or continuous current batteries that were mostly used by asylum medical superintendents in treating the insane from the 1870s onward.

Some thought galvanic current increased blood flow to the brain, others that it decreased it, some considered it was stimulative, and others thought it had a sedative effect. Battery experimentation was certainly not widespread amongst British asylum superintendents, but the results of those that did were closely monitored. Psychiatric publications like the *Journal of Mental Science* kept English readers up to date with experiments from across Europe and America. Electrical currents were used to test pain threshold and insensitivity in hysteria patients, for example, but with the development of neurology and increased asylum research on the brains of the insane, the application of galvanic electricity for insanity was increasingly focussed on the head as a means of influencing the brain.[70] In the 1880s, Joseph Wiglesworth of the Rainhill Asylum, Merseyside, published his experiments with a sophisticated galvanic battery that was capable of increasing the current in small increments. He tried repeated applications on eleven female patients. In each case flexible electrode plates were placed on the forehead and the nape of the neck, with each patient receiving repeat treatments. Only in three cases did the galvanic treatment lead to a clear improvement, though, and these concerned melancholic symptoms. His conclusion: 'The use of galvanism to the head is a proceeding which is certainly *not* going to revolutionize the treatment of insanity.'[71] Alexander Robertson, physician to the Glasgow City Parochial Asylum, tried Faradic current at first but later concentrated on galvanic current—but drew few conclusions from his experiments with both. He wrote up one case, that of a 50-year-old dealer in old clothes named Margaret. She suffered from melancholia and delu- sions of suspicion and unseen agency. He applied a galvanic current to her head on multiple occasions over several months, and she reported feeling better. It made 'her think the voices are in her head and not real'. He noted that 'so convinced is she of the benefit she is deriving from the battery that she asks to have her hair cut very short again in order that the current may produce its full effects'. Indeed, at the end of the treatment Margaret herself remarked, 'What a good that battery has done me.'[72]

The results of such published experiments were contradictory in their conclusions as well as in their interpretations of the galvanic effect on the mind and body. By the end of the 1890s battery therapy was largely dis- carded in British asylums, though electroshock therapy would remerge in the aftermath of the First World War with the treatment of shellshock.[73] We can clearly detect the spread of patient awareness about the practice through the late nineteenth and early twentieth century. Unlike Margaret's experi- ence, patient opinions on the use of batteries were usually highly negative. In 1892 Mary Hannah Lough, twenty-seven, said she felt 'batteries of galvanism sent from some miles away' and that people were galvanizing her through the floors. Around the same time, Martha Robinson, a long-term dementia patient in Lancaster Moor, complained that 'she is worked on by a galvanic battery'.[74] While in these cases the persecutors were unseen agents, Roland Livsey, twenty-five, accused his medical attendants. One of them wrote in his case notes, '[Livsey] says I have an electric battery & keep galvanizing him & have caused him to have nervous debility.' Ada Chadwick Gosling also complained that the doctor had 'touched her' with electricity and thereby 'spoilt her life'.[75] In Lancaster Moor in 1906 we find Bedelia Lord, forty-five, who believed that batteries were used on her body at night and had an evil influence over her, and that 'the doctors play on her with electricity: they can read her thoughts'. The West Riding Asylum dealt with

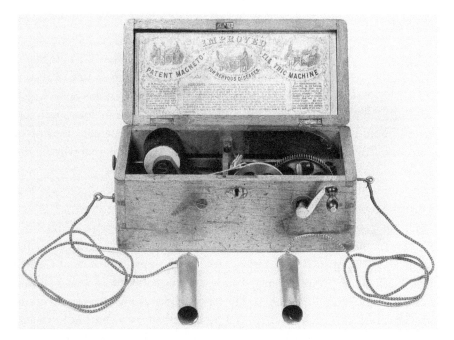

Figure 6 Magneto-electric machine for domestic use.
Credit: Wellcome Collection

a particularly troublesome ex-patient, a journalist who was admitted as a criminal lunatic and attempted to obtain summonses against the staff for electrical ill-treatment. On his release he published a pamphlet of his complaints, and although he subsequently moved abroad, he still claimed they continued to work upon him with batteries.[76]

It was not all in the imagination. There is some evidence of patients being 'worked on' by asylum staff as a punishment or restraint rather than as a therapy. The boundaries were clearly blurred as to whether applying a battery to deter patients from 'dirty, violent, destructive and erotic practices' was really a treatment. This came to a head at the Norfolk Lunatic Asylum in 1909, for instance, when several patients gave evidence to lunacy commissioners on the matter. The medical superintendent conceded that staff may have applied a galvanic battery to a patient 'for violence to an Attendant'. One patient reported, 'I used to think it was strengthening my nerves but now I think it was for punishment.' The commissioners ordered that, from then on, only the superintendent could sanction the use of batteries.[77] The application of batteries to test the fraudulent insane was also recommended by some. In 1870, David Nicolson, Assistant Medical Officer at Portland Prison, Scotland, suggested that a small galvanic battery had a 'wonderful influence' on prisoners faking madness. This might explain the complaints of Lancaster Moor patient James Cairns, thirty-three, who in 1911, was convinced 'the prison authorities put an electric machine on to his brain which controlled his actions & gave him shocks'. But Nicolson was absolutely clear it should not be used indiscriminately and definitely not as a means of detection.[78] Such abuses were rare, and medical staff were generally careful and cautious, but suspicions and fears were understandable.

While in the cases above the battery was another tool used by diabolical *external* agents, some patients also complained of having batteries placed *inside* them. Annie Kate Mary Eshelley, thirty-three, heard voices from within her and thought that there was an electric battery in her head.[79] One long-term patient in Bristol Lunatic Asylum, a shipwright named George Joseph Silman, expressed similar concerns about batteries for years. He was initially diagnosed with dementia but this was later changed to mania. When first admitted in March 1890, he said he had a battery in his head that had been turned on and that he also heard voices. He had lodged a complaint with the police about it. After a while in the asylum he reported that the battery was thankfully working less upon him, but he never lost the delusion and feared that his life was slowly draining away. Over the thirty-six years he spent in the asylum his concern shifted gradually from the battery in his head to electrickery more generally as mains electricity became more widespread and evident.[80] How did people think the batteries got there? The delusion perhaps derived from concerns over the galvanic experiments already described. It was a short cognitive leap from having the electrodes placed on the forehead and nape of the neck to the notion that the source of electricity was actually physically transferred into the head. Richard Wright, forty-one, was convinced that he had been drugged by someone who then installed the battery inside him.[81]

We heard in a previous chapter about visceral insanity with regard to abdominal pain and, by the end of the century, similar physical suffering was also interpreted in terms of battery work. Clouston had a female epileptic patient who had painful twitches in the limbs and would point to them and say, 'look how it works on me', meaning the unseen batteries she blamed for her condition. Another female patient who complained of being 'worked on' at night by her neighbours subsequently blamed it on the medical staff once she was removed to the asylum. She was found to be suffering from heart disease and had attacks of angina. Clouston also had a 44-year-old patient suffering from visceral melancholia brought on by over-work and business anxieties, who believed his pain and sleeplessness were due to people likewise 'working on him'. He made a full recovery and later reflected on his illusion or delusion, which he attributed to a 'morbid fancy'. He explained how 'his sensations had been most uncomfortable, that he used to feel sudden pains, to twitch and jerk and jump up in bed, and had imagined those motor and sensory nervous symptoms meant that he was worked on by a battery'.[82]

Popular concerns about batteries among asylum patients were also likely fuelled by the rise of the commercial, domestic 'medical battery' that delivered low dose electric shocks.[83] The iron core, switches, and wires that made up a medical battery were housed in a wooden container around the size of a modern shoebox, though some were small enough to be carried in a large coat pocket. They were made possible as consumer items due to the development of dry cell batteries by the 1890s which did not need to be tampered with and topped up with conductive fluids—a task that most were reluctant to undertake. The 'feeding' of wet cell batteries could strike some as troublingly alchemical. One Dublin asylum patient who complained that a couple living near him sent electrical shocks to his teeth and were electrically 'tightening up' his testicles, said he saw them carrying a jar and a can for the battery: 'it is a curious-looking thing to see a woman carrying up a jar of water and it corked', he commented.[84]

British local newspapers contained regular advertisements for mail order medical batteries bearing claims that they were an essential part of household medicine. In 1886, for instance, adverts appeared for Chambers' Voltaic Battery, which delivered 'electricity as a healing power' for just four shillings. Then there was Dr Lowder's Medical Magneto-Electric Battery, promoted as the 'Great Health Restorer... The blood is the life, but electricity is the life of the blood'. In 1910 the blurb for the British Electric Institute's Ajax Dry Cell Body Battery claimed that 'it pours its life-giving current into your weakened nerve cells', making nervous and physical wrecks healthy and strong again.[85] It is important to note that such medical batteries were usually advertised for bodily health and not for mental illness. Instructions advised placing the electrodes on the part of the body that was affected rather than the head, while faradic batteries with their mild shocks became popular in facial cosmetic treatments and hair stimulation as well. Perhaps it was anxiety over medical batteries that led Thomas Sheen, in 1888, to think that an electrical battery was continually being placed every night on his feet, legs, hands, and private parts.[86]

Suspect devices

The growing influence of the telephone, from the Greek 'distant voice', provided a new cognitive paradigm for people to negotiate. People may have sometimes thought they heard voices communicating with them down the telegraph wires but all it could actually do was transmit the sound of dits and dahs (recorded as dots and dashes). With the telephone voices really were calling in from a distance. That must have been pretty mind blowing to deal with for some. When patients said they heard voices down the telephone were they now real or imaginary? There was another seismic difference between these two electronic forms of communication in terms of the relationship between physical spaces and internal dialogues. The telephone would come to be in the home, in intimate spaces, blurring the psychical boundary between domestic security and external supernatural threat. Elizabeth Ann Ainsworth believed a telephone had been placed down the chimney and connected to her ear. She said it 'caused her eyes to twist in her head' and she constantly got out of bed to look for the telephone and the men who had put it there. Around 1886, James Maguire, aged sixty, pulled down the fireplace in his house looking for such a telephone and thought there was 'another in the downspout of his house' by which he heard all that his neighbours were saying.[87]

Alexander Graham Bell may have invented the telephone in 1876, which he demonstrated in public by using existing telegraph lines, but it was only with the expiry of his telephone patents in 1894 that telephone companies and customers began to expand significantly, albeit tentatively. By 1890, the British National Telephone Company had a modest 50,000 subscribers and ten years later there were still only 0.005 telephones per 100 of the population as a whole. Britain was comparatively slow on the uptake. In Germany, there were 0.5 telephones per 100 of the population by 1900 while America was far in advance of everyone else. By 1920 some 39 per cent of American farms and 34 per cent of non-farm households possessed phones.[88] While the advent of the telephone was the subject of history books as early as 1910, the social history of the early years of the telephone has received surprisingly little attention, and its reception by the working classes has been described as an 'irrecoverable history'.[89] But like the adoption of other mass technologies, the asylum records provide some interesting insights into the early public response—if not the actual experience of using them.

As with domestic electricity, anxieties about telephones preceded actual ownership. As early as 1883, Clouston noted in his clinical lectures on insanity that among his patients experiencing 'monomania of unseen agency' were those who believed enemies called them 'bad names through the walls by telephones'.[90] A year later, George Savage, the superintendent at Bethlem, reported that his attendants 'hear of every variety of telephonic communication' on the wards. One patient accused Savage of possessing a range of telephones and microphones that allowed him to read the thoughts of every patient whenever he wanted.[91] As this indicates, one view of the telephone was that it was another new tool of the fiendish persecutorial 'other', which became jumbled up with the other invisible forces already mentioned in this chapter. Emily Walton Nichols in Lancaster Moor, 'says she has been hypnotized…says a man applies a telephone wire to her left breast at night when she is asleep'. She also came to think that two men suggested immoral ideas to her through the telephone, and that 'they mesmerize her from a distance'.[92] Letters from patients in the Royal Edinburgh Asylum included one complaining of being plagued by 'this telephone work'. Another written by a cook suffering from mania said he was haunted by a 'speaking Telephane'. A 38-year-old alcoholic draper explained how he was 'telephonated': 'About 10 o'clock at night sitting in the same public house I heard the voices for the first time, they threatened violence, I looked about the front shop to see where the parties were. Could see no likely persons…I took the train to Edinburgh trying to get rid of the voices.'[93]

For those suffering from auditory hallucinations the telephone enabled some of them to make sense of the voices they heard, particularly those that appeared to come from a long distance away rather than from the other side of the wall. This was a type of hallucination that psychiatrists had long identified, and which was also associated with notions of divine communication. In 1892 Maria Hammerton, aged forty, a hairdresser's wife from Atherton, Manchester, was under the impression that there were telephones in the property next door and that people from Preston and other places were 'jeering & talking about her through the telephone'.[94] The telephone could also be a paralysing device of control. In 1892, Alice Fullalove, forty-two, said 'she must not see anyone unless the telephone says so', while Fanny Mounsey, the wife of a Lancaster shoe and bootmaker, believed she was being persecuted night and day by her neighbours using telephones and 'tommy talkers' (kazoos), and that they continually called her bad names through these telephones and urged her to cut her throat.[95] Patients mostly described *receiving* communications, but when it came to the otherworld then there was more talk of being the caller, of being in control. While in Lancaster Moor Asylum Mary Ann Culshaw believed she was pregnant with the Holy Ghost and had 'a telephone put up to God'. Thomas Hamer, forty-eight, similarly had a telephone to Heaven through which he spoke to the Supreme Being, but John Walsh and Joseph Jackson also believed they had telephone communications with Hell, with Jackson hearing celestial music down the line but also receiving alarming calls that he must go to the inferno. A woman in Prestwich Asylum said she was able to telephone the dead.[96]

The telephone voices could also appear to be produced internally, convincing some that they had telephones in their heads and bodies. Edward Jackson, aged twenty, was one such patient who, in 1892, suffered from hallucinations of hearing and was worried about the harm the two telephones in his head were causing him. A 36-year-old female servant admitted to Richmond Asylum, Dublin, in 1902, thought she was a telephone in the sense that the 'telephone' worked within her, 'humbugging' her with a lot of questions. She heard it in her throat and mouth rather than her ears. As she explained to Conolly Norman, 'The telephones speak to me from my voice inside (laying her hand on her chest). It is like my own voice; it is someone speaking with my voice. I hear it in my mouth.' Norman observed her moving her lips when she said she was hearing the voice, and when he suggested to her that she had been talking to herself, she was quite clear, 'No, someone moved my lips.'[97] A few such patients pondered long and hard on how the intrusive technology worked and came up with their own sophisticated explanations. Psychiatrists described this as a 'systematized' delusion in that the patient could argue at length in coherent debate and rebut counter explanations in detailed and lucid terms. One of Savage's Bethlem patients in the early 1880s explained that he beieved that people, through the use of telephones, could basically read his mind. One of the voices he heard explained to him that they could do this by picking up pulsations from his brain, but the man had developed another theory that they were able to interpret his own imperceptible movement of the organs of speech. He believed that when he thought particularly hard and vehemently he felt his tongue move slightly.[98] The commercial clerk in the West

Riding Asylum we met earlier, T.S., was voracious in his reading to find the scientific origin of the mysterious forces behind his condition, and the telephone was his breakthrough discovery:

> He ransacked every book, periodical, and newspaper he could lay his hands upon; and eagerly questioned the medical officers as to the probabilities of mesmerism, electro-biology, witchcraft, odyle, electricity, and magnetism being the means employed. We well remember his excited expression one day when, handing us a newspaper, he indicated a passage bearing upon the telephone and phonograph, of which he had for the first time heard, and which he convincingly and triumphantly regarded as the solution to the whole mystery of his case.[99]

The phonograph represented another category shift in cognitive thinking compared with the telephone. It was not just the shock of hearing disembodied voices that had to be negotiated but the notion that the act of recording somehow captured the essence of being, created an archive of the self, that it was a soul stealer, a ghost machine. Indeed, at the time, cultural commentators referred to the cylinder recordings as repositories or dungeons of ghosts that briefly haunted the spaces in which they were played— for as long as the machine was cranked.[100] The phonograph was invented by Thomas Edison in 1877. Sound was etched onto a cylinder covered in tin foil or wax and then played back using a listening stylus. This was followed up in the 1880s by Alexander Graham Bell's graphophone, and then in the 1890s Emile Berliner introduced the gramophone with its flat circular discs or records. But it was the name 'phonograph' that stuck in the popular mind as a generic term for these various early recording machines. So, even in 1904, the case notes for William McLean observed that 'he is annoyed continually by phonographs & that the noise prevents him sleeping at night', and that 'he hears whispers thro' phonograph all day'.[101] It attracted the same sorts of patient concerns as telephones, particularly with regard to aural hallucinations. People claimed they were controlled by phonographs or were possessed by them. In 1889, Mary Jane Dunkling, a patient in Lancaster Moor said her inside was a phonograph and that she consequently had the spirit of prophecy.[102]

It seemed conceivable within the existing framework of thinking about occult powers that if people could take possession of the recordings of others, then they could use them as a new infernal tool of control over an individual's free will. A Dublin asylum patient, a 39-year-old butcher, who had various hypochondriacal delusions, started to receive profound supernatural messages while in the workhouse. 'It all began through the phonograph', he explained. 'Some years ago when the phonograph was new I was asked to speak into the phonograph that I might hear my own voice. I did so, and they have got hold of my phonogram and are always interfering with it. I was sent here [the asylum] because my phonogram was exposed to the public and everybody could work upon it.' On another occasion, he explained, 'You can do anything with a man's phonogram by putting it into an electrical battery.'[103]

People had already had to confront the technological reproduction and capture of the self with the advent of the camera, of course. The cultural impact of the camera, like the telegraph, coincided with the rise of spiritualism, and by the early 1860s the manipulation of photographic images and the use of double exposures, created the genre of spirit photography, which blurred the boundaries between science and the supernatural. But what concerns us here is the capture of the essence of life and not the afterlife. In American folk magic at this time it was a not uncommon belief that witches used photographs in vengeful image magic, for instance, and likewise, that witches could be attacked by shooting a photograph of them with a silver bullet. While there is little reference to this practice in British folklore, there were evidently similar concerns. A gardener's wife told the Somerset folklorist Frederick Elworthy that she had heard 'twas terrible onlucky' to have one's photograph taken and that 'volks never didn live long arter they be a-tookt off'. This was the camera as evil eye.[104] One of Conolly Norman's patients, the former soldier in the Royal Field Artillery mentioned earlier, was convinced that the man who controlled him through telegraphy and hypnotism had 'got hold of the dry plate of my photograph, and makes use of it to influence me and communicate with me'. Conolly Norman observed that the man's belief was 'contemporary in form' but 'in essence, the old notion of witchcraft' in terms of witches obtaining power over their victims through possession of a portion of their body or clothing.[105]

The asylum records suggest, though, that by the 1880s there were few worries about photography. While only a small percentage of the population possessed cameras there were photographic studios in towns and people became habituated to seeing photographs in newspapers. In the 1890s film processing services also began to appear on the high street, with the likes of Boots establishing a nationwide network of 'photographic chemists'.[106] The idea of the family photograph came of age. Many people in rural and urban areas would have seen enthusiastic amateur photographers setting up their cameras capturing landscapes and taking portraits of picaresque rustics. By the late nineteenth century, it was also increasingly common for asylum patients to be photographed for their records.[107]

But there may have been more anxiety about cameras than the asylum records suggest. As with some people's reluctance to openly express their convictions of having been bewitched, so patient refusal to be photographed might have been indicative of unspoken fears.

In 1895, a new revolution in photography occurred when the first pocket camera produced by Kodak went on the market. Priced relatively cheaply at $5 it came in a leather-covered wooden box and used a roll of film that could be easily processed in Boots and other high-street chemists. It also had a reflecting viewfinder. It is not surprising, then, that with the proliferation of these cameras the old anxieties about the influencing machine arose once again. In 1901 a 36-year-old fireman on an Atlantic liner went to see Conolly Norman about his mental unsoundness, which exhibited itself in hallucinations of persecution. He had already spent time in an English county asylum and had been discharged while unrecovered. The man told Norman that, 'they started those pocket reflecting Kodaks with me three years ago, and illuminated my whole system and brain and intellect. They upset my head by this. They drew my mind and imagination; they took my mind out on the breath.' He said he had seen the blue flash of light when they illuminated his head.[108] But the impact of the Kodak on the public consciousness was overshadowed by a new scientific breakthrough the same year—the discovery of Röntgen rays or X-rays by German physicist Wilhelm Conrad Röntgen (1845–1923). Before its medical value was fully realized the X-ray was first promoted as a technological attraction and the media had a field day. In 1896 startling images of X-rayed hands wearing rings were printed by the popular press as well as in medical journals. There were public exhibitions and talks up and down the country.[109] As one journalist observed:

> Never has a scientific discovery so completely and irresistibly taken the world by storm... The performances of Rontgen's rays are obvious to the 'man in the street'; they are repeated in every lecture-room; they are caricatured in comic prints; hits are manufactured out of them at the theatres; nay, they are personally interesting to every one afflicted with a gouty finger.[110]

This 'photography of the invisible' readily conjured up once again the elision of the physical and the spiritual, the 'vanishing point between science and the occult'.[111]

The 'X-ray craze' started to peter out by 1898 but over the next few years it is likely hundreds of people up and down the country developed delusions of unseen persecution regarding X-rays or added the technology to their mental list of existing concerns. Patients at the Royal Edinburgh Asylum were soon writing letters in which they blamed their troubles on the X-rays. In 1897 we find Maria Jago in Lancaster Moor complaining that people were examining her brain by X-rays.[112] A couple of years later, Joseph Carroll, thirty-five, was deeply depressed because of technological persecution. He complained of being acted upon by electricity and heard voices saying vile things, which he said were produced by a phonograph. And then the new discovery added to his woes. His case notes record that 'he cannot work because people are using Rontgen Rays to see his thoughts & putting all sorts of wrong ideas into his head'. He accused his work foreman of using the rays to discover his secrets. Most complaints about X-rays were mixed up with such general electrical preoccupations. Joseph Frost, thirty-seven, suffered from the belief that electricity was 'put on' him by neighbours and that they also exposed him to X-rays.[113] We continue to find asylum patients mentioning X-rays into the early years of the twentieth century.

Unlike audio technologies, photography and the X-ray were static, they captured the living but did not replicate life lived. That all changed with the arrival of the cinematograph ('writing in movement') and motion pictures. The world's first public demonstration of a movie, by the Lumières brothers in Paris, was in, you guessed it, 1895. The technology developed swiftly and in Britain, as elsewhere, people's first viewing of projected film would have been at a fairground, town hall, or music hall, with existing magic lantern operators swiftly adopting the new technology. Permanent cinemas proliferated from around 1908 onward, by which time the wonder may have worn off and the new mass form of entertainment had established itself as a familiar fact of life.[114]

It is between the first shows in 1896 and the rise of the cinema that we find asylum records indicating how the experience of seeing motion pictures helped some people explain the unusual mental impressions they experienced. In 1902, the post-office employee in Richmond Asylum, Dublin, who we heard from earlier, who believed unseen agents had an 'ether connection' and wires by which they exerted control, also said they used it to reproduce scenes on his brain 'like a cinematograph'. Conolly Norman was intrigued by another of his patients, a plumber by trade, who in 1903 talked of seeing 'animated pictures' on the walls of his room when alone. The man explained that they were just like the cinematograph pictures he had once seen in the Empire Music Hall. They were mostly figures of people, and he described them as 'thrown before' him by some kind of machinery. The plumber's understanding was shaped by a 'systematized' delusion of technology mixed with notions of sympathetic magic. 'If any enemy of yours get hold of your photograph', he continued, 'they can use it in animation to injure and torment you. They may have got hold of my photograph for all I know.' The process of being 'animated' in this way was initiated by the use of electricity, an arc lamp or telephone pole. The whole thing was done for annoyance and torment, and 'it is going on in the city every other day', he complained.[115] At the Royal Asylum at Perth, Scotland, in 1907, there was also a female patient suffering from mania who professed that she could call up pictures in the fashion of a cinematograph—'waving her hands in front of the wall of her room she asked for a subject, and, failing a suggestion, proceeded to describe moving pictures with great emotional display'.[116]

★   ★   ★

French psychiatrist, Jules Séglas, writing in 1895, was certain that that there was an intellectual and cultural divide between those who continued to feel persecuted by witches, devils, and magic, and those whose delusions of persecution were concerned with magnetism, hypnotism, and technology. The former were uncultivated, he stated, while the latter lived in a 'more civilised environment'.[117] Conolly Norman, who was much inspired by the work of Séglas, and was one of the very few superintendents to think deeply about such matters, came to a different conclusion. In an article entitled 'Modern Witchcraft: A Study of a Phase of Paranoia' (1905) he observed with regard to his patients who believed they were controlled by phonograms or photographs that, 'in all we have so striking a coincidence with the machinery of witchcraft that it is difficult to believe that we are merely in face of an accidental resemblance'.[118] Whereas Séglas talked of two cultures, Norman saw the shared recrudescence of an ancient, universal mental connection. This was perceptive, but with another century and more of hindsight with regard to technological developments we can see a third way. Science and magic had never been incompatible or mutually exclusive and the popular response to the technological revolution of the nineteenth and early twentieth centuries provides further confirmation. The fears and concerns about technology were not primeval responses but essentially human and modern. And, on this note, let us end the chapter with the impressive ambition of a 34-year-old cotton mill stoker from Accrington, named James Meredith. In 1890 he was driven with technological zeal and entrepreneurial desire. He was 'going to run a new mill by electric power through wires 12,000 times finer than hair and 15,000 horse power'. He was in an asylum, though, as he also believed his sister and mother were full of devils.[119]

Epilogue

A century on from the last days of the asylum the Western approach to mental illness is very different. The term 'insanity' has gone the same way as 'madness' and has been largely abandoned by the medical profession, though it remains integral to legal definitions of criminal responsibility. The deinstitutionalization or 'decarceration' of mental health care in recent decades, the provision of psychiatric beds in general hospitals, the emphasis on care in the community, and the development of new psychiatric drugs, have transformed the lives of sufferers and have also helped change popular attitudes towards mental illness. Over the same period socio-cultural attitudes towards the supernatural and unorthodox faiths have also changed significantly, though not in the linear, progressive manner the old psychiatrists confidently mapped out. While state education and healthcare are now universal, the last century has not experienced an immersive wave of mass scientific rationalism roll across the West, or some Darwinian rooting out of supernatural beliefs from society at large. The worldviews held by our nineteenth- and early twentieth-century asylum patients are still recognizable today in contemporary mass culture. While people in the West rarely express fears about neighbourhood witches these days, and large-scale possessions are (currently) a thing of the past, a significant minority of people still believe in ghosts, for instance, and ghost hunting has become a staple of late-night television in the United States and Britain in recent years. As I write, British newspapers are printing photographs of providential cloud formations representing Queen Elizabeth II. New expressions of the supernatural have also continued to emerge. The most influential is obviously the belief in UFOs and extra-terrestrial visitations. Since the days when Hélène Smith told Théodore Flournoy of her remarkable Martian experiences, many thousands have claimed to have had alien encounters. Film and television have represented alien visitations as perfectly reasonable in myriad imaginative ways.

Fear of Unseen Agency is alive and well in various supernatural forms. The QAnon conspiracy raises once again the collective and individual fear of Satanic political plotting, and it elides with the 'reptilian overlords' conspiracy theory promoted by a former British TV presenter. As to the reception of technology, the recent beliefs regarding 5G and chemtrails, and the concerns over the unseen agents held responsible, are not dissimilar to the worries about infernal machines and electricity expressed by asylum patients. The rise of the Internet and social media creates large, global, virtual communities of such believers, helping to amplify the unorthodox beliefs and convictions born of individual anxieties, delusions, and bare-faced lies. Contrast this with the isolated nineteenth-century asylum patients desperately trying to promote their conspiracies or proclaim their divinity through letters that were either censored or thrown in the bin by superin-tendents. With regard to religion, millions of Christian evangelicals con-tinue to believe in the imminent Second Coming of Christ, while self-styled prophets have thrived, in contemporary America in particular, just as they did in the days of the Millerite 'madness'. Whole new faith systems such as Scientology continue to emerge without being condemned by the medical profession as outbreaks of mass insanity—as were the early LDS Church and Spiritualism. Many small cults and religious sects have also come and gone, some ending in tragic circumstances.

If we engage in a little magical thinking ourselves, what would the early psychiatrists have made of all this if they could have travelled forward in time? How would an application of nineteenth-century psychiatric classifi-cation and diagnoses to such contemporary Western developments pan out? Who today would be placed in an asylum on these terms? These are rhet-orical questions, of course, a bit of casual historical what-iffery. Yet they do raise profound issues about our relationship with the past and what it means to be modern over the last 200 years.

The pathologizing of the supernatural and radical religion during the nineteenth century was essentially an attempt to delineate, instigate, and map a new stage in Western society. The fostering of the right sort of faith would engender wellbeing, and harmonize religion with science, thereby facilitating rather than hindering the march of humanity. It was not about some cynical policy of mass mind control, but rather a medical movement to try and transition populations to adjust mentally to the perceived chal-lenges of progress. Yet, what has actually happened during the twentieth and twenty-first centuries is the mass normalization of the supernatural and the heterodox, a fundamental decoupling of belief from insanity. Today it is not so much the medical or legal profession but the mass media that shapes public conceptions of what beliefs are insane or not. The media defines the ever-expanding boundaries of what is considered acceptable to believe in— and, more importantly, what beliefs are given uncritical public platforms.

The contemporary Western world has not become re-enchanted from some notional disenchantment in the Enlightenment past. That is a flawed and artificial construct. Rather the enchanted mind has become depathologized and unchained since the nineteenth century. The supernatural is now widely accepted reality. By and large, people freely live by their own spiritual and ritual belief systems, which can be highly idiosyncratic and creative, without hindrance from the medical profession and the state. Friends, families, neighbours, and the authorities do not have the power to make interventions as they did over a century ago, unless there is a clear danger to life—the life of the believer, the lives of those around them, or wider society. From the perspective of many early psychiatrists this would be considered a dystopian state of affairs. Naïve or noble, repressive or responsible, the asylum movement evidently failed in achieving its aims. But the issues the psychiatrists grappled with concerning the supernatural have certainly not gone away.

Endnotes

PART I INTRODUCTION

1. John Sibbald, 'Insanity in Modern Times', *The Journal of Mental Science* 23 (1878) 544.
2. See, for example, H.C. Erik Midelfort, *A History of Madness in Sixteenth-Century Germany* (Stanford, CA, 1999); David Lederer, *Madness, Religion and the State in Early Modern Europe: A Bavarian Beacon* (Cambridge, 2006).
3. See Mark S. Micale, *Hysterical Men: The Hidden History of Male Nervous Illness* (Cambridge, MA, 2008), pp. 8–22; Sander L. Gilman, Helen King, Roy Porter, G.S. Rousseau, and Elaine Showalter, *Hysteria Beyond Freud* (Berkeley, CA, 1993).
4. See, for example, David Healy, *Mania: A Short History of Bipolar Disorder* (Baltimore, MA, 2008); Lisa M. Hermsen, *Manic Minds: Mania's Mad History and its Neuro-Future* (New Brunswick, 2011); Petteri Pietikäinen, *Madness: A History* (London, 2015); G.E. Berrios, 'Dementia during the Seventeenth and Eighteenth Centuries: A Conceptual History', *Psychological Medicine* 17 (1987) 829–37.
5. On Pinel's books, career and influences see, for example, Jan Goldstein, *Console and Classify: The French Psychiatric Profession in the Nineteenth Century* (Cambridge, 1987); Dora B. Weiner, 'Mind and Body in the Clinic: Philippe Pinel, Alexander Crichton, Dominique Esquirol, and the Birth of Psychiatry', in G.S. Rousseau (Ed.), *The Languages of Psyche: Mind and Body in Enlightenment Thought* (Berkeley, CA, 1990), pp. 331–402; Louis C. Charland, 'Lost in Myth, Lost in Translation: Philippe Pinel's 1809 Medico-Philosophical Treatise on Mental Alienation', *International Journal of Mental Health* 47 (2018) 245–9.
6. Phillipe Pinel, *Traité médico-philosophique sur l'aliénation mentale* (Paris, 1809), pp. 353–4.
7. See, Michel Foucault, *History of Madness*, trans. Jonathan Murphy and Jean Khalfa (London, 2009); Jacques Postel, *Naissance de la psychiatre* (Paris, 1981); Patrick Vandermeersch, 'The Victory of Psychiatry over Demonology. The Origin of the Nineteenth Century Myth', *History of Psychiatry* 2 (1991) 351–63; John Waller, *Leaps in the Dark: The Making of Scientific Reputations* (Oxford, 2004), pp. 191–213.
8. *American Journal of Insanity* 3 (1846–7) 78; Joseph Workman, *Demonomania and Witchcraft* (1871), p. 17; Workman, 'Demonomania and Witchcraft', *American Journal of Insanity* 28, 2 (1871) 175–93. On Workman's career, see C.G. Stogdill, 'Joseph Workman, M.D., 1805-1894', in *Canadian Medical Association Journal* 95 (1966) 917–23.

9. Esquirol, *Mental Maladies*, pp. 34, 41, 42.
10. Esquirol, *Mental Maladies*, p. 42.
11. John Charles Bucknill and Daniel H. Tuke, *A Manual of Psychological Medicine* (London, 1858), p. 46.
12. E.T. Wilkins, *Insanity and Insane Asylums* (Sacramento, CA, 1872), pp. 10–29.
13. Wilkins, *Insanity*, p. 9; Andrew Scull, *The Insanity of Place / The Place of Insanity: Essays on the History of Psychiatry* (London, 2006), p. 117; Andrew Skull, *The Most Solitary of Afflictions: Madness and Society in Britain, 1700–1900* (New Haven, 1993), p. 362; David Wright, 'Getting Out of the Asylum: Understanding the Confinement of the Insane in the Nineteenth Century', *Social History of Medicine* 10 (1997) 142.
14. See Skull, *The Most Solitary of Afflictions*, pp. 334–63.
15. For an overview of this approach see, for example, Alexandra Bacopoulos-Viau and Aude Fauvel, 'The Patient's Turn Roy Porter and Psychiatry's Tales, Thirty Years On', *Medical History* 60 (2016) 1–18; Flurin Condrau, 'The Patient's View Meets the Clinical Gaze', *Social History of Medicine* 20 (2007) 525–40.
16. See Owen Davies, 'Finding the Folklore in the Annals of Psychiatry', *Folklore* 133 (2022) 1–24.
17. Louise Hide, *Gender and Class in English Asylums, 1890–1914* (Basingstoke, 2014), ch. 5.

CHAPTER 1

1. Claude-François Michéa, 'De la sorcellerie et de la possession démoniaque dans leurs rapports avec le progrès de la physiologie pathologique', *Revue contemporaine* 25 (1862) 533.
2. William Lecky, *History of European Morals* (London, 1869), Vol. 2, p. 93. More generally see Jan Machielsen, *The War on Witchcraft: Andrew Dickson White, George Lincoln Burr, and the Origins of Witchcraft Historiography* (Cambridge, 2021).
3. E. Hoyt, *Antiquarian Researches; Comprising a History of the Indian Wars in the Country Bordering Connecticut River* (Greenfield, 1824), p. 179.
4. Charles Mackay, *Memoirs of Extraordinary Popular Delusions* (London, 1841), vol. 2, pp. 168, 205.
   Peter Melville Logan, 'The Popularity of "Popular Delusions": Charles Mackay and Victorian Popular Culture', *Cultural Critique*, 54 (2003), pp. 213–41.
5. H.C. Erik Midelfort, 'Witch Craze? Beyond the Legends of Panic', *Magic, Ritual, and Witchcraft* 6, 1 (2011) 11–33.
6. See, Merry E. Wiesner-Hanks, *What Is Early Modern History?* (Cambridge, 2021); Christa Tuczay, 'The Nineteenth Century: Medievalism and Witchcraft', in Jonathan Barry and Owen Davies (Eds.), *Witchcraft Historiography* (Basingstoke, 2007), pp. 52–69.
7. See Richard Noakes, *Physics and Psychics: The Occult and the Sciences in Modern Britain* (Cambridge, 2019), pp. 21–33; Peter Lamont, 'Reflexivity, the Role of History, and the Case of Mesmerism in Early Victorian Britain', *History of Psychology* 13 (2010) 393–408; Alison Winter, *Mesmerism and Popular Culture in Early Victorian England* (Cambridge, 1994).

8. Kathleen M. Grange, 'Pinel or Chiarugi?', *Medical History* 7, 4 (1963) 373; Goldstein, *Console and Classify*, p. 76.

9. Johann Gaspar Spurzheim, *Outlines of the Physiognomical System of Drs. Gall and Spurzheim* (London, 1815), p. 102.

10. Roger J. Cooter, 'Phrenology and British Alienists, c.1825–1845. Part II: Doctrine and Practice', *Medical History* 20, 2 (1976) 136–7; Martin Staum, 'Physiognomy and Phrenology at the Paris *Athénée*', *Journal of the History of Ideas* 56 (1995) 455.

11. Joseph Ennemoser, *The History of Magic*, trans. William Howitt (London, 1854), vol. 2, p. 329.

12. John Campbell Colquhoun, *History of Magic, Witchcraft, and Animal Magnetism* (London, 1851), vol. 2, p. xi.

13. John Campbell Colquhoun, *Isis Revelata: An Inquiry into the Origin, Progress, and Present of Animal Magnetism* (Edinburgh, 1836), Vol. 2, p. 105. See also, 'On Mesmerism in Connection with Mental Philosophy', *The Phrenological Journal and Magazine of Moral Science* 17 (1844) 347–9.

14. 'Lettre de M. Despine', *Bulletin de l'académie Royal de Médicine* 2 (1837–8) 631; John Abercrombie, *Pathological and Practical Researches on Diseases of the Brain and Spinal Cord*, 2nd ed. (Edinburgh, 1829), pp. 428–31.

15. *The Westminster Review* 61 (1854) 307.

16. Wouter J. Hanegraaff, *Esotericism and the Academy: Rejected Knowledge in Western Culture* (Cambridge, 2012), pp. 273–7; Owen Davies, *Magic: A Very Short Introduction* (Oxford, 2012), pp. 38–9.

17. Matthew H. Kaufman, 'Peter David Handyside's Diploma as Senior President of the Royal Medical Society', *Res Medica* 268 (2004) 34–5; Thomas Stone, *Observations on the Phrenological Development of Burke, Hare, and Other Atrocious Murderers* (Edinburgh, 1829).

18. Thomas Stone, 'Witchcraft and Mesmerism', *London Polytechnic Magazine* (1844) 88.

19. Spurzheim, *Phrenology, or the Doctrine of the Mental Phenomena* (Boston, MA, 1833), Vol. 1, pp. 235–6.

20. George Combe, *A System of Phrenology*, 3rd ed. (London, 1830), p. 318.

21. Thomas Forster, *Sketch of the New Anatomy and Physiology of the Brain and Nervous System of Drs. Gall and Spurzheim* (London, 1815), p. 56.

22. Jean Bodin, *De la demonomanie des sorciers* (Paris, 1580), preface. For more context see, Jonathan Pearl, 'Humanism and Satanism: Jean Bodin's Contribution to the Witchcraft Crisis', *Canadian Review of Sociology* 19, 4 (1982) 541–8.

23. Heather Munsche and Harry Whitaker, 'Eighteenth Century Classification of Mental Illness: Linnaeus, de Sauvages, Vogel, and Cullen', *Cognitive and Behavioral Neurology* 25, 4 (2012) 224–39; Alicja Kacprzak, 'La nomenclature médicale de François Boissier de Sauvages en tant que pré-terminologie du XVIIIe siècle: point de vue linguistique', *Çédille, revista de estudios franceses* 10 (2014) 193–205.

24. François Boissier de Sauvages, *Nosologie méthodique: dans laquelle les maladies sont rangées par classes, suivant le système de Sydenham, & l'ordre des botanistes* (Paris, 1771), vol. 2, pp. 739–45.

25. Sauvages, *Nosologie méthodique*, p. 742.

26. Jan Machielsen, *Martin Delrio: Demonology and Scholarship in the Counter-Reformation* (Oxford, 2015).

27. Martinus Martini, *Dissertatio Inauguralis Practico-Medica De Dæmonomania Et Variis Ejus Speciebus* (Vienna, 1782); L.A. Magyar, 'Die siebenbürgische "Vampir KrankHeit" ', *Communicationes de historia artis medicinae* 186–7 (2004) 49–61; Fiona Subotsky, *Dracula for Doctors: Medical Facts and Gothic Fantasies* (Cambridge, 2020), pp. 144–5.

28. Sauvages, *Nosologie méthodique*, p. 742.

29. Alexander Ross, *Arcana Microcosmi, Or, The Hid Secrets of Man's Body Discovered* (London, 1652), p. 103.

30. James Makittrick Adair, *Commentaries on the Principles and Practice of Physic* (London, 1772), p. 342.

31. Engelbert Kämpfer, *Amoenitatum exoticum* (Lemgo, 1712); Bernd Roling, 'Northern Anger: Early Modern Debates on Berserkers', in Karl A.E. Enenkel and Anita Traninger (Eds.), *Discourses of Anger in the Early Modern Period* (Leiden, 2015), p. 233. On the changing interpretation of this culture-bound syndrome see, for example, Hissei Imai, Yusuke Ogawa, Kiyohito Okumiya, and Kozo Matsubayashi, 'Amok: A Mirror of Time and People. A Historical Review of Literature', *History of Psychiatry* 30 (2019) 38–57.

32. Eglé Sakalauskaité-Juodeikiené, Dalius Jatuzis, and Saulius Kaubrys, '*Plica polonica*: From National Plague to Death of the Disease in the Nineteenth Century', *Indian Journal of Dermatology Venereology and Leprology* 84, 4 (2018) 1–5.

33. William Cullen, *Nosology: Or, a Systematic Arrangement of Diseases, by Classes, Orders, Genera, and Species* (Edinburgh, 1800), p. 133.

34. William F. Bynum, Stephen Lock, and Roy Porter (Eds.), *Medical Journals and Medical Knowledge: Historical Essays* (London, 1992).

35. Cited in Roderick McConchie, *Discovery in Haste: English Medical Dictionaries and Lexicographers 1547 to 1796* (Berlin, 2019), p. 181.

36. See, for example, Maria Conforti, 'Creating Italian Medicine. Language, Politics and the Venetian Translation of Three French Medical Dictionaries in the Early 19th Century', *La Révolution française* 13 (2018) 1–14.

37. Abraham Rees, *The Cyclopædia; Or, Universal Dictionary of Arts, Sciences, and Literature* (London 1819), Vol. 11, n. p.

38. See, Jason Semmens, ' "I Will Not Go the Devil for a Cure": Witchcraft, Demonic Possession, and Spiritual Healing in Nineteenth-Century Devon', *Journal for the Academic Study of Magic* 2 (2004) 132–55; Owen Davies, 'Wesley's Invisible World: Witchcraft and the Temperature of Preternatural Belief', in Robert Webster (Eds.), *Perfecting Perfection: Essays in Honor of Henry D. Rack* (Eugene, OR, 2015), pp. 166–70.

39. James Heaton, *The Demon Expelled: Or, The Influence of Satan, and the Power of Christ, displayed in the Extraordinary Affliction, and Gracious Relief of a Boy* (Plymouth Dock, 1820); Heaton, *The Extraordinary Affliction and Gracious Relief of a Little Boy* (Plymouth, 1822); Heaton, *Farther Observations on Demoniac*

Possession, and Animadversions on Some of the Curious Arts of Superstition, &c. (Frome, 1822).

40. Heaton, *The Extraordinary Affliction*, pp. 126–7.

41. *Encyclopaedia Perthensis; Or Universal Dictionary*, 2nd ed. (Edinburgh, 1816) vol. 14, p. 226. Heaton cites p. 293, but it is the same quote as p. 226 in the second edition of the *Encyclopaedia*.

42. Heaton, *The Extraordinary Affliction*, p. 54.

43. John E. Lesch, 'Systematics and the Geometric Spirit', in Tore Frängsmyr, J.L. Heilbron, and Robin E. Rider (Eds.), *The Quantifying Spirit in the 18th Century* (Berkeley, CA, 1990), pp. 99–100.

44. Philippe Pinel, *Nosographie philosophique, ou La méthode de l'analyse appliquée à la médecine* (Paris, 1807),Vol. 3, p. 92.

45. Jean-Étienne Dominique Esquirol, 'Démonomanie', in A.J.L. Jourdan et al., *Dictionnaire des Sciences Médicales* (Paris, 1814), vol. 8, pp. 294–318.

46. Esquirol, *Mental Maladies*, p. 44.

47. Esquirol, 'Démonomanie', p. 297.

48. Michel Marescot, *Discours veritable sur le faict de Marthe Brossier de Romarantin, prétendue démoniaque* (Paris, 1599).

49. Esquirol, 'Démonomanie', p. 306; Esquirol, *Mental Maladies*, p. 243.

50. Christian Martin, 'Bodin's Reception of Johann Weyer in *De la Démononmanie*', in Howell A. Lloyd (Ed.), *The Reception of Bodin* (Leiden, 2013), p. 121. On early modern mass possessions see, for example, Brian Levack, *The Devil Within: Possession and Exorcism in the Christian West* (New Haven, CT, 2013); Sarah Ferber, *Demonic Possession and Exorcism in Early Modern France* (London, 2004).

51. Esquirol, 'Démonomanie', p. 306.

52. Alexander Morison, *Cases of Mental Disease with Practical Observations on the Medical Treatment* (London, 1828), p. 69.

53. J.B. de Saincric, 'Médicine philosophique : De la démonomanie', in François Vatar Jouannet and J.B. de Saincric, *Le Musée d'Aquitaine: recueil uniquement consacré aux sciences, à la littérature et aux arts* (Bordeaux, 1823), pp. 130–40.

54. Cited in Craig E. Stephenson (Ed.), *On Psychological and Visionary Art: Notes from C.G. Jung's Lecture on Gérard de Nerval's Aurélia* (Princeton, NJ, 2015), p. 23.

55. Antonio Fossati, *Del suicidio nei suoi rapporti colla medecina legale* (Milan, 1831), p. 70; Mario Maj and Filippo M. Ferro (Eds.), *Anthology of Italian Psychiatric Texts* (2002), p. 17.

56. Alexander Morison, *Cases of Mental Disease, with Practical Observations on the Medical Treatment. For the Use of Students* (London, 1828), pp. 3, 75–7; Amariah Brigham, *Observations on the Influence of Religion upon the Health and Physical Welfare of Mankind* (Boston, MA, 1835), p. 290.

57. Louis-Francisque Lélut, *Du démon de Socrate: Spécimen d'une application de la science psychologique à l'histoire* (Paris, 1836). See Zrinka Stahuljak, *Pornographic Archaeology: Medicine, Medievalism, and the Invention of the French Nation* (Philadelphia, PA, 2013).

58. Jean Céard, 'Démonologie et Démonopathies au temps de Charcot', *Histoire des sciences médicales* 28, 4 (1994) 337.

59. Calmeil, *De la folie*, Vol. 2, p. 504.

60. Calmeil, *De la folie*, Vol. 2, pp. 242–400; *Journal of Psychological Medicine and Mental Pathology* 2 (1849) 221–2.

61. Claude-François Michéa, 'Démonomanie', *Nouveau dictionnaire de médecine et de chirurgie pratique* (Paris, 1860), Vol, 11, p. 126.

62. Ritti, 'Démonomanie', pp. 684–5.

63. Calmeil, *Folie*, Vol. 1, p. 163, For details of the case see, Moshe Sluhovsky, *Believe Not Every Spirit*, p. 238.

64. François Emmanuel Foderé, *Traité du délire appliqué a la médicine, a la morale et a la législation* (Paris, 1817), Vol. 1, pp. 361, 368; 'An Analysis of Guislain's Work on Insanity', *Journal of Psychological Medicine* 6 (1853) 434.

65. Michéa, 'De la sorcellerie', 526–66.

66. *The Works of Francis Bacon, Baron of Verulam, Viscount St. Alban* (London, 1740), p. 310.

67. For a problematic modern comparison between the demonological texts on witch suicide and contemporary knowledge, see J. Lönnqvist and Kalle A. Achté, 'Witchcraft, Religion and Suicides in the Light of the Witch Hammer and Contemporary Cases', *Journal of Death and Dying* 5 (1974) 115–25.

68. Michéa, 'De la sorcellerie', 543.

69. For analysis of the case see Ferber, *Demonic Possession and Exorcism*, pp. 89–113.

70. Bénédict Morel, *Études cliniques: traité théorique et pratique des maladies mentale* (Paris, 1853), Vol. 2, p. 164.

71. Michéa, 'De la sorcellerie', p. 566.

72. Forbes Winslow, 'Modern Developments of the Marvellous', *Journal of Psychological Medicine* 13 (1860) 542.

73. William T. Gairdner, *Insanity: Modern Views as to its Nature and Treatment* (Glasgow, 1885), pp. 11, 12.

74. Joseph Guislain, *Leçons orales sur les phrénopathies* (Ghent, 1852), Vol. 1, p. 203; *The British and Foreign Medico-chirurgical Review* 38 (1866) 349. See also W.H.O. Sankey, *Lectures on Mental Diseases* (London, 1866), pp. 76–7.

75. *The Penny Mechanic*, 24 December 1836, 63.

76. Johannes B. Friedreich, *Zur Bibel: naturhistorische, anthropologische und medizinische Fragmente* (Nuremberg, 1848), Vol. 1, pp. 312–14; N. Parker, 'On Lycanthropy or Wolf-Madness, a Variety of Insania Zoanthropica', *The Asylum Journal of Mental Science* 1 (1855) 53.

77. Thiago Cardoso Vale and Francisco Cardoso, 'Chorea: A Journey through History', *Tremor and Other Hyperkinetic Movements* 5 (2015) 1–6; Kélina Gotman, *Choreomania: Dance and Disorder* (Oxford, 2018).

78. See H.C. Erik Midelfort, *A History of Madness in Sixteenth-Century Germany* (Stanford, 1999), pp. 32–6.

79. Gotman, *Choreomania*, pp. 35–7.

80. The term borrows from Elaine Showalter, *Hystories: Hysterical Epidemics and Modern Culture* (New York, 1997).

81. See, H.C. Erik Midelfort, 'Charcot, Freud, and the Demons', in Kathryn A. Edward (Ed.), *Werewolves, Witches, and Wandering Spirits: Traditional*

Belief & Folklore in Early Modern Europe (Kirksville, 2002), pp. 199–217; Ferber, 'Charcot's Demons', pp. 123–5; Jean Céard, 'Démonologie et Démonopathies au temps de Charcot', *Histoire des Sciences Médicales* 28, 4 (1994) 337; Herman Westerink, 'Demonic Possession and the Historical Construction of Melancholy and Hysteria', *History of Psychiatry* 25 (2014) 337; Mary James, 'Hysteria and Demonic Possession', in Basiro Davey, Alastair Gray, and Clive Seale (Eds.), *Health and Disease: A Reader*, 2nd ed. (Basingstoke, 1995), pp. 55–61; Michael R. Finn, 'Retrospective Medicine, Hypnosis, Hysteria and French Literature, 1875-1895', in G. Rousseau, M. Gill, D. Haycock, and M. Herwig (Eds.), *Framing and Imagining Disease in Cultural History* (Basingstoke, 2003), pp. 173–90; Per Faxneld, *Satanic Feminism: Lucifer as the Liberator of Woman in Nineteenth-Century Culture* (Oxford, 2017, pp. 208–13.

82. There is a vast literature, but see, for example, Goldstein, *Console and Classify*; Mark Micale, *Approaching Hysteria: Disease and Its Interpretations* (Princeton, NJ, 1995); Asti Hustvedt, *Medical Muses: Hysteria in Nineteenth-Century Paris* (London, 2012); Nicole Edelman, *Les métamorphoses de l'hystérique: Du début du XIXe siècle à la Grande Guerre* (Paris, 2003).

83. Midelfort, 'Charcot', pp. 203–4.

84. Diana P. Faber, 'Jean-Martin Charcot and the Epilepsy/Hysteria Relationship', *Journal of the History of the Neurosciences* 6 (1997) 275–90.

85. William J. Morton, 'Hystero-Epilepsy—Its History, etc', *Medical Record* 18 (1880) 247.

86. J. Georges Didi-Huberman, *Invention of Hysteria: Charcot and the Photographic Iconography of the Salpêtrière* (Cambridge, MA, 2004); Jonathan W. Marshall, *Performing Neurology: The Dramaturgy of Dr Jean-Martin Charcot* (New York, 2016), pp. 123–7; Péricles Maranhão-Filho, 'The Art and Neurology of Paul Richer', *Arquivos de Neuro-Psiquiatria* 75 (2017), 484–7; Kélina Gotman, *Choreomania: Dance and Disorder*, pp. 146–51.

87. Jean-Martin Charcot and Paul Richer, *Les démoniaques dans l'art* (Paris, 1887), p. vi.

88. *Journal of Mental Science* 33 (1888) 584.

89. Guillemain, *Diriger les consciences*, p. 220; Micale, *Approaching Hysteria*, pp. 265–6; Roberta Vittoria Grossi, 'Demonic Possession and Religious Scientific Debate in Nineteenth-Century France', in Giuseppe Giordan and Adam Possamai (Eds.), *The Social Scientific Study of Exorcism in Christianity* (Cham, 2020), pp. 33–52.

90. *Dublin Review* 103 (1888) 210–11.

91. Charles Richet, 'Hysteria and Demonism: A Study in Morbid Psychology', *Popular Science Monthly* 17 (1880) 86–93. See, for example, Julien Bogousslavsky and François Boller, 'Jean-Martin Charcot and Art: Relationship of the "Founder of Neurology" with Various Aspects of Art', in Stanley Finger, Dahlia W. Zaidel, François Boller, and Julien Bogousslavsky (Eds.), *The Fine Arts, Neurology, and Neuroscience: Neuro-Historical Dimensions* (San Diego, CA, 2014), pp. 185–99.

92. Luckhurst, *The Invention of Telepathy*, pp. 100–3.

93. Fredrik Björnström, *Hypnotism: Its History and Present Development*, trans. Baron Nils Posse (New York, 1889), p. 3; L.R. Regnier, *Hypnotisme et croyances anciennes* (Parish, 1891); Barrett Wendell, *Stelligeri and other Essays Concerning America* (New York, 1893), p. 86.

94. Christopher G. Goetz, Michel Bonduelle, and Toby Gelfand, *Charcot: Constructing Neurology* (Oxford, 1995), p. 183; Jennifer Hecht, *The End of the Soul: Scientific Modernity, Atheism, and Anthropology in France* (New York, 2003), pp. 250–1.

95. Philippe Galanopoulos, 'La Bibliothèque diabolique du docteur Bourneville (1882-1902)', *Vesalius: Acta Internationales Historiae Medicinae* 17, 2 (2011) 89. See also Céard, 'Démonologie et Démonopathies au temps de Chacot', 337–43.

96. Désiré Magloire Bourneville and Edouard Teinturier, *Le sabbat de sorciers* (Paris, 1882), p. 25.

97. Céard, 'Démonologie et Démonopathies au temps de Chacot', 339.

98. *Procès verbal fait pour délivrer une fille possédé e par le malin esprit, à Louviers* (Paris, 1883); Paul Provotelle, 'Françoise Fontaine, possédée de Louviers (1591)', *Annales médico-psychologiques* 9th S., 4 (1906) 353–68. For a more recent study of the case see, Anita M. Walker and Edmund H. Dickerman, 'The Haunted Girl: Possession, Witchcraft and Healing in Sixteenth-century Louviers', *Proceedings of the Annual Meeting of the Western Society for French History* 23 (1996) 207–18.

99. De Certeau, *Possession*, pp. 213–26; Ferber, *Demonic Possession*, pp. 139–44; Rapley, *A Case of Witchcraft*, pp. 212–14.

100. Johann Weyer, *Histoires, disputes et discours des illusions et impostures des diables, des magiciens, infâmes, sorcières et empoisonneurs* (Paris, 1885).

101. Emanuel Garcia, 'Johann Weyer and Sigmund Freud: A Psychoanalytic Note on Science, Narcissism, and Aggression', *American Imago* 46 (1989) 21.

102. On Johann Weyer's work see most recently, Michaela Valente, '"Against the devil, the subtle and cunning enemy": Johann Wier's *De praestigiis daemonum*', in Jan Machielsen (Ed.), *The Science of Demons: Early Modern Authors Facing Witchcraft and the Devil* (Abingdon, 2020). See also, Stuart Clark, *Thinking with Demons: The Idea of Witchcraft in Early Modern Europe*, pp. 198–203; Claudia Swan, *Art, Science, and Witchcraft in Early Modern Holland: Jacques de Gheyn II (1565–1629)* (Cambridge, 2005), pp. 157–75.

103. Christian Martin, 'Bodin's Reception of Johann Weyer in De la Démonomanie', in Howell A. Lloyd (Ed.), *The Reception of Bodin* (Leiden, 2013), pp. 117–37.

104. Arnold, *Observations*, p. 321.

105. Olivier Walusinski, *Georges Gilles de la Tourette: Beyond the Eponym*, pp. 339–41; Goldstein, *Classify*, pp. 355–7.

106. Joseph Guislain, *Traité sur les phrénopathies, ou Doctrine nouvelle des maladies mentales*, 2nd edition (Brussels, 1835), p. vii; Joseph Guislain, *Leçons orales sur les phrénopathies, ou Traité théorique et pratique des maladies mentales* (Ghent, 1853), Vol. 1, p. 287.

107. *La Morale indépendante*, 10 September 1865, 46. On Axenfeld, see Goetz, *Charcot: Constructing Neurology*, pp. 43–5.

108. George Alexander Gibson, *Life of Sir William Tennant Gairdner* (Glasgow, 1912), p. 214; Alexandre Axenfeld, *Jean Wier et la sorcellerie* (Paris, 1866), p. 77.

109. See Philip C. Almond, *England's First Demonologist: Reginald Scot and 'The Discoverie of Witchcraft'* (London, 2011).

110. Almond, *England's First Demonologist*, pp. 61, 63.

111. Gairdner, *Insanity*, p. 61. See also Daniel Hack Tuke, *Chapters in the History of the Insane in the British Isles* (London, 1882), pp. 37–8.

112. *Journal of Mental Science* 29 (1883) 135; *Journal of Mental Science* 32 (1886) 259.

113. A.R. Urquhart, 'Current Opinion on Medico-Psychological Questions in Germany', *Journal of Mental Science* 40 (1894) 208.

114. Pierre Briquet, *Traité clinique et thérapeutique de l'hystérie* (Paris, 1859), pp. 268–71.

115. John Stearne, *A Confirmation and Discovery of Witch-Craft* (London, 1648), p. 48.

116. William Alexander Hammond, *A Treatise on the Diseases of the Nervous System* (New York, 1871), p. 626.

117. Jacques Fontaine, *Discours des marques des sorciers* (Paris, 1611). On early modern witch marks in French works see, Katherine Dauge-Roth, *Signing the Body: Marks on Skin in Early Modern France* (Abingdon, 2020); Hélène Hotton, 'Les marques du diable et les signes de l'Autre. Rhétorique du dire démonologique à la fin de la Renaissance', PhD Thesis, Montreal University, 2011.

118. John Michell Clarke, 'On Hysteria', *Brain: A Journal of Neurology* 15 (1892) 548.

119. Clarke, 'On Hysteria', 549.

120. Michèle Ouerd, 'Dans la forge à cauchemars mythologiques: sorcières, praticiennes et hystériques', *Les Cahiers de Fontenay* 11–12 (1978), 139–215; Monique Schneider, *De l'exorcisme á la psychanalyse: Le Féminin expurgé* (Paris, 1979). See Sarah Ferber, 'Charcot's Demons: Retrospective Medicine and Historical Diagnosis in the Writings of the Salpêtrière School', in Marijke Gijswijt-Hofstra and Hilary Marland Hans de Waardt (Eds.), *Illness and Healing Alternatives in Western Europe* (London, 1997), pp. 128–30.

121. Gairdner, *Insanity*, pp. 53–6.

122. See, for example, M. Géraud, 'Emil Kraepelin: A Pioneer of Modern Psychiatry: On the Occasion of the Hundred and Fiftieth Anniversary of his Birth, *Encephale* 33 (2007) 561–7.

123. George Trumbull Ladd, *Outline of Physiological Psychology* (New York, 1891), p. 3.

124. See Peter Lamont, *Extraordinary Beliefs. A Historical Approach to a Psychological Problem* (Cambridge, 2013), pp. 19–34.

125. George Miller Beard, *The Psychology of the Salem Witchcraft Excitement of 1692* (New York, 1882), p. v. On Beard's interpretation see Marion Gibson, *Witchcraft Myths in American Culture* (London, 2007), pp. 104–6.

126. Beard, *Psychology of Salem*, p. 28.

127. *The Detroit Lancet* 6 (1882) 185.

128. William James, *The Principles of Psychology* (New York, [1890] 1910), vol. 2, p. 309; William James, *Manuscript Lectures* (Cambridge, MA, 1988), pp. 71–8. See also, Robert D. Richardson, *William James: In the Maelstrom of American Modernism: A Biography* (Boston, MA, 2006), pp. 346–7.

129. Jean Baptiste M. Parchappe, 'Recherches historiques et critiques sur la démonologie et la sorcellerie au quinzième siècle (le Maillet des sorcières), *Revue de Rouen* (1843) 193–200, 287–94, 350–37. A transcript can be read at the excellent *Histoire de la folie* website http://www.histoiredelafolie.fr/psychiatrie-neurologie/parchappe-du-vinay-demonologie-et-sorcellerie-au-xve-siecle-le-maillet-des-sorcieres-article-paru-dans-la-revue-de-rouen-et-de-la-normandie-rouen-11e-annee-1er-semestre-143-pp; Richardson, *William James: In the Maelstrom*, p. 347.

130. James, *Manuscript Lectures*, p. 72.

131. William James, *Essays in Psychical Research* (Cambridge, MA, 1986), p. xxiv.

132. James, *Manuscript Lectures*, p. 72.

133. Cited in Lachapelle, *Investigating the Supernatural*, p. 67.

134. Hayward, *Resisting History*, pp. 61–4; Lachapelle, *Investigating the Supernatural*, pp. 65–71.

135. Cited in Lachapelle, *Investigating the Supernatural*, p. 66.

136. Elizabeth R. Valentine, 'Spooks and spoofs: relations between psychical research and academic psychology in Britain in the inter-war period', *History of the Human Sciences* 25 (2012) 67–90; Régine Plas, 'Psychology and psychical research in France around the end of the 19th century', *History of the Human Sciences* 25 (2012) 91–107; Maria Teresa Brancaccio, 'Enrico Morselli's Psychology and "Spiritism": Psychiatry, psychology and psychical research in Italy in the decades around 1900', *Studies in History and Philosophy of Science* 48 (2014) 75–84; Lynn L. Sharp, *Secular Spirituality: Reincarnation and Spiritism in Nineteenth-century France* (Lanham, 2006), pp. 133–9; Oppenheim, *The Other World*, pp. 236–49.

137. See Andreas Sommer, 'Psychical research and the origins of American psychology: Hugo Münsterberg, William James and Eusapia Palladino', *History of the Human Sciences* 25 (2012) 23–44; Sommer, 'Are you afraid of the dark? Notes on the psychology of belief in histories of science and the occult', *European Journal of Psychotherapy & Counselling* 18 (2016) 105–22; Lamont, *Extraordinary Beliefs*, pp. 181–95; Heather Wolffram, *The Stepchildren of Science: Psychical Research and Parapsychology in Germany, c. 1870–1939* (Amsterdam, 2009), p. 41.

138. G. Stanley Hall, 'A Study of Fears', *The American Journal of Psychology* 8 (1897) 147–249.

139. Owen Davies, *A Supernatural War: Magic, Divination, and Faith during the First World War* (Oxford, 2018), pp. 2–3.

140. Mark S. Micale (Ed.), *Beyond the Unconscious: Essays of Henri F. Ellenberger in the History of Psychiatry* (Princeton, NJ, 1993), pp. 341–61.

141. Pierre Janet, 'Un cas de possession et l'exorcisme moderne', *Bulletin des Travaux de l'Université de Lyon* 8 (1894–1895) 41–57. See also, Stefan Andriopoulos, *Possessed: Hypnotic Crimes, Corporate Fiction, and the Invention of Cinema* (Chicago, IL, 2008), pp. 71–3.

142. Henry Meige, 'Les possédés des dieux dans l'art antique', *Nouvelle iconographie de la Salpêtrière* 7 (1894) 35–64.

143. Sigmund Freud, *Pre-Psycho-Analytic Publications and Unpublished Drafts*, trans. James Strachey (London, 1966), p. 41. See also William J. McGrath, 'Retrospective Medicine in Breuer and Freud's "Studies on Hysteria": The Assault on Medieval Superstition', *The Annual of Psychoanalysis* 21 (1993) 39–56; Kathleen Duffy, *Freud's Early Psychoanalysis, Witch Trials and the Inquisitorial Method: The Harsh Therapy* (Abingdon, 2020); Midelfort, 'Charcot, Freud', pp. 208–14; Peter Swales, 'A Fascination with Witches', *The Sciences* 27 (1982) 221–5.

144. Quoted in Arij Ouweneel, *Freudian Fadeout: The Failings of Psychoanalysis in Film*, p. 56. See also Duffy, *Freud's Early Psychoanalysis, Witch Trials and the Inquisitorial Method*, ch. 5.

145. See, for example, Antonio Melechi, *Fugitive Minds: On Madness, Sleep and other Twilight Afflictions* (London, 2003), pp. 24–5.

146. Quoted in Ouweneel, *Freudian Fadeout*, p. 57.

147. Ernest Jones, 'On the Nightmare', *American Journal of Insanity* 66 (1910) 383–417.

148. Ernest Jones, *On the Nightmare* (London, [1931] 1949), pp. 190, 232, 211.

149. Gregory Zilboorg, *A History of Medical Psychology* (New York, 1941), pp. 148–55.

150. Juliette Wood, 'The Reality of Witch Cults Reasserted: Fertility and Satanism', in Barry and Davies (Eds.), *Witchcraft Historiography*, p. 80.

151. Thomas Szasz, *The Manufacture of Madness: A Comparative Study of the Inquisition and the Mental Health Movement* (New York, 1970), p. 78. See Peter Elmer, 'Science, Medicine and Witchcraft', in Barry and Davies (Eds.), *Witchcraft Historiography*, pp. 33–52; Vandermeersch, 'The Victory of Psychiatry over Demonology'.

152. N.P. Spanos, 'Witchcraft in Histories of Psychiatry: A Critical Analysis and an Alternative Conceptualization', *Psychological Bulletin* 85 (1978) 417–39; T.J. Schoeneman, 'The Mentally Ill Witch in Textbooks of Abnormal Psychology: Current Status and Implications of a Fallacy', *Professional Psychology: Research and Practice* 15 (1984) 299–314. See also, T.J. Schoeneman, S. Brooks, C. Gibson, J. Routbort, and D. Jacobs, 'Seeing the Insane in Textbooks of Abnormal Psychology: The Uses of Art in Histories of Mental Illness', *Journal for the Theory of Social Behaviour* 24 (1994) 111–41.

153. Midelfort, 'Charcot, Freud'.

154. *Journal of Psychological Medicine and Mental Pathology* 2 (1849) 230.

CHAPTER 2

1. Thomas Bakewell, *The Domestic Guide, in Cases of Insanity* (Newcastle, 1805), p. 85.

2. Lisetta Lovett, 'Thomas Bakewell (1761–1835): Madhouse Keeper and Moral Therapist', *Journal of Medical Biography* 15, 4 (2007) 188–94; William Ll. Parry-Jones, *The Trade in Lunacy: A Study of Private Madhouses in England in the Eighteenth and Nineteenth Centuries* (London, 1972), pp. 93–4.

3. Bakewell, *Domestic Guide*, pp. viii, ix.

4. Davies, *Witchcraft, Magic, and Culture*, pp. 7–8.

5. Reprinted in *The Medical and Physical Journal*; John Vaughan, 'Remarkable Case of Madness; Communicated by Dr. John Vaughan, of Wilmington', *The Medical and Physical Journal* 8 (1802) 311–15.

6. Vaughan, 'Remarkable Case of Madness', 313, 315.

7. Esquirol, 'Démonomanie', p. 308; Esquirol, *Maladies Mentales*, Vol. 1, p. 504.

8. Esquirol, 'Démonomanie', pp. 302–3; Esquirol, 'Démonomanie', p. 304.

9. Esquirol, 'Démonomanie', pp. 237–8.

10. Alexandre Brière de Boismont, 'Observation de démonomanie; deux ans de durée; guérison instantanée (7 mars 1843)', *Annales médico-psychologiques* 2 (1843) 111. For confirmation of this see Owen Davies, 'Witchcraft accusations in France 1850–1990', in Willem de Blécourt and Owen Davies (Eds.), *Witchcraft Continued: Popular Magic in Modern Europe* (Manchester, 2004), pp. 107–32; Judith Devlin, *The Superstitious Mind: French Peasants and the Supernatural in the Nineteenth Century* (New Haven, CT, 1987); William Pooley, 'Magical Capital: Witchcraft and the Press in Paris, c.1789–1939', in Karl Bell (Ed.), *Supernatural Cities: Enchantment, Anxiety and Spectrality* (Woodbridge, 2019), pp. 25–44.

11. Brigham, *Observations on the Influence of Religion*, p. 290. For confirmation see Davies, *America Bewitched*; Ann Goldberg, *Sex, Religion, and the Making of Modern Madness: The Eberbach Asylum and German Society, 1815–1849* (Oxford, 1999), p. 52.

12. Maurice Macario, 'Etudes cliniques sur la démonomanie', *Annales Medico-Psychologiques* 1 (1843) 440–85. See Vandermeersch, 'The Victory of Psychology over Demonology', 9–11; Macario, 'Etudes cliniques sur la démonomanie', 441.

13. Macario, 'Etudes cliniques sur la démonomanie', 475.

14. Charles Louandre, 'De mouvement Catholique en France depuis 1830', *La revue des deux mondes* 5 (1844) 484.

15. Hervé Guillemain, *Diriger les consciences guérir les âmes: Une histoire compare des pratiques thérapeutiques et religieuses (1830–1939)*, pp. 16–22, 55–65; Goldstein, *Console and Classify*, pp. 206–9; Olivier Bonnet, 'Faire la biographie d'un charlatan? Frère Hilarion, fondateur d'asiles d'aliénés au XIXe siècle', *Cahiers d'histoire* 47 (2002) 27–43.

16. Bouchet, 'Surveillant, infirmier et gardien', *Annales médico psychologiques* 3 (1844) 60.

17. Hervé Guillemain, 'Déments ou demons? L'exorcisme face aux sciences psychiques (XIXe-XXe siècles', *Revue d'histoire de l'Église de France* 87 (2001) 441, n. 11.

18. See, Catherine-Laurence Maire, *Les possédées de Morzine 1857–1873* (Lyon, 1981); Jacqueline Carroy, *De la possession à l'hystérie* (Paris, 1981); Ruth Harris, 'Possession on the borders: The 'mal de Morzine' in nineteenth-century France', *Journal of Modern History* 69 (1997) 451–78; Nicole Edelman, *Les métamorphoses de l'hystérique* (Paris, 2003); Jean-Christophe Richard, *Les Possédées de Morzine*, 2 vols (Bossey, 2010–2016).

19. César Chiara, *Les diables de Morzine en 1861, ou Les nouvelles possédées* (Lyon, 1861), pp. 20, 21.

20. Joseph Arthaud, *Relation d'une hystéro-démonopathie épidémique observée a Morzine* (Lyon, 1862), pp. 73–4.

21. Augustin Constans, *Relation sur une épidémie d'hystéro-démonopathie en 1861*, 2nd ed. (Paris, 1863), p. 106.

22. Constans, *Relation sur une épidémie*, p. 70.

23. See, for example, 'Hystero-Demonopathy in Savoy', *The Intellectual Observer* 7 (1865) 374–7; 'The Devils of Morzine', *Living Age* 85 (1865) 227–35 (reprinted from the *Cornhill Magazine*); *The Journal of Mental Science* 13 (1867) 258–61.

24. Philippe Kuhn, 'L'épidémie hystéro-démonopathique', *Annales médico psychologiques* 4th S. 6 (1865) 37.

25. Kuhn, 'L'épidémie hystéro-démonopathique', 34.

26. Maire, *Les possédées*, p. 105.

27. Barbara Chitussi, 'Hystéro-Démonpathie et Personnalité Multiple: Le Cas de Verzegnis', *European Yearbook of the History of Psychology* 2 (2016) 116–17; 'Epidemic of Hysterical Demonomania', *The American Journal of Insanity* 36 (1879–1880) 230; Fernando Franzolini, L'epidemia di ossesse (istero-demonopatie) in Verzegnis : Studiata dai dottori Giuseppe Chiap e Fernando Franzolini', *Rivista Sperimentale de Franiatra* 5 (1879) 89–169; Luciana Borsatti, *Le indemoniate. Superstizione e scienza medica—Il caso di Verzegnis* (Udine, 2002); Barbara Chitussi, 'Introduction', *European Yearbook of the History of Psychology* 2 (2016) 89–94.

28. Franzolini, L'epidemia di ossesse', 169.

29. Chitussi, 'Introduction', 92.

30. Esquirol, 'Demonomanie', p. 298.

31. Oonagh Walsh, ' "The Designs of Providence": Race, Religion and Irish Insanity', in J. Melling and B. Forsyth (Eds.), *Insanity, Institutions and Society, 1800–1914* (London, 1999), pp. 223–43; Alice Mauger, *The Cost of Insanity in Nineteenth-Century Ireland: Public, Voluntary and Private Asylum Care* (Cham, 2018), p. 225.

32. *A Report of the Proceedings of Three Public Meetings, which were held in the City of Cork* (Cork, 1825), p. 41. On Halloran's career see Brendan Kelly, *Hearing Voices: The History of Psychiatry in Ireland* (Newbridge, 2016).

33. *A Report of the Proceedings of Three Public Meetings*, pp. 89–90.

34. Karl Wilhelm Ideler, *Versuch einer Theorie des religiösen Wahnsinns: ein Beitrag zur Kritik der religiösen Wirren der Gegenwart* (Halle, 1848–1850).

35. See Goldberg, *Sex, Religion, and the Making of Modern Madness*, pp. 37–41; Otto M. Marx, 'German Romantic Psychiatry. Part II', in Edwin R. Wallace and John Gach (Eds.), *History of Psychiatry and Medical Psychology* (New York, 2008), pp. 343–5.

36. Ann Goldberg, *Sex, Religion, and the Making of Modern Madness*, p. 68.

37. Brigham, *Observations on the Influence of Religion*, pp. 303, 304, 305.

38. Pliny Earle, *A Visit to Thirteen Asylums for the Insane in Europe* (Philadelphia, PA, 1841), p. 119.

39. W.C. Ellis, *A Treatise on the Nature, Symptoms, Causes, and Treatment of Insanity* (London, 1838), p. 67.

40. James Cowles Prichard, *A Treatise on Insanity and Other Disorders Affecting the Mind* (London, 1835), p. 142. See, Jonathan Andrews, 'Cause or Symptom? Contention Surrounding Religious Melancholy and Mental Medicine in Late-Georgian Britain', *Studies in the Literary Imagination* 44 (2011) 82–4.

41. Prichard, *A Treatise on Insanity*, p. 143.

42. Prichard, *A Treatise on Insanity*, p 149.

43. Theodore M. Porter, 'Quantity and Polity: Asylum Statistics and the Drive for Medical Evidence', in Jed Z. Buchwald (Ed.), *A Master of Science History: Essays in Honor of Charles Coulston Gillispie* (Dordrecht, 2012), pp. 327–41.

44. Borthwick Institute, BOO6/2/2/1- BOO6/2/3/2.

45. *The British and Foreign Medico-chirurgical Review* 26 (1860) 294; cited from *Statistique des établissements d'aliénés en France, de 1842 à 1853* (Paris, 1857).

46. Frédéric Carbonel, 'L'asile pour aliénés de Rouen: Un laboratoire de statistiques morales de la Restauration à 1848', *Histoire & mesure* 20 (2005) 11; Henri Dagonet, *Notice statistique sur l'aliénation mentale dans le départment du Bas-Rhin* (Strasburg, 1859), pp. 27, 18; John Webster, 'Stéphansfeld asylum', *Journal of Psychological Medicine* 5 (1852) 360.

47. Fiona Godlee, 'Aspects of Non-Conformity: Quakers and the Lunatic Fringe', in W.F. Bynum, Roy Porter, and Michael Shepherd (Eds.), *The Anatomy of Madness* (London, 1985), Vol. 2, pp. 73–86.

48. Samuel Tuke, *Description of the Retreat, an Institution near York, for Insane Persons of the Society of Friends* (York, 1813), pp. 208–9.

49. Prichard, *A Treatise on Insanity*, p. 151.

50. See, J. Andrews, 'Cause or Symptom? Contentions Surrounding Religious Melancholy and Mental Medicine in Late-Georgian Britain', *Studies in the Literary Imagination* 44 (2011) 68–9; Paul Laffey, 'John Wesley on Insanity', *History of Psychiatry* 12 (2001) 467–79; Jessica Leaf, 'Credulity, Superstition and Fanaticism'? An Examination of the Relationship between Evangelical Revivalism, Madness and the Age of Reform', *Midlands Historical Review* 2 (2018), n.p.

51. James Cornish, 'Remarkable Effects of Fanaticism on the Inhabitants of Several Towns in Cornwall', *London Medical and Physical Journal*, 31 (1814) 376–7. For context on the Revival see, David Luker, 'Revivalism in Theory and Practice: The Case of Cornish Methodism', *The Journal of Ecclesiastical History* 37 (1986) 603–19; David Hempton, *Methodism: Empire of the Spirit* (New Haven, CT, 2005), pp. 25–7.

52. Henry D. Rack, 'Charles Wesley and the Supernatural', *Bulletin of the John Rylands Library* 88 (2006), 59–79; Owen Davies, 'Wesley's Invisible World: Witchcraft and the Temperature of Preternatural Belief', in Robert Webster (Ed.), *Perfecting Perfection: Essays in Honor of Henry D. Rack* (Eugene, OR, 2015), pp. 147–73; Karl Bell, *The Magical Imagination: Magic and Modernity in Urban England, 1780–1914* (Cambridge, 2012), pp. 52–5.

53. Marjorie Levine-Clark, 'Dysfunctional Domesticity: Female Insanity and Family Relationships among the West Riding Poor in the Mid-Nineteenth Century', *Journal of Family History* 25 (2000) 349.

54. *The New York Journal of Medicine* 10 (1848) 372–4. See also, Herman Albert Norton, *Religion in Tennessee, 1777–1945* (Knoxville, TN, 1981), pp. 23–5.

55. J. Spencer Fluhman, '*A Peculiar People': Anti-Mormonism and the Making of Religion in Nineteenth-Century America* (Chapel Hill, NC, 2012), pp. 49–66.

56. Nathaniel Bingham, *Observations on the Religious Delusions of Insane Persons* (London, 1841), p. 142.

57. Carl Ulrik Sondén, 'Anteckningar och reflexioner angående den epidemiska religiösa ecstas, som härskade i Sverige år 1841 och 1842', *Hygiea* 12 1843: 1–4; Carl Ulrik Sondén, *Anteckningar öfver den epidemiska religiösa ecstas, som härskade i Sverige åren 1841–1842* (Stockholm, 1843); Carl Ulrik Sondén, 'Memoir on an Epidemic Religious Ecstasy which Prevailed in Sweden in 1841 and 1842', *The Dublin Journal of Medical Science* 24 (1843) 226–37; Samuel Hanbury Smith, *Sketch of the Epidemic Religious Monomania which Occurred in Sweden, in the Year 1841 and 1842* (Columbus, OH, 1850); Peter Aronsson, 'Pigornas rop och överhetens diskurs. Ett tolkningsförsök av en väckelse på 1840-talet', *Scandia* 55 (1989) 245–88.

58. Roger Qvarsell, *Ordning och behandling. Psykiatri och sinnessjukvård i. Sverige under 1800-talets första hälft* (Umeå 1982), p. 64.

59. Aronsson, 'Pigornas rop och överhetens diskurs', 248.

60. See, for example, Samuel Wright, 'An Experimental Inquiry into the Physiological Action of Ergot of Rye', *Edinburgh Medical and Surgical Journal* 52 (1839) 308–10.

61. Aronsson, 'Pigornas rop och överhetens diskurs', 256–7; Smith, *Sketch of the epidemic religious monomania which occurred in Sweden*, p. 504.

62. Kristina Tegler Jerselius, *Den stora häxdansen: vidskepelse, väckelse och vetande I Gagnef 1858* (Uppsala, 2003); *The Athenæum* 30 October (1858), 552.

63. See R.L. Numbers and J.S. Numbers, 'Millerism and Madness. A Study of "Religious Insanity" in Nineteenth-Century America', in Ronald L. Numbers and Jonathan M. Butler (Eds.), *The Disappointed: Millerism and Millenarianism in the Nineteenth Century* (Knoxville, TN, 1993), pp. 92–119; Cynthia M.A. Geppert, 'Religious Insanity: A Diagnosis at the Intersection of 19th Century American Religion and Psychiatry', *J Nerv Ment Dis.* 207 (2019) 785–91.

64. William Miller and Joshua V. Himes, *Views of the Prophecies and Prophetic Chronology, selected from Manuscripts of William Miller* (Boston, MA, 1842), p. 57.

65. 'Report of the Board of Visitors, of the Trustees and of the Superintendent of the New Hampshire Asylum for the Insane', *The American Journal of the Medical Sciences* 7 (1844) 151, 151.

66. Pliny Earle, 'On the Causes of Insanity', *The American Journal of Insanity* 3–4 (1846–47), 207.

67. 'Memorial of D.L. Dix, praying an appropriation of land for the relief of the insane', *Index of Miscellaneous Documents Printed by Order of the Senate of the United States* (Washington, 1850), p. 2.

68. Morel, 'Rapports sur les établissements d'aliénés des États-Unis et de l'Angleterre', *Annales médico-psychologiques* 9 (1847) 301–2.

69. *The Christian Parlor Magazine* (1846) 370–1.

70. *The Pennsylvania Journal of Prison Discipline and Philanthropy* 4 (1849), 81.

71. Numbers and Numbers, 'Millerism and Madness', 99.

72. See, Andrew R. Holmes, 'The Ulster Revival of 1859: Causes, Controversies and Consequences', *The Journal of Ecclesiastical History* 63 (2012) 488–515; Daniel Ritchie, 'The 1859 Revival and its Enemies: Opposition to Religious Revivalism within Ulster Presbyterianism', *Irish Historical Studies* 40 (2016) 66–91; Janice Holmes, *Religious Revivals in Britain and Ireland, 1859–1905* (Dublin, 2000).

73. Holmes, 'Ulster Revival', 494.

74. Henry Mac Cormac, 'Some Remarks on the Ulster Revival, so Named, of 1859', *Journal of Mental Science* 10 (1865), 165, 164.

75. Mac Cormac, 'Some Remarks', 161.

76. Holmes, 'Ulster Revival', 503. See Daniel Richie, 'William McIlwaine and the 1859 Revival in Ulster: A Study of Anglican and Evangelical Identities', *Journal of Ecclesiastical History* 65 (2014) 803–26; David N. Livingstone, 'Darwin in Belfast: The Evolution Debate', in John Wilson Foster and Helena Chesney (Eds.), *Nature in Ireland: A Scientific and Cultural History* (Montreal, 1997), pp. 387–8.

77. W.M. M'Ilwaine, 'Ulster Revivalism; a Retrospect', *Journal of Mental Science* 6 (1860) 198.

78. James G. Donat, 'Medicine and Religion: On the Physical and Mental Disorders that Accompanied the Ulster Revival of 1859', in W.F. Bynum, Roy Porter, and Michael Shepherd (Eds.), *Anatomy Of Madness* (Abingdon, 1988), Vol. 3, pp. 125–50; David Bebbington, *Victorian Religious Revivals: Culture and Piety in Local and Global Contexts* (Oxford, 2012), pp. 159–93.

79. Bucknill and Tuke, *Manual of Psychological Medicine*, 4th ed., p. 99.

80. [Frederick A. Packard], *Relations of Religion to what are called Diseases of the Mind* (Philadelphia, 1850), pp. 8–9, 41. Packard's authorship is attested in *The Presbyterian Magazine* 1 (1851), 533. See also Ronald L. Numbers, *Science and Christianity in Pulpit and Pew* (Oxford, 2007), pp. 99–100.

81. [Packard], *Relations of Religion*, p. 8.

82. Forbes Winslow, 'Religious Insanity', *Journal of Psychological Medicine and Mental Pathology* 3 (1850), 283–92.

83. *American Journal of Insanity* 7 (1851) 287.

84. *American Journal of Insanity* 7 (1851) 287.

85. W. Lauder Lindsay, 'The Causes of Insanity in Arctic Countries', *British and Foreign Medico-Chirurgical Review* 45 (1870) 228. See also, Fluhman, 'A Peculiar People', p. 62.

86. 'Religious Insanity', *Proceedings of the Medical Society of London* 2 (1874–1875) 52–5.

87. Bruce J. Evensen, *God's Man for the Gilded Age: D.L. Moody and the Rise of Modern Mass Evangelism* (Oxford, 2003).

88. *Sheffield Daily Telegraph*, 6 March 1875; *Wigton Advertiser*, 24 April 1875.

89. Cited in *The Galaxy* 21 (1876) 702.

90. Theodore W. Fisher, 'Insanity and the Revival', *Boston Medical and Surgical Journal* 97 (1877) 59.

91. *The Galaxy* 21 (1876) 702.

92. George H. Savage, 'Religious Insanity and Religious Revivals. Effects of the "Mood and Sankey Services"', *The Lancet* 28 August 1875, 303–4.

93. George H. Savage, *Insanity and Allied Neuroses, Practical and Clinical*, 3rd ed. (London, 1891), pp. 53, 52.

94. *British Medical Journal*, 23 September 1882, 588.

95. See Hayward, *Resisting History*; Hayward, 'Neurology and the Resurgence of Demonology in Edwardian Britain' *Bulletin of the History of Medicine* 78 (2004) 37–58.

96. Tine Van Osselaer, 'Stigmata, Prophecies, and Politics: Louise Lateau in the German and Belgian Culture Wars of the Late Nineteenth Century', *Journal of Religious History* 42 (2018) 591–610; Tine Van Osselaer, Andrea Graus, Leonardo Rossi, and Kristof Smeyers, *The Devotion and Promotion of Stigmatics in Europe, c.1800–1950: Between Saints and Celebrities* (Leiden, 2020); Richard D. E. Burton, *Holy Tears, Holy Blood: Women, Catholicism, and the Culture of Suffering in France, 1840–1970* (Ithaca, NY, 2004); Michael E. O Sullivan, *Disruptive Power: Catholic Women, Miracles, and Politics in Modern Germany, 1918–1965* (Toronto, 2018).

97. Ruth Harris, *Lourdes: Body And Spirit in the Secular Age* (London, 1999); Emilie Garrigou-Kempton, 'Hysteria in Lourdes and Miracles at the Salpêtrière: The Intersection of Faith and Medical Discourse in Late Nineteenth-Century French Literature', PhD thesis, University of Southern California, 2016; Roberta Vittoria Grossi, 'Demonic Possession and Religious Scientific Debate in Nineteenth-Century France', in Giuseppe Giordan and Adam Possamai (Eds.), *The Social Scientific Study of Exorcism in Christianity* (Cham, 2020), pp.33–52; Guillemain, *Diriger les consciences*, pp. 192–226.

98. Shane McCorristine, *Spectres of the Self: Thinking about Ghosts and Ghost-Seeing in England, 1750–1920* (Cambridge, 2010), pp. 49–50.

99. See Gretchen A. Adams, *The Specter of Salem: Remembering the Witch Trials in Nineteenth-Century America* (Chicago, IL, 2008), pp. 82–5.

100. J.P. Williams, 'Psychical Research as Psychiatry in late Victorian Britain: Trance as Ecstasy or Trance as Insanity', in W.F. Bynum, Roy Porter, and Michael Shepherd (Eds.), *The Anatomy of Madness: Essays in the History of Psychiatry* (London, 1985), pp. 233–55; Janet Oppenheim, *'Shattered Nerves': Doctors, Patients, and Depression in Victorian England* (New York, 1991); Roger Luckhurst, *The Invention of Telepathy, 1870–1901* (Oxford, 2002), pp. 95–8; Claudie Massicotte, *Trance Speakers: Femininity and Authorship in Spiritual Séances, 1850–1930* (Montreal, 2017), pp. 49–50; Owen, *The Darkened Room*, pp. 147–51; Molly McGarry, *Ghosts of Futures Past: Spiritualism and the Cultural Politics of Nineteenth-Century America* (Berkeley, CA, 2008), pp. 121–54; Erika White Dyson, 'Spiritualism and Crime: Negotiating Prophecy and Police Power at the Turn of the Century', PhD thesis, Columbia University, 2010, 235–7; Pascal Le Maléfan, Renaud Evrard, and Carlos S. Alvarado, 'Spiritist Delusions and Spiritism in the Nosography of French Psychiatry (1850–1950)', *History of Psychiatry* 24 (2013) 477–91.

101. Andrew Wynter, *The Borderlands of Insanity: And Other Allied Papers* (New York, 1875), p. 290. On Wynter see the DNB.

102. Philibert Burlet, *Du spiritisme considéré comme cause d'aliénation mentale* (Lyon, 1863); Philibert Burlet, 'Du spiritisme considéré comme cause d'aliénation mentale', *Gazette médicale de Lyon* (1862), 557–60; http://www.histoiredela-folie.fr/psychiatrie-neurologie/philibert-burlet-du-spiritisme-considere-comme-cause-dalienation-mentale-lyon-imprimerie-de-richard-cie-1863-1-vol-in-8-2-ffnch-57-p-1-ffnch. On Arthaud's influence see, Frédéric Scheider, 'Aliénisme et catholicisme à Lyon au XIXe siècle: les missions de Joseph Arthaud (1813–1883)', PhD thesis, University of Lyon, 2005. See also, Lynn L. Sharp, *Secular Spirituality: Reincarnation and Spiritism in Nineteenth-century France* (Lanham, MD, 2006), p. 71.

103. Allan Kardec, *Qu'est-ce que le spiritisme?* (Paris, 1865), p. 70; Le Maléfan, Evrard, and Alvarado, 'Spiritist Delusions and Spiritism', 480–1.

104. Bainbridge, 'Religious Insanity in America', 234, 227.

105. Alfred Cridge, *Epitome of Spirit-Intercourse: A Condensed View of Spiritualism* (Boston, MA, 1854), p 85. On the Cridges see Ann Braude, *Radical Spirits: Spiritualism and Women's Rights in Nineteenth-century America*, 2nd ed. (Bloomington, IN, 2001), pp. 1–2, 129–31.

106. Joel Tiffany, 'Tiffany's Review of the Treatment Spiritualism has Received from the Hands of its Opponents', *Tiffany's Review: Devoted to the Investigation of Spiritual Science* 4 (1859), 470. For details on Tiffany's life, see https://www.findagrave.com/memorial/117096989/joel-tiffany.

107. Lyttleton Forbes Winslow, *Recollections of forty years; being an account at first hand of some famous criminal lunacy cases* (London, 1910), p. 366.

108. Lyttleton Forbes Winslow, *Spiritualistic Madness* (1877) p. 6.

109. *The Lancet*, 10 March 1877, 363.

110. Eugene Crowell, *The Identity of Primitive Christianity and Modern Spiritualism* (New York, 1874), Vol. 1, p. 340.

111. Eugene Crowley, *Spiritualism and Insanity* (Boston, MA, 1877), pp. 3, 5.

112. M. J. Baratoux, 'Les possédées de Plédran', *Progrès médical*, 9 July 1881, 550–1.

113. W, Herbert Packer, 'Demoniacal Possession', *Journal of Mental Science* 28 (1882–1883) 279.

114. Charles Lasègue and Jules Falret, 'La folie à deux ou folie communiquée', *Archives générales de médecine* 30 (1877) 257–97.

115. See Terry Castle, *The Female Thermometer: Eighteenth-Century Culture and the Invention of the Uncanny* (Oxford, 1995), pp. 208–14; Robert A. Faguet and Kay F. Faguet, 'La Folie à Deux', in Claude T.H. Friedmann and Robert Faguet, Eds., *Extraordinary Disorders of Human Behavior* (New York, 1982), pp. 1–14.

116. Evariste Marandon de Montyel, 'Contribution A l'Étude de la Folie A Deux', *Annales Medico-Psychologiques* 6 S. Vol. 5 (1881) 28–52. On de Montyel, see Brian Michèle, 'Marandon de Montyel, 1851–1908 : critique de l'asile : sa vie, son œuvre', PhD Thesis, Faculté de médecine Paris-Sud, 1987.

117. Reverchon and Pagè, 'La Famille Lochin', *Annales Medico-Psychologiques* 6 S. Vol. 8 (1882) 18–35.

118. Dr Lapointe 'Une famille entière atteinte simultanément de démonomanie', *Annales Medico-Psychologiques* 7th S. Vol. 4 (1886) 350–70.

119. See, Pauline M. Prior, *Madness and Murder: Gender, Crime and Mental Disorder in Nineteenth-Century Ireland* (Dublin, 2008), pp. 179–94; Brendan D. Kelly, 'Folie à plusiers: Forensic cases from nineteenth-century Ireland', *History of Psychiatry* 20 (2009) 47–60. See also Brendan Kelly, *Hearing Voices: The History of Psychiatry in Ireland* (Newbridge, 2016).

120. 'Obituary: Oscar Thomas Woods', *Journal of Mental Science* 52 (1906) 841; *Greenock Telegraph and Clyde Shipping Gazette*, 11 August 1888.

121. *Kerry Evening Post*, 1 February 1888; *Kerry Evening Post*, 14 July 1888.

122. Oscar T. Woods, 'Notes of a case of *folie à deux* in five members of one family', *Journal of Mental Science* 34 (1889) 536.

123. *Kerry Evening Post*, 14 March 1888.

124. Woods, 'Notes of a case of *folie à deux*', 538.

125. *Kerry Evening Post*, 11 and 14 July 1888; Prior, *Madness and murder*, p. 186.

126. *Kerry Evening Post*, 1 February 1888.

127. Woods, 'Notes of a Case', 538. See also Oscar Woods, 'Notes of some cases of *Folie à Deux* in several members of the same family', *Journal of Mental Science* 43, 183 (1897) 822–5.

128. Daniel Hack Tuke, 'Folie à deux', *Brain: A Journal of Neurology* 10 (1888) 410–11, 421.

129. For example, Peugniez, *L'Hystérie chez les enfants*, pp. 170–9.

130. Davies, *A Supernatural War*.

CHAPTER 3

1. Mitchell, Arthur. 'On Various Superstitions in the North-west Highlands and Islands of Scotland, Especially in Relation to Lunacy'. *Proceedings of the Society of the Antiquaries of Scotland* 4 (1860–62): 255–88; Daniel Hack Tuke, *Chapters in the History of the Insane in the British Isles* (London, 1882), p. 43.

2. Eigen, *Witnessing Insanity*, p. 101.

3. Cited in Eigen, *Witnessing Insanity: Madness and Mad-doctors in the English Court* (New Haven, CT, 1995), p. 90.

4. See Houston, *Madness and Society in Eighteenth-Century Scotland* (Oxford, 2000), p. 332; Alex Leff, 'Clean Round the Bend—The Etymology of Jargon and Slang Terms for Madness', *History of Psychiatry* 11 (2000) 155–62.

5. Porter, *Mind-Forg'd Manacles*, p. 19.

6. See Steve King, *Sickness, Medical Welfare and the English Poor, 1750–1834* (Manchester, 2018).

7. Cited in Goldstein, *Console and Classify*, p. 153.

8. Porter, *Mind-Forg'd Manacles*, p. 31. See also Allen Thiher, *Revels in Madness: Insanity in Medicine and Literature* (Ann Arbor, MI, 1999), pp. 9–11.

9. Owen Davies, 'Finding the Folklore in the Annals of Psychiatry' *Folklore* 133 (2022) 1–24.

10. Thomas Joseph Pettigrew, *On Superstitions Connected with the History and Practice of Medicine and Surgery* (London, 1844), pp. 132–6.

11. Esquirol, *Mental Maladies*, p. 50; Edward Jarvis, *Mania Transitoria* (Boston, MA, 1869), p. 28; Paul Tobia, 'The Patients of the Bristol Lunatic Asylum in the Nineteenth Century 1861–1900', PhD thesis, University of the West of England, 2017, 123.

12. See, for example, John Gideon Millingen, *Aphorisms on the Treatment and Management of the Insane* (Philadelphia, PA, 1842), p. 34. On puerperal insanity see Hilary Marland, *Dangerous Motherhood: Insanity and Childbirth in Victorian Britain* (Basingstoke, 2004); Irvine Loudon, 'Puerperal Insanity in the 19th Century', *Journal of the Royal Society of Medicine* 81 (1988) 76–9.

13. 'Fright a frequent cause of insanity, and sometimes a cure', *American Journal of Insanity* 3–4 (1846–47) 280–9.

14. *Sketches in Bedlam; or Characteristic traits of insanity*, 2nd ed. (London, 1824), pp. 183–4.

15. James G. Kiernan, 'Etiology of Insanity', *The Detroit Lancet* 6 (1882) 501–2.

16. *Northampton Mercury*, 8 September 1911.

17. David Wright, ' "Childlike in his innocence": Lay attitudes to "idiots" and "imbeciles" in Victorian England', in David Wright and Anne Digby (Eds.), *From Idiocy to Mental Deficiency: Historical Perspectives on People with Learning Disabilities* (London, 1996); Steven J. Taylor, ' "She Was Frightened while Pregnant by a Monkey at the Zoo": Constructing the Mentally Imperfect Child in Nineteenth-Century England', *Social History of Medicine* 30 (2017) 756–7; Steven J. Taylor, *Child Insanity in England, 1845–1907* (London, 2017), p. 36.

18. Lee Y. Olsen, 'Imagination and Deformation: Monstrous Maternal Perversions of Natural Reproduction in Early Modern England', PhD thesis, University of Arizona, 2011; David M. Turner, *Disability in Eighteenth-century England: Imagining Physical Impairment* (Abingdon, 2012), pp. 36–42.

19. *Census of Ireland, 1871. Part II. Vol. 1: The Status of Disease* (Dublin, 1873), pp. 23, 26.

20. J.G. Ballentine, 'Teratogenesis: an inquiry into the causes of monstrosities III. The Theories of the Past', *Edinburgh Medical Journal* 42 (1896), 250–5; Katherine Angell, 'Joseph Merrick and the Concept of Monstrosity in Nineteenth Century Medical Thought', in Holly Lynn Baumgartner and Roger Davis (Eds.), *Hosting the Monster* (Amsterdam, 2008), pp. 131–53; Emily Williams Kelly (Ed.), *Science, the Self, and Survival after Death: Selected Writings of Ian Stevenson* (Lanham, MD, 2013), pp. 293–313.

21. Robert Burton, *The Anatomy Of Melancholy* (Oxford, 1638), p. 64; John O'Reilly, *The Nervous and Vascular Connection Between the Mother and Foetus in Utero* (New York, 1864), p. 66.

22. T.C. Duncan, 'A Case of Monstrosity', *The United States Medial Investigator* 4 (1867) 76.

23. Quoted in Fisher, 'Does Maternal Mental Influence', 254.

24. *The Humboldt Medical Archives* 1 (1867–1868) 363.

25. G.J. Fisher, 'Does Maternal Mental Influence Have any Constructive or Destructive Power in the Production of Malformations or Monstrosities at any Stage of Embryonic Development?', *American Journal of Insanity* 26 (1869–70) 242.

26. Fisher, 'Does Maternal Mental Influence', 281.

27. Édouard Séguin, *Idiocy: and Its Treatment by the Physiological Method* (New York, 1866), p. 41.

28. Bakewell, *The Domestic Guide, in Cases of Insanity*, p. 103.

29. Jonathan Andrews, 'Letting Madness Range: Travel and Mental Disorder c. 1700-1900', in Richard Wrigley and George Revill (Eds.), *Pathologies of Travel* (Amsterdam, 2000), pp. 25–89.

30. Mark Harrison, 'From medical astrology to medical astronomy: sol-lunar and planetary theories of disease in British medicine, c. 1700-1850', *The British Journal for the History of Science* 33 (2000), 25–48.

31. Graeme Yorston and Camilla Haw, 'Old and Mad in Victorian Oxford: A Study of Patients aged 60 and Over Admitted to the Warneford and Littlemore Asylums in the Nineteenth Century', *History of Psychiatry* 16 (2005) 408; J. Webster, 'The Influence of Weather on Disease and on the Human Frame', *The London Lancet* 2 (1859) 136.

32. Francis Skae, 'On Insanity Caused by Injuries to the Head and Sunstroke', *Edinburgh Medical Journal* 11 (1866) 687–94; Andrews, 'Letting Madness Range', p. 51.

33. Diane Teresa Carpenter, 'Above all a Patient should never be Terrified: An Examination of Mental Health Care and Treatment in Hampshire 1845–1914', PhD thesis, University of Portsmouth, 2010, 97; *The Monthly Weather Report of the Meteorological Office for the Year 1884* (London, 1885), pp. 69, 77.

34. Alexander Morison, *Outlines of Lectures on the Nature, Causes, and Treatment of Insanity*, 4th ed. (London, 1848), p. 278; *Carlisle Patriot*, 3 September 1869; J. Crichton Browne, 'The Etiology of Insanity', *The British and Foreign Medico-Chirurgical Review* 40 (1867) 194.

35. Skae, 'On Insanity Caused by Injuries'.

36. See Catherine Beck, 'Patronage and Insanity: Tolerance, Reputation and Mental Disorder in the British Navy 1740–1820', *Historical Research* 94 (2021) 77–8.

37. William Battie, *On Madness* (London, 1758), p. 47.

38. James Mitchell, 'On the Coup de Soleil', *The Monthly Journal of Foreign Medicine* 1 (1828) 385–91.

39. *Sunderland Daily Echo and Shipping Gazette*, 27 July 1881; *Dundee Evening Telegraph*, 24 September 1898.

40. See Anna Marie Roos, 'Luminaries in Medicine: Richard Mead, James Gibbs, and Solar and Lunar Effects on the Human Body in Early Modern England', *Bulletin of the History of Medicine* 74 (2000) 433–57; Harrison, 'From medical astrology to medical astronomy'.

41. Richard Mead, *Medica sacra* (London, 1755), p. xv.

42. Pierre Foissac, 'The Influence of the Lunar Phases on the Physical and Moral Man', trans W.H. Tingley, *St. Louis Medical and Surgical Journal* 13 (1855) 502–11.

43. Mitchell, 'Coup de Soleil', 385.

44. Andrew Marshal and Solomon Sawrey, *The Morbid Anatomy of the Brain in Mania and Hydrophobia* (London, 1815), p. 153; John Haslam, *Observations on Madness and Melancholy*, 2nd ed. (London [1808, 1809), pp. 215–16; Anon., *Familiar Views of Lunacy and Lunatic Life* (London, 1850), p. 27.

45. Haslam, *Observations*, p. 216.

46. Haslam, *Observations*, p. 216; Niall McCrae, *The Moon and Madness* (Exeter, 2011).

47. Margaret Barnet, 'Matthew Allen, M.D. (Aberdeen) 1783–1845', *Medical History* 9 (1965) 16–28; Valerie Pedlar, ' "No place like Home": Reconsidering Matthew Allen and His "Mild System" of Treatment', *John Clare Society Journal* 13 (1994) 33–9.

48. Matthew Allen, *Cases of Insanity*, p. 104; John Thurnam, *Observations and Essays on the Statistics of Insanity* (London, 1845), pp. 115–16.

49. *Thirteenth Annual Report of the Trustees of the State Lunatic Hospital at Worcester* (Boston, MA, 1846), pp. 79–80.

50. *Good Words* (1862) 116.

51. Forbes Winslow, 'Medical Jurisprudence of Insanity. Part 1', *Journal of Mental Science* 9 (1856) 159.

52. Forbes Winslow, *Light and its Influence* (London, 1867), p. 150.

53. Thomas S. Kirkbride, 'Remarks on the Construction, Organisation and General Arrangements of Hospitals for the Insane', *The American Journal of Insanity* 11–12 (1854–55) 157.

54. *Asylum Journal of Mental Science* 2 (1856) 126.

55. M.A. Riva, L. Tremolizzo, M. Spicci, C. Ferrarese, G. De Vito, G.C. Cesana, and V.A. Sironi, 'The Disease of the Moon: The Linguistic and Pathological Evolution of the English Term "Lunatic" ', *Journal of the History of the Neurosciences* 20 (2011) 70–1.

56. John Douglas Blaisdell, 'A Frightful, But Not Necessarily Fatal, Madness: Rabies in Eighteenth-century England and English North America', Iowa State University, PhD, 1995, 30–1.

57. 'An Account of the diseases of Doggs and several Receipts for the Cure of their Madness, and of those bitten by them. Extracted from the papers of Sr Theodore Mayern', *Philosophical Transactions* 16 (1686) 408.

58. See the overview by William Lauder Lindsay, 'Madness in Animals', *Journal of Mental Science*, Vol. 17 (1871) 181–206.

59. Daniel Peter Layard, *An Essay on the Bite of a Mad Dog*, 3rd ed. (London, 1768), pp. 98, 99–100.

60. Layard, *An Essay on the Bite of a Mad Dog*, p. 28.

61. Cited in Blaisdell, 'A frightful, but not necessarily fatal, madness', 91.

62. W. Lauder Lindsay, 'Spurious Hydrophobia in Man' [part 2], *Journal of Mental Science* 24 (1879) 54. See also, Jessica Wang, *Mad Dogs and Other New Yorkers: Rabies, Medicine, and Society in an American Metropolis, 1840–1920* (Baltimore, 2019), pp. 61–4.

63. Nick Pemberton and Michael Worboys, *Rabies in Britain: Dogs, Disease and Culture, 1830–2000* (Basingstoke, 2007), p. 16.

64. Esquirol, *Des maladies Mentales*, Vol. 1, p. 226.

65. Samuel Argent Bardsley, *Medical Reports of Cases and Experiments: With Observations, Chiefly Derived from Hospital Practice* (London, 1807), pp. 236–305.

66. M. Tenon, *Mémoires sur les hôpitaux de Paris* (Paris, 1816), p. 216; *The Medical Times*, 6 November 1858, 486.

67. George Fleming, *Rabies and Hydrophobia: Their History, Nature, Causes, Symptoms, and Prevention* (London, 1872), pp. 28–68; Stephanie Howard-Smith, 'Mad Dogs, Sad Dogs and the "War against Curs" in London in 1760', *Journal for Eighteenth Century Studies* 42 (2019) 101–18.

68. *Gentleman's Magazine* 30 (1760) 353.

69. Cited in Howard-Smith, 'Mad Dogs', 104.

70. Oliver Goldsmith, *Essays and Poems* (Glasgow, 1819), p. 79.

71. *Cases and Cures of the Hydrophobia: Selected from the Gentleman's Magazine* (London, 1807), p. 67.

72. Christopher Nugent, *An Essay on the Hydrophobia* (London, 1753), p. 84; Armand Trousseau, *Lectures on clinical medicine, delivered at the Hotel-Dieu, Paris* (Philadelphia, PA, 1867), vol. 1, p. 691.

73. William Maryan, *A Treatise Explaining the Impossibility of the Disease termed Hydrophobia* (London, 1809), pp. iii–iv.

74. Maryan, *A Treatise*, p. 40.

75. *The Medical and Physical Journal* 22 (1809) 344.

76. Lauder Lindsay, 'Madness in Animals', 181.

77. Claude-Charles Pierquin, *Traité de la folie des animaux, de ses rapports avec celle de l'homme et les législations actuelles* (Paris, 1839), Vol. 2, pp. 5, 354–7.

78. Laurel Braitman, 'Animal Madness: A Natural History of Disorder', PhD, MIT, 2013, 43–5.

79. Pemberton and Worboys, *Rabies in Britain*, p. 93. See also B. Griffin, 'Mad Dogs and Irishmen': Dogs and Rabies in the Eighteenth and Nineteenth Centuries', *Ulster Folklife* 40 (1994) 1–15.

80. W. Lauder Lindsay, 'Spurious Hydrophobia in Man', *Journal of Mental Science* 23 (1878) 557.

81. *The Medical Times and Gazette*, 22 June 1878, 683.

82. Charles Dulles, 'Report on Hydrophobia', in Thomas M. Dolan, *M. Pasteur and Hydrophobia* (1890) p. 8.

83. Lauder Lindsay, 'Spurious Hydrophobia in Man' [part 2], 56.

84. Charles Dulles, 'Report on Hydrophobia', in Thomas M. Dolan, *M. Pasteur and Hydrophobia* (1890) p. 8; *American Lancet* 13 (1889) 227.

85. Sarah N. Cleghorn, 'Witchcraft and Hydrophobia', *Journal of Zoöphily* 23 (1914) 38.

86. Macdonald, *Mystical Bedlam*, pp. 139–40, 209.

87. William Falconer, *A Dissertation on the Influence of the Passions upon Disorders of the Body*, 2nd ed. (London, 1791), p. 110.

88. John Sinclair (Ed.), *The Statistical Account of Scotland* (London, 1792), Vol. 2, 496.

89. John Crichton, 'Case of the Leaping Ague of Angus-shire', *Edinburgh Medical and Surgical Journal* 31 (1829) 299–301.

90. John Sinclair (Ed.), *The Statistical Account of Scotland* (London, 1792), vol. 4, p. 5; John Sinclair (Ed.), *The Statistical Account of Scotland* (London, 1797), Vol. 19, p. 373; Alexander Tweedie (Ed.), *A System of Practical Medicine* (Philadelphia, PA, 1840), Vol. 2, p. 330.

91. John Thomson, *An Account of the Life, Lectures, and Writings of William Cullen*, Vol. 2, pp. 706–8; The Consultation Letters of Dr William Cullen (1710–1790) at the Royal College of Physicians of Edinburgh, ID3672; http://www.cullenproject.ac.uk/docs/3672/.

92. Joseph Wright, *The English Dialect Dictionary* (Oxford, 1905) Vol. 3, p. 669; John Ewart, *Tentamen medicum inaugurale, de chorea* (Edinburgh, 1786), p. 5.

93. For a history of epilepsy see Owsei Temkin, *The Falling Sickness: A History of Epilepsy from the Greeks to the Beginnings of Modern Neurology*, 2nd ed. (Baltimore, MD, 1994); Leo Kanner, 'The Names of the Falling Sickness. An Introduction to the Study of the Folklore and Cultural History of Epilepsy', *Human Biology* 2 (1930) 109–27.

94. Alexander Gordon, *Observations on the Efficacy of Cold-bathing in the Prevention and Cure of Diseases* (Aberdeen, 1786), p. 24; 'Report Upon the Number of Sick at their own Homes, and Summary of the Total Sick in Ireland on the Night of the 30ᵗʰ of March, 1851', *The Census of Ireland for the Year 1851* (Dublin, 1854), part 3, p. 111.

95. Fiona Godlee, 'Aspects of Non-Conformity: Quakers and the Lunatic Fringe', in W.F. Bynum, Roy Porter, and Michael Shepherd (Eds.), *The Anatomy of Madness* (London, 1985), vol. 2, pp. 73–82.

96. Haslam, *Observations on Madness*, p. 262; Nathaniel Bingham, *Observations on the Religious Delusions of Insane Persons*, p. 56; Marshall Hall, 'On the Theory of Convulsive Diseases, and Especially of Epilepsy', *Botanico-Medical Recorder* 16 (1848) 289.

97. C.H. Hardy, 'Imitative Epilepsy', *London Medical Gazette* 11 (1833) 247–8; Thomas Watson, 'Lectures on the Principles and Practice of Physic', *London Medical Gazette*, 28 May (1841), 371; Haygarth, *Of the Imagination*, p. 48.

98. Roos, 'Luminaries in Medicine', 445.

99. On the new school of thinking see, K. Sidiropoulou, A. Diamantis, and E. Magiorkinis, 'Hallmarks in 18th- and 19th-century Epilepsy Research', *Epilepsy & Behavior* 18 (2010) 151–61.

100. Richard Mead, *A Treatise Concerning the Influence of the Sun and Moon upon Human Bodies* (London, [1704] 1748), p. 39.

101. *Thirteenth Annual Report of the Trustees of the State Lunatic Hospital at Worcester*, p. 79. Also John Gideon Millingen, *Aphorisms on the Treatment and Management of the Insane* (Philadelphia, 1842), p. 11.

102. Cesare Lombroso, 'The Influence of Meteorological Conditions on Insanity', *The Half-yearly Abstract of the Medical Sciences* 46 (1868) 48–9; Owen Davies and Francesca Matteoni, *Executing Magic*, p. 14.

103. Jacques-Joseph Moreau, 'De l'étiologie de l'épilepsie', *Mémoires de l'Académie de Médecine* 18 (1854) 94–6; *The British and Foreign Medico-chirurgical Review* 16 (1855) 37.

104. Robert Boyd, 'Observations on Epilepsy', *The Asylum Journal of Mental Science* 3 (1857), 282.

105. Arthur Foss and Kinsey Trick, *St. Andrew's Hospital, Northampton: The First 150 Years (1838–1988)* (Cambridge, 2007), p. 195.

106. William Newnham, *Essay on Superstition: Being an Inquiry into the Effects of Physical Influence on the Mind* (London, 1830), p. 132.

107. Mark R. Taylor, 'Norfolk Folklore', *Folklore* 40 (1929) 116.

108. Mead, *Medica Sacra*, pp. 73–93; Thomas C. Upham, *Jahn's Biblical Archaeology* (Andover, 1823), p. 217.

109. See Anthony Ossa-Richardson, 'Possession or Insanity? Two Views from the Victorian Lunatic Asylum', *Journal of the History of Ideas* 74 (2013) 553–75.

110. On the Lukins affair see, Jonathan Barry, *Witchcraft and Demonology in South-West England, 1640–1789* (London, 2012), pp. 206–56; Davies, *Witchcraft, Magic and Culture*, pp. 20–2.

111. Heaton, *The Extraordinary Affliction*, pp. 19, 100.

112. Heaton, *The Extraordinary Affliction*, p. 30.

113. CRH female casebook, 1889, vol. 4.

114. Isaac Nicholson, *A Sermon against Witchcraft, Preached in the Parish Church of Great Paxton, in the County of Huntingdon, July 17, 1808* (London, 1808), p. ii. For an examination of the case see, Stephen Mitchell, 'A case of witchcraft assault in early nineteenth-century England as ostensive action', in Willem de Blécourt and Owen Davies (Eds.), *Witchcraft Continued: Popular Magic in Modern Europe* (Manchester, 2003), pp. 14–29.

115. John Wesley, *Primitive Physic*, 22nd ed (Philadelphia, PA, 1791), pp. 106–7.

116. *Culpeper's Complete Herbal: To which is Now Added, Upwards of One Hundred Additional Herbs* (London, 1816), pp. 245, 254, 306, 141.

117. Marie Trevelyan, *Folk-lore and Folk-stories of Wales* (London, 1909), p. 314.

118. Davies, *A People Bewitched*, p. 57.

119. Thomas Joseph Pettigrew, *Substance of a Clinical Lecture on a Case of Hydrophobia* (London, 1834), p. 30; *British Medical Journal*, 24 June 1865, 650.

120. *Staffordshire Advertiser*, 2 October 1819. On Morison see, Michael Brown, 'Medicine, Quackery and the Free Market: The "War" against Morison's Pills and the Construction of the Medical Profession, c. 1830-c1850', in Mark Jenner and Patrick Wallis (Eds.), *Medicine and the Marketplace in Early Modern England and its Colonies* (Basingstoke, 2007), pp. 238–61.

121. *Leicester Herald*, 17 November 1838; *Weekly Chronicle* (London), 1 January 1848; *Oxford Chronicle and Reading Gazette*, 28 August 1847; W.R. Hunter, 'William Hill and the Ormskirk Medicine', *Medical History* 12 (1968) 294–7.

122. Robert Hamilton, *Remarks on Hydrophobia: Or, the Disease Produced by the Bite of a Mad Dog* (London, 1798), vol. 1, pp. 160–1; Amanda Vickery, *The Gentleman's Daughter: Women's Lives in Georgian England* (New Haven, CT, 1998); Alan Mackintosh, *The Patent Medicines Industry in Georgian England: Constructing the Market by the Potency of Print* (London, 2018), pp. 91–3.

123. Job Lewis Smith, *Report of a Case of Hydrophobia* (New York, 1856), p. 54.

124. Stephanie Cox, Clare Hocking, and Deborah Payne, 'Showers: From a Violent Treatment to an Agent of Cleansing', *History of Psychiatry* 30 (2019) 58–76; Foucault, *Madness and Civilization*, pp. 158–60.

125. Wesley, *Primitive Physic*, p. 107.

126. James Vaughan, *Two Cases of Hydrophobia; With Observations on that Disease* (London, 1778), p. 23.

127. Robert Hunt, *Popular Romances of the West of England* (London, 1865), Vol. 2, p. 51.

128. Pinel, *Traité médico-philosophique sur l'aliénation mentale* (1801), pp. 272–6.

129. James Freeman, *Medical Reflections on the Water Cure* (London, 1842), p. 44; *Annual Report of the Central Kentucky Lunatic Asylum [Anchorage, Kentucky]* (Frankfort, 1883), pp. 86–95.

130. Marie Trevelyan, *Folk-lore and Folk-stories of Wales* (London, 1909), pp. 314–15.

131. Emily Donoho, 'The Madman amongst the Ruins: The Oral History and Folklore of Traditional Insanity Cures in the Scottish Highlands', *Folklore* 125 (2014) 26.

132. *Inverness Courier*, 31 August 1871.

133. François Boissier de Sauvages, *Les Chefs-d'oeuvres de Monsieur de Sauvages ou Recueil de dissertations* (Lyon, 1770) Vol. 1, p. 80.

134. *Mémoires publiés par l'académie de Marseille* 9 (1812) 15; J.F. Fauchier, 'Réflexions sur la coutume barbare d'étouffer les hydrophobes', *Journal de médecine, chirurgie, pharmacie* 35 (1816) 25; P.-F. Saint-Georges Ransol, *Mémoire philosophique sur la rage: suivi de réflexions relatives aux préjugés du ontai vendéen sur la médecine* (Bourbon-Vendée, 1833), pp. 56, 57; *West Kent Guardian*, 18 August 1838.

135. Thomas Michael Dolan, *The Nature and Treatment of Rabies*, 2nd ed. (London, 1879), pp. 230–4. See also, DiMarco, *The Bearer of Crazed and Venomous Fangs*, pp. 176–91.

136. D. Campbell, 'A Case of Hydrophobia', *Edinburgh Medical and Surgical Journal* 23 (1825) 238–42.

137. G.M. Brumwell, 'Case of Hydrophobia Following the Bite of a Cat', *British Medical Journal* 14 October 1871, 434.

138. James Vaughan, *Two Cases of Hydrophobia; With Observations on that Disease* (London, 1778), p. 16.

139. *Freeman's Journal*, 2 March 1841. My thanks to Clodagh Tait for the reference to this trial.

140. Pemberton and Worboys, *Rabies in Britain*, p. 17; Wang, *Mad Dogs*, p. 71.

141. See Davies, *Witchcraft, Magic and Culture*, pp. 23–6; Francis Young, *English Catholics and the Supernatural, 1553–1829* (London, 2013), pp. 226–8. See also Francis Young, 'Bishop William Poynter and Exorcism in Regency England', *British Catholic History* 33 (2016) 278–97.

142. Guillemain, *Diriger les consciences guérir les âmes*, p. 60.

143. Thomas John Graham, *Modern Domestic Medicine: A Popular Treatise*, 9th ed. (London, 1844), pp. 427–8; Owen Davies, 'Wesley's Invisible World: Witchcraft and the Temperature of Preternatural Belief', in Robert Webster (Ed.), *Perfecting Perfection: Essays in Honor of Henry D. Rack* (Eugene, OR, 2015), p. 170.

144. 'L'eau et la ontaine de Saint-Jacut', *Revue des Traditions Populaires* 27 (1912) 252; Yvan Lebrun and Franco Fabbro, *Language and Epilepsy* (London, 2002), pp. 21–5.

145. J. Camille Gorcy, *Essai sur l'hydrophobie* (Paris, 1812), p. 18.

146. *Messager des sciences et des arts de la Belgique* (Ghent, 1833), vol. 1, 443; *The Western Mail*, 9 November 1898.

147. Marius Touron, 'Les toucheurs contre la rage, descendants du grand Saint Hubert', *Revue des Traditions Populaires* 16 (1901) 379–80; Eugène de Courcillon, *Le Curé Manqué: Or, Social and Religious Customs in France* (New York, 1855), p. 54.

148. Nicholas Carlisle, *A Topographical Dictionary of the Dominion of Wales* (London, 1811), n.p.

149. *Bell's New Weekly Messenger*, 27 August 1848.

150. Peter Roberts, *The Cambrian Popular Antiquities: Or, An Account of Some Traditions, Customs, and Superstitions, of Wales* (London, 1815), p. 243.

151. Richard Carew, *The Survey of Cornwall* (London, 1602), p. 123.

152. Robert Hunt, *Popular Romances of the West of England* (London, 1865), Vol. 2, pp. 50–2; *Reynolds's Newspaper*, 17 January 1869.

153. Donoho, 'The Madman amongst the Ruins' 30–4; Houston, *Madness and Society*, pp. 297–8.

154. James Young Simpson, *Clinical Lectures on Diseases of Women* (Philadelphia, PA, 1863), p. 452.

155. Thomas Pennant, *A Tour in Scotland, and voyage to the Hebrides* (Chester, 1774), p. 382. See Ceri Houlbrook, 'The Wishing-tree of Isle Maree: The Evolution of a Scottish Folkloric Practice', in Ceri Houlbrook and Natalie Armitage (Eds.), *The Materiality of Magic* (Oxford, 2015), pp. 123–43; Ceri Houlbrook, *The Magic of Coin-Trees from Religion to Recreation: The Roots of a Ritual* (Cham, 2018), pp. 27–32.

156. Davies, *A People Bewitched*, pp. 128–9.

157. *Transactions of the Society of Antiquaries of Scotland* 3 (1831) 138.

158. John F. Bigge, 'Local Superstitions at Stamfordham', *Transactions of the Tyneside Naturalists' Field Club* 5 (1860–1862) 96–7; James Hardy (Ed.), *The Denham Tracts: A Collection of Folklore* (London, 1895), Vol. 2, pp. 221–3.

159. *The Zoophilist*, 1 May 1888, 9; Jonathan Ceredig Davies, *Folk-Lore of West and Mid-Wales* (Aberystwyth, 1911), p. 287.

160. See Davies, *America Bewitched*, p. 36; Wang, *Mad Dogs and Other New Yorkers*, pp. 106–11.

161. Reprinted in *Medical Brief* 23 (1895) 1528.

162. Moritz Romberg, *A Manual of the Nervous Diseases of Man* (London, 1853), vol. 2, p. 138.

163. Margaret Lonsdale, *Sister Dora: A Biography* (Leipzig, 1880), pp. 191–2.

164. William T. Walker, 'Hydrophobia—Is it a Specific Disease?', *Virginia Medical Monthly* 22 (1893) 1106.

165. *Lancashire Evening Post*, 7 October 1891.

166. Lauder Lindsay, 'Spurious Hydrophobia' [part 2], 54; Charles P. Russell, 'Some Popular Superstitions of Hydrophobia', *The Popular Science Monthly* 6 (1875) 182–3.

167. *Edinburgh Evening News,* 9 October 1884.

168. *Buckinghamshire Examiner,* 25 February 1898; *Lancashire Evening Post,* 7 October 1891.

169. See Richard Sugg, *Mummies, Cannibals, and Vampires: The History of Corpse Medicine from the Renaissance to the Victorians* (London, 2011); Owen Davies and Francesca Matteoni, *Executing Magic in the Modern Era: Criminal Bodies and the Gallows in Popular Medicine* (Basingstoke, 2017).

170. Robert James, *A Treatise on Canine Medicine* (London, 1760), p. 14; Layard, *An Essay on the Bite of a Mad Dog,* p. 51.

171. *Bury and Norwich Post,* 16 October 1866. For another reference to the practice at the time, see, Charlotte Latham, 'West Sussex Superstitions Lingering in 1868', *The Folk-Lore Record* 1 (1878) 43.

172. Tuke, *Chapters in the History of the Insane,* p. 23; Mark Finnane, *Insanity and the Insane in Post-Famine Ireland* (London, 1981), pp. 129–30; Elizabeth Malcolm, '"The House of Strident Shadows": The Asylum, the Family and Emigration in Post-Famine Rural Ireland', in Greta Jones and Elizabeth Malcolm (Eds.), *Medicine, Disease and the State in Ireland, 1650–1940* (Cork, 1999), p. 186. The springs have seen a resurgence of activity in recent years from those suffering from mental and physical health problems; https://www.irishtimes.com/news/health/recovering-well-1.556572.

173. 'The Curability of Insanity', *British Medical Journal,* 18 February 1871, 171.

CHAPTER 4

1. Edward H. Sieveking, 'Presidential Address', *Medico-chirurgical Transactions* 72 (1889) 10.

2. See Dana Y. Rabin, 'Searching for the Self in Eighteenth-Century English Criminal Trials, 1730-1800', *Eighteenth-Century Life,* 27, 1 (2003), 87; James E. Moran, *Madness on Trial: A Transatlantic History of English Civil Law and Lunacy* (Manchester, 2019).

3. This section on the Devil is based on Owen Davies, 'Talk of the Devil : Crime and Satanic Inspiration in Eighteenth-Century England', self-published (2007), https://uhra.herts.ac.uk/bitstream/handle/2299/13377/Talk_of_the_Devil2.pdf?sequence=2.

4. J. Towers, *An Enquiry into the Extent of the Power of Juries, on Trials of Indictments or Informations, for Publishing Seditious, or other Criminal Writings, or Libels* (London, 1785), p. 61. Towers added a further commentary to the papers of F. Maseres published in 1776.

5. See, for example, *OBP,* June 1747, Rachael Pickett (t17470604-31); *OBP,* May 1763, John Marsh (t17630518-39).

6. *OBP,* March 1741, Sarah Palson (t17410325-68); *OBP,* September 1742, William Edwards (t17420909-2).

7. *Ordinary's Accounts* (www.oldbaileyonline.org, 2005), 1748, George Cock (oa17480622).

8. *OBP*, December 1812, John Chaplin (t18121202-32).

9. Paul S. Seaver, 'Suicide and the Vicar General in London: A Mystery Solved?', in Jeffrey Rodgers Watt (Ed.), *From Sin to Insanity: Suicide in Early Modern Europe* (New York, 2004), pp. 37–8. See also Michael Macdonald and Terence Murphy, *Sleepless Souls: Suicide in Early Modern England* (Oxford, 1990); Michael Macdonald, 'The Secularisation of Suicide in England, 1660–1800', *Past and Present* 111 (1986) 50–100; Michael Macdonald, 'Suicide and the Rise of the Popular Press in England', *Representations* 22 (1988) 36–55.

10. Worcestershire QSR 1/1/394/23; OBP, February 1730, Hannah Burridge (t17300228-22).

11. *The Times*, 2 August 1817.

12. *OBP*, December 1752, Anne Fox (t17521206-15); *OBP*, October 1745, William Beeson (t17451016-21); *OBP*, October 1772, Christopher Curd (t17721021-47).

13. For several examples from eighteenth-century suicide cases see Macdonald and Murphy, *Sleepless Souls*, p. 212, esp. n. 140.

14. *OBP*, April 1714, Richard Chapman (t17140407-21); *OBP*, July 1731, Edward Stafford (t17310714-52); *OBP*, June 1815, Isaac Foy (t18150621-43).

15. Dana Y. Rabin, *Identity, Crime and Legal Responsibility in Eighteenth-Century England* (Basingstoke, 2004), p. 93; Rabin, 'Searching for the self', 100.

16. *Ordinary's Accounts*, 1752, William Descent (oa17520922); 1747, Robert Radwell (oa17470121).

17. Houston, *Madness and Society*, pp. 303, 307.

18. E. Gillespy, *A Disquisition upon the Criminal Laws; Shewing the Necessity of Altering and Amending them* (Northampton, 1793), p. 32.

19. Prince, *Self-Murder*, p. 63.

20. Thomas Humphries, *A Preservative from Criminal Offences; or the power of godliness to conquer the reigning vices of sensuality and profaneness* (Shrewsbury, 1776), p. 46.

21. *OBP*, December 1758, Samuel Cordwell (t17581206-26).

22. On the Hadfield case see, Rabin, *Identity, Crime and Legal Responsibility*, pp. 142–64; Richard Moran, 'The Origin of Insanity as a Special Verdict: The Trial for Treason of James Hadfield (1800)', *Law and Society Review* 19 (1985) 487–519; Steve Poole, *The Politics of Regicide in England, 1760–1850: Troublesome Subjects* (Manchester, 2000), pp. 120–8.

23. *Attempt on the Life of the King. The Trial of James Hadfield* (London, 1800), p. 19.

24. *Attempt on the Life of the King*, pp. 22, 26.

25. Roger Smith, *Trial by Medicine: Insanity and Responsibility in Victorian Trials* (Edinburgh, 1981), p. 14; Eigen, *Witnessing Insanity*, pp. 48–51.

26. See Eigen, *Witnessing Insanity*, p. 42.

27. F. Elrington Ball, *The Judges in Ireland, 1221–1921* (New York, 1927), pp. 257–8, 340.

28. For context on religious politics and masculinity in Irish courts at the time see, Katie Barclay, *Men on Trial: Performing Emotion, Embodiment and Identity in Ireland, 1800–45* (Manchester, 2018).

29. The case has garnered little interest among historians, but see Mary Hatfield, *Growing Up in Nineteenth-Century Ireland: A Cultural History of Middle-Class*

Childhood and Gender (Oxford, 2019), pp. 59–62. The account here is based on: *Report of the Trial of the Rev. John Carroll* (Dublin, 1824); *The Waterford Mirror*, 9 Aug 1824; *Enniskillen Chronicle and Erne Packet*, 12 August 1824; *Saunders's News-Letter*, 7 August 1824; *Fife Herald*, 29 July 1824; *Fanaticism! Cruelty!! Bigotry!!! The particulars of the horrible murder of Catharine Sinnott, a child under four years of age, by the Rev. John Carroll, an Irish Catholic priest, under pretence of performing a miracle, by casting devils out of the child* (London, 1824); Irish National Archives CSO/RP/1824/509.

30. *Report of the Trial of the Rev. John Carroll*, p. 21; William H. Grattan Flood, *History of the Diocese of Ferns* (Waterford, 1916), pp. 35, 141.

31. *Report of the Trial of the Rev. John Carroll* (Dublin, 1824), p. 10.

32. *Report of the Trial of the Rev. John Carroll*, p. 20.

33. *Report of the Trial of the Rev. John Carroll*, pp. 15; William Henry Grattan Flood, *History of the Diocese of Ferns* (Waterford, 1916). pp. 141, 187.

34. *Report of the Trial of the Rev. John Carroll*, pp. 23, 24, 25.

35. Irish National Archives CSO/RP/1832/5143; CSO/RP/1833/1274; CSO/RP/1833/2637; CSO/RP/1833/3298; CSO/RP/1833/6282.

36. Miranda Gill, *Eccentricity and the Cultural Imagination in Nineteenth-Century Paris* (Oxford, 2009), pp. 240–3.

37. James Gregory, 'Local Characters': Eccentricity and the North-east in the Nineteenth Century', *Northern History* 42 (2005) 163–86.

38. Maudsley, *Natural Causes and Supernatural Seemings*, p. 151.

39. 'Gooch on Insanity', *Quarterly Review* 41 (1829) 183; John Conolly, *An Inquiry concerning the Indications of Insanity* (London, 1830), pp. 136, 137, 139.

40. Prichard, *A Treatise on Insanity* (1837), p. 273; Alexander Watson, *A Medico-legal Treatise on Homicide by External Violence* (Edinburgh, 1837), p. 340.

41. Watson, *A Medico-legal Treatise on Homicide*, p. 338.

42. *Caledonian Mercury*, 2 January 1832.

43. James Simpson, *Necessity of Popular Education; As a National Object; With Hints on the Treatment of Criminals, and Observations on Homicidal Insanity* (London, 1834), p. 336.

44. Simpson, *Necessity of Popular Education*, p. 346; Prichard, *A Treatise on Insanity* (1837), p. 273.

45. Katherine D. Watson, *Forensic Medicine in Western Society: A History* (London, 2011); Goldstein, *Console and Classify*, p. 163.

46. *The London University Calendar* (London, 1859), p. xxxv.

47. Taylor, *Manual of medical jurisprudence*, p. 643.

48. Katherine D. Watson, *Medicine and Justice: Medico-Legal Practice in England and Wales, 1700–1914* (Abingdon, 2020), p. 120.

49. David W. Jones, 'Moral Insanity and Psychological Disorder: The Hybrid Roots of Psychiatry', *History of Psychiatry* 28 (2017) 267.

50. W. Lauder Lindsay, 'The Histology of the Blood in the Insane', *The Journal of Psychological Medicine and Mental Pathology* 8 (1855), 81; David Skae, 'A Rational and Practical Classification of Insanity', *The Journal of Mental Science* 9 (1863) 312.

51. William Augustus Guy, *Principles of Forensic Medicine* (London, 1844), p. 258; Alfred Swaine Taylor, *A Manual of Medical Jurisprudence*, 2nd ed. (London, 1846), pp. 639–40. On Taylor's relations with Guy see, Helen Barrell, *Fatal Evidence: Professor Alfred Swaine Taylor & the Dawn of Forensic Science* (Barnsley, 2017), pp. 43–4.

52. Wilhelm Griesinger, *Mental Pathology and Therapeutics*, trans. C. Lockhart Robertson and James Rutherford, London, 1867), p. 117.

53. See, for example, Joel Peter Eigen, *Mad-Doctors in the Dock: Defending the Diagnosis, 1760–1913* (Baltimore, MD, 2016); Watson, *Forensic Medicine in Western Society*, pp. 72–125; Karl Bell, ' "She Was Full of Evil Spirits": Occult Influence, Free Will, and Medical Authority in the Old Bailey, circa 1860–1910', *Preternature* 6 (2017) 310–36; Jill Newton Ainsley, ' "Some mysterious agency": Women, Violent Crime, and the Insanity Acquittal in the Victorian Courtroom', *Canadian Journal of History* 35 (2000) 37–56; Ciara J. Toole, 'Medical Diagnosis of Legal Culpability: The Impact of Early Psychiatric Testimony in the Nineteenth Century English Trial', *International Journal of Law and Psychiatry* 35 (2012) 82–97.

54. Henri Legrand du Saulle, *La folie devant les tribunaux* (1864), pp. 395–7; Joseph Arthaud, *Réflexions sur l'état mental de C. Feuillet, condamné par la cour d'assises pour crimes d'empoisonnement* (Lyon, 1854).

55. Christian Legault, 'Comprendre le "criminel fou" dans la France du XIXe siècle: le meurtre Jobard (1851)', *Strata* 8 (2018) 3–24; 'Homicidal Monomania', *The Journal of Psychological Medicine and Mental Pathology* 5 (1852) 423–35.

56. See Ian Dowbiggin, *Inheriting Madness: Professionalization and Psychiatric Knowledge in Nineteenth Century France* (Oxford, 1991), esp. pp. 62–8.

57. Goldstein, *Console and Classify*, pp. 189–97, 155. I look forward to seeing the results of Will Pooley's fascinating research on French murder trials involving witchcraft belief.

58. Charles-Auguste Bihorel, 'On the Doubtful Cases of Insanity in a Clinical and a Medico-Legal Point of View', *Journal of Psychological Medicine* 5 (1871) 817.

59. See, Eric J. Engstrom, *Clinical Psychiatry in Imperial Germany: A History of Psychiatric Practice* (Ithaca, NY, 2003); Heather Wolffram, 'Crime and hypnosis in fin-de-siècle Germany: The Czynski case', *Notes and Records* 71 (2017), 213–26; Christian Müller, *Verbrechensbekämpfung im Anstaltsstaat. Psychiatrie, Kriminologie und Strafrechtsreform in Deutschland, 1871–1933* (Göttingen, 2004).

60. For a detailed study see, Owen Davies, *Murder, Magic, Madness: The Victorian Trials of Dove and the Wizard* (London, 2005).

61. Bell, ' "She was full of evil spirits" ', 310–11.

62. On the case see Kate Summerscale, *The Suspicions of Mr. Whicher: Or The Murder at Road Hill House* (London, 2008).

63. *The Solicitors' Journal and Reporter*, 22 July 1865, 854; *The Fortnightly Review* 1 (1865), 764.

64. On hag-riding and sleep paralysis in Dorset and Somerset see, Owen Davies, 'Hag-riding in Nineteenth-Century West Country England and Modern Newfoundland: An Examination of an Experience-Centred Witchcraft Tradition', *Folk Life* 35 (1996) 36–53.

65. *Frome Times*, 22 March 1871; *Salisbury and Winchester Journal*, 22 July 1871; *Southern Times and Dorset Herald*, 22 July 1871.

66. The genealogies for all the people involved in the case have been researched by an ancestor of Tennant, Richard Ratcliffe, https://d23iiv8m8qvdxi.cloudfront. net/wp-content/uploads/2016/07/The-Full-Story-of-the-Murder-of-My-Great-Great-Grandmother-Ann-Tennant-of-Long-Compton.pdf; https:// www.ourwarwickshire.org.uk/content/article/the-murder-of-my-great-great-grandmother-ann-tennant-of-long-compton-part-one.

67. Details of the trial from *Warwick and Warwickshire Advertiser*, 18 December 1875.

68. On Parsey's career see, Alastair Robson, *Unrecognised by the World at Large: A biography of Dr Henry Parsey* (Kibworth Beauchamp, 2016).

69. *Sun*, 19 June 1862; https://www.oldbaileyonline.org/browse.jsp?id=def1-657-18620616&div=t18620616-657#highlight.

70. Roger Smith, *Trial by Medicine*, pp. 104–5.

71. F. Whitwell, 'The Law of Insanity', *British Medical Journal* 23 November 1878, 784.

72. *Reports of the superintendent and chaplain of Broadmoor Criminal Lunatic Asylum, with statistical tables, for the year 1876* (London, 1877), p. 3; Reports *upon Broadmoor Criminal Lunatic Asylum for the Year 1890* (London, 1891), p. 18.

73. William Bathurst Woodman and Charles Meymott Tidy, *A Handy-book of Forensic Medicine and Toxicology* (London, 1877), p. 829.

74. Bell, ' "She was full of evil spirits" ', 314–15; Davies, *America Bewitched*, pp. 159–79.

75. Thomas Stevenson (Ed.), *The Principles and Practice of Medical Jurisprudence by the Late Alfred Swaine Taylor*, 3rd ed. (London, 1883), vol. 2, p. 574.

76. *American Journal of Insanity* 8 (1852) 382.

77. See, for example, *The Jurist*, 9 December 1848.

78. *Reports of Cases Heard and Determined by the Judicial Committee and the Lords of Her Majesty's Most Honourable Privy Council* (London, 1846–9), vol. 6, pp. 341–70; John Batty Tuke and Charles R.A. Howden, 'The Relations of the Insanities to Criminal Responsibility and Civil Capacity', *Edinburgh Medical Journal* 16 (1904) 435–41.

79. Susanna L. Blumenthal, 'The Deviance of the Will: Policing the Bounds of Testamentary Freedom in Nineteenth-Century America', *Harvard Law Review* 119 (2006), 959–1034.

80. John A. Clark (Ed.), *Pennsylvania Law Journal Reports* (Philadelphia, PA, 1873), Vol. 5, pp. 86–93; *American Journal of Insanity* 8 (1852) 383–5. For further examples see, Davies, *America Bewitched*, pp. 163–6.

81. Clark (Ed.), *Pennsylvania Law Journal Reports*, p. 92.

82. *Reports of Cases Decided in the Supreme Court of the State of Indiana* (Philadelphia, PA, 1855), vol. 5, p. 138.

83. Davies, *America Bewitched*, p. 165; Dyson, 'Spiritualism and Crime', p. 228.

84. James Schouler, *A Treatise on the Law of Wills* (Boston, MA, 1887), p. 166.

85. *The Southwestern Reporter* (St Paul, 1887), vol. 4, pp. 235–37. The family history can be found here http://schildknecht.goldenagegraphics.net/main. php?cmd=album&var1=Schildknecht_1860s_e1940s/.

86. For a comprehensive account of the case see, Martyn Frost, *A Victorian Tragedy: The Extraordinary Case of Banks V Goodfellow* (London, 2018).

87. *Cumberland Pacquet, and Ware's Whitehaven Advertiser*, 23 February 1869.

88. Brian Sloan (Ed.), *Landmark Cases in Succession Law* (Oxford, 2019), pp. 51–71; Denzil Lush, 'Banks v Goodfellow (1870)', https://www.step.org/step-journal/tqr-october-2012/banks-v-goodfellow-1870; Kenneth I. Shulman, Susan G Himel, Ian M Hull, Carmelle Peisah, Sean Amodeo, and Courtney Barnes, 'Banks v Goodfellow (1870): Time to Update the Test for Testamentary Capacity', *Canadian Bar Review* 95 (2017) 252–67.

89. Isaac F. Redfield, *The Law of Wills*, 2nd ed. (Boston, MA, 1866), Vol. 1, pp. 66–7. On Redfield's views and influence see Susanna L. Blumenthal, *Law and the Modern Mind: Consciousness and Responsibility in American Legal Culture* (Cambridge, MA, 2016); Erika White Dyson, 'Spiritualism and Crime: Negotiating Prophecy and Police Power at the Turn of the Century', PhD, Columbia University, 2010, 214–19.

90. R.M. Stover (Ed.), *The New York State Reporter* (Albany, NY, 1888), pp. 148–59.

91. Blewett Lee, 'Psychic Phenomena and the Law', *Harvard Law Review* 34 (1921) 628.

92. Edward C. Mann, *A Treatise on the Medical Jurisprudence of Insanity* (Albany, NY, 1893), p. 163.

93. *The Atlantic Reporter* 17 (1889), pp. 827–35; Mann, *A Treatise*, pp. 161–9.

94. George Helm Yeaman, 'Spiritualism in Wills', *The Albany Law Journal* 40 (18890189O), 385; Mann, *A Treatise*, p. 165. For further criticism see *The Medico-legal Journal* 7 (1889) 521–2.

95. Yeaman, 'Spiritualism in Wills', 385.

96. Ardemus Stewart, 'Belief in the Preternatural and its Effect upon Dispositions of Property', *The American Law Register and Review* 40 (1892) 584–5.

97. Redfield, *Leading American Cases*, p. 385.

98. Stewart, 'Belief in the Preternatural and its Effect upon Dispositions of Property', 584–5, 582–3, 585.

99. Joseph P. Guadnola, 'Insane Delusions—Phenomena Affecting Testamentary Capacity in the Execution of Wills', *Notre Dame Law Review* 5 (1930) 397; C. Lily Schurra, 'What Ghost up Must Come Down: The Highs and Lows of Psychic Mediums in Probate Law', *Quinnipiac Probate Law Journal* 29 (2016) 317.

100. R.A. Witthaus and Tracy C. Becker, *Medical Jurisprudence, Forensic Medicine and Toxicology* (New York, 1896), Vol. 3, p. 407.

101. Tony Ward, 'Law, Common Sense and the Authority of Science: Expert Witnesses and Criminal Insanity in England, ca. 1840–1940', *Social & Legal Studies* 6 (1997) 353–6; Tony Ward, 'A Terrible Responsibility: Murder and the Insanity Defence in England, 1908–1939', *International Journal of Law and Psychiatry* 25 (2002) 375.

PART 2 INTRODUCTION

1. *Fourth Annual Report of the Inverness District Lunatic Asylum* (Inverness, 1868), p. 22; Esquirol, 'Folie', in *Dictionaire des sciences médicales* 16 (1816), pp. 182–3. See Laure Murat, *The Man who Thought he was Napoleon: Toward a Political History of Madness*, trans. Deke Dusinberre (Chicago, IL, 2014).

2. For an overview see, Frank Larøi et al, 'Culture and Hallucinations: Overview and Future Directions', *Schizophrenia Bulletin* 40 (2014) 213–20.

3. See Vinzia Fiorino, 'La fiaba e la follia. Medicina, folklore e religione nelle rappresentazioni culturali della malattia mentale (1850-1915)', *Psychiatry Online Italia* (2012) http://www.psychiatryonline.it/node/2104; Davies, 'Finding the Folklore in the Annals of Psychiatry'.

4. On Gothic and horror representations of the asylum see for example, David Waldron, Sharn Waldron, and Nathaniel Buchanan, *Aradale: The Making of a Haunted Asylum* (Melbourne, 2020); Troy Rondinone, *Nightmare Factories: The Asylum in the American Imagination* (Baltimore, MD, 2019).

5. Peter Bartlett, *The Poor Law of Lunacy: The Administration of Pauper Lunatics in Mid-Nineteenth Century England* (London, 1999); David Wright, 'The Certification of Insanity in Nineteenth-Century England and Wales', *History of Psychiatry* 9 (1998) 267–90; Joseph Melling and Bill Forsythe, *The Politics of Madness: The State, Insanity and Society in England, 1845–1914* (Abingdon, 2006), 23–46. On the certification process in Ireland see Catherine Cox, *Negotiating Insanity in the Southeast of Ireland, 1820–1900* (Manchester, 2012), pp. 73–97.

6. David Wright, 'Delusions of Gender?: Lay Identification and Clinical Diagnosis of Insanity in Victorian England', in Jonathan Andrews and Anne Digby (Eds.), *Sex and Seclusion, Class and Custody: Perspectives on Gender and Class in the History of British and Irish Psychiatry* (Amsterdam, 2004), p. 166.

7. *Seventh Report of the Derbyshire County Pauper Lunatic Asylum* (Derby, 1859), p. 14; J.C. Bucknill, 'On Medical Certificates of Insanity', *Journal of Mental Science* 7 (1860) 85.

8. See, Charles Palmer Phillips, *The Law Concerning Lunatics, Idiots, & Persons of Unsound Mind* (London, 1858), pp. 205–7.

9. Lyttleton S. Winslow, *Manual of Lunacy: A Handbook* (London, 1874), pp. 61–2.

10. Susan Margaret Burt, '"Fit objects for an asylum": The Hampshire County Lunatic Asylum and its Patients, 1852–1899', PhD thesis, University of Southampton, 2003, 123–47.

11. Jonathan Andrews, 'Case Notes, Case Histories, and the Patient's Experience of Insanity at the Gartnavel Royal Asylum, Glasgow, in the Nineteenth Century', *Society for the Social History of Medicine* 11 (1998) 255–81.

12. My thanks to Ceri Houlbrook for her work in searching and transcribing case notes from Prestwich Asylum, South Yorkshire Asylum in Sheffield, Lancaster Moor Asylum, and Parkside Asylum.

13. Andrews, 'Case Notes, Case Histories', 266.

14. See Roy Porter, *Stories of the Insane: A Social History of Madness* (London, 1987); Geoffrey Reaume, 'From the Perspective of Mad People', in Greg Eghigian (Ed.), *The Routledge History of Madness and Mental Health* (2017), pp. 277–97.
15. Louise Wannell, 'Patients' Relatives and Psychiatric Doctors: Letter Writing in the York Retreat, 1875–1910', *Social History of Medicine* 20 (2007) 297–313; Allan Beveridge, 'Voices of the Mad: Patients' Letters from the Royal Edinburgh Asylum, 1873–1908', *Psychological Medicine* 27 (1997); Catharine Coleborne, 'Families, Patients and Emotions: Asylums for the Insane in Colonial Australia and New Zealand, c. 1880–1910', *Social History of Medicine* 19 (2006) 425–42; Coleborne, *Madness in the Family: Insanity and Institutions in the Australasian Colonial World, 1860–1914* (Basingstoke, 2010), pp. 88–107.
16. Carpenter, 'Above all a Patient Should Never be Terrified', 95.
17. David Wright, 'Getting Out of the Asylum', 143.
18. C. Lockhart Robertson, 'A Descriptive Notice of the Sussex Lunatic Asylum, Hayward's Heath', *The Journal of Mental Science* 6 (1860) 253–3; Claire Chatterton, ' "Always Bear in Mind that you are in your Senses": Insanity and the Lunatic Asylum in the Nineteenth-Century—From Keeper to Attendant to Nurse', in Thomas Knowles and Serena Trowbridge (Eds.), *Insanity and the Lunatic Asylum in the Nineteenth Century* (London, 2015), pp. 85–99.
19. Bucknill and Tuke, *Manual of Psychological Medicine*, 4th ed. (1879), p. 700.
20. Bucknill and Tuke, *Manual of Psychological Medicine*, 4th ed. (1879), p. 727.
21. Bucknill and Tuke, *Manual of Psychological Medicine*, p. 756. See also Benoît Majerus, 'The Straightjacket, the Bed, and the Pill: Material Culture and Madness', in Eghigian (Ed.), *The Routledge History of Madness*, pp. 264–7; Madeline Bourque Kearin, 'Dirty Bread, Forced Feeding, and Tea Parties: The Uses and Abuses of Food in Nineteenth-Century Insane Asylums', *Journal of Medical Humanities* (2020), advanced online publication.
22. Bucknill and Tuke, *Manual of Psychological Medicine*, 4th ed. (1879), p. 702.
23. Phil Fennell, *Treatment Without Consent: Law, Psychiatry and the Treatment of Mentally Disordered People since 1845* (London, 1996), pp. 37–48.

CHAPTER 5

1. Prestwich ADMF2/23 (1910), patient 15,026.
2. See, for example, Paul Tobia, 'The Patients of the Bristol Lunatic Asylum in the Nineteenth Century 1861-1900', PhD Thesis, University of the West of England, 2017, 123; Charlotte MacKenzie, 'A Family Asylum: A History of the Private Madhouse at Ticehurst in Sussex, 1792–1917', PhD Thesis, University of London, 1986, 505; Edward B. Renvoize and Allan W. Beveridge, 'Mental Illness and the Late Victorians: A Study of Patients Admitted to Three Asylums in York, 1880–1884', *Psychological Medicine* 19 (1989) 22; Diane Teresa Carpenter, 'Above all a Patient should never be Terrified: An Examination of Mental Health Care and Treatment in Hampshire 1845–1914', PhD thesis, University of Portsmouth, 2010, 96–7; Allan Beveridge, 'Madness in Victorian Edinburgh: A Study of

Patients admitted to the Royal Edinburgh Asylum under Thomas Coulson, 1873–1908', *History of Psychiatry* 6 (1995) 38; Renvoize and Beveridge, 'Mental illness and the late Victorians', 21.

3. The literature is large but for some major overviews see, Hugh McLeod, *Religion and the Working Class in Nineteenth-Century Britain* (Basingstoke, 1984); Callum G. Brown, *Religion and Society in Twentieth-Century Britain* (London, 2006); John Wolffe, *God and Greater Britain: Religion and National Life in Britain and Ireland 1843–1945* (London, 1994); Keith D.M. Snell and Paul S. Ell, *Rival Jerusalems: The Geography of Victorian Religion* (Cambridge, 2000); Julie Melnyk, *Victorian Religion: Faith and Life in Britain* (Westport, CT, 2008).

4. See Catherine Cox, Hilary Marland, and Sarah York, 'Emaciated, Exhausted, and Excited: The Bodies and Minds of the Irish in Late Nineteenth-Century Lancashire Asylums', *Journal of Social History* 46 (2012) 500–24.

5. Quoted in Cox, Marland, and York, 'Emaciated, Exhausted', 506.

6. G.K. Nelson, *Spiritualism and Society* (New York, 1969), pp. 167, 161, 285; Gerald O'Hara, *Dead Men's Embers* (York, 2006), p. 300; Owen Davies, *Ghosts: A Social History* (London, 2010), Vol. 5, pp. ix–x.

7. See, for example, Sue Morgan and Jacqueline de Vries (Eds.), *Women, Gender and Religious Cultures in Britain, 1800–1940* (London, 2010); David Blackbourn, *Marpingen: Apparitions of the Virgin Mary in Nineteenth-Century Germany* (New York, 1993); Susan O'Brien, 'French Nuns in Nineteenth-Century England', *Past & Present* 154 (1997) 142–80.

8. *First annual report of the joint lunatic asylum for the counties of Monmouth, Hereford, Brecon, Radnor, and city of Hereford* (Abergavenny, 1854), p. 25.

9. Maudsley, *The Pathology of Mind*, 3rd ed. (New York, 1880), p. 418; Henry Maudsley, 'Delusions', *Journal of Mental Science* 9 (1863) 13.

10. Lewis, *Text-Book of Mental Diseases*, p. 194.

11. William W. Ireland, *The Blot Upon the Brain: Studies in History and Psychology* (New York, 1886), pp. 40–1; Enrico Toselli, 'Sulla religiosità degli epilettici', *Archivio italiano per le malattie nervose* 16 (1879) 69–102; James C. Howden, 'The Religious Sentiment in Epileptics', *Journal of Mental Science* 18 (1873) 483–97.

12. Henry Maudsley, *Natural Causes and Supernatural Seemings* (London, 1886), p. 172.

13. See most recently, Ian Bone and Simon Dein, 'Religion, spirituality, and epilepsy', *Epilepsy & Behavior* 122 (2021) 108–219.

14. A. Brierre de Boismont, *Hallucinations: Or, the Rational History of Apparitions, Visions, Dreams, Ecstasy, Magnetism, and Somnambulism*, 2nd ed (Philadelphia, PA, 1853), pp. 188, 211; Maurice Macario, *Des Hallucinations* (Paris, 1846).

15. Hammond, *Treatise on Insanity*, p. 248.

16. John Thompson Dickson, *The Science and Practice of Medicine in Relation to Mind* (London, 1874), p. 358.

17. SYA NHS3/5/1/11 (1896), patient 4574; LMA HRL/4/12/2/25 (1906), p. 176.

18. Prestwich ADMF2/23 (1910), patient 15,153.

19. Robert Boyd, 'Diseases of the Nervous System. No. IV. Mania', *Journal of Psychological Medicine* 3 (1877) 274; Prestwich ADMF2/15 (1903), patient 12,793.

20. Shane McCorristine, *William Corder and the Red Barn Murder: Journeys of the Criminal Body* (Cham, 2014); Rhodri Hayward, 'Policing Dreams: History and the Moral Uses of the Unconscious', in Daniel Pick and Lyndal Roper (Eds.), *Dreams and History: Interpretation of Dreams from Ancient Greed to Modern Psychoanalysis* (London, 2004), pp. 161–5; Maureen Perkins, *The Reform of Time: Magic and Modernity* (London, 2001), pp. 59–83; Davies, *Witchcraft, Magic and Culture*, pp. 137–9; Nicola Brown, 'What is the Stuff that Dreams Are Made Of?', in Nicola Brown, Carolyn Burdett, and Pamela Thurschwell (Eds.), *The Victorian Supernatural* (Cambridge, 2004), pp. 163–5.

21. Geoffrey Cubitt, *The Jesuit Myth: Conspiracy Theory and Politics in Nineteenth-Century France* (Oxford, 1993); Jules Séglas, *Leçons cliniques sur les maladies mentales*, pp. 506, 587, 592, 652.

22. John Wolffe, 'The Jesuit as Villain in Nineteenth-century British Fiction', *Studies in Church History* 48 (2012) 308–20.

23. Prestwich ADMF2/22 (1908), patient 14,602; LMA HRL/4/12/3/15 (1889), p. 88; LMA HRL/4/12/3/34 (1910), p. 46.

24. See Owen Davies and Ceri Houlbrook, *Building Magic: Ritual and Re-enchantment in Post-Medieval Structures* (Cham, 2021), pp. 77–9.

25. Prichard, *A Treatise*, p. 372.

26. *Belfast Weekly News*, 30 December 1871.

27. Crichton DGH1/5/21/4/1 (1876), p. 343.

28. José A. Ferrer Benimeli, 'Freemasonry and the Catholic Church', in Henrik Bogdan and Jan A.M. Snoek (Eds.), *Handbook of Freemasonry* (Leiden, 2014), pp. 142–3.

29. *London Evening Standard*, 19 April 1884.

30. Prestwich ADMM2/4 (1893), patient 8785; Prestwich ADMM2/19 (1908), patient 12,809; LMA HRL/4/12/2/13 (1884).

31. LMA HRL/4/12/2/7 (1877), patient 9883; LMA HRL/4/12/3/11 (1883), p. 75; LMA HRL/4/12/3/34 (1911), p. 214.

32. Beveridge, 'Voices of the mad', 902.

33. LMA HRL/4/12/2/11 (1882), patient 11,539; Prestwich, ADMF2/24 (1911), patient 15,348; Prestwich, ADMM2/13 (1902), patient 11,071.

34. See Leslie Howsam, *Cheap Bibles: Nineteenth-Century Publishing and the British and Foreign Bible Society* (Cambridge, 1991); Mary Wilson Carpenter, *Imperial Bibles, Domestic Bodies: Women, Sexuality, and Religion in the Victorian Market* (Athens, 2003); Rachel Teukolsky, *Picture World: Image, Aesthetics, and Victorian New Media* (Oxford, 2020), pp. 154–66; F.K. Prochaska, 'Body and Soul: Bible Nurses and the Poor in Victorian London', *Historical Research* 60 (1987) 336–48.

35. Howden, 'The Religious Sentiment in Epileptics', 485; J. Hawkes, 'Delusions and Hallucinations', *The Lancet* 17 December (1870), 848.

36. Crichton DGH1/5/21/4/2 (1885), p. 191.

37. *Nineteenth Annual Report of the Suffolk Lunatic Asylum* (Woodbridge, 1857), p. 8.

38. Crichton DGH1/5/21/4/5 (1891), pp. 761–3; LMA HRL/4/12/2/5 (1872), patient 8946.

39. Davies, *Supernatural War*, pp. 179–83. See also Brian Malley, 'The Bible in British Folklore', *Postscripts* 2 (2006) 241–72.

40. LMA HRL/4/12/2/12 (1883).

41. Prestwich ADMM2/1 (1891), patient 8024; Prestwich ADMF2/18 (1905); Prestwich ADMM2/6 (1895), patient 9264; Prestwich ADMM2/16 (1905), patient 11,881.

42. Thomas Inman, *Ancient Faiths Embodied in Ancient Names*, 2nd ed. (London, 1873), Vol. 2, p. 523.

43. LMA HRL/4/12/2/5 (1872), patient 8814; LMA HRL/4/12/2/20 (1901), p. 266; *Manchester Evening News*, 6 December 1876; *Preston Chronicle*, 16 February 1878.

44. LMA HRL/4/12/2/9 (1879), patient 10,570; LMA HRL/4/12/2/11 (1882), patient 11,669; LMA HRL/4/12/2/15 (1888), p. 178.

45. *The Sessional Papers Printed by Order of the House of Lords* 19 (1859) p. 11.

46. LMA HRL/4/12/2/11 (1882), patient 11,613; Parkside, NHM 8/1/2/74a (1907).

47. Prestwich, ADMF2/15 (1902), patient 12,717; *Manchester Courier and Lancashire General Advertiser*, 5 February 1904.

48. SYA NHS3/5/1/9 (1892), patient 3904; SYA NHS3/5/1/9 (1892), patient 4005; Crichton DGH1/5/21/3/2 (1885), p. 195; Prestwich ADMM2/11 (1902) patient 10,647.

49. Crichton DGH1/5/21/4/1 (1885), p. 187.

50. Bevan Lewis, *Text-Book*, p. 195.

51. Crichton DGH1/5/21/4/3 (1887), p. 125; SYA NHS3/5/1/10 (1895), patient 4345; SYA NHS3/5/1/4 (1883), patient 2028.

52. Martin Spence, *Heaven and Earth: Reimagining Time and Eternity in Nineteenth-Century British Evangelicalism* (Cambridge, 2015), p. 256. See also David W. Bebbington, 'The Advent Hope in British Evangelicalism since 1800', *Scottish Journal of Religious Studies* 9 (1988) 103–14; Davies, *A Supernatural War*, pp. 40–8.

53. Prestwich, ADMM2/3 (1892), patient 8367; Prestwich, ADMF2/10 (1898), patient 11,456.

54. Prestwich, ADMF2/9 (1897), patient 11,104; LMA HRL/4/12/2/10 (1880), patient 10,980.

55. William Cullen Bryant II and Thomas G. Voss (Eds.), *The Letters of William Cullen Bryant* (New York, 1977), Vol. 2, p. 374.

56. Henry Heavisides, *The Annals of Stockton-on-Tees: With Biographical Notices* (Stockton-on-Tees, 1865), pp. 44–5. See also, Thomas Richmond, *The Local Records of Stockton and the Neighbourhood* (Stockton, 1868), p. 106.

57. *Western Mail*, 22 December 1874.

58. *The Pall Mall Budget*, 24 December 1874, 32; *The Saturday Review of Politics, Literature, Science and Art*, 26 December 1874, 825. On Girling see Philip Hoare, *England's Lost Eden: Adventures in a Victorian Utopia* (London, 2005); Kristof Smeyers, 'A Christ in Curls: The Contested Charisma of Mary Ann Girling (1827–1886)', *Women's History Review* 29 (2020) 18–36.

59. Leonard D. Smith, 'Insanity and Ethnicity: Jews in the Mid-Victorian Lunatic Asylum', *Jewish Culture and History* 1 (1998) 32–3.

60. BPA BOO6/2/2/2, patient 85; SYA NHS3/5/1/17 (1905), patient 6831.

61. Beveridge, 'Voices of the Mad', 901.

62. Maudsley, *Pathology of Mind*, p. 418. For a controversial study of twentieth-century Christ delusions and cure see Milton Rokeach, *The Three Christs of Ypsilanti* (New York, 1964).

63. Morison, *Cases of Mental Disease*, pp. 70–2.

64. LMA HRL/4/12/2/21 (1902), p. 4.

65. Parkside NHM 8/5/10/74 & 287 (1897); Bevan Lewis, *Text-Book of Mental Diseases*, p. 198; Beveridge, 'Voices of the mad', 904.

66. Crichton DGH1/5/21/4/1 (1880), page 455; LMA HRL/4/12/3/13 (1886), p. 6; SYA NHS3/5/1/9 (1893), patient 4798.

67. Davies, *Witchcraft, Magic and Culture*, p. 105; Owen Davies, 'The Witch of Endor in History and Folklore', *Folklore*, forthcoming 2023.

68. Maudsley, 'Delusions', 13.

69. Claire Hilton, *Civilian Lunatic Asylums During the First World War: A Study of Austerity on London's Fringe* (Cham, 2021), p. 241.

70. LMA HRL/4/12/3/14 (1888), p. 191.

71. *Eighteenth Annual Report of the Suffolk Lunatic Asylum* (Woodbridge, 1856), p. 4.

72. LMA HRL/4/12/2/30 (1910), patient 24,017; Prestwich ADMM2/20, patient 12,915.

73. Carol Engelhardt Herringer, *Victorians and the Virgin Mary: Religion and Gender in England, 1830–85* (Manchester, 2008); Carol Engelhardt Herringer, 'The Virgin Mary', in Gareth Atkins (Ed.), *Making and Remaking Saints in Nineteenth-Century Britain* (Manchester, 2016), pp. 44–59.

74. Prestwich ADMF2/19 (1906), patient 13,954; Prestwich ADMF2/22 (1909), patient 14,872.

75. Prestwich ADMF2/3 (1892), patient 9724.

76. LMA HRL/4/12/2/12 (1883); LMA HRL/4/12/2/22 (1903), p. 5.

77. LMA HRL/4/12/2/14 (1886).

78. Prestwich ADMM2/4 (1893), patient 8811.

79. LMA HRL/4/12/2/13 (1884); Prestwich ADMF2/12 (1901) patient 12,126; Prestwich ADMF2/15 (1903) patient 12,851.

80. LMA HRL/4/12/2/23 (1904), p. 39; SYA NHS3/5/1/12 (1897), patient 5691.

81. Parkside, NHM 8/2/4/219 (1882).

82. Prestwich ADMF2/17 (1904), patient 13,445; Parkside, NHM 8/5/7/137 (1886–1889).

83. LMA HRL/4/12/2/12, 1883.

84. Crichton DGH1/5/21/4/6 (1891), p. 161; LMA HRL/4/12/2/10 (1881), patient 11,245; Prestwich ADMF2/10 (1897), patient 11,262; Prestwich ADMM2/6, 1894, patient 9172; SYA NHS3/5/1/11 (1895), patient 4491; Crichton DGH1/5/21/4/7 (1893), p. 365.

85. Davies, *Supernatural War*, pp. 55–63.

86. Prestwich ADMF2/18 (1904), patient 13,525.

87. See, for example, *The Children's Hymnal* (London, 1881), p. 15.

88. SYA NHS3/5/1/10 (1893), patient 4865; SYA NHS3/5/1/10 (1895), patient 5130.

89. *The Enlarged Songs and Solos* (London, 1879), pp. 34, 3; *Salvation Songs* (London, 1889), p. 30.

90. Howden, 'Religious Sentiment in Epileptics', 486.

91. Howden, 'Religious Sentiment in Epileptics', 490.

92. Howden, 'Religious Sentiment in Epileptics', 489.

93. LA QAM/1/30/27 (1881).

94. Morag Allan Campbell, '"This Distressing Malady": Childbirth and Mental Illness in Scotland 1820-1930', PhD Thesis, University of St Andrews, 2020, 168; Prestwich ADMF2/15 (1903), patient 12,784.

95. Parkside NHM 8/1/2/48a (1905); LMA HRL/4/12/2/7 (1876), patient 9786.

96. Dickson, *The Science and Practice of Medicine*, p. 193.

97. SYA NHS3/5/1/4 (1883), patient 2434; LMA HRL/4/12/2/8 (1878), patient 10,275.

98. William Booth, *In Darkest England and the Way Out* (New York, 1890), pp. 14, 158, 159. See also Pamela J. Walker, *Pulling the Devil's Kingdom Down: The Salvation Army in Victorian Britain* (Berkeley, CA, 2001).

99. See Sarah Bartels, *The Devil and the Victorians: Supernatural Evil in Nineteenth-century English Culture* (London, 2021); Bell, *The Magical Imagination, passim*; Davies, *Witchcraft, Magic and Culture*, pp. 32–5, 178–9; James Obelkevich, *Religion and Rural Society: South Lindsey 1825–1875* (Oxford, 1976), pp. 276–9; Ulrika Wolf-Knuts, 'The Devil between Nature and Culture', *Ethnologia Europaea* 22 (1992) 109–14; Ülo Valk, *The Black Gentleman, Manifestations of the Devil in Estonian Folk Religion* (Helsinki, 2001).

100. LMA HRL/4/12/2/10 (1881), patient 11,402; SYA NHS3/5/1/18 (1906), patient 7841; Prestwich ADMF2/7 (1895), patient 10,573; Robert Boyd, 'Observations on Puerperal Insanity', *Journal of Mental Science* 16 (1870) 155.

101. SYA NHS3/5/1/4 (1884), patient 2203.

102. LMA HRL/4/12/2/17, p. 309; LMA HRL/4/12/3/18 (1894), p. 220; Hilary Marland, 'Under the Shadow of Maternity: Birth, Death and Puerperal Insanity in Victorian Britain', *History of Psychiatry* 23 (2012) 85; Prestwich ADMF2/11 (1898), patient 11,573.

103. LMA HRL/4/12/2/13 (1885); Crichton DGH1/5/21/4/3 (1888) p. 717; Prestwich ADMM2/20 (1910), patient 13,123. On black dog folklore and diabolic associations see, Bob Trubshaw (Ed.), *Explore Phantom Black Dogs* (Loughborough, 2005); Mark Norman, *Black Dog Folklore* (London, 2015); Jonathan Woolley, 'Hounded Out of Time: Black Shuck's Lesson in the Anthropocene', *Environmental Humanities* 10 (2018) 295–309.

104. Gordon Parker, 'The History and Development of Australia's Black Dog Institute', *Revista Brasileira de Psiquiatria* 35 (2013) 75–80.

105. Prestwich ADMM2/20 (1910), patient 13,123; J. Hawkes, 'Delusions and Hallucinations', *The Lancet* 17 December 1870, 848; LMA HRL/4/12/3/2 (1866), p. 215; Prestwich ADMF2/2, 1891, patient 9425; LMA HRL/4/12/2/12 (1883).

106. LMA HRL/4/12/2/17 (1893), p. 239.

107. Darren Oldridge, 'Fairies and the Devil in Early Modern England', *The Seventeenth Century* 31 (2016) 1–15; Charles P.G. Scott, 'The Devil and His Imps: An Etymological Inquisition', *Transactions of the American Philological Association* 26 (1895) 79–146.

108. *London Evening Standard*, 17 April 1855. For context see Philip Lockley, *Visionary Religion and Radicalism in Early Industrial England: From Southcott to Socialism* (Oxford, 2013); Margaret Makepeace 'From bad feet to blasphemy: the life of Charles William Twort', https://blogs.bl.uk/untoldlives/2019/04/from-bad-feet-to-blasphemy-the-life-of-charles-william-twort.html.

109. *Liverpool Mail*, 13 August 1853.

110. Davies, *Dove and the Wizard*, pp. 132–3.

111. LMA HRL/4/12/3/3 (1869), patient 8317; LMA HRL/4/12/3/7 (1879), p. 189; Prestwich, ADMF2/7 (1895), patient 10,546.

112. Bingham, *Observations on the religious delusions of insane persons*, p. 175.

113. Prestwich ADMF2/18 (1905), patient 13,567; Prestwich ADMF2/16 (1904), patient 13,126.

114. Prestwich, ADMM2/20 (1910), patient 13,128; Prestwich, ADMF2/21 (1907).

115. Renvoize and Beveridge, 'Mental illness and the late Victorians', 25.

116. SYA NHS3/5/1/8 (1890) patient 3556; SYA NHS3/5/1/9 (1892) patient 3880.

117. Harriet Sturdy, 'Boarding-out the Insane, 1857-1913: A Study of the Scottish System', PhD thesis, University of Glasgow, 1996, 142, 229.

118. Parkside NHM 8/5756/1/23 (1873).

119. Parkside, NHM 8/1/2/101a (1909); Parkside, NHM 8/1/1/37a (1889).

120. LMA HRL/4/12/2/27 (1908), p. 211.

121. Parkside NHM 8/1/2/46a (1905).

122. Clouston, *Clinical Lectures on Mental Diseases* (London, 1883), pp. 64–65, 252, 251.

123. SYA NHS3/5/1/8 (1890) patient no. 4242.

124. SYA NHS3/5/1/8 (1890) patient no. 4238; A. Campbell Clark, 'Clinical Illustrations of Puerperal Insanity', *The Lancet* 21 July (1881) 97.

125. F.W. Mott, *Tabes in Asylum and Hospital Practice* (London, 1903), p. 44. See also Louise Hide, 'Making sense of pain: delusions, Syphilis, and somatic pain in London County Council Asylums, c. 1900', *Interdisciplinary Studies in the Long Nineteenth Century* 15 (2012) n.p.; Allan Ingram, *The Madhouse of Language: Writing and Reading Madness in the Eighteenth Century* (London, 1991).

126. Dickson, *Science and Practice of Medicine*, p. 357.

127. LMA HRL/4/12/2/(1872) patient 8782.

128. Parkside, NHM 8/1/2/73a (1908).

129. *Sheffield Daily Telegraph*, 7 September 1883; SYA NHS 3/5/1/4, 1883. On Dale James see, Ronald Church, 'The History of Dermatology in the Sheffield Region', *British Journal of Dermatology* 91 (1974) 347–52.

130. S.C. Williams, *Religious Belief and Popular Culture in Southwark c. 1880–1939* (Oxford, 1999), pp. 130, 132–4.

131. Dorothy Entwistle, '"Hope, Colour, and Comradeship": Loyalty and Opportunism in Early Twentieth-Century Church Attendance among the Working Class in North-West England', *Journal of Religious History* 25 (2001) 32–5.

CHAPTER 6

1. Prestwich ADMF2/1 (1891), patient 9139.

2. *Third Annual Report of the Inverness District Lunatic Asylum* (Inverness, 1867), p. 22.

3. Owen Davies, 'Finding the Folklore in the Annals of Psychiatry'.

4. *Fifth Report of the Somerset County Asylum for Insane Paupers 1852* (Wells, 1853), p. 24; *Thirteenth Report of the Somerset County Pauper Lunatic Asylum 1860* (Wells, 1861), p. 18.

5. Robert Boyd, 'Diseases of the Nervous System'. No. IV. Mania', *Journal of Psychological Medicine* 3 (1877) 272, 287; Robert Boyd, 'Diseases of the Nervous System. No. V. Partial Insanity', *Journal of Psychological Medicine* 4 (1878), 84.

6. *First Annual Report of the County and City of Worcester Pauper Lunatic Asylum* (Worcester, 1854), p. 40; *Second Annual Report of the County and City of Worcester Pauper Lunatic Asylum* (Worcester, 1855), pp. 20, 31. On the asylum's history see, Frank Crompton, *Lunatics: the mad poor of Worcestershire in the long nineteenth century: writing 'History from below' of patients in a Pauper Lunatics Asylum* (Worcester 2013); Frank Crompton, *Doctor Sherlock's casebook: patients admitted to the Worcester City and County Pauper Lunatic Asylum at Powick August 1854 to March 1881* (Worcester, 2016).

7. Prestwich ADMM2/1 (1891), patient 8106; Prestwich ADMF2/5 (1893), patient 10,162.

8. See Davies, *Witchcraft, Magic, and Culture*; Thomas Waters, *Cursed Britain*; Andrew Sneddon and J. Fulton, 'Witchcraft, the Press and Crime in Ireland, 1822–1922', *Historical Journal* 62 (2019) 741–64.

9. Owen Davies, *A People Bewitched*; Owen Davies and Simon White, 'Witchcraft and the Somerset Idyll: The Depiction of Folk Belief in Walter Raymond's Novels', *Folklore* 126 (2015); Owen Davies, 'Researching Reverse Witch Trials in Nineteenth- and Early Twentieth-Century England', in Jonathan Barry, Owen Davies, and Cornelie Usbourne (Eds.), *Cultures of Witchcraft in Europe from the Middle Ages to the Present* (Cham, 2018), 215–33.

10. *Twentieth Report of the General Board of Directors of Prisons in Scotland* (Edinburgh, 1859), p. 62.

11. *Kelso Mail*, reprinted in the *Inverness Courier*, 2 July 1845.

12. NRS JC26/1845/177; Archibald Broun, *Reports of Cases Before the High Court and Circuit Courts of Justiciary in Scotland* (Edinburgh, 1846), Vol. 2, pp. 484–5.

13. Garthnavel Royal Hospital HB13/5/75, patient number 27.

14. LMA HRL/4/12/2/15 (1888), p. 324.

15. LMA HRL/4/12/2/23 (1904), p. 64; Prestwich ADMM2/19 (1908), patient 12,682.

16. SAC D/H/men/17/2/7 (1883), p. 448. On Billy Brewer see, Davies, *A People Bewitched*, pp. 65–76.

17. Prestwich ADMF2/23 (1910), number 15150.

18. *The Report of the Committee of Visitors, and Medical Superintendents of the Devon County Lunatic Asylum, for the Year 1871* (Exeter, 1872), p. 17; *West Somerset Free Press*, 18 February 1871.

19. LMA HRL/4/12/3/5 (1874); Prestwich ADMF2/18 (1905), patient 13,627; Prestwich ADMM2/7 (1896), patient 9485.

20. LMA HRL/4/12/2/12 (1884).

21. Prestwich ADMF2/2 (1891), patient 9396. She was still in the asylum, or had been readmitted, in 1911; Prestwich ADMF2/2 (1891), patient 9411.

22. LMA HRL/4/12/3/17 (1893), p. 283; Prestwich ADMF2/18 (1905), patient 13,536.

23. *Seventeenth Annual Report on the Health of Salford* (Salford, 1885), p. 63.

24. Prestwich ADMF2/7 (1894), patient 10,491.

25. Quoted in John Carter Wood, *Violence and Crime in Nineteenth-Century England: The Shadow of our Refinement* (London, 2004), p. 104.

26. Prestwich ADMM2/3 (1892), patient 8408; Prestwich ADMF2/4 (1893), patient 9969; Prestwich ADMF2/9)1896), patient 11,024.

27. *Warwick and Warwickshire Advertiser*, 18 December 1875; Crowell, *Spiritualism and Insanity*, p. 10.

28. *Fourteenth Annual Report of the Suffolk Lunatic Asylum* (Woodbridge, 1852), p. 8.

29. J.C. Bucknill, 'On Medical Certificates of Insanity', *Journal of Mental Science* 7 (1860) 85–6.

30. *Shields Daily Gazette*, 26 September 1904; *Shields Daily Gazette*, 15 October 1904.

31. *Shields Daily Gazette*, 29 October 1904.

32. D/H/men/17/2/7 (1883), patient 3203.

33. Waters, *Cursed Britain*, p. 85.

34. LMA HRL/4/12/3/34 (1910), p. 71; LMA QAM/1/30/27 (1886), patient 13,420.

35. Prestwich ADMF2/2 (1891), patient 9396.

36. Crichton DGH1/5/21/4/7 (1893) p. 525.

37. SYA NHS3/5/1/17 (1904), patient 6604. See, for example, Mirjam Mencej, *Styrian Witches in European Perspective: Ethnographic Fieldwork* (London, 2015), pp. 61–2.

38. Thomas E. Waters, 'Encounters with the Supernatural: Belief in Witchcraft and Ghosts in Victorian and Edwardian Oxfordshire and Warwickshire', PhD thesis, Oxford University, 2010, 114, 120.

39. West Riding Pauper Lunatic Asylum C85/3/6/14, pp. 211–12. Ritty's story is told in Davies, *Murder, Magic, Madness*, pp. 190–2.

40. LMA HRL/4/12/2/12 (1883); Prestwich ADMF2/16 (1904), patient 13,178.

41. LMA HRL/4/12/3/5 (1874).

42. LMA HRL/4/12/3/10 (1883), p. 205.

43. Donoho, 'Appeasing the saint in the loch', 303.

44. John Clendinning, 'Hallucination and Epilepsy', *The Lancet*, 12 March 1842, 811.
45. LMA HRL/4/12/3/4 (1871), patient 8742; LMA HRL/4/12/3/11 (1884), p. 164.
46. See Elaine Murphy, 'Workhouse Care of the Insane, 1845–90', in Pamela Dale and Joseph Melling (Eds.), *Mental Illness and Learning Disability Since 1850* (London, 2006), pp. 24–46; Peter Bartlett, 'The Asylum, the Workhouse, and the Voice of the Insane Poor in Nineteenth Century England. International', *Journal of Law and Psychiatry* 21 (1998); Cara C. Dobbing, 'The Circulation of Pauper Lunatics and the Transitory Nature of Mental Health Provision in Late Nineteenth Century Cumberland and Westmorland', *Local Population Studies* 99 (2017) 56–65.
47. *The Twenty-Third Report of the Commissioners in Lunacy* (London, 1869), p. 23.
48. Prestwich ADMF2/2, 1891, patient 9411.
49. LMA HRL/4/12/3/3 (1869), patient 8244; SYA NHS3/5/1/15 (1902), patient 6002; Prestwich ADMM2/4 (1893), patient 8803.
50. SYA NHS3/5/1/13 (1898), patient 5175; LMA HRL/4/12/3/11 (1884), p. 163.
51. LMA HRL/4/12/3/11 (1884), p. 206; LMA HRL/4/12/3/3 (1868), patient 8144; SYA NHS3/5/1/11 (1896), patient 5343.
52. SYA NHS3/5/1/8 (1891), patient 3644; LMA HRL/4/12/3/9 (1882); LMA HRL/4/12/3/2 (1867), patient 7695.
53. See Davies, *Witchcraft, Magic and Culture*; Davies, *A People Bewitched*; Waters, *Cursed Britain*.
54. Parkside Asylum case book for private patients (1899–1910): NHM 8/1/2/15a, 1901.
55. SYA NHS3/5/1/15 (1901), patient 6600; Crichton DGH1/5/21/4/8 (1894), p. 677.
56. LMA HRL/4/12/3/21 (1896), p. 267; Crichton DGH1/5/21/4/5 (1890), p. 225.
57. Waters, 'Encounters with the Supernatural', 121; LMA HRL/4/12/3/7 (1879).
58. LMA HRL/4/12/3/6 (1876); LMA HRL/4/12/2/9 (1879), patient 10,700.
59. Prestwich ADMF2/20 (1906), patient 14,110.
60. Bucknill and Tuke, *Manual of Psychological Medicine*, 2nd ed, pp. 567, 582.
61. LMA HRL/4/12/2/28 (1910), patient 24,092.
62. Lyttelton Forbes Winslow, *Mad Humanity: Its Forms, Apparent and Obscure* (London, 1898), p. 39; LMA HRL/4/12/3/10 (1883).
63. Prestwich ADMF2/21 (1908), patient 14,419; LMA HRL/4/12/3/29 (1904), p. 150; Prestwich ADMF2/8 (1896), patient 10,970.
64. *Kerry Evening Post*, 11 July 1888; *Kerry Evening Post*, 4 February 1888; Prior, *Madness and Murder*, p. 192.
65. Donoho, 'Appeasing the saint in the loch', 304; Prestwich ADMF2/11 (1899), patient 11,808.
66. Philip Leidy and Charles K. Mills, 'Reports of Cases of Insanity from the Insane Department of the Philadelphia Hospital', *Journal of Nervous and Mental Disease* 14 (1887) 46–8.
67. See, for example, Alexandra Warwick, 'Ghosts, Monsters and Spirits, 1840-1900', in Glennis Byron and Dale Townsend (Eds.), *The Gothic World* (Abingdon, 2014), pp. 373–4.

68. SYA NHS3/5/1/10 (1893), patient 4833; LMA HRL/4/12/2/25 (1906), p. 208; Prestwich, ADMM2/20 (1909), patient 13,076.

69. LMA HRL/4/12/2/5 (1871), patient 8618; Parkside NHM 8/5/11/6 (1899); Prestwich ADMF2/20 (1906), patient 14,063; Prestwich, ADMF2/13 (1901), patient 12,297.

70. Owen Davies, *The Haunted: A Social History of Ghosts* (Basingstoke, 2007); Sasha Handley, *Visions of an Unseen World: Ghost Beliefs and Ghost Stories in Eighteenth-Century England* (London, 2007); Martha McGill, *Ghosts in Enlightenment Scotland* (Woodbridge, 2018)); Shane McCorristine, *Spectres of the Self: Thinking about Ghosts and Ghost-Seeing in England, 1750–1920* (Cambridge, 2010). See also Roger Clarke, *A Natural History of Ghosts: 500 Years of Hunting for Proof* (New York, 2015); Susan Owens, *The Ghost: A Cultural History* (London, 2017).

71. LMA HRL/4/12/3/4 (1870), patient 8516; LMA HRL/4/12/3/12 (1885), p. 80; Prestwich ADMF2/13 (1901), patient 12,152.

72. LMA HRL/4/12/3/18 (1894), p. 244; Prestwich ADMF2/21 (1907), patient 14,313; LMA HRL/4/12/3/17 (1892), p. 11; Crichton DGH1/5/21/4/3 (1888), p. 661.

73. Prestwich ADMF2/13 (1901), patient 12,291.

74. Crichton DGH1/5/21/4/6 (1891), p. 13.

75. LMA HRL/4/12/3/6 (1875), p. 25; LMA HRL/4/12/3/18 (1894), p. 157; Crichton DGH1/5/21/4/7 (1893), p. 653.

76. SYA NHS3/5/1/17 (1904), patient 7408; SYA NHS3/5/1/17 (1905), patient 7470.

77. LMA HRL/4/12/2/20 (1900), p. 196; Prestwich ADMM2/8 (1897), patient 9866.

78. Gillian Bennett, *Alas, Poor Ghost! Traditions of Belief in Story and Discourse* (Logan, 1999), pp. 49–50, 98–101.

79. LMA HRL/4/12/2/10 (1881), patient 11,396.

80. Mott, *Tabes in Asylum*, p. 84.

81. Prestwich ADMF2/4 (1893), patient 9939; Prestwich ADMF2/24 (1911), patient 15,328.

82. LMA HRL/4/12/2/19 (1896), p. 70; LMA HRL/4/12/3/3 (1869), patient 8364.

83. Davies, *The Haunted*, pp. 14–15; Mary Wilson Carpenter, *Health, Medicine, and Society in Victorian England* (Santa Barbara, CA, 2010), p. 164.

84. LMA HRL/4/12/3/6 (1876), p. 71; Prestwich ADMF2/14 (1902), patient 12,530.

85. Davies, *The Haunted*, p. 40. On talking with and at ghosts in a contemporary context see Caron Lipman, *Co-habiting with Ghosts: Knowledge, Experience, Belief and the Domestic Uncanny* (London, 2014), pp. 117–33.

86. LMA HRL/4/12/2/15 (1888), p. 240; Prestwich ADMM2/19 (1909), patient 12,905; Prestwich ADMM2/10 (1900), patient 10,390.

87. LMA HRL/4/12/3/8 (1880), p. 68; Prestwich ADMM2/19 (1908), patient 12,741.

88. Clendinning, 'Hallucination and Epilepsy', 811; Davies, *Witchcraft, Magic and Culture*, p. 23.

89. LMA HRL/4/12/2/8 (1878), patient 10,207.

90. Prestwich ADMF2/6 (1894), patient 10,399; LMA HRL/4/12/3/11 (1885), p. 320.

91. LMA HRL/4/12/2/13 (1885).

92. Davies, *The Haunted*, p. 6; LMA HRL/4/12/3/9 (1881), p. 105.

93. Prestwich ADMF2/9 (1897), patient 11,172; Crichton DGH1/5/21/4/3 (1887), p. 121.

94. W. Beresford, 'Notes on a Portion of the Northern Borders of Staffordshire', *The Reliquary* 7 (1866–7), 101; Thomas Sternberg, *The Dialect and Folk-Lore of Northamptonshire* (London, 1851), pp. 131–2. See, Francis Young, *Suffolk Fairylore* (Norwich, 2019), pp. 79–95; Simon Young, 'Three Notes on West Yorkshire Fairies in the Nineteenth Century', *Folklore* 123 (2012) 223–30; Simon Young, 'Fairies and Railways: A Nineteenth-Century Topos and its Origins', *Notes and Queries* 59 (2012) 401–3; Simon Young and Ceri Houlbrook (Eds.), *Magical Folk: British and Irish Fairies: 500 AD to the Present* (London, 2017).

95. Simon Young, *The Boggart: Folklore, History and Dialect Studies* (Exeter, 2022); Simon Young, 'Joseph Wright Meets the Boggart', *Folk Life* 56 (2018) 1–13; Simon Young, 'Public Bogies and Supernatural Landscapes in North-Western England in the 1800s', *Time and Mind* 13 (2020) 399–424.

96. Campbell, '"This Distressing Malady"', 169; Lancashire Archives, LM HRL/4/12/2/20, p. 11.

97. Barclay, *Men on Trial*, pp. 185–8.

98. Margaret Bennett, 'Balquhidder Revisited: Fairylore in the Scottish Highlands, 1690-1990', in Peter Narváez (Ed.), *The Good People: New Fairylore Essays* (New York, 1991), p. 96.

99. See Simon Young, 'Some Notes on Irish Fairy Changelings in Nineteenth-Century Newspapers', *Béascna* 8 (2013) 34–47; Simon Young, 'Fairy impostors in County Longford in the Great Famine', *Studia Hibernica* 38 (2012) 181–99.

100. *Report of the Commissioners Appointed to take the Census of Ireland, for the Year 1841* (Dublin, 1843), pp. xxxii–xxxiii.

101. For meticulous accounts of the case see Angela Bourke, *The Burning of Bridget Cleary: A True Story* (London, 1999); Joan Hoff and Marian Yeates, *The Cooper's Wife is Missing: The Trials of Bridget Cleary* (New York, 2000).

102. Prior, *Madness and Murder*, pp. 188–9.

103. G.H. Kinahan, 'Notes on Irish Folk-Lore', *Folk-Lore Record* 4 (1881) 112.

104. Leland L. Duncan, 'Fairy Beliefs and other Folklore Notes from County Leitrim', *Folklore* 7 (1896) 162; Edith Balfour, 'A Week in the West of Ireland', *The Living Age* 247 (1905) 236.

105. See, for example, Lizanne Henderson and Edward J. Cowan, *Scottish Fairy Belief: A History* (East Linton, 2001); Diane Purkiss, *At the Bottom of the Garden: A Dark History of Fairies, Hobgoblins, and Other Troublesome Things* (New York, 2000); Richard Sugg, *Fairies: A Dangerous History* (London, 2018); Katharine Briggs, *The Fairies in Tradition and Literature* (London, 1967); Jeremy Harte, *Explore Fairy Traditions* (Loughborough, 2004).

106. Prestwich ADMF2/1 (1891); G.A. Doody, A. Beveridge, and E.C. Johnstone, 'Poor and Mad: A Study of Patients Admitted to the Fife and Kinross District Asylum Between 1874 and 1899', *Psychological Medicine* 26 (1996) 893–4.

107. Crichton DGH1/5/21/4/1 (1885), p. 571.

108. LMA HRL/4/12/3/13 (1887), p. 130; Crichton DGH1/5/21/4/4 (1889), p. 53; LMA HRL/4/12/3/19 (1895), p. 62.

109. LMA HRL/4/12/3/12 (1885), p. 47; LMA HRL/4/12/3/12 (1886), p. 309.

110. LMA QAM/1/30/27 (1864), patient 7149; Prestwich ADMM2/14 (1903).

111. Lady Wilde, *Ancient Legend, Mystical Charms, and Superstitions of Ireland* (Boston, MA, 1888), p. 258.

112. LMA HRL/4/12/3/29 (1904), p. 250; Crichton DGH1/5/21/4/7 (1892), pp. 141–3; Prestwich ADMF2/11 (1898).

113. Crichton DGH1/5/21/4/1 (1885), p. 571.

114. Vinzia Fiorino, 'La fiaba e la follia. Medicina, folklore e religione nelle rap-presentazioni culturali della malattia mentale (1850-1915).' Pyschiatry Online Italia (2012) http://www.psychiatryonline.it/node/2104; Davies, 'Finding the Folklore in the Annals of Psychiatry'.

CHAPTER 7

1. LMA HRL/4/12/3/33 (1909), p. 144.

2. Louis Waldstein, *The Subconscious Self and its Relation to Education and Health* (London, 1897), p. 133; *Journal of Mental Science* 44 (1898) 853; Renvoize and Beveridge, 'Mental illness and the late Victorians', 25.

3. Waldstein, *The Subconscious Self*, p. 134.

4. Savage, *Insanity and Allied Neuroses*, p. 242.

5. See Bernhard Rieger, *Technology and the Culture of Modernity in Britain and Germany, 1890–1945* (Cambridge, 2005).

6. Quoted in Peter Broks, *Media Science before the Great War* (Basingstoke, 1996), p. 28.

7. See Owen Davies, *Magic: A Very Short Introduction* (Oxford, 2012), pp. 103–6.

8. See Steven Connor, *Dream Machines* (London, 2017); Jeffrey Sconce, *The Technical Delusion: Electronics, Power, Insanity* (Durham, 2019).

9. Victor Tausk, 'On the Origin of the "Influencing Machine" in Schizophrenia', trans. Dorian Feigenbaum *Psychoanalytic Quarterly* 2 (1933) 519–56.

10. Crichton DGH1/5/21/4/5 (1890), p. 117; Conolly Norman, 'Notes on Hallucinations. II' *Journal of Mental Science* 49 (1903) 281–2.

11. Mike Jay, *The Influencing Machine: James Tilly Matthews and the Air Loom* (London, 2012); Thomas Roske, Bettina Brand-Claussen, Zoe Beloff, Rod Dickinson, Mike Jay, and Verena Kuni, *Air Loom: Der Luft-Webstuhl und andere gefährliche Beeinflussungsapparate/ The Air Loom and Other Dangerous Influencing Machines* (Heidelberg, 2006).

12. John Haslam, *Illustrations of Madness* (London, 1810), p. 38.

13. Haslam, *Illustrations*, pp. 43–4.

14. Amy Milne-Smith, 'Shattered Minds: Madmen on the Railways, 1860–80', *Journal of Victorian Culture* 21 (2016) 21–39; Edwin Fuller Torrey and Judy Miller, *The Invisible Plague: The Rise of Mental Illness from 1750 to the Present* (New Brunswick, 2001), p. 165; *St Louis Medical and Surgical Journal* cited in 'Railway Travelling a Cause of Disease', *American Journal of Insanity* 22 (1865) 269–70.

15. Bucknill and Tuke, *Manual of Psychological Medicine*, 4th ed. p. 200; Crichton DGH1/5/21/4/5 (1890), p. 369.
16. LMA HRL/4/12/2/7 (1876), patient 9780; LMA HRL/4/12/2/29 (1908), patient 23,131.
17. LMA HRL/4/12/2/12 (1884); Savage, 'Some Uncured Cases', p. 231.
18. Beveridge, 'Voices of the mad', 903.
19. Norman, 'Notes on Hallucinations. I', 50.
20. 'Scenes from the Life of a Sufferer: Being the Narrative of a Residence in Morningside Asylum', *Hogg's Instructor* 2 (1854) 327.
21. Noakes, *Physics and Psychics*, pp. 28–33. More generally, see William Hughes, *That Devil's Trick: Hypnotism and the Victorian Popular Imagination* (Manchester, 2015); Peter Lamont, *Extraordinary Beliefs: A Historical Approach to a Psychological Problem* (Cambridge, 2013), pp. 63–126; Winter, *Mesmerised*.
22. *Liverpool Mail*, 16 December 1843.
23. *Medical Times and Gazette,* 24 January 1852.
24. Clouston, *Clinical Lectures*, p. 251. For the history of a detailed first-person account of mesmeric-magnetic persecution see, Burkhart Brückner, 'Animal Magnetism, Psychiatry and Subjective Experience in Nineteenth-Century Germany: Friedrich Krauß and his *Nothschrei*', *Medical History* 60 (2016) 19–36.
25. LMA HRL/4/12/2/14 (1886); LMA HRL/4/12/2/11 (1883), patient 11,937; LMA HRL/4/12/2/17 (1893), p. 330.
26. Crichton DGH1/5/21/4/3 (1888), p. 773; LMA HRL/4/12/2/10 (1881), patient 11,444.
27. LMA HRL/4/12/3/24 (1899), p. 223; LMA HRL/4/12/3/21 (1896), p. 294.
28. Norman, 'Modern Witchcraft', 119, 120.
29. Alan Gauld, A *History of Hypnotism* (Cambridge, 1992).
30. L. Edward Purcell, 'Trilby and Trilby-Mania: The Beginning of the Best Seller System', *Journal of Popular Culture* 11 (1977) 62–76; Leighton, 'The Trilby Phenomenon and Late Victorian Culture'; Daniel Pick, *Svengali's Web: The Alien Enchanter in Modern Culture* (New Haven, CT, 2000); Lara Karpenko, 'Purchasing Largely: Trilby and the *Fin de Siècle* Reader.' *Victorians Institute Journal* 34 (2006) 215–41; Hilary Grimes, *The Late Victorian Gothic: Mental Science, the Uncanny, and Scenes of Writing* (Farnham, 2011), 61–83; Mary Elizabeth Leighton, 'The Trilby Phenomenon and Late Victorian Culture', PhD, University of Alberta, 2003.
31. Jeanette Leonard Gilder, *Trilbyana: The Rise and Progress of a Popular Novel* (New York, 1895), pp. 25–6.
32. *Punch* 30 November 1895, 253.
33. Ruth Harris, *Murder and Madness: Medicine, Law, and Society in France at the Fin de Siècle* (Oxford, 1989), ch. 5; Heather Wolffram, 'Crime and hypnosis in fin-de-siècle Germany: The Czynski case', *Notes and Records* 71 (2017), 213–26; Kaat Wils, 'From transnational to regional magnetic fevers: The making of a law on hypnotism in late nineteenth-century Belgium', *Notes and Records* 71 (2017) 179–96.
34. Crichton DGH1/5/21/4/3 (1888), p. 450.

35. LMA HRL/4/12/3/29 (1904), p. 245; LMA HRL/4/12/2/23 (1904), p. 24.

36. *Edinburgh Medical Journal* 38 (1893) 643.

37. George Robertson, 'The Use of Hypnotism among the Insane', *Journal of Mental Science* 39 (1893) 12.

38. Pinel, *Traité médico-philosophique*, 2nd ed. (1809), pp. 116, 223.

39. LMA HRL/4/12/2/5 (1872), patient 8771.

40. Lewis, *Text-Book of Mental Diseases*, pp. 313–14.

41. Crichton DGH1/5/21/4/1 (1867), p. 159; SYA NHS3/5/2/1 (1887), patient 97.

42. N. Parker Willis, *The Rag-Bag, A Collection of Ephemera* (New York, 1855), p. 192. See also Jeffrey Sconce, *Haunted Media: Electronic Presence from Telegraphy to Television* (Durham, NC, 2000), p. 25; Anthony Enns, 'The Undead Author: Spiritualism, Technology and Authorship', in Tatiana Kontou and Sarah Willburn (Eds.), *The Ashgate Research Companion to Victorian Spiritualism and the Occult* (London, 2012), pp. 60–2; Cathy Gutierrez, *Plato's Ghost: Spiritualism in the American Renaissance* (Oxford, 2009), pp. 45–77.

43. LMA HRL/4/12/2/5 (1872), patient 8862; LMA HRL/4/12/2/20 (1900), p. 136.

44. LMA HRL/4/12/2/9 (1879), patient 10,598.

45. Prestwich ADMM2/6 (1894), patient 9173; SYA NHS3/5/1/10 (1894), patient 4365.

46. See Luckhurst, *The Invention of Telepathy*, pp. 137–8; Pamela Thurschwell, *Literature, Technology, and Magical Thinking, 1880–1920* (Cambridge, 2001), p. 25. See also, Jill Galvan, *The Sympathetic Medium: Feminine Channeling, the Occult, and Communication Technologies, 1859–1919* (Ithaca, NY, 2010).

47. Lewis, *Text-Book of Mental Diseases*, p. 319.

48. Norman, 'Notes on Hallucination', 272–3.

49. See, Tim Armstrong, *Modernism, Technology, and the Body: A Cultural Study* (Cambridge, 1998), pp. 13–36; Martin Willis, *Mesmerists, Monsters, and Machines: Science Fiction and the Cultures of Science in the Nineteenth Century* (Kent, 2006); Linda Simon, *Dark Light: Electricity and Anxiety from the Telegraph to the X-Ray* (Orlando, FL, 2004); Courtenay Raia, *The New Prometheans: Faith, Science, and the Supernatural Mind in the Victorian fin de Siècle* (Chicago, IL, 2019); David E. Nye, *Electrifying America: Social Meanings of a New Technology, 1880–1940* (Cambridge, MA, 1990); Carolyn Thomas de la Peña, *The Body Electric: How Strange Machines Built the Modern Era* (New York, 2003); Theo Paijmans, *Free Energy Pioneer: John Worrell Keely* (Kempton, 2004); Iwan Rhys Morus, 'The Measure of Man: Technologising the Victorian Body', *History of Science* 37 (1999) 249–82; Louise Hide, 'Making Sense of Pain: Delusions, Syphilis, and Somatic Pain in London County Council Asylums, c. 1900–19', *Interdisciplinary Studies in the Long Nineteenth Century* 15 (2012) 1–8.

50. LMA HRL/4/12/2/23 (1904), p. 28; LMA HRL/4/12/2/28 (1909), patient 23,303; W.R. Dawson, 'Notes on a Year's Asylum Work', *The Dublin Journal of Medical Science* 118 (1904) 114.

51. LMA HRL/4/12/3/33 (1909), p. 219.

52. LMA, HRL/4/12/2/30 (1910), patient 23,952; *Electricity* 1 June 1892, 234.

53. LMA HRL/4/12/2/16 (1889), p. 187; CRH, DGH1/5/21/4/5 (1890), p. 65; LMA HRL/4/12/3/17 (1893), p. 310.
54. LMA HRL/4/12/2/15 (1887), p. 4; LMA HRL/4/12/3/21 (1896), p. 339; LMA HRL/4/12/2/28 (1910), patient 23,727.
55. Crichton DGH1/5/21/4/1 (1884), p. 676; LMA HRL/4/12/2/20 (1899), p. 76.
56. LMA HRL/4/12/3/33 (1908), p. 46; LMA HRL/4/12/2/30 (1910), patient 24,114; SYA NHS3/5/1/15 (1902), patient 5977.
57. Graeme Gooday, *Domesticating Electricity: Technology, Uncertainty and Gender, 1880–1914* (London, 2008), pp. 65–73. On the pace of electrification in Britain in the twentieth century see, Paul Brassley, Jeremy Burchardt, and Karen Sayer (Eds.), *Transforming the Countryside: The Electrification of Rural Britain* (London, 2017). Philip Smith, *Punishment and Culture* (Chicago, IL, 2008), pp. 142–69.
58. Prestwich ADMM2/9 (1899), patient 1088; SYA NHS3/5/1/13 (1899), patient 5377; LMA HRL/4/12/2/28 (1908), patient 23,174.
59. LMA HRL/4/12/3/32 (1907), p. 8.
60. LMA HRL/4/12/2/30 (1909), patient 23,680.
61. SYA, NHS3/5/1/11 (1896), patient 5481; LMA HRL/4/12/2/13 (1885); SYA NHS3/5/1/15 (1902), patient 6731.
62. LMA HRL/4/12/3/14, (1888), p. 85; LMA HRL/4/12/3/30 (1905), p. 164.
63. Norman, 'Notes on Hallucinations. II', 284; Jules Séglas *Leçons cliniques sur les maladies mentales et nerveuses: (Salpêtrière, 1887–1894)* (Paris, 1895), p. 15.
64. Mott, *Tabes in Asylum*, p. 118.
65. Prestwich ADMF2/17 (1904), patient 13,453.
66. Crichton DGH1/5/21/4/8 (1894), p. 677.
67. Wright, 'Delusions of Gender?', p. 166; SYA NHS3/5/1/17, 1904, patient 6568.
68. LMA HRL/4/12/3/33 (1908), p. 113; LMA HRL/4/12/3/31 (1906), p. 202.
69. Although not an influence here, it is worth noting that Jules Verne's science fiction masterpiece *20,000 Leagues under the Sea*, which was first published in English in 1873, introduced the idea of electric balls that were miniature Leyden jars in construction, which were fired from a gun to kill animals.
70. On asylum brain research see Jennifer Wallis, *Investigating the Body in the Victorian Asylum: Doctors, Patients, and Practices* (Cham, 2017), pp. 141–81.
71. Joseph Wiglesworth, 'On the Use of Galvanism in the Treatment of Certain Forms of Insanity', *The Journal of Mental Science* 33 (1888) 394.
72. Alexander Robertson 'Case of Insanity of Seven Years' Duration: Treatment by Electricity', *Journal of Mental Science* 30 (1884) 56, 57.
73. A.W. Beveridge and E.B. Renvoize, 'Electricity: A History of Its Use in the Treatment of Mental Illness in Britain during the Second Half of the 19th Century' *British Journal of Psychiatry* 153 (1988) 157–62; Timothy W. Kneeland and Carol A.B. Warren, *Pushbutton Psychiatry: A History of Electroshock in America* (2002); Edward Shorter and David Healy, *Shock Therapy: A History of Electroconvulsive Treatment in Mental Illness* (New Brunswick, 2007).
74. LMA HRL/4/12/3/16 (1892), p. 78; LMA QAM/1/30/27 (1874), patient 9263.
75. LMA HRL/4/12/2/25 (1906), p. 102; LMA HRL/4/12/3/26 (1901), p. 80.

76. LMA HRL/4/12/3/31 (1906), p. 91; Frederic P. Hearder, 'An Analysis of 131 Male Criminal Lunatics Admitted to the West Riding Asylum, Wakefield, during the Years 1884-1896', *Journal of Mental Science* 44 (1898) 70.

77. Cherry, *Mental Health Care in Modern England*, pp. 140-1.

78. LMA HRL/4/12/2/30 (1911), patient 24,152; David Nicolson, 'Feigned Insanity; with Cases', *The Journal of Mental Science* 15 (1870) p. 563.

79. LMA HRL/4/12/3/27 (1902), p. 27.

80. Paul Tobia, 'The Patients of the Bristol Lunatic Asylum', 5–6, 177–8.

81. LMA HRL/4/12/2/26 (1907), p. 115.

82. Clouston, *Clinical Lectures*, pp. 80, 251, 81.

83. Anna Wexler, 'The Medical Battery in the United States (1870-1920): Electrotherapy at Home and in the Clinic', *Journal of the History of Medicine and Allied Sciences*, 72 (2017)166–92; de la Peña, *The Body Electric*, pp. 97–8.

84. Norman, 'Modern Witchcraft', 121.

85. *Sheffield Weekly Telegraph*, 17 April 1886; *Brighton Gazette*, 19 April 1890; *Sheffield Weekly Telegraph*,14 May 1910.

86. LMA, HRL/4/12/2/15 (1888), p. 290.

87. LMA HRL/4/12/3/32 (1907), p. 196; LMA HRL/4/12/2/14 (1886).

88. Data from Briggs and Burke, *Social History of the Media*, p. 122; Stephen Broadberry, *Market Services and the Productivity Race, 1850–2000: British Performance in International Perspective* (Cambridge, 2006), p. 112; Fischer, *America Calling*, p. 93.

89. Jessica Kuskey, 'Listening to the Victorian Telephone: Class, Periodicals, and the Social Construction of Technology', *Nineteenth-century Contexts* 38 (2016) 18. On the social history of telephones see also, Ithiel de Sola Pool (Ed.), *The Social Impact of the Telephone* (Cambridge, MA, 1977); Claude S. Fischer, *America Calling: A Social History of the Telephone to 1940* (Berkeley, CA, 1992); Asa Briggs and Peter Burke, *A Social History of the Media: From Gutenberg to the Internet*, 2nd ed. (Cambridge, 2005); Jessica Kuskey, 'Listening to the Victorian Telephone: Class, Periodicals, and the Social Construction of Technology', *Nineteenth-century Contexts* 38 (2016) 3–22.

90. Clouston, *Clinical Lectures*, p. 251.

91. Savage, *Insanity and Allied Neuroses*, pp. 241–2.

92. LMA HRL/4/12/3/30 (1904), p. 7.

93. Beveridge, 'Voices of the Mad', 906.

94. LMA HRL/4/12/3/16 (1892), p. 171.

95. LMA HRL/4/12/3/16 (1892), p. 294; LMA HRL/4/12/3/27 (1902), p. 130.

96. LMA HRL/4/12/3/16 (1892), p. 292; LMA HRL/4/12/2/27 (1908), p. 206; LMA HRL/4/12/2/21, (1903), p. 144; LMA HRL/4/12/2/27 (1908), p. 114; Prestwich ADMF2/16 (1903), patient 13,061.

97. LMA HRL/4/12/2/17 (1892), p. 181; Norman, 'Notes on Hallucinations. II', 281.

98. Savage, *Insanity and Allied Neuroses*, p. 241.

99. Lewis, *Text-Book of Mental Diseases*, p. 315.

100. John M. Picker, *Victorian Soundscapes* (Oxford, 2003), pp. 119–20.

101. LMA HRL/4/12/2/23 (1904), p. 37.

102. LMA HRL/4/12/3/14 (1889), p. 290.

103. Norman, 'Modern Witchcraft', pp. 123, 124.

104. Davies, *America Bewitched*, p. 43; Davies, *A People Bewitched*, p. 162.

105. Norman, 'Notes on Hallucinations. II', 274, 276.

106. Annebella Pollen, 'Marketing Photography: Selling Popular Photography on the British High Street', in Stephen Bull (Ed.), *A Companion to Photography* (Hoboken, 2020), pp. 214–16.

107. Katherine D.B. Rawling, '"The Annexed Photos were Taken Today": Photographing Patients in the Late-Nineteenth-century Asylum', *Social History of Medicine* 34 (2021) 256; Carol Berkenkotter, *Patient Tales: Case Histories and the Uses of Narrative in Psychiatry* (Columbia, 2008), pp. 51–70.

108. Norman, 'Notes on Hallucinations. II', 289.

109. Sylvia Pamboukian, '"Looking Radiant": Science, Photography and the X-ray Craze of 1896', *Victorian Review* 27 (2001) 56–74; Allen W. Grove, 'Röntgen's Ghosts: Photography, X-Rays, and the Victorian Imagination', *Literature and Medicine* 16 (1997) 141–73; Simone Natale, 'The Invisible Made Visible: X-rays as Attraction and Visual Medium at the End of the Nineteenth Century', *Media History* 17 (2011) 345–58.

110. Cited in Natale, 'The Invisible made Visible' 345–6.

111. Roger Luckhurst, *The Mummy's Curse: The True History of a Dark Fantasy* (Oxford, 2012), p. 175.

112. L. Beveridge, 'Voices of the mad', 901–2; MA HRL/4/12/3/23 (1897), p. 56.

113. LMA HRL/4/12/2/20 (1899), p. 101; LMA HRL/4/12/2/22 (1904), p. 203.

114. Richard Abel (Ed.), *Encyclopedia of Early Cinema* (London, 2005), pp. 281–3.

115. Norman, 'Notes on Hallucinations. II', 281; Norman, 'Modern Witchcraft: A Study of a Phase of Paranoia', *Journal of Mental Science* 51 (1905) 121, 122.

116. A. R. Urquhart, 'The Morison Lectures—On Insanity, with Special Reference to Heredity and Prognosis', *Journal of Mental Science* 53 (1907) 288.

117. Jules Séglas *Leçons cliniques sur les maladies mentales*, p. 506.

118. Norman, 'Modern Witchcraft', 124.

119. LMA HRL/4/12/2/16 (1890), p. 227.

Index

For the benefit of digital users, indexed terms that span two pages (e.g., 52–53) may, on occasion, appear on only one of those pages.